ADD Kaleidoscope:

The Many Facets of

Adult

Attention Deficit Disorder

Joan Andrews, M.S., L.E.P.
Denise E. Davis, M.S., M.F.C.C.

A.D.D. Kaleidoscope
The Many Facets of Adult Attention Deficit Disorder

by
Joan M. Andrews and
Denise E. Davis

Published by: **Hope Press**
P.O. Box 188
Duarte, CA 91009 U.S.A.

For other books by Hope Press see insert card in the back.

The ideas in this book are based on the author's personal experience with ADD and as such are not to be considered medical advice. This book is not intended as a substitute for psychotherapy or the medical treatment of Attention Deficit Hyperactivity Disorder and the various medications described can only be prescribed by a physician. The reader should consult a qualified health care professional in matters realting to health and particularly with respect to any symptoms which may require diagnosis or medical advice.

Library of Congress Cataloging-in-Publication

Andrews, Joan, 1939-
    ADD kaleidoscope : the many facets of adult attention deficit disorder / Joan Andrews, Denise E. Davis
       p. cm.
    Includes bibliographical references and index.
    Cover title: A.D.D. kaleidoscope.
    ISBN 1-878267-03-5 (paperback)
    1. Attention-deficit disorder in adults. I. Davis, Denise E. (Denise Evelyn), 1957- . II. Title. III. Title: A.D.D. kaleidoscope
RC394.A85A53   1997
616.85'89 — —dc21
                                     97-2618
                                       CIP

FOREWORD

The ADD Kaleidoscope: The Many Facets of Adult Attention Deficit Disorder, by Joan Andrews and Denise Davis, is a wonderfully rich presentation of what it is like to be an adult with Attention Deficit Disorder. The years of experience the authors have had with this disorder shows on every page. The modern tools of medical science, from brain scans to molecular biology, are beginning to provide us with greater insights into the cause of ADD. It is clear that it is a genetic disorder, that the symptoms often persist into adulthood, and that the genes involved affect many different brain chemicals, including dopamine, serotonin and norepinephrine. These defects especially impact the function of the frontal lobes of the brain. Since the frontal lobes are involved in attention span, motivation, organization, planning, memory, learning, motor activity, and the self-correction of one's mistakes, individuals with ADD can have problems in all of these areas.

Andrews and Davis describe many new areas not usually covered by other books, including the effect of ADD on problems with temper control, addictive behaviors, domestic violence and criminal behaviors. While this collection of problems can have a devastating impact on many areas of one's life, the authors also emphasize that ADD can have a positive influence on drive, energy level and creativity. ADD is a complex, genetic behavioral disorder. Because it affects behavior instead of something physically obvious, like height or eye color, it is often misdiagnosed and often ridiculed and claimed to be a non-existent entity. This is particularly tragic, because the treatment of this disorder can dramatically improve people's lives. That treatment can involve medication, or it can involve the hundreds of non-medical approaches and suggestions the authors so well describe. A combination of both can be particularly effective.

Anyone with ADD, a relative with ADD, or simply with an interest in human behavior, will benefit from reading these pages.

David E. Comings, M.D.
City of Hope National Medical Center
Author of *Tourette Syndrome and Human Behavior*

<u>Joan's Acknowledgements</u>

To my husband…

    for his patience

To my children and grandchildren

    Dina, for her emotional support

    David, for his technical support

    Sue, Max and Mario, for the lightness in life

<u>Denise's Acknowledgements</u>

This book is lovingly dedicated to my mother, Mary Lee Hayden Davis, whose infinite compassion touched all who knew her, and to my father, Robert Dean Davis, whose genes and zest for life have filled me to the brim.

I'm forever grateful to all of my family and friends who have stood by my side throughout the adventure of writing this book.

PROLOGUE

A Word to Our Readers

ADD Kaleidoscope: The Many Facets of Adult Attention Deficit Disorder is a book that can be used by professionals as well as laypeople who are curious about Attention Deficit Disorder, who want to explore it for themselves, who believe that others in their lives may have the condition, or who have interest in specific topics within the ADD world.

The book is organized into chapters that can be easily read. Each chapter is meant to stand alone as a quick reference. Each chapter deals with a subject that is important and relevant to ADD adults, their families, their employers and their therapists. We have found that a simple, direct writing style that invites you to read without overwhelming you works best.

There is a questionnaire about ADD included in Chapter 1, a checklist regarding Domestic Violence and ADD in Chapter 7, and checklists for Employees, Employers, and Co-Workers with ADD in Chapter 11. We have included these as checkpoints along the way, as well as an opportunity to self-test in the privacy of your own living room before taking a next step.

As we reviewed current literature on adult ADD, we became aware of several important topics addressed in our book which are just now beginning to reach the awareness of ADD adults and professionals.

ADD and Addictions – Our book contains two chapters on addiction and recovery. We explore both in detail, with concrete information and proposed solutions.

ADD and Domestic Violence – We have a full chapter that discusses ADD's role in domestic violence and the patterns that are triggered in couples and families. We also offer solid methods of obtaining solutions.

ADD, Education and the Workplace – These two chapters thoroughly explore the problems caused by ADD in the educational process and in the workplace. We explain the difficulties encountered and, more specifically, how the Americans with Disabilities Act (ADA) of 1995 can be used to provide protection and to promote success. A checklist to assist in determining ADD in the workplace is included.

ADD and Crime Connection – This chapter deals specifically with ADD characteristics among the prison population. It also discusses the prognosis for an ADD adult in jail and paints scenarios before and during prison and upon release. This chapter concludes with specific recommendations for rehabilitation programs that work.

As we write this book, we find that the ADD field is changing rapidly as our knowledge of brain chemistry deepens. This is an exciting time to be at the forefront of whirlwind advances in psychology, science and technology. We hope that you find our book illuminating, thought-provoking and helpful.

Joan's Story

All my life I have been covering up certain things that I thought were just quirks of my personality. I realized that I had a terrible memory. Not only would dates and numbers disappear, but I would also lose entire chunks of memory, even with pleasant experiences, such as a vacation or a visit with friends. They would just be gone.

I get lost. No, that is a real understatement. I don't just get lost, I get totally disoriented and often don't have a clue as to where I am or which way to turn. I have a terrible time starting projects. It feels as though it takes an unbelievable amount of energy just to begin something. Once into a project, if I don't keep going and finish it, I never get it completed. In elementary school my handwriting would change from day to day.

Did I tell anyone about these quirks? No, for a couple of reasons. One, I didn't understand that they could be connected, and two, I managed to push them down, becoming the master of coping techniques. I developed coping techniques for saving myself from getting lost. Whenever I go somewhere new I write directions for myself to the place. I also write directions to get home as I can't simply reverse the process. I take lots of pictures on visits and trips to protect myself from my memory void. At the office I make multiple copies and file things in two or three places so I have a better chance of retrieving things. I type rather than write.

However, all these quirks left me with a question in the back of my mind. What was wrong with me? When I began to connect the ADD adult symptoms with my own pattern in life, I felt a huge sense of relief. "Oh, that is what is going on with me!" Beyond that, it gave me a different way to understand the patterns in my family.

For me, understanding I had ADD was a relief, a burden lifted and a way to understand my life.

Denise's Story

I am an ADD adult. I was probably an ADD child and adolescent, but since I didn't show academic problems or severe outward behavioral signs, I "passed" without being detected as ADD. I had more of the inattentive symptoms than the hyperactive symptoms.

I was not diagnosed with ADD until I was thirty years old. A therapist mentor of mine noted that I would reach a certain level of performance and then hit a plateau that I could never seem to go beyond. She suggested I consider testing and I did so, wanting to prove that I wasn't ADD . . . after all, I had already succeeded in my life.

Well, after dragging my feet through testing and then through the medical maze, I finally began to wonder whether this might be true for me. Not only is it true that I am an ADD adult, but I thank my mentor for having the perception and strength to bring it to my attention in a way that forced me to face myself.

ADD affects every area of our lives; with education and treatment I have grown to understand ADD in my own life and in the lives of my clients, family and friends. The co-authoring of this book is the opportunity to share with you the rich information we have gleaned so far on the ADD trail.

ADD Kaleidoscope:
The Many Facets of Adult Attention Deficit Disorder

Chapter 1

An ADD Adult? Who, Me?

As a child, did you find comments on your report cards from your teachers in elementary school or even junior high that you simply "were not working up to your potential?" In fact, if you laid your report cards end to end, would you find a clear pattern of comments from your early years that noted you had "trouble paying attention," were "a daydreamer," often "talked out in class," had "problems with written reports?" In your adult life as a mother or father, or in your job or career, do you realize that you are doing an okay job, but you *could* do better?

Have you had a gut-level feeling all of your life that something is wrong with you, but you don't know what it is? Have you often felt that somehow you are vaguely "crazy," but can't explain it and certainly would never think of asking your doctor or counselor, because you couldn't explain why you feel this way? You function in society, and to others you probably look absolutely normal. However, there is a deep, hidden part of you that knows that something is just not right.

Maybe you have a hard time understanding things that you really should catch the first time around. Maybe you need to ask your spouse to explain a plot line in a movie that your ten-year-old son easily understands. Maybe you absolutely crave physical activity or even dangerous activities, such as driving too fast. Maybe you try and try to listen to co-workers in meetings or to friends in conversations, but no matter how hard you try, you find yourself drifting off. Even if you dig your fingernails into the palm of your hand or cross your feet a certain way to remind yourself to pay attention, it still doesn't work.

Maybe you lose time. You step into the shower, or sit down on the bed to put on a shoe, and find that a few minutes or even much longer has been lost. This chapter is designed to give you a quick and easy look at the world of the ADD adult. If you are ADD, you won't read past this first chapter unless it catches your interest and you recognize yourself in these pages. If you are not ADD, you may want to read on because you'll recognize someone you know.

There is no one quick and easy medical test to identify the ADD adult. There is no blood test or skin test that will give us a diagnosis. (We will be talking about medical tests that are now experimental or projected for the future in a later chapter, but at this time nothing is available.) The ADD adult is usually diagnosed through a battery of tests, and this battery will be different depending on whether you see a psychiatrist, neurologist or educational psychologist. More and more professionals are becoming aware of the uniqueness of ADD. Interestingly, when given sufficient information, the ADD adult is often accurate in his self-diagnosis. Somehow, at the very core of himself, he recognizes the ADD pattern and, surprisingly, he is seldom wrong.

Typically, if an ADD adult comes into the office and says, "I read your article," "I saw a recent TV special on ADD adults," "I found myself in tears because of the relief I felt," or "For the first time in my life I realized that I was not alone, that other people have what I have been so carefully hiding all my life," he is usually right in his own diagnosis. So read on, let us give you the skeleton of what makes up an ADD adult's profile. See for yourself if you fit the pattern.

At first, the adult ADD condition seems impossible to diagnose. ADD adults can present many different patterns, and the ADD pattern can even be dramatically different within one family, between brothers and sisters, or children and parents; however, it is really not that hard. Let's get very basic.

We'd like you to think of a continuum. A continuum is a line with "normal" being represented in the middle and the ends of the continuum representing the extremes. ADD adults typically fall at one end of the continuum or the other – not in the nice, easy, normal middle range. There are a bunch of problems that are common among ADD people. Just remember that they can occur at either end of the continuum. Have we lost you? . . . It is really not that hard.

The ADD Continuum

As you look at this list ask yourself, "Where do I fall on the continuum?" Are you typically at one end or the other, or do you flip from one end to the other? If so, you most probably *are* an ADD adult. Of course, this diagnosis is very unscientific and subjective at this point – but we are just beginning the exploration of the answers to your questions.

Spacy or a Daydreamer

Can't pay attention throughout a conversation; floats or drifts off.

Tunnel Vision

Becomes totally absorbed in a book or TV – must often be touched to break concentration.

Disorganized

Clutter everywhere; desk, room or office a mess.

Compulsively Neat

Everything has its place; clutter drives this person crazy.

Hyperactive

Restless, unable to sit still, moves arms, legs, fidgets. Finger tapping, foot tapping, shifting positions frequently.

Hypoactive

The original "couch potato," often misunderstood as being lazy or unmotivated, often feels lethargic.

Impulsive/Spontaneous

Overextends credit; quick to buy a new car, a new boat, change jobs. Impulsive decisions regarding relationships.

Compulsive/Overly Cautious

Takes a long time to research and re-research any purchase or to make any decision at all.

Temper/Anger Outbursts

Quick to blow up, yell, or may do a slow burn and then erupt. Behavior often shows up as a need for dangerous activities (sky diving, speeding, bungee jumping, etc.)

No Emotion at All

Doesn't show any emotions, including temper (or happiness). Often early family history didn't allow emotions to show.

Mood Swings

Moods range from happy to down. Moods often bounce around in the same day.

Low Level of Depression

The world looks flat or gray; this person seldom recognizes the feeling as depression since he has always felt that way.

Problems Began in Elementary School

Problems learning to read, write or do math; often placed in special education or had many tutors.

Problems Began in Adolescence

Elementary school was a breeze. In adolescence, there was a dramatic change, and academic or behavioral problems began.

Problems Understanding

Privately she may feel "dumb"; has problems understanding concepts in books, things people tell her or written directions. Feelings of being "dumb" remain even though others may see her as successful.

Quick to Comprehend

No difficulties in ability to understand material (written or spoken). May even jump several steps ahead (in comprehension) of where the speaker or text is at the time.

Terrible Memory

Loses keys, glasses; can't remember names. Whole chunks of time (early childhood or earlier events) drop out, leaving a black hole.

Excellent and Specific Memory

Able to recall exact years and dates; a whiz at games like Jeopardy.

Have we caught your interest? Are you still with us? Then read on. ADD adults can have any number of symptoms, and they can present themselves in any configuration of clusters. See if you can find yourself in any of the real life histories on the next few pages. The descriptions are presented in bold type with their stories to follow.

Description: ***Woman, spacy, disorganized, problems understanding, mood swings***

Sally is thirty-four years old, married, works as a bank teller and is a mother of three school-aged children. She did just okay in school, and two of her children need help on a nightly basis with homework. She has had a lot of problems with her marriage.

When Sally was in elementary school, teachers told her mother that she seemed bright. They were mystified because no matter how hard they tried to help her, she just never "worked up to her potential." By high school, Sally's counselor told her mother (as an aside) that Sally should consider a trade school, since she would "never make it in college." Since there are no secrets in families, Sally eventually heard her mother relating her counselor's words to her favorite aunt. Of course, she was devastated, and, instead of pursuing a dental degree, she didn't even consider college. She took a job in a bank and was trained on the teller line. She always had to check and double check her work so that she wouldn't make silly errors, and her performance reviews were mediocre because of her mistakes. *No matter how hard she tried to do an excellent job*, she found she was just barely hanging on.

Sally married at age twenty-one and soon had three children. She found that working and trying to take care of the house and kids was almost too much. Fortunately, she married a nice guy who did help a lot and loved Sally very much. However, Fred felt he was at the end of his rope too. Sally was one of those women who had pronounced mood swings about three weeks out of every month. She had been told that this was related to her hormonal cycle; however, birth control pills, other medication, herbs and vitamins had not helped. When Sally was in her "moody cycle" she was angry, explosive or in tears most of the time.

As hard as this was on Fred and the kids, believe it or not, it was even harder on Sally. When Sally was in the middle of one of her moods, she had *no way of evaluating what was happening*. Instead, she felt that whatever particular mood she was feeling was absolutely appropriate. No one could possibly convince her that she was wrong. *However*, and this is a *big* however, on the next day after the explosion was over, she felt terrible. She hated herself. She asked herself, "Why did I blow up?" She knew she was wrong. She lived with the constant guilt that she might be damaging her children or destroying her marriage, but the cycle would repeat itself over and over in her life.

Sally is an ADD adult. She has always had problems processing information. The tasks at work are difficult for her. She has mood swings which accelerate before her menstrual cycle and make it impossible for her to be a successful spouse and mother. Does this sound familiar? If you are a man, does this sound like your wife?

Description: ***Male, impulsive, need for danger, minor difficulty processing***

John is twenty-two years old and in college. He is doing okay academically and is satisfied with his progress. His main concern is his lack of ability to keep a relationship.

John always had to work to get good grades in high school. He complained loudly to his parents that he was working too hard. Actually, he probably spent twice the amount of time needed by his buddies to pull grades of A's and B's. He kept on plugging, though, and not only graduated from high school with a GPA of 3.6, but did quite well on his SATs.

John is dark-haired, well-built and has been told he is "cute," "handsome," and a "stud." However, he can't seem to hook up with just one woman. He can't even begin to think of a long-term relationship because he can't even get to first base. He hasn't had one date in college. He always seems to blurt out something that hurts women's feelings, and then he feels stupid. He has had many women simply look at him with amazement and then disgust when he tries to start what he considers to be an "interesting" conversation.

John has another side to him as well. Since adolescence, he has needed to drive as fast as possible in his car (did you know a VW bus can go eighty-seven m.p.h. down a winding road?) He needed to water-ski as fast as his friends would tow him and try that one jump over and over, until he finally broke his arm.

As a little kid, he was climbing trees, jumping off cliffs, and he knew the staff at the local emergency room by their first names. John's mother was always pleading with him to "knock it off." She was legitimately afraid she would get a call from the sheriff or police informing her that he had taken one chance too many. John laughed her off but secretly, inside himself, he was a little afraid too.

He knew that there was almost a compulsion that forced him into dangerous activity about once a month, or even more often. He knew that there was a calmness and centering that happened for him after the terrific adrenaline rush associated with danger had passed. He found himself living more and more for this calmness.

John is an ADD adult. He has major problems with impulsivity, which cause many of his blunders and general ineptitude in social situations. In addition, he absolutely craves danger for the calming effect it produces as a result of the adrenaline surges. Sound familiar?

Description: *Male, hyperactive, compulsive*

Peter is fifty-two years old and is a very successful and well-known stockbroker/financial planner (only for the "very" rich and famous). He is currently working on his third marriage and has no children. For fun, he trains for triathlons and, not too surprisingly, competes at the national level.

Peter is fiercely competitive in all areas of his life. When he began running, he began with 5Ks, but quickly moved up to triathlons (for the challenge). He absolutely lives for running and the thrill of competition. His office walls are covered with pictures of himself and other competitors in the heat of the race.

Peter is just as competitive in his business life, and he constantly lives on the edge of danger and excitement in his business ventures. No one in the business is willing to take more risks or is as brilliant as Peter. Just don't ever get in his way. Unfortunately, his bloodlust in the business world makes him cut ethical corners once in a while. His "corners" are nothing that the IRS could ever prove, but he knows that he has pulled one over on the world. His business motto (which hangs in his secret den at home) is *Crush and Destroy.*

Peter will talk loudly and at length about his love of running and the competition he finds in triathlons. What he doesn't admit to clients and business partners is that he feels *driven* to run. When he is running, he feels alive and able to cope with the world. Peter thrives on the thought of an upcoming competition. He loves the heat and rush of blood as he participates. To him, this is life! Don't ever get in the way of his scheduled runs. Even the most important business crisis takes a back seat to his sport.

But inside, Peter has a small glimmer of fear that he doesn't share with anyone. He recognizes that he is driven. Once, just once, when he was twenty-four, he had a knee injury. His choice was to stop running forever or have arthroscopic surgery. Of course, he chose the surgery. This required a two-week period of immobility, then physical therapy, a knee brace, and again physical therapy for a solid year before he was able to run again.

He went crazy during this time. He lost clients at work because he was short and nasty with them. His edge, his shark-like business sense, disappeared, and he felt more like a jellyfish floating through the water but making no impact on anything. His income dropped from $200,000 per year to below $100,000. He couldn't sleep at night. He developed a craving for sugar and chocolate. He tried to talk to his doctor about how he was feeling but was told to "relax" and heal. No one understood the agony that he was experiencing. He felt as though he was on pins and needles. His very skin crawled at times. He was losing his edge. What was happening? He was not just frightened, he was absolutely terrified of never feeling "normal" (to him) again.

Finally, his knee healed. He began to work out slowly and cautiously. He was fine. He went back to 5Ks, then 10Ks, then, after a year-and-a-half, was once again entering a triathlon. He was back! His career was moving ahead. He was making money. His life was saved!

Peter is an ADD adult who is extremely hyperactive. He self-medicates and keeps his hyperactivity under control by running; thus the hyperactivity becomes an asset in his business life. The extreme training and running actually changes the chemical balance in his brain and produces a focused and calming effect. Have you known a Mr. "Crush and Destroy" in your life?

Description: *Male, problems processing and understanding, impulsivity*

Dave is only eighteen years old and is currently serving time in the criminal justice system.

Dave was a cute little boy in elementary school. His mother always dressed him in clean jeans and polo shirts. He always came to school with his hair combed and his face scrubbed. But . . . Dave had problems staying in his seat and quickly became known as the class clown. When he was asked to copy sentences from the board or take dictation, it was an absolute nightmare for him! He tried so hard! He didn't mean to erase and leave those huge gaping holes in his papers. He just couldn't help it. By second grade, his teacher and his mom knew that reading was going to be a struggle as well, but Dave's teachers liked him. He didn't have a mean bone in his body. He worked hard, and his parents faithfully spent hours and hours sitting at the kitchen table helping him with his homework. Sometimes he didn't really need that much help, but he did need them to stay with him and say, "Dave, pay attention. Let's get this done. Stop playing with the dog. *Pay attention.*"

When Dave reached the age of eleven, he began to get a little more defiant and testy with his teachers and his parents. He wasn't quite the same hardworking, lovable little boy any longer. When he reached twelve, and adolescence hit with full force, his real problems began. Dave's parents describe the change by saying that Dave went from Dr. Jekyll to Mr. Hyde. Dave began cutting school, swore at his teachers, and his grades fell to the C and D level. Dave told his parents that he hated them. He began wearing black clothing, listening to heavy metal music, and he shaved off part of his hair.

Dave's parents were flabbergasted and actually paralyzed by the change. They didn't know what to do next. What happened to their sweet, hardworking son? Initially, they thought it was just adolescence. They tried one counselor, then another, but nothing helped. By age sixteen, Dave was continuing on the same path and soon added truancy to his list of problems. Suddenly he refused to go to school at all. His parents asked for help from the vice principal, the counselor, the principal and, finally, the police. There was no help. There was nothing that would "make" Dave go to school. However, his parents were told that they could be in a lot of trouble if they couldn't make Dave go to school. Dave's mom lost weight and spent day after day crying alone in the house about her son and what had happened to him.

Dave continued his truancy and defiance. He moved out of the house at seventeen and lived with a friend (who was twenty-three) in a garage. He refused to even talk to his parents. His friends looked like something out of horror comic books.

Before too long, Dave's parents answered a knock on their front door, and the police were on the doorstep. The police asked questions regarding Dave's whereabouts. A local liquor store had been robbed. Dave's parents didn't know much about his life but, once again, they were warned that they were responsible for him until he turned eighteen. Dave's parents tracked him down to his garage and offered help. Dave's mother cried. Dave refused and told both his mother and father he could take care of himself. Dave's parents again went to the social workers and police for help, but they came away feeling that Dave's problems were *their* fault.

This pattern continued. The police visited Dave's parents on several occasions. When Dave was eighteen, the final knock was heard at the door. The police once again asked if they knew where Dave was. Of course, they gave the police his garage address, but Dave had left town. The police recited a whole list of crimes, mainly dealing with violent and impulsive acts on Dave's part. The parents were devastated.

Finally, a year later, Dave was apprehended by the police and put in jail. He was eighteen-and-a-half and therefore tried in the adult justice system. Dave called his parents from the phone in jail. This time he sounded more like his old self. He sounded more like the little boy they had known until adolescence hit. Dave was sad, sorry for what he had done, and in tears when he called his parents.

He told them he didn't know what had happened to him. He explained that for those years, he had felt so angry he didn't know what to do. He told his parents he was angry at them, people at school and people in the world. The only thing he knew to do was to pull away and hurt people. For that period of time he didn't care about his parents or the other people he hurt. He felt an overwhelming compulsion to rob and strike out at the world. Looking back, he said he couldn't understand what he had done. He couldn't understand what had happened to him. It was almost as though another person had taken over his body for those violent teenage years.

But Dave is eighteen-and-a-half and, in the eyes of our justice system, an adult. He was tried in the criminal justice system and sentenced to four years in a federal prison.

Dave is an ADD male who had learning problems in school that were never identified and treated appropriately. When he reached adolescence, the surge of adolescent hormones took over. His main reaction was one of anger and rage. He was also very impulsive – certainly the anger and impulsivity was an explosive combination. Have you ever known the heartache of a troubled adolescent?

Description: *Female, processing problems, depression, disorganization*

Adele is forty years old. She is married and has two children, but the marriage has been rocky for years. She holds an important position as a corporate executive and deals with overseas trading. This position requires her to work with high-powered people in the business world and to be responsible for huge sums of money, often numbering into the millions.

Adele has an excellent reputation in the business world. People talk about her with awe. Her salary is above six figures. To her co-workers and superiors she can do no wrong. All her life she has been told by her supervisors, as she moved up the corporate ladder, that she was very intelligent. However, she knows only too well that she is really *not* as intelligent as people think. She has simply been able to fool people for many years. In fact, she often thinks of herself as a "fake" and lives in constant terror of someone finding this out. She knows she has had difficulty understanding and processing information all her life. She has had to work extremely hard and has spent many long nights studying to understand the principles of international trading.

Nothing ever comes easy to her. She feels that she is barely hanging onto all of her high-powered business dealings by her fingernails. She has the feeling that if she is given just one more assignment or one more client, she will lose the whole thing and her career will fall down around her head like a house of cards – then everyone will know the truth about her!

Adele has another secret as well. She is totally disorganized. However, this is a well-kept secret at work. No one, not even her secretary, knows just how scattered she really is. She dictates memos and relies heavily on her secretary to keep her appointments scheduled and to find memos and papers. She has a secret drawer in her desk where she scoops papers and memos from the top of her desk – there to stay for weeks and weeks until they are forgotten entirely.

At home, she can't keep up her charade. She must let down somewhere. Her desk is a mess; clutter engulfs her house. She can't find her checkbook and can't manage to pay her bills on time. This enrages her husband, who has begun to feel that she simply doesn't care about him, or else she is being vindictive and punishing him for his one brief affair.

As Adele gets older, she realizes that her body is beginning to show signs of stress. She has backaches and constant stomach problems, very likely caused by anxiety. The tension across the back of her shoulders feels like a steel band. She has a wide range of moods, including periods of depression. She worries about her children. They are hard workers, making A's in school, but they also seem to be driven.

She knows she is not happy. Life is too much work. How long can she hang on? Will her children grow up and feel the same way she does? This is no way to live.

Description: *Male, problems processing, depression, spacy*

Jim is twenty-two years old and is now working as a stock boy at K-Mart. He is doing well. His boss likes him, he is happy to put in extra hours, and he never causes trouble.

Jim was a cute little boy with red hair and a brush of freckles across his nose. His parents thought that his habit of beginning a sentence and then stopping and repeating the same subject, or changing subjects, was "cute." Actually, Jim had a delay of about five seconds in his speech pattern. He would begin to say something simple, such as, "I want to go up the street and . . . (five-second gap) . . . Oh! I want to go up the street and play with John."

Jim was identified as having a "learning disability" when he began to have problems with reading and writing in second grade. He was placed in a resource program and was maintained in that program until he graduated from high school.

When a student graduates from high school, the implication is that he is ready for the world – not true in Jim's case. He had graduated only because he had been carefully and lovingly moved along through the grades. He had no real life skills, and the big world was terrifying and frightening to him.

After graduation, at age seventeen, Jim needed to find a job. He looked clean-cut and friendly. He was quickly hired as a stock boy at a local market. Soon the boss realized that Jim couldn't remember a sequence of three orders, such as, "take the soup back to the soup aisle, pick up a bunch of celery, and bring in the carts from the parking lot." Jim would invariably forget two of the three orders. Jim's boss didn't understand this stuff about "learning disabilities." What a bunch of baloney, anyway! This kid was just lazy and didn't want to work, so Jim was fired, as he was fired from the next ten or eleven jobs. Jim didn't know what was happening. He knew in his heart that he was a nice person. He knew he tried his best. He knew he really wanted to work, but nothing was going right.

Finally, Jim found a job that seemed to work for him. He was hired to bag groceries in a small, exclusive grocery store that catered to an older but wealthy clientele. This was perfect. Jim had finally found his niche. He was able to put the groceries in the bags. He walked the old folks out to their cars, and he put the groceries in the trunk. He said things such as, "It's a nice day. How do you like the weather? It looks like rain. How is your granddaughter?" He was clean and neat and everybody liked him. The owner knew that he was a bit "slow," but that was okay

Jim was succeeding in life. He had made friends with one of the girls who attended his church, so he was even dating on Saturday nights. What heaven! He made a friend of another boy who worked at the gas station down the street from the grocery store, and they often ate their lunch together in a small park with lots of trees and cool shade.

Jim had a big heart. He trusted people. He had been supported by parents who loved him. He had been helped by learning disability specialists during his years in high school who understood that he was "learning disabled." Jim didn't have a mean bone in his body, and what's more, he liked to help people feel as good as he did. He had a job and was conscientious. He was saving his money under the paper liner in his underwear drawer and was on the road to being a grown man.

Jim's mother suggested that he needed to start a bank account and added him to her combination checking and savings accounts so she could keep an eye on his earnings. This sounded wonderful. Jim scooped up all his cash and went down to the bank with his mother. He had managed to accumulate $546 and some change. They added his name to his mother's accounts.

His mother mentioned that some day he might like to save his money for a car. Jim heard that statement and the next day decided he needed a car – *now*. After all, he was working, he had money, and he had a bank account. He marched right down to the local used car lot and bought himself a blue pick up truck. He forged his mother's name ahead of time and signed his own name. After all, it was his own money! He proudly drove the truck off the lot.

The next day, Jim was telling his friend at the gas station about his truck and the friend sadly said, "Gee, I wish I had a truck."

Jim replied, "I'll buy you a truck too." He and his friend marched down to a different car lot and, once again, he forged his mother's name, signed his own name and bought his friend a truck. Fortunately for Jim, he had only forged his mother's name and not an employer's name on the check. He had absolutely no concept that he had done something wrong by tapping into her personal bank account. Even though his mother explained it to him several times and drew him a picture, he never did understand why he had to return not only his friend's pick up truck but his own truck as well.

Jim is an ADD/learning disabled adult. The school recognized his learning disability and supported him, but nothing was ever done about the ADD specifically. Thus Jim was truly not prepared to cope with the outside world, since he had never had the opportunity to see if medication would make a difference.

Summary

Do you see any similarities between any of these stories and your own life? Do you recognize yourself as being at either end of the ADD continuum or moving back and forth along the continuum, even on the same day? Are you still interested? Are things beginning to fall into place? Again, we are still at the exploring stage, so keep an open mind and see what you think.

Adult Attention Deficit Disorder Questionnaire

Below is an ADD questionnaire that will help you identify where you are on the ADD continuum. Each category has a rating scale from 1 to 5, with 5 being *the highest rating*. For example, if you are reading about Hyperactivity and think, "Yes, this really is me," then you would rate yourself as a 5. If that category doesn't fit, you would be a 1 – or somewhere in between.

This questionnaire is subjective. That means the numbers are not hard and fast, and after rating yourself you will not be able to say, "Bingo! Yes, that is me!" It is simply meant to give you more information at this stage as you pursue your exploration of ADD.

Adult Evaluation for Attention Deficit Disorder

The following rating scale is written in a narrative form to provide the rater with a comprehensive look at ten different categories that typically affect ADD adults. A rating scale from 1 to 5 has been used. A number 5 indicates that a high degree of that behavior is present, and a number 1 indicates that it is almost non-existent in that adult.

Although this scale does require the rater to provide a numerical score from 1 to 5, it does not have a total score that must be met to qualify as an adult with ADD. Rather it is intended to provide a sufficiently broad range of information for both the rater and the adult being evaluated to consider how the adult is affected by the characteristics of ADD.

1. **Present in Childhood**

For some people, academic difficulties extend as far back as school entrance. Comments on early report cards from teachers typically include such statements as "has difficulty paying attention in class," "is easily distracted," and the most prevalent comment of all, "is not working up to potential." Very often there are incidences of early temper outbursts with real temper tantrums in evidence, as well as mischievous behavior. There can also be difficulty with written reports and assignments.

For other adults, the academic area has escaped any impact, and the signs of ADD that extend into childhood are sometimes more subtle but present, nevertheless. Sometimes adults recall having difficulty with concentration; they may even have had a somewhat "spacy" reputation in the early years, or may have been clearly hyperactive with a high degree of motor restlessness in evidence.

Special Notes

RATING SCALE: 1___ 2___ 3___ 4___ 5___

2. Inattention

Adults with ADD typically have experienced difficulty concentrating and paying attention all their lives.

While they were in school they often tended to "drift off" during lectures and resorted to coping techniques, such as taking notes or doodling, which served to focus their attention. In conversation with friends or business associates, they will often feel themselves lose their trains of thought or "float off" and, when they pull themselves back with effort, will only find the same tendency occurring over and over again. They will very often describe themselves as becoming "bored" with conversations, since they really can't explain the phenomenon that is occurring, and sometimes will find themselves far ahead of the conversation, almost second-guessing the person.

Special Notes:

RATING SCALE: 1___ 2___ 3___ 4___ 5___

3. Processing of Information

Adults who have Attention Deficit Disorder usually have difficulty with processing information. They often have the feeling that they should be able to understand something, but that it eludes them. They often need to have things such as new concepts or information explained more than once. One adult mentioned that he found himself asking people to "tell me a different way." He was instinctively attempting to use more than one modality to acquire information.

There appears to be a discrepancy between the level of intellectual ability, or how "smart" they are, and how well they can understand information. Obviously, this causes a great deal of frustration and usually seriously affects self-image. This is often not apparent to the outside world, but the ADD adult is very conscious of this difficulty.

Special Notes:

RATING SCALE: 1___ 2___ 3___ 4___ 5___

4. Hyperactivity/Hypoactivity

Adults who have Attention Deficit Disorder fall into one side of a continuum or the other when this category is considered. They may either appear to be "hyperactive," with much activity and motor restlessness present, or they may have a "spacy" or daydreaming presentation and generally appear vague and lethargic.

On this section, if an adult falls into either the "hypo-" or "hyperactive" end of the continuum, mark a 5.

Hyperactivity

Hyperactive adults usually exhibit a varied degree of motor activity. This can range from a foot or leg jiggling in a rather unobtrusive manner to the entire body rocking or moving. At times the adult will shift his entire body position while sitting in a chair. It can include such things as constantly (and almost compulsively) touching the face or hair. It can move into more serious behaviors such as pulling out hair, eyebrows or eyelashes.

Hyperactive adults usually fill their lives completely so they have no idle time. If there is an extremely high degree of hyperactivity, the person may use jogging, biking or some other strenuous physical exercise to correct the internal system. This can be the classic workaholic who always must be doing something. At times hyperactive adults become sensitive to their high degree of movement and utilize some strong coping strategies. They can actually train themselves to look calm on the outside when they describe that, in actuality, they may be "going one hundred m.p.h." on the inside. Very often hyperactive adults will maintain this level of activity and then "crash" and come to a dead halt.

Hypoactivity

On the other end of the continuum are ADD adults who have been described all their lives as "lazy" or "unmotivated." These people desperately want to do well and succeed, but just can't get up the momentum to make his or her life work. They speak about things taking an unbelievable amount of effort, and beginning a task or project is often seen as an insurmountable task. They have difficulty with "follow-through."

Special Notes:

RATING SCALE: 1___ 2___ 3___ 4___ 5___

5. **Impulsivity**

One of the easiest forms of impulsivity to recognize is impulsive speech, which takes the form of constantly interrupting friends and co-workers. The ADD adult is often not even aware that it is occurring. Other indicators of impulsivity are spending beyond one's financial limits, owning many adult toys (such as cars and boats) and leaving jobs and/or school without thinking through the consequences.

Adults tend to mask this tendency as their early family upbringing comes into play. They have been taught at an early age that this type of impulsivity is not good; thus they temper their impulses and try to remain in a socially acceptable range.

One way to discern if this is indeed a problem area is to track the person's school or employment history. There is often a long series of school moves or changes of employment – the person appears to have a good reason for those moves, but when viewed objectively, the pattern remains.

Special Notes:

RATING SCALE: 1___ 2___ 3___ 4___ 5___

6. **Short and Hot Temper**
    An ADD adult may be subject to flashes of temper or rage attacks that erupt with little or no warning. Often they describe these episodes of rage as being "white hot" or "red flashes" and are unable to control their reactions until the attack is past. Once it passes, they often experience a feeling of calm.

    Adults often find that they must do their best to hide or modify their tempers in order to exist in society. They can be extremely successful for awhile. This can be disastrous to relationships, as the temper may not surface until the adult has passed the courtship phase and is into a relationship or marriage.

    At other times the adult may have been raised in a family where temper was not allowed to surface. By repressing temper, several things may occur. He may appear to be absolutely flat emotionally. He may allow temper to slowly build to a point where he explodes. He may experience physical complaints such as back pain or gastrointestinal upsets.

Special Notes:

RATING SCALE: 1___ 2___ 3___ 4___ 5___

7. **Disorganization/Compulsively Neat**
    Again, this category is on a continuum. On one end of the continuum people are disorganized and scattered. On the other end of the continuum they can be compulsively organized to the point that much rigidity is in evidence. On this section an adult who is either very disorganized or compulsively neat would be rated a 5.

    Disorganization
    On the disorganized side of the continuum, people often find their desks at work piled high by the end of the day, or have a system where they claim they can always find things, but certainly no

one else could. Often there is a feeling that a task facing them is almost insurmountable, since the energy that it takes to begin something is significant. They know that the task itself is well within their ability levels, but actually beginning the task feels like hitting a brick wall. These people generally are known as procrastinators and drive spouses and significant others crazy by this behavior.

Compulsively Neat

The compulsively neat person often reacts with anger if anything is out of place. Clutter distracts these people; thus the rigidity. However, it is interesting that sometimes a person will be compulsively neat at work, insisting that everything be organized and perfect, while that same person may be a "total slob" or disorganized at home. Often the ADD adult will rely on a secretary at work or the spouse at home to keep things in order.

Special Notes:

RATING SCALE: 1___ 2___ 3___ 4___ 5___

8. Mood Swings

Mood swings can occur as often as two or three times a day or more. They can vary widely from person to person. Women appear to be more plagued by mood swings than men, but not always. It may have some connection with female hormones, but this is not documented at this time. There is also a strong possibility that men tend to hide this characteristic not only from others, but from themselves, so they actually are not consciously aware that the moods are occurring.

The mood swings are typically described as a feeling of being "up" or normal, and then something small – an action or thought – will send the person plunging into depression. Often this depression will last and present problems in itself. Depression can become so deep that suicide is contemplated. The fear of such a depression is often present for ADD people. ADD adults often find that as their mood swings on the "up" or high side there is a feeling of elation or of almost manic energy. They often use these periods as periods of high creativity and accomplishment. They often strongly resist letting go of this feeling.

At times ADD adults try to avoid the mood swings by including heavy physical activity in their lives, such as jogging or bicycling. They are usually aware that a panic sets in if an injury or the weather prevents their normal exercise regime from taking place. Symptoms may accelerate as age or injury make exercise impossible.

Special Notes:

RATING SCALE: 1___ 2___ 3___ 4___ 5___

9. **Low Stress Tolerance**

ADD adults typically handle stress in one of two ways. They may approach it as a "high" and use it to create energy which, at times, can be almost manic in nature. For example, they may do such things as staying up all night working on a project.

On the other end of the continuum ADD adults may fear stress, since it causes depression. When stress becomes extreme, many of these adults retreat to the house or the bedroom and stop functioning for a period of time. They will go to great lengths to avoid people. This can even extend to being unwilling to make or receive phone calls.

Stress can often produce physical symptoms as well. It is very common to find ADD adults with gastrointestinal upsets, headaches and, occasionally, back pain.

Special Notes:

RATING SCALE: 1___ 2___ 3___ 4___ 5___

10. **Heredity**

ADD is usually genetic in nature, and once an adult becomes familiar with the ADD indicators, she will say, "That's just like my dad," or "That's just like my mom." At times an adult ADD evaluation is begun because the adult has brought her child in for an evaluation. During the conversation the adult realizes that many of the same traits are present in her life, causing difficulties. Aunts, uncles and other siblings often have the ADD characteristics as well.

Special Notes:

RATING SCALE: 1___ 2___ 3___ 4___ 5___

Chapter 2

Is ADD Just a Fad?
What's All the Fuss?

Are we talking about the new yuppie disease of the nineties? Is ADD just a figment of some social welfare-do-gooder's imagination? No! Unequivocally, no! No, in the strongest terms that we can state!

Attention Deficit Disorder is a *biochemical malfunction of the brain*. ADD is a very real disorder. Let us begin with what we do know about Attention Deficit Disorder. We know that in an ADD adult the brain chemistry is somehow incorrect. As medical science understands it now, there appears to be a chemical deficiency in the frontal lobe of the brain, such that the normal functions of the frontal lobe – attention, planning, organization, long-term goals, self-criticism – are missing. The system within the brain that regulates the ability to clamp down on the thoughts that are scattered in a million different directions is *poor*. The brain system that allows us to control our focus and pay attention is *deficient*. The ability to control the impulsiveness that makes us interrupt our boss in an important business meeting is *lacking*. The ability to pull ourselves out of a mental slump or a depression is *not present*. While all of these different aspects of ADD are separate and unique, they are all caused by the chemical deficiency within the brain that translates into lack of control for ADD adults.

All of the signals the brain gives to its various parts are transmitted by a very complex chemical network. These chemicals activate neurons that actually communicate with each other through the release and reception of specific neurotransmitters. When the chemical source is intermittent, the information that is being transmitted comes across as on-and-off bits of information as well.

The chemicals the brain produces represent an unbelievably intricate and complex network. To illustrate the complexity of the entire chemical chain of events, think back to your childhood. As a child did you ever set up a string of dominos in a long line? When you flicked the first domino with your finger the entire row fell over in a sequence. Our brains act in much the same way. One brain chemical triggers another chemical and yet another. These interactions are sequential, and they also move from the simple to the complex. To make it even more awe-inspiring, each chemical in the brain represents a very specific set of interactions. The main chemicals thought to be implicated in the ADD condition are dopamine and norepinephrine. Another chemical thought to be involved in ADD is serotonin. Each of these chemicals seems to have a fairly specific function. When we talk about dopamine, we are talking about a chemical which is thought to be the main culprit in the ADD adult's difficulty with attention span and concentration. Serotonin is essential for restful sleep and feelings of well-being. When serotonin levels are low, aggression, depression and irritability may result. There is also an interaction between chemicals that occurs and initiates a chain of events that scientists are still struggling to fully understand. You can see how the entire subject quickly becomes extremely complicated.

For our purposes, it is important to have a basic understanding of the overall framework of the chemical system, but beyond that, it is best left to the ADD adults who are scientifically oriented and/or curious. For those, we recommend any text on brain function.

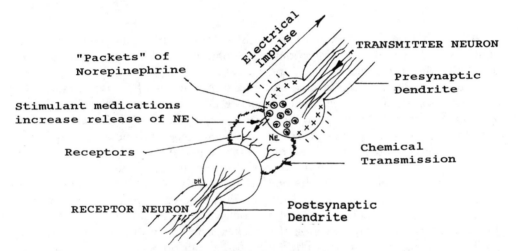

Neurological Pathway System in the Brain

This illustration is an enlargement of a neuro-pathway system in the brain. It shows the gap, called the synapse, between the neurotransmitter sites. It also shows the receptor sites on each side of the neuro-pathway that enter into the process. Without some kind of biochemical intervention, the electrical activity that activates the chemical messengers that carry all the summary input through the brain doesn't cross the synapse in a regular manner. To make matters more complicated, the brain function or amount of electrical activity available to an ADD adult can vary from day to day. One day the ADD adult may feel "on" and experience much less difficulty in life and at work, but the very next day (or hour!) he may find himself almost unable to think and function. Until the electrical malfunction of the ADD condition is understood, ADD adults will often feel that they are slightly "crazy." After all, how could their ability to think and perform not only change, but change *radically*, from one day to the next?

Let's end this section with what we *don't* know about the brain. This applies whether we are discussing an ADD brain or just the brain itself. We have mentioned that the brain is incredibly complex and an absolute marvel in its ability to function. This is an understatement, but it is difficult to find words that adequately express the marvel that is the sponge-like gray matter that sits in our skulls. All scientists are well aware that the understanding of brain chemistry is still in its infancy. To give you an illustration of just where the art of brain research stands, let us relate a comment made by a noted psychiatrist at an ADD conference. He said, "What we know about the chemistry of the brain is the equivalent of a teaspoon of water. What we don't know is the equivalent of the ocean." That is pretty awesome.

Thus, at this stage of the game, we are able to identify the symptoms of ADD and even visually look at the electrical patterns thrown off by an ADD adult's brain using one of our newest tools, the PET Scan (Positron Emission Tomography). However, we are not able to pinpoint with precise accuracy the exact chemical mechanism that is responsible for ADD or the precise combination of genes. Beyond that, we are certainly not able to determine with precision which medication will work for any specific ADD adult. We are able to make suppositions and scientific guesses as to which class of medications will probably work best for an ADD adult, but that is as far as it goes. Once you understand the complexity of the brain and our understanding (or lack of understanding), clearly you will get a gut-level appreciation of the need for a trial-and-error search for correct medication. This will also allow you to understand our chapter on medication in a whole different light.

Why is ADD Such a Big Deal Now?

Even though the "official" naming of ADD (or hyperactivity) appeared in the literature as early as the late 1890s, it seems as though ADD has always been a part of the human condition. However, there seem to be several reasons that ADD is not only being researched and recognized, but becoming more of a problem in this day and age.

Changes in Society

Let's take, for example, a young male adolescent with a high degree of hyperactivity and impulsivity in the late 1800s. If school was difficult for this adolescent, there were plenty of alternate career opportunities possible – working on the family farm or making his fame and fortune on a merchant ship were alternatives – and it was not at all uncommon for a young male to leave home to make his way in the world. These adolescents were not "stuck" in a school setting which was often extremely difficult for them. The case is different now.

Today our young people are required to remain in a structured and highly academic school setting. They are stuck! Vocational education, which promoted welding, woodworking or auto mechanics, was prevalent in years past but is long gone. Now there is literally no way out for many ADD adolescents as they approach adulthood.

In the case of ADD females, the recognition that they could possibly have been suffering from ADD didn't come until years and years after the ADD condition had been documented in males. This is because with females, ADD typically takes on a different presentation. Instead of being boisterous, hard-to-manage and troublemakers, females tend to have a much quieter brand of ADD, more on the inattentive side. That does not mean that it presents problems that are any less severe, just more difficult to spot. In fact, that is still the case today, and many ADD females are never diagnosed. Instead, they are often the dreamers who sit in the back of the classroom, lost in thought and lost in education.

In the past we had little understanding of mental health and certainly no concept of ADD. There was often a skeleton or two in the family closet, such as a crazy relative locked away. There were many instances in the romantic novels of that period's young women pining away in seclusion or routinely falling ill with the "vapors." This could easily have been an ADD adolescent who was unable to cope with the world, instead retreating into herself. There was often a family member, usually a male (but not always), who had a lust for adventure and who left home to go West. In fact, Columbus was probably ADD – who else would have gotten on a rickety ship and sailed off the edge of the world? It is easy to see that our society in the early years offered many opportunities which allowed a higher degree of mobility, excitement and physical labor. This is certainly not the situation today.

Another factor operating today is the pressure that is present in our society. We live in a terribly pressure-filled environment. Our highways are packed, our cities are crowded and air quality is poor. We are surrounded by people and noise pollution. Most interesting of all, we have become so accustomed to the lives we live, we are not aware of the stress and, therefore, do not take measures to deal with it. The rash of shootings on the crowded freeways that occurred in the early 1990s, the increase in homelessness, the gang situation – all attest to the pressure as well as add to it. To make matters worse, pressure or stress exacerbates the severity of the ADD symptoms.

All these ingredients added together operate like a gigantic stew which, after years of simmering quietly, is about ready to boil over and make a real mess.

Genetic Factors

It is generally recognized that ADD has been present in the human race since the dawn of time. This means that even among cavemen our ADD adult population was represented. In prehistoric days it was most probably the impulsive ADD male who braved the raging blizzard, killed a woolly mammoth and saved the tribe from starvation. However, the ADD caveman who lived in the next cave to the right was probably killed by another woolly mammoth when he attempted the same maneuver. The ADD males who survived and those who died (and weren't able to reproduce) probably provided some sort of natural balance within the race.

In the early history of the United States, there was a good deal of violence. The young, hot-tempered male often wouldn't live into adulthood. Probably many of the "quick-draw artists" of the Old West, as well as many of the outlaws, were ADD adolescents and adults. In addition, we had the early soldiers of the frontier – the cavalry was required to be bold, and a high degree of impulsivity would need to be present for a young man to choose to go off and fight Indians. There is a high probability of ADD there too. What happened to them? They died, usually at an early age.

As we move forward into history we have the devastating and terrible ground wars which took a tremendous toll of young, active men. History tells us that the Civil War, when the deaths on the side of the North and South are counted, killed as many men as WWII. In World War I, even though it was devastating, we lost only 109,000 men. This was soon followed by WWII, which was responsible for the deaths of 400,000 males in their prime. Korea and Vietnam added to the death toll, but because of the altered nature of warfare by that time, the numbers were not as high.

Let's take our young ADD male who had been drafted or enlisted in the service during that period of time. Doesn't it make sense that it was the young ADD male who stepped forward when volunteers were requested for the Airborne Division, the Navy Seals in WWII or the Green Berets in the 1960s? It was probably true that a higher proportion of ADD males were killed or disabled than men in the general population. Because young men comprise the age group that is sent to war, many of the ADD males were killed before they found a mate and produced children. This is a parallel to the phenomena that was present with our ADD cavemen. There was a sufficient number of ADD males killed, and therefore unable to reproduce, that provided a system of natural checks and balances that held civilization in a state of homeostasis.

Now let's look at society today and attempt to project into the future. We have some rather alarming information coming to us in a book by Dr. David Comings, a geneticist who has worked with the Tourette Syndrome population for many years. In his recently published book, *The Gene Bomb*, he states that there has been an increase in depression, suicide, alcohol and drug abuse, anxiety, Attention Deficit Hyperactivity Disorder and an increase in crime. To back up his hypothesis he supplies study after study, all of which have been published and thus authenticated in well-known scientific journals such as the *Archives of General Psychiatry* and the *American Journal of Epidemiology*, or which have been taken from official bodies such as the California Department of Justice.

In his introduction to *The Gene Bomb*, Dr. Comings provides a clean and simple summary of his hypothesis. He begins by stating that he doesn't believe that the behaviors listed above are due to the fact that our society is increasing in complexity. Instead he thinks that our complex society is actually selecting for the genes causing these behaviors.

In his research, he has documented that ADD is a polygenetic disorder. That means that there are a number of genes at work that cause the individual characteristics of ADD, and these genes are inherited from both sides of the family. As each generation grows up and has children there is a tendency for more genes to accumulate. This is certainly borne out in our practice. At times we have had the opportunity to evaluate three generations at one time. In these cases, if you know what to look for, you can see some mild evidence of ADD in the grandparents, but nothing that caused them any difficulty. In the parents the ADD is a little more pronounced, and although they may be successful in business, perhaps the disorder was responsible for them feeling that they never reached their potential. In the third generation, the children, who typically were the ones who prompted the evaluation in the first place, the ADD is obvious and often has caused behavioral problems as well as learning problems.

As these genes accumulate, we see more and more individuals who pose a danger to their own future. We see these behaviors as *problem behaviors*, which include being impulsive, compulsive, oppositional, addictive, easily bored, preferring instant gratification over long-term goals, tending to drop out of school early and becoming involved in teenage pregnancy. On the other hand, individuals who do not carry these genes tend to stay in school, go to college or develop useful skills prior to beginning a family.

Now comes the crux of Dr. Comings' hypothesis. Any living object that reproduces every fifteen to twenty-two years will increase its numbers faster than one that reproduces every twenty-three to thirty years. This earlier age of the first pregnancy tends to act as a powerful selective advantage for the genes involved. This premise is certainly borne out in our clinical practices. As we deal mainly with the ADD population, bear in mind that we are comparing ADD individuals with other ADD individuals, and thus are not even considering what is occurring with the so-called "normal" population.

In our practices it is not uncommon for our more severely ADD/learning disabled clients to have multiple children. These children are often from different mates, drugs have often been involved in the pregnancies, and the marriage is often not a stable environment where the children can be cared for and supported; instead, the children may be in foster care or are being raised by grandparents.

In comparison, our more high-functioning ADD adults who do not have a severe form of ADD typically have gone to college, received technical training or have become involved in a career, and the age of childbearing begins later in life. In fact, many women are now having their first child at thirty-five or even forty. They typically have only one or two children because, they report, they are very aware of the cost of raising and educating children and want to be able to give them every possible advantage in life.

While Dr. Comings' hypothesis is certainly thought-provoking and even somewhat frightening, it is in no way saying that society is doomed. His premise is that if we understand what is occurring in society, then we have the ability to make some changes and deal in a more informed manner with the emerging trends.

Is ADD Worldwide?

The other question that is often asked is, "Why is ADD a problem in just the United States? What about other countries?" It's there. We see ADD present in all races and cultures as "Americanized" adults and children are seen in the office. There is an annual international ADD conference, and ADD is increasingly recognized in countries outside of the United States.

However, in underdeveloped countries, survival is still the main concern. When people are worried about putting food on the table or a roof over their heads, ADD isn't considered. It isn't life-threatening, so it is well below food and survival on a person's hierarchy of needs. In addition, many of the conditions that were once present in the U.S., with men needing to participate in dangerous and bloody battles, still remain in those countries. Many of the ADD young men may still be killed at a regular rate, thinning the remainder of ADD adults who exist in underdeveloped societies and preventing the transmission of the genes.

Attention Deficit Disorder has clearly been around since the late 1800s and most probably throughout human history. Due to the change in society, it is now a problem area that must be addressed.

Does Medical Science Recognize ADD?

The answer is unequivocally yes. In fact, to those of us working in the ADD field, this question is so basic and has been answered in so many different ways that we considered omitting this section entirely. Unbelievably, however, we still get calls from people asking if ADD really exists, or they ask if problems with attention or concentration really don't apply to everyone, and isn't ADD overdone anyway?

Let's start from the beginning and see if we can't clear up this question once and for all. For many, many years, there was no way to medically verify that ADD not only existed, but was a very specific biochemical malfunction in the brain.

To answer this question we needed to wait until medical science and technology evolved to the point where science – in particular, the science of brain chemistry – was able to document that ADD does exist. The first definitive medical study to be done on ADD, now considered a landmark study, was done by Dr. Alan Zemetkin at the National Institute of Mental Health in 1990. The title of his study was "Cerebral Glucose Metabolism in Adults with Hyperactivity of Childhood Onset."

Dr. Zemetkin used the PET Scan (Positron Emission Tomography) for this study. He had two technicians administer a radioactive glucose solution intravenously to fifty normal adults and twenty-five hyperactive adults while they performed an auditory attention task. After a period of time, the PET Scan was used to photograph images of the subject's brains, and twenty-eight images or "slices" were obtained from each subject. Dr. Zemetkin was able to determine that in the brains of the ADD adults there was a significant decrease in cerebral glucose metabolism. What does this mean? It means that their brains were less active.

Dr. Zemetkin also noted differences in cerebral glucose metabolism between ADD adults and the "normal" control subjects *specifically in regions of the brain that have "been postulated to be important in the control of preparation for motor activity, motor activity itself, inhibition of inappropriate response, and attention."* What does this mean? ADD adults have difficulty controlling motor activity, are impulsive and have difficulty paying attention.

Since Dr. Zemetkin's famous study there have been many more PET Scan studies. Unfortunately, the PET Scan has some drawbacks, so is not available for routine tests of just anyone suspected of being ADD. For one thing, the glucose that is fed intravenously into the system is radioactive – not very, but still radioactive. In fact, some universities and research centers that have PET Scans for research purposes have cyclotrons in their basements so they can prepare radioactive "soup" for their research patients. In addition, we are talking about a huge outlay of money for the equipment – a PET Scan typically costs somewhere between $1,600 and $2,200. Obviously, it is not readily available to the common man or woman, but to prove the point that ADD is truly a medical condition, the PET Scan is unbeatable.

In addition to the PET Scan, we can also look at the position taken by the federal government regarding ADD. It is tremendously slow and ponderous in its willingness to recognize anything. After the recognition has occurred, our government is even slower in bringing about laws on a specific subject. Once something is finally made law, it has been researched and documented thoroughly. In 1973 the government passed a law which impacted ADD adults. Section 504 of the Rehabilitation Act documented an adult's right to special modifications due to a handicapping condition. This law applies to ADD adults in colleges and universities and also in the workplace.

Next, the Americans with Disabilities Act (ADA) came into being. This act was set in place to protect the handicapped worker from discrimination in the workplace. ADD is considered to be one of the handicapping conditions under ADA, so now we have the federal government not only supporting the presence of ADD in adults, but offering protection to those ADD adults who need it as well.

We can also look to the medical and psychological communities for verification of the existence of ADD. In addition to articles found in medical and psychological research journals, we have the *Diagnostic and Statistical Manual (DSM)*, which is the very bible of psychologists and psychiatrists as they diagnose a person's condition. The *DSM*, now in its fourth revision (known as the *DSM-IV*), is a heavy paperback weighing ten to fifteen pounds. In it are described disorders of the human mind ranging from the mild to the severe.

ADD is included in the *DSM-IV*. In fact, ADD has undergone a very interesting progression, which will be described in detail a little later in this chapter. Basically, in the *DSM*, ADD began with hyperactivity being recognized only in children and ends with the full recognition that ADD extends into the adolescent and adult populations.

It has now been documented beyond any shadow of a doubt that ADD is a legitimate medical condition. It is biochemical in nature and a condition that is not visible to the naked eye. ADD people don't break out in splotches or spots. In fact, it is often termed a "hidden disability" because of this. But, even though its physical effects are "hidden," the chemical imbalance in the brain can cause significant difficulties in the ADD adult's daily life. As you research ADD and talk to your family members, if anyone dares to say to you – whether it is a psychiatrist, pharmacist, neighbor or family member – "That's just the yuppie disease of the nineties," stand tall! Know you have laws and medicine backing you up!

Have the fortitude to continue your own quest for understanding, and if there is the slightest chance that you are an ADD adult, don't stop asking questions and investigating until you have a firm diagnosis and are receiving treatment.

ADD in Adolescents and Adults Documented

When hyperactivity was identified as existing in children in the late 1890s, the psychological and medical researchers unilaterally indicated that it totally *disappeared* when the children reached adolescence. How about adulthood? Nope! It didn't appear there either.

This belief system went on for years until finally, Dr. Paul Wender from the University of Utah decided to do some additional research on the adult "hyperactive" population. You have to give Dr. Wender a lot of credit. He was one of the original medical researchers who stated that ADD only existed in children. It must have taken a great deal of internal fortitude and strength of character for him to admit clearly, loudly, and through many forthcoming research studies that *he had been wrong*! However, Dr. Wender was cautious. At first his studies indicated that only in a minuscule portion (three percent) of the population did the "hyperactivity" of childhood continue into adolescence and adulthood. True to the scientific spirit, however, he kept researching, and other psychologists and physicians followed closely behind. Finally, the percentage began to increase, and by the early 1990s, the percentage of children who carried ADD characteristics over into adolescence and adulthood hit the eighty-three percent mark. Currently, some researchers place the percentage even higher. Dr. Stephen Copps, medical director of the National Professional Consortium in ADD, and a physician in Georgia, feels that the figures are most probably at one hundred percent. However, he clarifies that that does not mean the adult would qualify for the *DSM IV* criteria for ADD, because in adulthood compensation has taken place to the extent that the qualifications might not be met.

We now have a large amount of information regarding ADD in adulthood. Noted scientific journals of psychology and medicine have studies that not only document the biochemical nature of the ADD condition, but *absolutely and without question* verify its presence in adulthood.

Why Has Adult ADD Been Such a Secret?

At the time Dr. Wender was conducting his research studies and was identifying the presence of ADD in adults, Ciba, the pharmaceutical company that manufactures Ritalin, was almost to the end of its patent. When a new drug emerges on the market, pharmaceutical companies spend hundreds of thousands of dollars holding inservices for physicians and in publicity campaigns; however, by the time the adult ADD area emerged, Ritalin was an old drug. Ciba was not willing to spend funds for publicity. This is one of the realities of business.

Therefore, for the first six or seven years after ADD in adulthood was documented, there was no publicity about it. There were no newspaper articles, radio spots or magazine articles and certainly no books on adult ADD. Slowly, adults with ADD began to link together through letters to share experiences. Finally, the first ADD adult newsletter was published, and then another and another; books soon followed. The adult ADD movement is truly a grassroots movement that has swelled to its present size because of the ADD adults themselves and their need for information, as well as their need to share experiences.

What Happens to ADD Adults?

If you are an intelligent adult and at all curious, you must be asking yourself, "Just how is it that 'hyperactivity' that had plagued a child in school and caused many problems in the ability to learn could remain hidden in adulthood?"

To understand the adult ADD population, we must again note that there is a huge amount of variability in the way ADD can manifest itself, and there is a continuum in the severity of the condition. Thus an individual may have any number of ADD characteristics, which can each range from mild to severe.

ADD adults may have been hampered by some of the ADD characteristics while in school, but as adults they have instinctively recognized their difficulties and *migrated toward careers* that placed them in life situations that worked to their advantage. For example, a little boy who might have had difficulty sitting still in a classroom and even more difficulty paying attention to the teacher, but *who was bright,* would instinctively move into a career field that maximized his strengths and minimized his weaknesses. Adults who have careers in real estate, architecture or medicine, as examples, all have the ability to create a high degree of mobility in their chosen fields with a minimal requirement to sit still and pay attention.

One physician who elected to be a trauma surgeon in the emergency room is a rather dramatic example. This particular surgeon is an ADD adult with a limited attention span. He made his way through medical school by forming study groups. When he graduated and needed to choose his area of specialty, he picked trauma surgery. The blood, guts and chaos of the emergency operating room caused an adrenaline surge that kept him focused while the victim was being patched up and shipped off to another part of the hospital for further medical care. This surgeon admitted that he would never have been able to complete a three- or four-hour operation. He recognized that his attention span was too limited. Trauma surgery in the ED was the perfect setting for him to be successful.

ADD adults who are not bright, or who have severe learning disabilities, problems with impulsiveness or serious episodes of rage or depression often can't exist in society. This segment of the ADD population makes up a proportion of our jail population and will be discussed in detail in Chapter 10.

ADD adults have often learned to cope with most situations in their lives, though. The ADD adult who just happens to be hyperactive will often engage in many sports, hire someone to perform tedious tasks, or marry an understanding person who doesn't complain when awakened in the morning at 5:00 a.m. by a foot or leg jiggling and the entire bed moving.

What Causes ADD?

Basically, the causes of ADD fall into two main clusters. The first cluster, and the one understood to be primarily responsible for ADD, is the genetic factor. The second cause is some type of trauma to the brain, which may occur at any point in life.

Genetic Factor

Let's refresh your memory about the genetic type of ADD covered in detail earlier in the chapter. Genetic ADD is usually described as the "true" ADD and probably accounts for eighty to ninety percent of the ADD population. In this type of ADD, if you know what to look for, you can spot evidence of ADD (although it may be subtle) in the family history. You can also spot signs of ADD (they are often subtle) in the early educational history.

ADD Caused by Birth Trauma

Birth is a natural process. When all goes well, a wrinkled, noisy infant emerges and life moves forward. But in some cases there are problems – often lightweight problems. A little person becomes "stuck" in the birth canal and needs some assistance from forceps or a suction device to emerge into the world. Perhaps there is a little trouble catching the initial first breath, and suction is applied or some oxy-

gen is used. The attending physician does his or her job well and there are no further problems.

In some cases, though, the new little person encounters more serious problems
coming into the world. In the birth process, when things begin to go wrong, they
can go wrong very quickly and require emergency procedures. Sometimes forceps
are used and the soft plates of the skull are shifted. Sometimes there are bruises.
Even though the physical symptoms of trauma disappear, a difficult delivery can
cause ADD-like symptoms as the child moves into the school years. Suddenly an
infant at home stops breathing and he or she is found unmoving, the skin tinged
with blue. The baby is revived and placed on a fetal monitor until the trouble is
well past, but the oxygen deprivation can cause ADD-like symptoms as well.

At times hyperactivity is obvious to the mother even when the fetus is still *in
utero*. It is not uncommon at all for mothers to accompany children into the office
and tell tales of practically non-stop kicking and moving since feeling the first
signs of life. Because of this level of activity and the twisting and turning, the
infant can be predisposed to injury at birth by a breech presentation or by having
the cord wrapped around his or her neck.

We have heard two mothers' stories in the office which certainly illustrate
what can occur. One mother related the following story: After four or five hours of
labor the fetal monitor attached to her baby indicated that he was in distress.
Suddenly vital signs came back into the normal range, only to just as suddenly
move into the danger area again. After several minutes the obstetrician decided
that there must be some danger to the infant and performed an emergency C-section. When the infant boy emerged, he was grasping the umbilical cord with one
tiny hand and alternately squeezing and releasing pressure on the cord.

Just recently, a mother of an eighteen-year-old girl told the story of her daughter's birth, which also required an emergency C-section. In her case, the baby
seemed to be in a very normal position for delivery when suddenly, *in utero*, she
twisted and, according to the mother, had her head aimed at the mother's breast-
bone. The mother had the sensation that the infant was trying to escape in the
wrong direction and was kicking furiously. The mother went to the emergency
room because she was having difficulty breathing due to the pressure in her chest.
An emergency C-section was done.

After hearing this particular story we laughingly asked the girl if she had directional problems, and she related that she is a disaster in this area. We wondered if
this was perhaps the earliest case of an ADD person getting lost that we had ever
heard.

Of course, there are times when a physician doesn't do his or her job correctly,
but, for the most part, things just happen! For all life forms – humans, puppies, kit-
tens – the stages of infancy are the most hazardous. Sometimes, no matter how
carefully you guard against problems, they simply occur.

Genetics Plus Injury

As our very active ADD children move into the terrible twos and the fear-
some fours we find a higher degree of motor activity or impulsivity than is found
in the non-ADD population. At about this age all children are experimenting

and testing their environments. This means that they fall out of trees, fall from playground jungle gyms, fall out of windows, run into sharp table edges, etc. It just seems that the ADD children do these things with more gusto and often sustain more serious injuries.

A five-year-old was brought into the office for an ADD evaluation due to severe learning problems. After taking the family history, it was clear that the father had many symptoms of ADD himself. However, he was a successful businessman, and the ADD had been very low-level and never problematic in his life. The mother was asked about the five-year-old's early history, and she mentioned a head injury that had occurred when he was three. The mother had climbed into the family van and waved good-bye to her husband, son and daughter who were standing in the garage. She backed carefully out of the driveway and drove down the street, only to see a neighbor frantically waving her down as she approached the corner. Her three-year-old son had broken away from his father, ran down the driveway, hooked his arm over the bumper of the van, and had been dragged about fifty yards down the street. Yes, he suffered head injuries in the process. Was this a good mother? Yes, most certainly! Was this an impulsive ADD three-year-old? Yes, most certainly!

Another boy, this time at the age of seven, was brought into the office for an evaluation. The mother explained that she was terribly worried that her son would die in an accident, and she went on to say that he seemed to be extremely impulsive. One story she told certainly verified the impulsivity. This little boy, at the age of five, suffered head injuries from running *into* a car. Yes, you read that correctly. The car didn't run into him, *he* ran into the car. He was running down his driveway at full speed and ran into the street, hitting the side of a car that was passing by the front of his house.

In another example, the *Los Angeles Times* in California carried a front page story of a four-year-old who was being babysat by an older couple. They had taken him to one of the local California piers to enjoy the sun and watch the people. The little boy became entranced with the sea gulls on the pier. Soon, without warning, he had chased a sea gull *right off the end of the pier* and was in the water. This particular story had a happy ending. The elderly couple jumped off the pier into the water and rescued the boy. He hadn't even been identified as ADD (yet), but it is not unlikely.

Insult to the Brain in Young Children

Sudden infection can produce a high fever. Anything that produces an injury to the brain, whether it is a fall, a lack of oxygen or an extremely high fever, has the potential to cause ADD-like symptoms or make a pre-existing ADD condition more severe (this is *not* to say that ADD symptoms will always result). The tricky thing here is that the child often appears to make a full recovery. Everything appears to be just fine, but . . . when the child is in first or second grade, learning problems begin to be obvious. The parents scratch their heads and say, "There are no learning problems in our family. What is happening?"

Because the illness or injury occurs before school age and before school problems are apparent, the parents or the school don't recognize where the problems might have begun. This often delays appropriate treatment for the child. It is not unusual for an ADD condition (which often has some misbehavior as a component) to be incorrectly seen as "psychological" in origin, particularly if a divorce is imminent or there are other problems in the family. The school may recommend that the parents solely pursue psychological counseling, and the possibility of a medical condition is never considered. This fruitless search for help for a medical problem incorrectly seen as psychological can go on for many years.

Injuries to Adolescents and Adults

The same information holds true for this age group as well. Adolescents who are injured in car accidents with a resulting coma that lasts twelve or more hours can certainly have ADD symptoms. Adolescents who suffer concussions from being repeatedly hit on the head by a surfboard or from multiple knocks on the head during football season can also have ADD symptoms. If they are ADD by virtue of their genetics, an injury or accident can make it worse.

Let us tell you another story. A mother called the office and arranged to have her thirty-five-year-old son flown down to the office for an ADD evaluation. She explained that he was once considered to be brilliant but was deteriorating. From a position in international sales, he had slid to the point that he found it impossible to work even as a "high-tech handyman," since he couldn't keep his appointments and schedules straight. He would sit at his computer for hours daily attempting to write out a simple schedule.

When this adult came into the office, his symptoms were so severe that, when he came in, he had the typical "look" of a hospital inpatient. He was questioned about his early history. It seemed that there was a low-level of genetic ADD that was present, but it never caused any significant academic difficulty. He entered college and was in intensive math/science classes and doing extremely well. The semester prior to graduation, he was piloting a small plane (for relaxation and fun) and crashed. The crash left him in a coma for two weeks. At first, he seemed to recover, and the college did graduate him (with honors) due to his past academic record. However, his abilities deteriorated over time. In this case, a mild ADD condition was made worse by a head trauma in adulthood.

What About Drug Babies?

In the early and mid-1990s, the private and public schools were beginning to feel the impact of babies born to mothers who used drugs during pregnancy. Fathers are now coming under fire too. Researchers are beginning to feel that prolonged use of drugs by fathers may have altered the sperm in some way which caused damage to the infant.

School psychologists in public schools are complaining of their caseloads and state that these infants (now first or second graders) often have pronounced learning problems and often "look like" ADD children. In fact, drug children that we are beginning to see in the office seem to have even more severe learning and behavioral problems than the purely genetic ADD child.

Summary

ADD is a well-documented, very real medical condition that is characterized by an underarousal of the brain. In most cases it is caused by a genetic factor in the family; however, there are cases where ADD-like symptoms appear due to some sort of trauma to the brain or that the trauma to the brain may make the effects of a genetic ADD condition much more severe.

We realize that ADD has been present in the human race since the days of the cavemen. ADD is present in all races and ethnic groups and encompasses all levels of intelligence. Changes in society have caused some of the typical ADD characteristics to be much more problematic in this day and age than ever before.

ADD has been with us since the dawn of time. It will continue to exist. With education and understanding about ADD and the possibilities for treatment we are standing at the door of a new, more hopeful era.

Chapter 3

ADD: *Not Just Hyperactivity But Much, Much More*

Initially, our understanding of ADD was quite limited and simplistic. We understood it to be a confusing, vague problem that somehow made some boys hyperactive. These same hyperactive boys also had trouble in school, especially when the ADD diagnosis grew to include the primarily inattentive type of ADD.

Next, the understanding of ADD broadened to include girls (who also had trouble in school).

The next jump in the evolution of our understanding came when ADD was recognized to cause difficulties in more areas of life than just academics. It caused problems with classmates in school, it caused kids to impulsively talk out of turn in the classroom, to fidget and generally get into trouble.

The biggest and most significant jump in our understanding of ADD came when new research identified that ADD didn't end at puberty. Instead, it continued in a large percentage of cases into adolescence and adulthood.

Finally, the understanding of ADD continued to expand and brings us to where we are today.

A Wider View of ADD

Our last chapter dealt with the chemical process of ADD and hopefully left you with a better understanding of the two main brain chemicals that seem to be affected by this condition – dopamine and serotonin.

Dopamine

Just as a refresher, remember that dopamine is typically the brain chemical we understand to be responsible for attention span and understanding, or processing, of information. In short, dopamine influences all the attributes of ADD that typically play an important role in school or in work settings.

Serotonin

The newest research on ADD has broadened our understanding of the total scope of the ADD condition. According to Dr. Comings' research into blood serotonin and tryptophan in Tourette Syndrome, we now know that ADD can and often does have a disastrous impact on a person's moods, level of depression, impulsiveness and tendency toward addictions. At this stage of our understanding, these problems are thought to relate more closely to a lack of the brain chemical serotonin.

Combinations

We also now know that ADD characteristics can occur in many different combinations. In fact, in an ADD family, each individual often has a unique set of ADD characteristics which can be thought of as being *as unique as an individual's fingerprint.*

Comorbidity

This is a technical word used to mean that the ADD condition might not occur alone. Comorbidity refers to co-existing conditions that an ADD person might have that are not caused by the ADD. Some examples of this multiple diagnosis, or comorbidity, include anxiety disorders, mood disorders (such as depression) or panic attacks. These comorbid conditions add yet another facet to the ADD individual's kaleidoscope.

Is ADD a Blessing or a Curse?

The Blessing

One of the ADD authors, Thomas Hartman, published a book entitled *Hunters in a Farmer's World* exclusively for ADD people. He put forth the premise that, for many, ADD is a blessing. He strongly supports the sense of adventure, high degree of creativity and positive benefit to the world that many ADD adults have contributed. In his book Mr. Hartman used the analogy of ADD people being hunters, but in this age, they are hunters who need to exist in a world of farmers. This concept has caught on with enthusiasm throughout the ADD adult community and is making quite a stir.

Let's look at some of his premises for a moment. ADD people tend to have a huge amount of energy. They are often driven to conquer new goals, not giving up, to move out and explore in the face of danger and adversity. This has a tremendously positive application for humanity as a whole.

As we become more "civilized" as a nation, our ADD adults move into the forefront of science, computers, business and the Internet. They may not be quite as visible today as were the explorers or mountain men of the past, but they are still with us. Our ADD adults are the adventurers and the entrepreneurs, the people who take risks and make things happen for us, whether behind the scenes or out on the stage. They typically have a high level of energy, love of life and often an extremely creative side.

One of the national Ch.A.D.D. (Children and Adults with Attention Deficit Disorder) publications discussed famous children and adults who, in retrospect, they believe were most probably ADD. These names are listed below. What do you think?

Hans Christian Anderson
Beethoven
Harry Belafonte
Alexander Graham Bell
Gregory Boyington
Wright Brothers
George Bush's children
Prince Charles
Cher
Agatha Christie
Winston Churchill
John Corcoran
Tom Cruise
Leonardo Da Vinci
Walt Disney
Thomas Edison
Albert Einstein
Dwight D. Eisenhower
Michael Farady
F. Scott Fitzgerald
Henry Ford
Zsa Zsa Gabor
Galileo
Danny Glover
Tracey Gold
Whoopie Goldberg
Stephen Hawkings
Mariel Hemingway
Dustin Hoffman
Bruce Jenner
"Magic" Johnson
John F. Kennedy
Robert Kennedy
Jason Kidd
John Lennon
Carl Lewis

Greg Louganis
James Clerk Maxwell
Steve McQueen
Mozart
David H. Murdock
Jack Nicholson
Luci Baines Johnson Nugent
Louis Pasteur
General George Patton
Edgar Allen Poe
Eddie Rickenbacher
Nelson Rockefeller
Rodin
Pete Rose
Nolan Ryan
Charles Shwab
George C. Scott
George Bernard Shaw
Tom Smothers
Suzanne Somers
Sylvester Stallone
Jackie Stewart
Thomas Thoreau
Alberto Tomba
Russell Varian
Jules Verne
Werner Von Braun
Lindsay Wagner
General Westmoreland
Weyerhauser Family
Russell White
Robin Williams
Woodrow Wilson
Henry Winkler
Wrigley
William Butler Yeats

In the past, ADD was seen as only a negative. We know now this is not true; it does have an extremely positive side. ADD adults are often the catalysts that make the world move ahead. However, and this is a rather big however, there are two things that we need to consider before we go too far telling everyone that ADD is truly a blessing.

The Other Side of the Coin: The Curse

The first thing to consider is the severity of the ADD symptoms in each person's case. If someone has the type of ADD that has produced learning problems, if he has been placed in special education classes all the way through school, if he can't find a job after school because he can't understand and process information, he does not consider ADD a blessing. In fact, this type of ADD is certainly not a blessing under any circumstances.

If the ADD is so severe that there is a high degree of impulsiveness that makes an adult unable to remain in college because she drops class after class, or can't hold a full-time job – this type of ADD isn't a blessing. If the ADD person can't sit still and listen, which prevents her from ever attending college, no matter how bright she is, then this type of ADD isn't a blessing. If a person has such difficulty with concentration that she is considered spacy or an "airhead," then this certainly isn't a blessing either. We also need to consider extreme moods and depression. These can be extremely severe in our ADD population; in no way could these things be considered a blessing.

The second factor to consider is exactly *how the ADD symptoms combine*. Not all ADD people act alike. They don't all have the same set of symptoms. Even within one family, they often will evidence different combinations of ADD symptoms. Some of these combinations create more problems in our world than others.

For example, a combination of ADD symptoms in Sally (from our first chapter) produced a young lady who is spacy, had problems in school with impulsivity and has a poor memory. This was a difficult combination for Sally. She did her best but worked most of her life as a file clerk. Sally's brother, Jack, on the other hand, had no problems in school, was hyperactive, didn't have problems processing information, but was very impulsive and rude. Oh yes, he also had quite a temper. Jack went to college, managed to alienate many of his fraternity brothers, but graduated with honors. He is currently a stockbroker making a six-figure income. His hyperactivity and impulsivity have worked to his advantage. What about his temper, you ask? He is so successful he has simply been able to get away with it. His secretary knows she needs to be one step ahead and that he is very difficult to work for, but he pays well.

There is an additional factor that may cause severe symptoms that needs to be explored. There is a subset of ADD adults who also carry the gene for a disorder called Gilles de la Tourette Syndrome (named for the man who first identified the condition). Adults who have Tourette Syndrome (TS) not only have ADD to contend with, but also experience a more severe form of the ADD symptoms. The body chemistry of adults with TS is more severely out of whack than just your normal ADD adults. These adults are often tremendously impulsive. Many often experience severe rages that come on in a flash, with little or no provocation and no warning. Some adults with TS swear or spit uncontrollably or have a fascination with knives. They make and carry knives and are generally obsessed with them. Some TS adults are fascinated by fire as well.

The difficulty begins in childhood for this population. Children with TS are typically not identified as having a biochemical problem. Somehow, most professionals and school administrators seem to be totally oblivious that this condition even exists; instead, these children are labeled as defiant or bad kids. If they are taken to professionals for an evaluation, often the diagnosis is Oppositional Defiant Disorder (ODD). They may be expelled from one school after another, kicked out of their homes and are often truly lost to society, since they are at the mercy of a biochemical condition that they and everyone else are unable to understand.

The most obvious signs of TS are motor and vocal tics. What is a tic? A motor tic is an involuntary or semivoluntary movement (beyond the person's control), such as the face contorting or an arm flailing wildly around in a circle. A vocal tic may take the form of uncontrollable foul language or even barking. However, the vocal tic may be a good deal more subtle, such as an incessant humming or a persistent throat clearing. Tics will change location and intensity. A child at ten or eleven years of age may evidence a very mild motor tic, like frequent squinting or blinking. In adolescence the tic may involve a shoulder shrugging motion. She may have an equally annoying habit of clearing her throat incessantly.

Why does Tourette Syndrome merit special consideration? There are three reasons:

1. It is often not diagnosed.
2. The behavior can be extreme and the victim is often viewed as a danger to self or society.
3. The body chemistry is typically more complicated to treat than a simple ADD condition.

How to Conceptualize ADD: Think of an Umbrella

People get confused with all the different ADD symptoms. Our concept of an umbrella is merely a visual symbol so that our readers can picture ADD more easily. To get an idea of just how broad the range of ADD symptoms are and how much ground it covers, *think of an umbrella (see illustration on the next page).*

Science and medicine are currently limited in their overall understanding of the workings of the brain and all its intricacies. With the diagnosis of ADD, we are really identifying the presence of a biochemical imbalance that may manifest itself in many different ways, or even in many different combinations. At this time, science and medicine do not have the capacity to provide a more precise diagnosis than the global term ADD (although this is sure to come).

Our ADD umbrella splits into two halves. One half of the umbrella covers problems or symptoms that get in the way of a person's ability to learn information or to perform in school or on the job. On the other side of the umbrella we have difficulties that appear in personality areas; areas that we don't completely understand. We are still learning a great deal from our ADD adults to help us in our quest to understand personality. Finally, the stem or the handle of our umbrella symbolizes ADD characteristics that may be present in any one individual from both the educational/work and the personality sides of the umbrella.

The Umbrella of Educational/Work Problems

The following pages describe each ADD characteristic. First, we'll start with the educational/work side of the umbrella. We've also described several case histories of adults who have had difficulties in educational areas that ultimately translate into problems in the workplace. These case histories are representative of a fairly wide sample of difficulties that adults incur and should give you an idea of

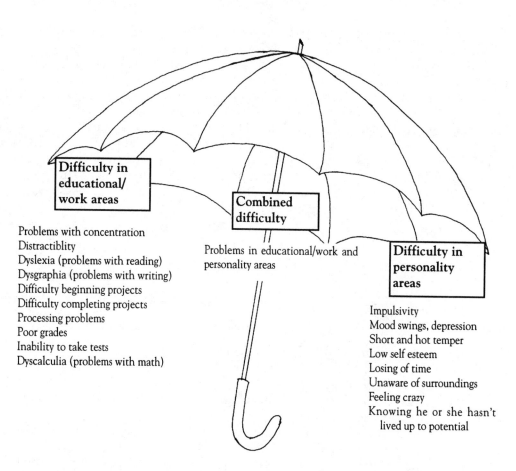

Difficulty in educational/ work areas

Problems with concentration
Distractiblity
Dyslexia (problems with reading)
Dysgraphia (problems with writing)
Difficulty beginning projects
Difficulty completing projects
Processing problems
Poor grades
Inability to take tests
Dyscalculia (problems with math)

Combined difficulty

Problems in educational/work and personality areas

Difficulty in personality areas

Impulsivity
Mood swings, depression
Short and hot temper
Low self esteem
Losing of time
Unaware of surroundings
Feeling crazy
Knowing he or she hasn't
  lived up to potential

the magnitude of some of these problems, as well as some of the coping strategies that have been used.

What About School?

If this is a book for adults, why are we talking about education? You are certainly through grade school, and at least some of you are saying as you read this, "Yuk! I never want to set foot in a school again!" In fact, many parents have told us that they feel an actual physical pain when they must go to their second or third grader's Open House to meet the teachers and to look at their children's schoolwork. Some tell us that even the smells that hit their noses as they pass through the front door or walk by the principal's office make them feel ill.

Adults may have navigated through school in some manner. They may have not completed high school, have graduated with a GED, or have more successfully moved through the system and gone on to higher education for either a master's or Ph.D. Various problems may have existed throughout their school years. During adulthood, many of these problems are still present in the working world, but often adults become experts at developing coping strategies and hiding their difficulties.

Reading, Writing and Spelling

Many ADD adults have problems in these areas. If they were very, very bright or if the problems weren't too severe, possibly no one ever recognized how hard they were working all of their lives. Perhaps these ADD adults may have been diagnosed as "dyslexic," placed in a learning disability class or had tutoring all of their school lives. Just how does this translate into problems in adulthood?

Well, if you couldn't put your thoughts down on paper when you were in school, chances are you aren't doing any better at work. Adults often hire secretaries or marry spouses who will cover for them in this area. They hire secretaries who can write letters or memos, or they simply avoid jobs where long reports are required. Some adults finally discover another tactic, which is bluffing their way through life.

Let us tell you the story of Tom, a good-looking guy in his mid-thirties who drives a black Corvette. This black Corvette certainly tells you something about his personality. He has a wife and children and a good job as a vice president in a local bank.

Tom had academic difficulties all through school. He had difficulty writing and spelling, although everyone continued to tell him that he was very bright. He received many comments, as many ADD adults do along the way, that he simply wasn't working up to potential.

Once he graduated from high school, he decided that college was not for him and he began working in a bank. He was so good on the teller line that he quickly moved up into management and excelled in the area of loans. He had a tremendous personality which made him extremely good with people. The bank began to prosper due to his skills and expertise.

One day he was in the office talking about ADD in his children, and he happened to mention that he was due to give a seminar for some important officers in the bank. He remarked that, although he couldn't spell or write, he certainly wasn't worried about the coming lecture. We asked him what he planned to do, and his reply certainly indicated a strong level of coping skills, as well as the facade of a strong ego.

When his audience was seated his first instruction was, "Pay close attention to what I am saying." Next he told them, "I have so much to say to you today that time is of the utmost urgency; therefore, I will not be writing entire sentences on the board; I will merely abbreviate. I understand that this may present a problem for some of you. If you don't understand my abbreviations, simply ask and I will be *glad* to explain them to you."

Tom took care of the difficulty with spelling and writing very nicely. No one ever learned his secret and he still remains an extremely valued member of the banking world.

You may be asking yourself, what is wrong with this? He's successful, he certainly has managed to pull off his charade – good for him! In Tom's case, this charade took a continuous and terrible toll on his ego. He admitted that all his life he felt dumb. To his way of thinking, his problems with spelling and writing had to be due to a lack of intellectual capacity. If he felt dumb, he needed something else to maintain his self-esteem, his ego. He eventually had a couple of affairs to reinforce his ego, and this pattern finally broke up his marriage.

A woman, Anne, although bright, had problems reading and processing and was a C-/D+ student all through school. Anne felt she could never even attempt college and settled for a job in a large discount chain. Because she truly was bright and a good worker, she was promoted from stock clerk to checker to manager. Anne finally reached a level in this particular chain, though, where she was told she couldn't go any higher without a degree. For the rest of her working life, her salary was between $20,000 and $30,000 per year, much lower than it would have been had she had a degree. This definitely placed her at a financial disadvantage. Worse, Anne continued to suffer self-esteem problems, always feeling inferior to the younger people on the management track who did have impressive degrees. She remained with the company but never felt she had reached her potential and was never happy in her life.

Processing Problems

ADD adults who have problems in processing information actually *aren't getting it*. A problem in processing means that *they are not understanding information in line with their IQ or level of mental ability*.

These are adults who know there is more there, but they can't reach it, no matter how hard they try. Often, way inside, they feel dumb or stupid. No matter how many times someone has told them they are smart, they can't believe it. On the job, in everyone else's opinion, they are doing well. They, themselves, feel that they are faking their performance. They feel that they are close to being "maxed out." They are certain that if anyone really knew what a tough time they were having processing or understanding the ins and outs of their jobs, they would be fired.

As we were beginning an ADD adult evaluation for a CEO of a large company that dealt with marketing, we heard this story. He looked us in the eye and said, "Before you test me, I want you to know something: I am ninety percent ego and ten percent ability. I'm just fooling everyone at work." This man had lived with his fear of failure and shame for years and years. Obviously, this was exhausting. After his evaluation, testing indicated that he was ADD but also that his IQ was in the *gifted* range. He was extremely capable, but he had a problem with processing information, so he was never able to see his level of capability.

It's easy to understand how difficulty with processing can cripple self-esteem. Until ADD adults can understand the concept of a problem in processing, often the only way it can be explained in their own minds is to say the familiar phrase, "I'm stupid." Tremendous effort must be expended to keep their processing problems a well-kept secret.

Concentration and Distractibility

ADD people who have problems in the areas of concentration or distractibility may or may not have had problems in reading, writing or math. Sometimes they have done quite well in academic subjects, but they are unable to keep their minds on what they are doing.

Concentration and distractibility go hand in hand. The person who is highly distractible has a tough time paying attention. Business meetings, conferences and even conversations can tax this person to his limit. These people typically find themselves floating off or spacing out during a conversation. No matter how sternly they remind themselves that they need to pay attention, invariably they will find themselves off in the ozone. In meetings, they might interrupt, make jokes or cause conflict if that is the only way they can maintain any level of focus. If they are intimidated by other people in the meetings, they'll often remain quiet, but they will be very distracted. Instead of listening, they'll find that they are counting dots on the ceiling, counting syllables in the conversation or creating a grocery list in their minds. If they are high enough in the company to be directing the meeting, sometimes they do much better because they can legitimately generate excitement. However, this is not always true. One CEO of a $3,000,000 company admitted that he had so much difficulty paying attention in business meetings, he hired someone to sit across the table from him in meetings and kick him under the conference table when he drifted off.

People who have difficulty with concentration are often troubled not only in the area of business, but with their marriage partners or significant others as well. These people have difficulty listening to a simple recital of what went on during the day. Because their minds wander, they may come back with comments not related to the ongoing conversation at all, and then change the subject entirely! What's the result? The spouse or significant other feels totally unloved, discounted, and as though what he or she said wasn't important at all.

Cliff, who had been identified as ADD, was talking about some of the problems he encountered with his wife prior to the ADD diagnosis and the administration of medication. Somewhat sheepishly, Cliff recounted the following story: He and his wife were on the first leg of a long vacation, and at the time of the incident they were walking through a revolving door in a large, plush hotel. His wife had been in tears on the airplane but hadn't been able to share what was wrong, since the plane was overcrowded and they couldn't sit together. Cliff had been very concerned about his wife and anxious to hear what was bothering her. She began to tell him what was on her mind as soon has they got out of the taxi; however, the colors, hustle and bustle of this huge hotel, as well as the revolving door, caused him to lose his concentration. His mind left his wife and floated to the events of the next day, so just after she said to him, "My best friend has been diagnosed with breast cancer," and added that she was afraid for herself as cancer ran in her own family, he answered, "We'll leave the hotel at 9:00 in order to connect with the tour shuttle at 9:30." He then went right on talking. Of course, she was devastated. Cliff didn't know anything about adult ADD at the time, so he couldn't even explain what had caused him to say such a thing. Six years later, she still gets tears in her eyes when she thinks about how lonely and devastated she felt at that moment.

Often ADD people exhibit a high level of distractibility. Sometimes they are so distractible that it is almost impossible for them to work in a traditional office setting. They find that a co-worker shifting in a chair, people moving around the office, or telephones ringing distract them. These people often do a minimal amount of work during the actual work day (although they typically look very busy), then pack up unfinished paperwork and do it at night when they can concentrate, instead of relaxing and spending time with their families. When a spouse complains about excessive work, the spouse is told that too much work is required on the job. It really isn't his or her fault that there is no time for family or fun.

Very often people who have this type of ADD are hard to spot, especially if they also fall on the hyperactive side of the continuum. One elementary school principal was always in action and had a lot of characteristics reminiscent of the Tasmanian Devil in Bugs Bunny cartoons. This principal would rush out his office door with a bang, and the entire staff was afraid that one day they'd find a child impaled on the other side of the doorknob. Years later, when his ADD was diagnosed, he admitted that a lot of the activity was to cover up the fact that it was impossible for him to do paperwork during the day. Instead, he'd rush around from room to room, talk to the teachers, discipline the students and wait until 4:00 when the teachers had all gone home to start his paperwork. He'd still be working at 9:00 or 10:00 at night and on occasion worked so late that he slept overnight at the school. His marriage didn't last very long either.

On the hypoactive side of the spectrum, we see the ADD adults who appear frozen in their seated or standing positions with an intent look on their faces, as if there's a radio transmission coming from another planet that only *they* can hear. Hypoactive ADD adults report a range – from their minds racing with the things they ought to do, to their minds moving as slowly as their bodies; the problem is that neither mind nor body kick into action. The concentration and distractibility problems of the hypoactive ADD adult may show themselves in a lack of motion or slow motion, rather than a flurry of activity. In the literature, this trait is labeled more as the *inattentive* part of the ADD profile.

Procrastination

An awful lot of ADD adults are procrastinators. When they're in school, they let a report or project wait until the very last minute. They often work until 2:00 in the morning the night before a project is due.

At first the pattern seems mysterious. When you ask these ADD adults if they are aware of the deadline that is approaching, they always say, "Yes." If you try to teach them tricks or techniques to help them finish their projects early with less strain, the attempt falls flat. Unbelievably, they usually do get things in by the deadline. Even so, bosses with this characteristic drive their secretaries crazy, since the ADD boss typically expects the secretary to work late too. If a spouse or significant other has agreed to type the report or a similar project, be assured that he or she will be working until the last second as well.

If the ADD adult usually gets things done – even though at the very, very, very last minute – then what's the problem?

Effects on co-workers and spouses: Eventually everyone, whether a co-worker who is inconvenienced because he must stay late for the twentieth time to type a project, or a spouse who is angry at the wife or husband remaining at work all night or working throughout the weekend again, feels that enough is enough! Typically, the people around the ADD adult who procrastinates run out of empathy. The procrastination occurs in a regular pattern. Nothing seems to make a difference. The conclusion ultimately reached by the co-worker or spouse is "You just don't care about anyone but yourself. What is wrong with you?"

Effects on employers: After seeing an employee work up to the very last minute on a project or report, an employer also begins questioning, "What's going on?" Typically she has two responses – she either finds herself getting more and more anxious seeing papers scattered all over desks and tables as our ADD adult rushes to meet the deadline, or she questions if the ADD adult really cares about the job. After all, if he really wanted to do a good job, wouldn't he start earlier? How can he do his best work under the strain of a deadline and a lack of sleep?

Why can't they get started? Energy: The ADD adult feels that it takes an insurmountable amount of energy to jump in and begin a project. Even though he knows he can complete a project, it feels like a mountainous effort is required just to get started!

What gets them going? Deadlines: As odd as it may seem, most ADD adults have found that if they attempt to complete a project early – well before the deadline – their overall product is often mediocre. They realize that if they wait until the last possible minute, the deadline creates an adrenaline surge that kicks in and makes their end products more creative and of higher quality. ADD adults often wish with all of their hearts that they weren't procrastinators. Typically, they're unable to explain their behavior to their bosses or spouses and, therefore, are continually in trouble.

In relationships, procrastination not only drives spouses crazy, but makes them feel their wishes are not important; they are discounted.

One ADD adult was a jack-of-all-trades. This guy could do anything, from hanging drywall to wiring and plumbing. He was an absolute genius and could figure out anything mechanical. However, his wife complained of stopped-up drains and lights that didn't work, all because the energy required to get into a large project was simply too much for her husband. At home there was never a deadline to kick him into gear.

ADD procrastinators typically bite off too much. Perhaps they do this to create the adrenaline surge. Let us tell you this story: Ed lived in an older house in a Southern California suburb. The house was so old, the main bathroom still had yellow tile with black trim, a lavender washbasin and a lavender cast iron tub and toilet (his wife always said someday she expected the Easter Bunny to pop out of the toilet!). The couple's daughter was getting married and wanted to have an old-fashioned wedding reception in the backyard with home-cooked food so everyone could be comfortable and have a good time.

Ed loved his daughter so he agreed to this plan. However, the house had fallen into such disrepair due to his pattern of procrastination that it needed major renovations before the wedding. One morning, our ADD adult (undiagnosed) walked into the kitchen with a sledgehammer and demolished a wall. The kitchen was the first to go. He had planned a new stove, new sink and new cabinets. The entire house also needed painting inside and out, and the grass had to be planted in the backyard.

Two nights before the wedding, Ed was still painting walls. The house was completed just in the nick of time for the wedding. Of course, he was exhausted (but also proud of himself that he'd made it!), but the bathroom was ignored and his wife tells us she's still looking for the Easter Bunny. His daughter was understandably on the verge of a nervous breakdown.

After the wedding, the wife, who is an intelligent lady, caught onto the concept of a deadline for her husband. She decided that she wanted a new can opener hung in the kitchen on the brand new cabinets. She had asked her husband to do it for three or four weeks, but nothing happened. Finally, very gently she said to him, "You know dear, I've looked at that can opener. I don't think it will be too hard to hang it on the new cabinets at all. I've looked for your drill, and I'm sure I can do it myself tomorrow. Don't you even worry about it." Guess what? Her husband was up at 6:00 a.m. and the can opener was hung within fifteen minutes. He was terrified that she would do it incorrectly and harm the new cabinets. She applied a deadline that worked for him, and it was done in a very gentle manner.

What would have happened if this man hadn't had a deadline? Very little. For example, he painted the outside of the same house three or four years later. There were no deadlines, such as another wedding coming up, an anniversary or a funeral to apply pressure. Thirty years later, the shutters were still unpainted and laying against the fence in the back yard.

Problems with Organizational Skills

Do you remember the character "Pig Pen" from the *Peanuts* comic strip? Pig Pen was followed around by a cloud of floating debris and dirt. When Pig Pen was in school, every time he opened his desk bits and pieces of things and general clutter surrounded him like a cloud. Pig Pen-grown-up is many of our ADD adults who have difficulty with organizational ability.

An ADD adult very often has no concept of how to organize. She may have trouble using an organizer or making a list of her itinerary for the day. She may look at her desk piled high with papers and is at a loss. Her boss complains about her lack of organization in her performance reviews. But there is still a problem, because if she cleans off her desk and files everything away neatly, she knows it will never stay that way.

An even bigger dilemma is that of finding things. She usually can't find something she has filed. Because her mind is disorganized, there is no logical or sequential system of filing that occurs naturally. If she has a job order for plants or a proposal for a landscaping project, she might file them under "L" for landscaping, or "S" because the contractor's name is Steve, or under "P" for plants. ADD adults often develop a healthy coping technique of making three copies of things and filing them under all three categories. Perhaps the most effective technique of all is to hire a secretary who does not have this same problem. Of course, the day she is out sick is a black day indeed.

Another difficulty exists with ADD adults who have problems with disorganization. Very often they find that they are distracted by any clutter at all, so not only is clutter a problem in terms of organizing their lives, but it also distracts them, which makes everything worse.

Problems with Memory

Because ADD adults have such a potentially devastating problem with memory, we have devoted an entire chapter to the subject of memory in this book, including both long- and short-term memory. For an in-depth discussion of short- and long-term memory and what you can do about it, please see Chapter 5.

Before you turn to the memory chapter (if you remember to), we would like to leave you with one thought: Most ADD adults who suffer from a poor memory tell us that the memory problems make them feel stupid. Invariably, they go through a whole process of asking themselves, "What's wrong with me?" "Why can't I remember?" Their conclusion is, at a very deep level, "I must be stupid." We would like you to copy the following statement on a card in block letters and post it around the house if you have a poor memory.

> # There is Absolutely NO Correlation Between Intelligence and Memory

This means that if you have a poor memory, it is only a poor memory. It has nothing to do with how smart you are. Memory relates to how much you can retrieve; it has nothing to do with your intellectual capacity.

Difficulty in Personality Areas

Moving to the other side of the umbrella, we next look at personality and the ADD adult. Some of the problems that fit under personality don't show up in childhood at all. However, we are seeing increasing numbers of children and adolescents who are demonstrating hyperactivity, aggression, major depression, anxiety and obsessive-compulsive traits. Dr. Comings notes in his book, *The Gene Bomb*, that the frequency of the above traits occurs more often in families and relatives with similar traits, which indicates a strong genetic link. While there are many ADD children who are depressed or who get into rituals or habits, it can be well into adolescence before these problems reach the level where they come to the attention of a parent or school personnel.

In childhood, it may be that the tight structures of school rules and parental expectations about chores (such as room cleaning) provide enough structure and rigidity that these problems do not pop up. At the beginning of adolescence, it may be that the hormones that are beginning to be released during puberty kick off or amplify some of these problems.

For the adolescent, there may be depression, excessive worry, overspending, impulsive shoplifting or an explosive temper. Because the controls and rules are still present and enforced by parents and schools, the full impact of the problem may still not be realized. Once the person reaches adulthood and is in college or in a work situation where there are fewer controls, the problems may cause real havoc in their lives.

For example, an ADD college student may have trouble getting up in the morning to go to class. In fact, he may sleep so soundly that he doesn't even hear his alarm clock. In college no one is there to wake him up five or six times and make sure he is out the door for that early class. After our ADD college student sleeps through a few classes, maybe six or seven, he may decide that the fraternity beer bust is more appealing than class. After all, who will know? The friends and beer will ease his mind. Before he knows it, he has dropped a class, and then another and another.

If our ADD adults are working, they may have been fired from one job after another for being late, not understanding instructions or for snarling at a customer. In their own minds, they are doing their best. They can't understand why the pattern keeps repeating itself.

Now ADD adults certainly aren't stupid. If they consistently find themselves dropping classes in college or getting fired from jobs, they are aware that something is wrong. They just can't put their finger on the exact problem. For years, their parents or teachers have probably tried to tell them that not getting the work done, sleeping through class or snarling at people is their problem. But ADD adults have a hard time seeing what they are doing. After all, they don't create problems on purpose! Their ability to see how their behavior impacts someone else is limited. It is sort of like their ability to interact with people and understand situations has stopped at the four-year-old level. They are often egocentric. This means they think about themselves and what is happening to them. They have a hard time seeing themselves or their problems from the other person's point of view.

ADD adults often struggle and struggle for years. Some will finally seek help from a professional. However, these adults often have a history of moving from one counselor to a therapist to a psychiatrist and back again, looking for answers because ADD is never considered. ADD adults have even been put on medication, or several different medications, by a well-meaning family practitioner or psychiatrist who, perhaps, is not familiar with ADD.

This process often leaves the ADD adult in a real dilemma. If counseling didn't work, if medication didn't work, what next? Is there any hope at all?

Impulsivity

Remember, ADD adults have a biochemical imbalance in their brain chemistry. Their brains fluctuate between underarousal and overarousal. This means the system that puts the brakes on what they say or do is not operating properly. Their brains may be like a runaway train with no "off" switch and no brakes, or a car with no gas in its tank.

Non-ADD people, without their conscious awareness, operate a system that can be described as *Ready, aim, fire*. They decide they want to do or say something. Next, they think about what it is they want to do or say. This may be accomplished in a matter of seconds, but they still think first. Finally, they fire – that is to say, they say what they meant to say, or do what they have intended.

ADD people operate in a different sequence. Because their brains fluctuate between over- and underarousal, their sequence is out of whack. Their system can be described as *Ready, fire, aim (see next page for illustration)*.

The ADD person intends to say something to a friend or co-worker. She blurts something out without thinking. Often she has said something so awful or hurtful that she is in real trouble. She feels terrible. "Why did I say that? What is wrong with me?"

Beyond saying things without thinking, impulsivity can include spending money when there is no money in the checkbook or when the credit cards are maxed out. Impulsivity can make an ADD adult walk off a job for no real reason at all. Maybe the job just felt boring that day or someone criticized him. He

walks off the job without thinking that there won't be money to feed the family or that he can't pay the rent.

Impulsivity can create the acquisition of adult toys. "I want it; therefore, I will buy it." One ADD adult had bought and sold twenty-three cars by the time he was thirty-one years old. Another adult had three cars, a boat and jet skis, but could barely pay the mortgage on the house.

Impulsivity often damages relationships. An ADD person who has problems with impulsivity can't stand to be in a situation she feels is boring. If she is in a good solid relationship with someone who cares, doesn't cheat on her and pays the bills, she thinks, "How boring." Boom! She is out of that relationship and into another. In her mind it is her "boring" partner who caused the problem. Her type of impulsivity demands a high level of excitement and intensity which is almost impossible to maintain in a long-standing relationship. This often dooms ADD adults to one marriage after another after another, with no hope for a long and happy life with one person.

Moods

Psychologists and psychiatrists have recognized for a long time that moods exist in people – so what's the difference when dealing with ADD adults? So what if they experience moods? What makes their moods different from the general population's?

ADD people often have unexplained moods which can be very perplexing to those around them. ADD people can go from high to low several times in the space of one day – or in the space of a few hours. These mood changes happen with no rhyme or reason. It may be something small, such as a comment in an ADD adult's work environment that causes not a mild shift in moods, but a sudden plunge into despair or a hot flash of rage. On the other hand, something small may send him on an energy high that creates an intensity that is difficult to explain to those around him.

Once a person is identified as having ADD, he is recognized as someone who has a biochemical imbalance of the brain. Rather than being seen as someone who is impacted by family problems or a troubled relationship, his difficulty is seen as medical, as biochemical.

In traditional therapy, if a person has excessive highs or lows, he may be placed on a mood-altering medication but will typically remain on that medication for no more than three months. During that time, the thought is that therapy is needed to assist him in working through whatever *caused* the moods.

In the treatment of ADD adults, the concept is very different. The diagnosis of ADD documents that a biochemical problem (typically a low level of serotonin when we are dealing with moods) is responsible. Often adults who are diagnosed with ADD and have excessive highs and lows need to be placed on mood-altering medications for a much longer period of time – sometimes for the rest of their lives. The diagnosis of ADD lays the foundation for understanding that environment alone hasn't caused the problem. Instead, it is the biochemical imbalance in the brain that has caused the problem.

Depression

In addition to moods, we may be talking about a low level of depression. This depression often goes unnoticed, as it has been present for the person's entire life. If she's always lived in a sort of haze or under a gray cloud, it is difficult for her to understand that she could feel any other way. In fact, it is difficult for the ADD person to grasp that she might be depressed. She has never considered herself depressed. After all, she's not in bed with the covers over her head. When depression is described to her as a gray feeling that pervades her life or a feeling that nothing is ever bright and happy, then she can identify and realize, yes, there probably is a low level of depression that has always been present in her life.

Temper

Here's another case where a biochemical imbalance can cause a huge problem in people's lives. For many ADD adults, temper takes one of two forms. It either builds slowly and then explodes in a white hot rage, or it is instantaneous, exploding with almost no warning. Temper in ADD adults can range from minor episodes, which are easily controlled, to major episodes. Some of these major episodes may be set off by something as commonplace as someone driving erratically on the freeway. After being cut off, the ADD adult may suddenly chase down the offending driver, running him off the road, jumping out of the car and breaking the car's windshield with a baseball bat.

Temper definitely can present problems in a family or in a relationship. ADD adults who have problems with temper often resort to verbal abuse and are so outraged with what is going on both inside and outside of themselves that they really don't know what they're saying or doing. Outbursts of temper can also extend to physical abuse or damage of property, such as holes in the walls, splintered doors or broken appliances. Very often, when there is a pattern of physical abuse in the family, it is evident in retrospect that the ADD adult's parents or extended family also had many symptoms of the ADD condition.

Loss of Time

As crazy as this may seem, ADD adults frequently experience a time loss or a time distortion. The amount of time lost can range from a couple of seconds to an hour or more. ADD adults generally report that "all of a sudden" they become aware they are standing still, and when they look at the clock they find that five to ten minutes, or even half an hour, has passed! In extreme cases, the amount of lost time has ranged up to two or three hours, or even an entire night. This seems to be different from the usual "loss of time" that most people experience when they are driving a familiar route and arrive at their destination miles away without remembering the trip – they have driven miles as though on auto-pilot. With ADD people, is almost as though they experience a period of unconsciousness. When they awaken, they find that time has simply passed.

Feeling Crazy

Throughout their lives, ADD adults tend to experience thoughts, moods, and events in their lives that they are at a loss to understand. Many times they lose jobs, become angry or depressed, lose relationships, and they are simply unable to put a finger on why the events have occurred. Somehow, at a very deep level, they realize that they feel different from most people; however, these feelings are subtle and difficult to explain. The ADD adult may go through life in silence outwardly, but somewhere deep inside seems to have a feeling that, somehow, he is "crazy."

Frequently, during the adult ADD evaluation ADD adults will confide to us (often with tears in their eyes), "I'm so relieved that I've found what is wrong with me. All my life I've either felt stupid or crazy."

In actuality, they're far from crazy. They're very much aware of the biochemical shifts that occur in their brain chemistry and know that somehow they are on a roller coaster for a good deal of their lives without any ability to step off, even at the end of the ride. They're not crazy, they're ADD adults.

Poor Social Skills

As non-ADD kids grow up, they learn how to get along with kids in the preschool sandbox by reading body language, facial expressions and gestures. Soon they learn that hitting, being mean or laughing at people makes kids stay away from them, so they slowly adapt and change their behavior. This is a very normal developmental process for children. By the time a child reaches adolescence, this skill of reading body language is finely tuned and she is very much aware of what is socially appropriate and inappropriate. Many ADD adults didn't have the ability to read social cues as children, nor do they develop it as adults. An ADD adult may say something too pointed to a friend, criticize more sharply than intended or interrupt frequently. However, he is unable to tell that he is offensive in what he says or does. He often fails to recognize the subtle cues from the other person so he does not interact appropriately in social situations and, more importantly, doesn't have a clue as to what is happening.

As stated previously, this inability to "read" people begins in childhood for the ADD adult. In childhood, however, the problem is obvious because kids are quick to comment with great directness by saying, "Go away!" "Shut up, you jerk!" or "I don't want to play with you." The social interaction is right out on the table, and the ADD youngster can more clearly get the message that kids his own age do or do not like him. This social skill difficulty can range from mild to more severe.

At the more severe end of the poor social skills continuum are the ADD people for whom *Asperger's Disorder* or mild *autism* is added to their diagnosis. We are currently watching the literature on these two neurological disorders that directly impair social skills and interactions. Asperger's Disorder became an official diagnosis with the publication of the *DSM-IV*. Its essential features include a severe impairment in social interactions and restricted, repetitive patterns of behavior, interests, and activities. Symptoms of attention deficit, impulsivity and distractibility are common in children with Asperger's Disorder (which occurs in about one in two hundred fifty people to one in six hundred fifty people, depending on the researcher), and they are often seen as socially "out of context" rather than socially isolated. Being "out of context" may include coming too close to others, being highly repetitive in speech or actions, asking inappropriate questions, or interacting with others only for one's own obsessive interests. People who are diagnosed with Asperger's are not able to modify their social behavior according to the environment.

Autism is a devastating disorder which includes severe social withdrawal and isolation, delayed onset of speech, and repetitious, ritualistic behaviors. It is important to note that these disorders are at the more severe end of the ADD continuum and that specialized treatment and support are available .

Assuming that neither autism nor Asperger's Disorder is present, as adults we become more "civilized" (fortunately or unfortunately). Non-ADD adults have learned the rules of social interaction and seldom make inappropriate confrontive comments. In contrast, ADD adults may say unkind things to acquaintances (whom they may really like) and either not be aware they've said anything wrong or wonder what in the world caused that person to be angry. Often they don't have a clue as to why they have difficulty with people, and non-ADD people may be unwilling to clue them in about their behavior.

A truly sensitive and kind ADD adult who also had Tourette Syndrome came in for some counseling because he couldn't understand why he kept upsetting people. He knew he only had a few friends and that he often turned off new acquaintances. He described one situation that had caused him a great deal of pain. He was receiving physical therapy for his back. His physical therapist was an attractive and friendly young woman, and they often chatted as he had his therapy.

One day, she came into the room and looked upset. His comment was, "Geez, what's the matter with you? You look like crap." Predictably, she became even more quiet and withdrawn. Exploring this with him in counseling, it was clear he meant to say, "I really care about you. Is something on your mind? Can I help?" (quite a different message). This is a classic example of an ADD adult who has never learned to read social cues from earliest childhood into adulthood and never learned how to modify what he said to people.

Problems with Directionality

Many ADD people get lost. They don't just get lost once, they get lost almost every time they get in the car. Even with directions, they have trouble finding their way to a new shopping center or even to a friend's house. Once they arrive somewhere, they absolutely, unequivocally can't reverse the directions to get home! These are the people who will circle off a freeway ramp and find they are totally disoriented. When walking to a store, they will become turned around. If they aren't careful, they will leave the store by a different door than they entered and be unable to find their cars. This is very embarrassing but is made even more devastating because ADD adults often pair getting lost with a feeling that they aren't smart. As we said in the section on memory, these are two very different things. This also applies to directionality – there is no correlation between getting lost and intelligence.

One directionality-impaired ADD adult had a terrible time. This man is a physician – he had completed medical school and had completed board certification in his field. He holds people's lives in his hands on a daily basis. Obviously, this man is intelligent and capable.

Let's call our physician Dr. Fred. Dr. Fred had an appointment at our office one evening. The first session, he arrived on time and he never mentioned he had problems with directionality. The next session, he was fifteen minutes late and quite angry. He walked in holding a Thomas Brothers Maps® book and was sputtering about his fiancée. Apparently, he had her talking him to his destination on his car phone. Usually she had the map book and simply told him to turn right or left. This particular night, she had an engagement and had left the house. She gave him directions and the map book. He couldn't read a map and did not have her on the other end of the phone to help guide him, and he was furious.

The last chapter of the story – and the funniest part – was during yet another visit to our office. Our office had relocated one block away. This particular night, Dr. Fred had his fiancée at home once again talking to him on his car phone. She also had our back line number and could call in for continuous directions. Dr. Fred was still a disaster. First, he couldn't find our street. Next, we got a second call – he couldn't find the building. Finally, she called back and said, "The problem is worse than it's ever been. Now he's not only lost, but he got out of his car and he's lost his car as well." His fiancée told us he was going through the bushes at the time he called her. He finally burst into the office half an hour later, shirt wet from perspiration and pieces of bush in his clothes.

Addictions

As humans, from the beginning of recorded time, we have a history of addictions. We have always been looking for something to take away the pain, to make us work longer or feel better. Even early cavemen learned how to ferment fruit. Peruvians learned that a certain leaf (coca) would increase their endurance and take away the pain of hard work.

As we look at ADD adults, their pattern of addictions fall into four categories.

ADD adults, by definition, have a recognized biochemical imbalance in their systems. Understandably, they would be even more prone to addictions than the rest of the population. While more scientific research on adults and addictions is emerging all the time, the main body of research has been done with the ADD adolescent population. That research clearly states that if an ADD adolescent is identified and placed on medication, there is a seventy percent to eighty percent greater chance that he *will not* become addicted to any illegal substance. We would guess that these figures would roughly apply to ADD adults as well.

Addictions in ADD adults fall into four broad categories which will be thoroughly discussed in Chapter 8.

- *Category 1*   *Positive Addictions (Exercise)*
- *Category 2*   *Non-Life-Threatening Addictions (Coffee)*
- *Category 3*   *Dangerous Substances – Non-Life-Threatening (Diet Pills)*
- *Category 4*   *Life-Threatening Addictions (Cocaine, Amphetamines)*

Problems Being Late

ADD adults are often late, understandably driving spouses and co-workers crazy. The obvious conclusion when someone is late is that he simply doesn't care about you or his job. With ADD adults, this really is not true. There are three main reasons that this continual pattern of lateness continues:

Too Many Things at the Last Minute: The ADD adult who falls on the hyperactive side of the continuum is always going and doing. If an appointment looms on the horizon, he's always trying to get the last three, four or five things done before he leaves the house. Invariably, this causes a time pressure as he rushes up to the deadline of when he is "supposed" to leave but still has two or three things to do. He thinks he can fit everything in, but in reality he can't, so he's often not only late, but frazzled when he arrives at his appointment.

Rules They Make up in Their Heads: Another interesting facet of the ADD adult's battle with lateness is the rules he makes up in his head. When you observe a pattern of many ADD adults, it becomes obvious that often they are late, but they are late by a specific number of minutes. An ADD adult may be ten minutes late to appointments, another may be seven minutes late, another a half an hour late. Somehow, in his head, he has arrived at a decision that it is "really okay to be late, as long as I am only ten (or seven or thirty) minutes late." This is a really interesting observation for the non-ADD adult, as she typically cannot understand what makes the ADD adult tick. If he can routinely be ten minutes late, why can't he be on time? However, there is something in the ADD adult person's brain that makes it almost impossible for many of them to be exactly on time.

Poor Memory: Sometimes the ADD adult's tendency to be late is coupled with a poor memory. Very often, he has good intentions of going somewhere but has forgotten the appointment or the meeting that is set to occur. Something out of the blue – possibly even a note in an organizer – will jog his memory into gear, and all of a sudden he will realize that he has five or ten minutes to get to the meeting. For the non-ADD adult, this gets old quick.

Lying and Cheating

Lying: Only bad people lie! Right? Wrong! Many ADD people lie. Usually, the lying begins at a very early age. It starts as an attempt to cover up things that they have forgotten to do, such as homework or classwork assignments, or things they've done impulsively, such as breaking a china platter or borrowing their father's favorite wrench and leaving it out in the rain. Often, because ADD kids are in trouble for years, the pattern of lying becomes so entrenched that parents say they always listen to the child with the mindset of "I can't trust this kid."

It is important to understand that this type of lying is not the same as pathological lying. It is not a symptom of a sick mind; it is a protective measure used by an ADD child.

Fortunately, the lying that occurs in childhood and early adolescence seldom seems to remain throughout adult life. Adults will often review their past history in amazement and say things such as, "I can't believe I lied all the time. I don't know why I did it." As adults, they are often law-abiding and upstanding citizens. The lying pattern is something they have been able to leave behind as they have become more and more successful in business and in their relationships.

Cheating: In school, ADD adolescents or young adults who have processing problems often cheat. At times, the cheating occurs when an ADD student become frustrated during a test. Her eyes land on her neighbor's paper, where the correct answer just "pops up." There it is! The other paper serves as a focus for her. She simply borrows the focus (and the answer) and puts it on her own paper.

Cheating can also be a sheer survival skill. ADD students who have real problems processing or understanding the course material eventually realize that without cheating, they will never in their wildest dreams "make it" in college. No matter how hard they study, the concepts will be there one minute, but slip out of their minds the very next minute.

ADD students begin to cheat out of desperation. Yes, they know it is wrong. Yes, they feel terrible about doing it. But it is the only thing they know to do to reach their goal of graduation or certification.

Few Friends, "Being a Loner"

There are two kinds of ADD loners. There are those who feel they'll go absolutely crazy without alone time (and to them it is an absolute necessity). There are others who are loners because they are social bumblers wishing desperately they had more friends. They just aren't sure how to make friends – or how to keep them.

ADD adults often require alone time on a daily basis. They find that they need to be alone after a hard day at work, or they need a half an hour to an hour of being totally alone before going to bed. This often presents problems in relationships. The non-ADD spouse is often quite upset and feels totally discounted in a relationship. She'll ask, "Why do you sit up and read? Wouldn't you rather come to bed? Don't you love me?"

The ADD spouse is unable to explain his need for alone time because he may not understand it himself. From as far back as childhood, he's felt guilty about needing the alone time. Now he feels even more guilty because he is not giving his spouse what she requires in a relationship. What's worse, there doesn't seem to be a good reason for his behavior.

Now, let's look at the other half of the ADD loners. These are the ADD adults who have had a great deal of difficulty interacting with people because they can't read social cues.

From the time little Tommy was three years old and playing in the preschool sandbox, he couldn't read the expression on Mary's face just before he smashed her sand castle with his foot. When she went screaming to the teacher, he had no clue as to what he'd done. In fourth grade, Tommy again didn't read the expression on Mary's face just before he leaned over to scribble on her paper. When she turned her back to him and took her paper up to the teacher, he again felt crushed and clueless. As a budding adolescent in ninth grade, Tommy didn't read Mary's facial expression just before he grabbed her backpack and threw it on the school roof. When she ran yelling into the vice principal's office, Tommy was floored to find that he was once again in trouble, not only with Mary, but with the vice principal. He was suspended.

Most kids learn from experience. Tommy doesn't. Tommy is one of those ADD kids for whom the social cues bounce off – over and over again. Is it any wonder that Tommy can't get Mary to go out with him as an adult? Is it any wonder that Tommy begins to wonder if he'll ever marry and have kids?

Many ADD people want to interact, but because of all the social disasters throughout their lives, they are never really accepted as one of the bunch. They always feel that they are standing on the outer edge of the group. They describe themselves as being on the outside, looking in. These ADD adults need help to identify the problems and learn how to "read" people. They can then learn how to make friends and keep relationships.

Summary

Remember, ADD adults come in all sizes, colors, and packages. There are a wide variety of symptoms that make up the umbrella term that we call Attention Deficit Disorder. No two ADD adults, such as a brother and a sister – even though they come from the same genetic pool – are alike. Each adult in the ADD family is totally unique and different from every other adult in the family. ADD in adults gives you a mix of symptoms that is rather like ordering from a Chinese menu. As you make up the profile of an ADD adult, you can pick one from column A, one from column B and one from column C (and don't forget column D, any comorbid conditions).

Before receiving a diagnosis of ADD, adults were at a loss to explain just why they were late, why they were so disorganized, why they needed time alone, why they were depressed and why they felt so different. With the diagnosis, they realize that there is a biochemical basis for most of their unique traits. For many ADD adults, the diagnosis of ADD gives them a tremendous amount of relief. Finally, they are able to make some sense out of their lives. Finally, they are able to say, not only to others, but to themselves, "I'm not stupid or crazy." Hallelujah!

Chapter 4

Education: *ADD's Impact*

You may be asking yourself why you should read a chapter on education. As an adult, you are most likely out of school. One way or another you have successfully (or unsuccessfully) negotiated the educational system. You may even be one of those ADD adults who, once you were through the educational process, promised yourself that you would never get near the door of a schoolroom ever again in your entire life. As we mentioned previously, many adults have told us that even the smell of a school corridor or the thought of their child's parent/teacher conference causes an immediate and intense stress reaction. Their feelings may run so deep that they find themselves even avoiding conferences with children's teachers to avoid the pain of sitting on the other side of the "dreaded" teacher's desk, having the teachers (Mr. or Ms. Authority Figure) tell them what is wrong with *their* children. The words may hit too close to what they, themselves, went through in similar classrooms years ago.

Basically, there are three reasons to understand the impact of ADD on your own education. One, it will certainly give you a lot of insights and help you make sense of some of the troubles that you experienced. Two, it will give you information and tools if you are considering going back for additional certification or a graduate degree. Three, many of the problems that you had in school, unfortunately, translate into current problems in the workplace. For example, if you had trouble reading, you may still resist reading technical material. If you were late on required papers, you may find that you still have a heck of a time meeting deadlines at work.

The truth is, many of our ADD adults admit that they are not only upset by their experiences in school, but very confused. In childhood, if they had the hyperactive type of ADD, their pediatrician may have labeled them as ADHD. They may have been on medication while in elementary school, only to find that the medication was abruptly discontinued at the onset of adolescence. They may have been labeled as learning disabled by the school system and shuttled off to special classes.

Now as adults they are being told that they have Attention Deficit Disorder. They are perplexed. Why didn't the school talk about Attention Deficit Disorder in their cases? Are ADD and learning disabilities one and the same?

Actually a great deal of confusion surrounds the entire area of ADD and education. Hopefully this chapter will provide clear answers to these questions.

How Does ADD Impact Education?

ADD can cause significant difficulties in academic areas: reading, math or written language. Adults who had severe problems in these areas may have been placed in a learning disability class called the Resource Specialist Program (RSP) or, if severe, in a Special Day Class (SDC) setting.

If the ADD was mild, or didn't carry with it the learning problems, it could have still caused difficulties in school. These problems could have shown up in a number of different areas – reading, math, writing, note taking, test taking, time management, short attention span, low frustration tolerance, a tendency to drop out of school, school phobia and truancy.

The ADD population with significant learning disabilities merits a closer look.

But the School Told Me I Was Learning Disabled

If you are one of those ADD adults who had severe problems learning to read, calculate or write and were in RSP or even SDC classes in school, we know one thing about you without ever meeting you. Life has been tough for you. Any first or second graders who sit in class and simply can't understand how to read or what the teacher is trying to get across in math begins to feel inferior to her peers. ADD adults talk about feeling "less than," stupid, dumb. If you had problems way back in elementary school, you took a blow to your self-esteem and felt a lack of confidence in your ability to be successful at an early age.

Are you confused? The school told you that you were "learning disabled." All your life you have thought of yourself this way. Now it's ADD. Which is which?

It is important to understand that we are talking about two separate conditions: ADD and learning disabilities.

Because the public school system (grades one through twelve) has shown a great deal of resistance to assisting with the identification of ADD in its students, any child with a problem in reading, math or written language is typically categorized under the catchall term of "learning disabled." This catchall term has caused many ADD children to be incorrectly labeled and, in many cases, has actually prevented the diagnosis of ADD.

What is the big deal? you may be asking yourself. Why does a label matter? It matters very much in this case. A true learning disability is a misfiring of the brain's neurotransmitters that deal with one or more of the particular centers that impact learning. A learning disabled person may have difficulty learning to read, write or understand math concepts. If a person has a true learning disability, the situation can't be changed or improved. The best course of action is to provide support in the form of tutoring or special classes as that person moves through school.

ADD children fall into an entirely different category. If they have problems in reading, math or written language, it is often caused by the ADD itself. The biochemical imbalance of ADD is the root of the problem. Once this is understood, treatment is possible. With medication, the ADD child's ability to improve her reading level, understand math concepts or perform tasks requiring written language is often greatly improved. In fact, there are many instances of dramatic improvements in academic areas once medication is administered. With the identification of ADD an entirely new path of treatment is possible, a treatment path far more effective than continued placement in special education classes alone.

What if the ADD child is not properly diagnosed? What if the school identifies a learning disability but never mentions the possibility of ADD? This is actually a frequent occurrence. Children with ADD often sit in RSP placements for years with only minimal improvement in their academic abilities. Unlike the child with true learning disabilities, ADD children often have a very strong sense that something is wrong with them. By the second or third grade an ADD child often comes home in tears, saying to his mother, "Something is wrong with my brain." He may be conscious that he can understand concepts, pay attention and sit still and listen much better on one day than another. This is a terrible burden for a child to bear, this deep understanding at a very basic level that something about him is not quite right. He often asks his parents, "What is wrong with me?" but there are no answers, and the ADD child's frustration continues.

As the ADD student reaches junior high or high school, he continues to feel "different." On the one hand, he may recognize that he is bright, but with this understanding comes the mystery – "Why can't I do better in school?" He begins to feel that he is doomed to failure. If he is still in RSP classes, he dislikes the "weird kids" who are in the same class and feels a real social stigma associated with the RSP placement. He may begin to drop out of several of his high school classes. Soon he has joined the losers who cut class and smoke pot on the outskirts of campus. If the learning problems are severe, he often drops out of school. He is definitely caught in a downward spiral with no hope.

If an ADD child is not properly diagnosed, there is actually a double negative that occurs. Not only is his learning impacted, but there is a tremendous loss of self-esteem. The first negative is that he doesn't learn. The second negative is that he feels terrible about himself.

ADD Can Cause Dyslexia, Dysgraphia and Dyscalculia

"But I'm dyslexic! I'm not 'learning disabled.' What about me?"

Let's be clear that we are dealing with educational jargon. As usual, something very simple to understand has been mystified and made to seem very complex. The labels themselves are causing the problems, so let's make it simple. When you think of elementary school and what kids are supposed to learn, most of us think of reading, writing and arithmetic. Well, someone has invented hard-to-pronounce, hard-to-spell labels for problems with reading, writing and arithmetic.

DYSLEXIA	=	Problems with Reading
DYSGRAPHIA	=	Problems with Written Language
DYSCALCULIA	=	Problems with Math

Simple, isn't it? The label means that someone is having trouble in one of these areas. But there is a catch – the label doesn't explain why he or she is having trouble.

If your child has a fever, the fever is an indication that something is wrong; your child is sick. If you take your child to a doctor and the doctor merely says, "It's a fever," and charges you fifty dollars, how would you feel? You would probably be upset. You already know that your child has a fever. You want the doctor to tell *why* your child has a fever.

If an adult has been labeled dyslexic, dysgraphic, or dyscalculic, it merely says that the adult has problems in one of these areas. It doesn't tell what is causing the problem or how to correct it.

Dyslexia – The term dyslexia seems to be understood by the general population as reversals of letters and numbers. In actuality, the word dyslexia is much broader than that definition and means that a person has difficulty with reading. The difficulty can encompass problems reading words or difficulty with sight vocabulary. It can mean problems with reading comprehension or not understanding what is being read. The specific difficulty then must be defined.

Dysgraphia – The ADD person who has problems putting her thoughts on paper suffers from dysgraphia. Many ADD adults are great talkers. They can expound on a variety of subjects and can get their points across with ease. Many ADD adults make great salespeople and are so verbally gifted that they could sell iceboxes to Eskimos. Because of their verbal skills they appear self-confident and self-assured. Friends and co-workers admire them for that skill.

But, the ADD adult with dysgraphia has a deep, dark secret. If someone puts a paper and pencil in front of her and she must write, she is in trouble. Often her writing skills are so poor that she avoids any writing like the plague. She usually doesn't understand why she has such trouble with writing, and there is a sense of shame about her secret. Often she will marry a spouse or hire a secretary who will write letters and memos for her and keep her secret.

The dysgraphic ADD adult cannot transfer her thoughts and ideas from her brain to the paper in front of her. This is due to a neurological pathway that is very often blocked for ADD adults.

When this adult was a kid, she could talk your arm off but couldn't copy sentences from the blackboard. She found herself in trouble because she didn't copy her homework assignments in her copy book. The teacher wouldn't believe that she couldn't do this simple task, and she was labeled as resistant or defiant. As she moved up into fifth or sixth grade, when she was required to write, she tended to use short choppy sentences which certainly didn't begin to represent the depth of her thought processes. But, this was the best she could do. Her spelling was often terrible as well, so she would use short, one-syllable words to avoid spelling errors. As an adult, her letters, memos and reports still have short, choppy sentences and one-syllable words. Her writing often looks as though she were still in fourth or fifth grade.

Dyscalculia – If an ADD person historically has problems with math, he is said to have dyscalculia. In elementary school a young child may *never* be able to learn the addition and subtraction facts by memory. He may hide this and develop ways to count on his fingers (without being obvious) all of his life. In elementary school a child may finally understand how to multiply or divide fractions, only to find a week or two later that his understanding of the process is entirely gone from his consciousness. He must go through the agony of learning the process once again. Suddenly, in fifth grade, our ADD student may find that he can't remember if he should start from the right or left when multiplying. How frustrating!

In high school or college our ADD student may be following the logic of Algebra 2. He understands the process. However, when working a long and complex test problem, he may experience the terrible frustration of making an unexplained number reversal, thereby getting a score of zero. The sequential nature of math may be very difficult. Of course he can understand step one and step two, but after that there is a giant hole. Just how does step three connect to the first two steps? He may experience the variable, or "on-and-off," nature of ADD. On one day, an algebraic equation makes perfect sense. He can see the beautiful logic involved. On the very next day, if his brain chemistry has changed, he may find that for him, there is no logic. It simply doesn't make sense.

For many ADD adults, math has been so frustrating that there is a deep fear that lasts throughout their adult lives. Often they will avoid jobs that have any math involved.

As an example, due to a divorce, one of our ADD adults needed to return to the work force after many years as a homemaker. She was dyscalculic and had been so traumatized as a child that, as a parent over the years, she had refused to help her own children with their math homework. She found a job in a small, very chic gift shop. Her panic surrounding math was so great that she was unable to ring up sales or make change. Even though the employer was kind and encouraging, her panic grew. After three days of crying, she decided to quit.

Does Medication Help?

Yes! The whole point of this chapter is to demonstrate the need for an early and accurate diagnosis of ADD, because medication often does make a tremendous difference.

ADD is a biochemical imbalance in the brain. This imbalance results in a decreased production of dopamine. Dopamine seems to be the brain chemical that is responsible for attention span, ability to focus and ability to process information. Difficulty with processing information means that the ADD adult is not understanding the material commensurate with her IQ. In very simple terms, if an ADD adult has an IQ or level of functioning that places her in the *Superior* range, her ability to understand material should also be in that same range. However, the ADD adult can sometimes understand information only at a *Low Average* range, and is not able to access or take advantage of her full intellectual capability. She is not processing information commensurate with her IQ. She often forms study groups to learn information. She may say to friends and co-workers, "Tell me that in a different way."

Because stimulant medications help to restore the biochemical balance of the brain, ADD adults often find that there is a significant increase in their ability to process information when medicated. Translated, this often means that their ability to read improves. Their ability to write or understand math may also improve.

To illustrate the differences that medication can make in an individual with dyslexia, dysgraphia or dyscalculia, we need to go back to children for our examples.

Why? ADD adults are notoriously slippery. Once ADD adults are identified and placed on medication, they will typically use their improvement in college grades or improvement at work as verification that the medication is working. They very seldom request additional standardized testing. In fact, if it is suggested, they generally refuse, saying that they don't have time in their busy schedules. Children are easier subjects to study because they are subject to their parents' wishes and can't get away from the ADD evaluators. Once children are evaluated for ADD, they are typically given the same academic battery six months or a year later to ascertain if academic growth has taken place. Thus we are able to quantify or measure the improvement in ADD children on medication.

No matter whether an ADD individual has problems in reading, writing or math, the medication often makes a huge difference. Remember, there are no promises. Every ADD individual is different, and it is impossible to predict just how the medication will work on any given individual, but often there are startling leaps in performance.

Reading and Medication

One case with rather surprising results involved a fifth grader who had moved into an affluent school district from a rural southern community. He was unable to keep up with his fifth grade class, and testing indicated that he was reading at a first grade level. Fortunately, he was obviously hyperactive and easily recognized as an ADD child, so he was placed on medication. In addition to medication, he received help from the Resource Specialist Program and improvement was rapid. At the end of the school year the fifth grader was retested and, unbelievably, he had gained *four years in his reading level in one year*. If the ADD condition had not been recognized and medication prescribed, most probably his reading level would have remained far below grade level.

Even though the gain of four years of reading in one year is certainly not a common occurrence, academic gains on medication are seen time after time. Once the biochemical imbalance is corrected, the student can learn at the level of his IQ. The use of medication doesn't make mental geniuses of anyone, but it does allow each person to "work up to his potential."

Writing and Medication

Many ADD adults are very verbal but can't put their thoughts on paper. At times the problem with written language can be so severe that it doesn't respond to medication. The area of ADD, medication and written language can best be understood if it is separated into four circumstances:

- When medication works on written language
- When medication doesn't work on written language
- Thank heaven for the computer!
- What if the computer doesn't work?

Difficulties in written language are one of the most common problems for ADD Adults

When medication works on written language – On medication, some ADD adults miraculously find that their thoughts flow smoothly. They can put their thoughts on paper, to write and think at the same time. If they are required to write research papers, job descriptions or letters to vendors, there is absolutely no problem as long as they are on their medication. However, they quickly notice that if they try to do written work when the medication is out of their systems, they are frustrated and back at square one. *They feel just like they did before ever taking the medication.* For these ADD adults, medication is just like wearing a pair of glasses. When the glasses are on (when the medication is in their systems) they can see (they can write). If the glasses (or medication) are off (out of their systems) their problems are still there. For these ADD people, all they need to do is remember to take their medication when they want to write. Very simple, very clean; the problem is solved.

When medication doesn't work on written language – For whatever reason, some ADD adults find that there is little change in this area, even if they take medication. When they are required at work or in a class to write something, it is almost impossible. They can't take notes in a meeting. They tend to write in very short, choppy sentences. Anyone reading their written work tends to question their intelligence or, even more importantly, their ability to perform on the job. If this type of ADD adult decides to return to graduate school for a master's degree or a Ph.D., the admissions committee reading his or her "required" written essays about "Why I Want to Return to School" will typically file it in the circular file.

Thank heaven for the computer – Thankfully, the computer seems to access a totally different neural pathway in the brain. Very often the ADD adult will find that written language flows easily if he simply learns to use a computer. The computer can improve an ADD adult's ability to copy notes from the blackboard, take comprehensive notes, write original material or compose his thoughts. A computer bypasses the difficulty – not all of the time, but a great deal of the time.

For an example of how dramatically a computer can assist an ADD person, let's take a look at an eighth grader who was in the office the day before we were writing this chapter. Sarah was ADD and on medication, but she didn't find that medication made any appreciable difference in her ability to write. (When she was in fifth grade her frustration with written language was obvious, and she took a computer keyboarding class at that time). She brought in a sample of a test she had taken, using paper and pencil, in her eighth grade science class. As a contrast she also brought in an essay that she had written for her English class using her computer. They are reproduced on the next page so that you can see the dramatic difference between her use of pencil and paper and her use of the computer.

What if the computer doesn't help? – There are some ADD people who simply can't put their thoughts on paper. With these people even a computer doesn't work. They can be "average," "bright" or "incredibly bright," and they still can't write. But let them talk and what comes out of their mouths is incredible. They paint pictures with words. They expound on esoteric subjects with ease. They could

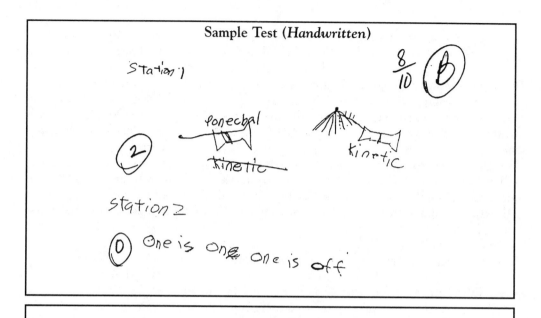

Sample Test (*Handwritten*)

Portion of Essay (*Computer*)

Endangered Cacti Report (rough draft)

Imagine this, you are a hiker in the Andes mountains, as you sit down on a bolder you think you see a cactus, but because you know that Cacti only live in the desert, you don't believe your eyes, so you rub them and take another look the cactus is still there!. Is that possible, or are there only cacti in the Andes mountains in fairy tails? Well believe it or not, there are cacti in the Andes mountains!

In fact the cacti can live in the deserts, mountain tops, jungles, tropical forests, and near oceans. Cacti live in the Americas from British Columbia to Massachusetts, and as far south as Chile. Two species live in Canada and at least one species is native to the lower 48 states except Maine, New Hampshire, and Vermont. Cacti can be found in countries bordering the Mediterranean Sea, Australia, Madagascar, Sri Lanka, and on Mount Kilimanjaro in East Africa. But most of the 2,000 species live in the Southwest United States. One fourth of all of the cacti are endangered. One reason is that some cacti are super picky about their habitat. For example, one species lives on a narrow strip of land 15 miles long, where there is a unique combination of rock and soil.

---

ace any test in the world if only they were allowed to give their answers orally. For this small segment of the ADD population, the key word is *accommodation*. These people need to know how to modify the requirements that they must meet. In school, there is protection under the Civil Rights Law (504). They are protected at work under the Americans with Disabilities Act (ADA). More information on these particular subjects can be found in Chapter 11 – Understanding ADD in the Workplace.

What About the Rest of My Life?

If you are an ADD adult who has had real problems in reading, math or written language, what can you do now? There are lots of things you can do and lots of avenues that are open to you. Do you need more schooling? Do you need job training?

You Mean I Might Be Able to Go Back to School?

In our technological age more schooling is often necessary to get a better job, advance on the job you have, or allow you to move into an entirely new career. Once your ADD is diagnosed and you are on medication, many of the ADD characteristics that prevented you from being successful in school, such as lack of concentration, inability to begin projects or inability to read for more than five minutes at a time, may simply not be a problem any more.

Jump Over the Block of Pain and Fear

For many of you who have had a terrible experience in the past with your education, going back to school is hard to think about. By now you are probably shaking your heads in disbelief that you could ever, possibly, in your wildest dreams be successful in school. Or, you may be getting that gut-wrenching feeling of fear and panic which quickly moves into anger or shame. Get ready to jump over the feelings and experiences of the past that have caused pain and fear. Let yourself open up to the possibility that the situation could be different.

Schools are Required to Help You!

Higher education is an entirely different entity than elementary school, junior high or high school. Adult programs in colleges operate under a different set of laws governing adults with learning problems and ADD. Most colleges have been willing to provide assistance for the ADD adult student. At this time, many colleges require a documented diagnosis of ADD.

But What Can I Really Expect College to Do for Me?

Admission to College – Many colleges provide a special registration packet for the student with ADD or learning disabilities. At other times ADD students fill out the "regular" application, but they identify the presence of ADD in the appropriate place on the application. The application is then given special consideration. In short, if you are identified as ADD, colleges view your application in a different light. They read your past transcripts differently and often have different admission standards to accommodate your pattern of disability.

Sometimes ADD students will be entitled to early or priority registration so that they can get first chance at the classes they need. This enables them to be successful in completing their course of study. To investigate the admission process as an ADD student, all you need to do is call the specific college for information. Believe us, more education, a higher degree, a certificate of competency – all are possible! This is true no matter what your past history!

All Alone on Campus? – Not by a long shot. If you have decided to take the big jump forward and enroll in college, you will not be alone. It is actually very simple to find the help you need. Find the Learning Disability Center (some colleges call it the Disabled Student Center), make an appointment, tell them you are ADD and need help. You will find people in most Disabled Student Centers friendly and willing to help.

Students who re-enter college and approach a college Disabled Student Center for the first time often call us back in absolute amazement. Some of their comments are "I can't believe it! They actually asked me how they could help," "They offered note takers for my lecture classes," "They offered me a tape recorder to use for the semester," "They offered to provide extra time on tests," "They said I could take my tests in a separate room with *no distractions*," "They let me know about the tutorial service on campus."

Colleges appear to be knowledgeable and willing to offer any legitimate help available. Of course, it goes without saying that colleges must work within budget constraints and financial limitations as they offer services.

What if you haven't been officially diagnosed with ADD, but you are pretty sure of the diagnosis? Some of the Learning Disability Centers provide an excellent diagnosis of ADD. If they cannot do the entire diagnosis, they will often be able to provide some of the required testing to supplement a private evaluation. A sample letter to a professor from the campus Learning Disability Center follows on the next page.

What Can I Expect from Individual Professors?

The ADA (Americans with Disabilities Act), Civil Rights Law (504) and the Learning Disability Centers are all there to provide you with protection and information. At the college level you are expected to take the initiative regarding your disability and how it impacts each class. You will need to ask yourself *specifically* what you need in each class from each teacher. In one lecture class the professor may write a clear outline on the overhead and lecture from the outline. You may have no trouble taking notes in that class. Another professor may be more free-flowing and difficult to follow. In that class you may need to request a note taker.

Do you need an untimed test to be able to think and get the information from your brain to the paper? Do you need to use a computer in class for essay tests because you simply cannot write with a pen or pencil? Do you need to learn information in a "different way"? You may need to ask for a tutor who can present material in a multi-sensory fashion (verbally, visually and kinesthetically).

It is usually a good idea to talk to your professors during their office hours and explain your unique disability. If it is apparent that you are a student who genuinely wants to learn the material, but are experiencing problems in one area or another, most professors are sympathetic and helpful. You need to be aware that the individual professor has the right to make a judgment about your request, so make sure it is logical and well-thought-out before presenting it. The Disabled Student Center can usually provide a good deal of assistance in these matters.

WeCare University

Date

To: PROFESSOR'S NAME, SUBJECT

From: LEARNING DISABILITY CENTER STAFF OR COUNSELOR

RE: NAME OF STUDENT AND I.D. NUMBER

(Name) was referred to the Learning Disability Center this semester with documentation that he/she has Attention Deficit Disorder (ADD).

Because of his/her learning difficulties, he/she may need special accommodations to insure improved performance. (Name) is having difficulty with the time constraints of testing situations and would benefit from an alternative test site with extended time.

We will be happy to assist you in arranging for these accommodations. Please feel free to contact us at 555-5555 regarding any questions you may have.

SIGNATURE of Counselor _____

Date _____

SPECIAL NOTE: The following are accommodations that are typically requested.

- Student needs to read test aloud in order to process information
- Student needs to use computer for essay tests
- Student needs permission to tape record lectures
- Student requires use of calculator during test
- Student requires extended time to take exams
- Student requires alternative location to take exams (usually the Learning Disability Center)
- Student needs to use an alternative test method to Scantron testing

---

Sample letter to professor from Learning Disability Center regarding special accommodations for a college student with ADD

A Word of Caution

The world is not perfect. People are not perfect. Systems are not perfect. Occasionally you may find that a professor is less than receptive to the idea that an adult has ADD and that the ADD is causing learning difficulty. It may be that the particular professor has been taken advantage of by other students who asked for special assistance. A case in point involves one ADD adult who was provided a note taker by the college's Learning Disability Center. This adult sent the note taker to class, but didn't go to class himself. Obviously, this didn't go over well with the professor and made it more difficult for the next student asking for special consideration.

Once in a while an undiagnosed ADD adult is not handled well by the college system. An example involves an African-American from a disadvantaged background who had been encouraged to try college by a close friend. This young man struggled and struggled but was unable to understand beginning algebra. He also found that his history class was simply beyond him. After receiving F's in both classes, he repeated the classes and raised both grades to C's.

At that point he approached the college Learning Disability Center and asked for some testing. The professional doing the testing didn't realize that the particular test had a cultural bias. In addition, ADD adults typically suffer from a depression of scores in certain areas due to the ramifications of ADD. The examiner completely misread the test results and diagnosed the young man as having a "low average" IQ. He suggested that he take some classes on "how to study."

The young man's friend brought him to us. Several more tests were administered, including a non-verbal test of intelligence. On this test our young man scored in the superior range of mental ability. Our diagnosis was that he had ADD and also specific difficulties in math and memory. We then suggested he return to the college Learning Disability Center with documentation of his disability for the proper assistance.

On to a Professional Career

If you are an ADD adult who has made it into college, or have finished college and are faced with an exam to qualify for higher education or a professional certification, read on. ADD adults taking LSATs, MCATs, Bar Exams, etc. all qualify for special modifications in the testing arrangement if needed. Initially, all that was required was a report or letter from a properly licensed professional verifying the ADD condition and a list of the tests administered in order to receive special accommodations.

Most probably due to the increase in identification of ADD in adults (including college students) the examining boards now require much more detail in the request for accommodations. In addition to listing specific tests that were administered, specific scores are now required and, beyond that, an explanation based on the test scores to verify that an individual needs the accommodations required.

Not surprisingly, the boards that administer the bar exams and medical licensing exams are the most particular and demand a good deal of documentation. In addition to specific tests and scores, they also require a full psychoeducational history which explains why the adult has not asked for accommodations prior to the current exam.

The following letter is a sample of the basic format that is typically still accepted by the Educational Testing Service (ETS) when a high school student is applying for accommodations on the PSAT, SAT or GRE. If the adult is applying for accommodations on a higher level exam, then a much more comprehensive letter will be needed.

Letterhead of Testing Professional

Date

To Whom It May Concern:

I recently completed a psychoeducational evaluation of (Name) and am writing this letter at his/her request.

(Name) has been diagnosed as having an Attention Deficit Disorder which has produced significant difficulty in her/his ability to attend appropriately for his/her age and complete tests in a timely manner.

The guidelines from the Admissions Testing Program for handicapped students state that the following information must be provided to qualify (Name) for special consideration.

1. **Nature of Disability**
   Attention Deficit Disorder, which causes significant impairment in focusing and concentration

2. **Tests Used in the Diagnosis**
   Wechsler Adult Intelligence Scale-Revised
   Bender Gestalt
   Woodcock-Johnson Psycho-Educational Battery-Revised
   Nelson-Denny Reading Test

3. **Need for Special Testing Arrangements**
   Due to the difficulty with attention span, (Name) requires that the SAT be administered with time-and-one-half given. Testing should be administered in a quiet, distraction-free setting.

(Name)'s test scores indicate the presence of an Attention Deficit Disorder, which is significantly impacting standard test scores.

Yours truly,

_____
Signature, License

Sample letter (on letterhead)

Can I Be ADD and Gifted??

Many of our ADD adults feel that they have never been able to reach their potentials in their careers. This is often a source of great mystery, since they had been told that they were very bright when in elementary school. For some, they may have been labeled *gifted* and placed in special classes. If they were able to do so well in school, why are they having such difficulty in their careers?

For our adult ADD population there are two separate aspects to this question:

1. Why was I never identified as gifted? All my friends were gifted. I always got straight A's in elementary school and junior high. All my teachers told me I should be in gifted classes.

2. I was identified as gifted, did well in elementary school, but in high school and college was only a C student. My SATs for college entrance were low. I had trouble passing the LSAT for law school. I have never approached what I consider to be my potential in my career.

ADD and Never Identified as Gifted

There is a definite problem with the identification process itself. Within the public school system the identification of being *gifted* is made by a test or a series of tests. The test performance of an ADD child will be skewed in a negative fashion due to difficulty with memory and spatial relationships, which are part and parcel of ADD; thus the ADD profile itself will often prevent an ADD child from reaching the gifted range. If the subtests on the various instruments could be adjusted and the tests influenced by ADD eliminated, the child is often performing well into the gifted range, but this is never acknowledged by the school system.

According to the public school standards, the child never quite meets the criteria for placement. The negative side of this has to do with damage to self-esteem. Even though the child may be a straight-A student and told by teacher after teacher that she is very bright, the question in her mind remains. *What is wrong with me? I can't be as bright as everyone says – after all, I "failed" the gifted test.*

ADD and Identified as Gifted

For the ADD adult many questions arise from her early school years. Often the gifted student who also has ADD is not challenged by the educational system until she reaches high school or, for some, graduate school. She is so bright that she is able to do well, even though she is only processing a portion of the material being presented. She may even be having difficulty reading the assignments in textbooks.

Some gifted students are highly motivated, competitive and will work long hours into the night on projects or assignments. They complain that they are spending three to four hours on homework assignments that their friends are completing in an hour or two, but they keep working.

The gifted ADD child may also fall on the other side of the continuum and decide that all the work is not worth it. The resistant ADD/gifted child may receive comments on his report cards that he is "lazy," "unmotivated" or is "not working up to his potential." However, it is seldom that this gifted child is recognized as someone who might have ADD.

In high school, gifted kids often find that the combination of a more demanding and rigorous academic curriculum plus the hormones of adolescence are too much. Again, some of them simply study harder, hide their frustrations and continue to plug away. They may be prone to bouts of anxiety and depression. With these students it is often low SAT scores that bring their parents into our office saying, "She is bright, she took an SAT preparation class – why is her Verbal Score only 300?" Often the PSAT or the SAT is the first time that gifted ADD youngsters are stopped cold. No matter how hard they study, how hard they try, they simply can't do better.

To compensate, they often develop alternative systems for themselves. One of our ADD adults who was in medical school realized that he could not read and absorb information in the textbook. His answer was to develop an alternative system – a study group. As he was quite charismatic, he drew his classmates together into a study group and typically received grades of A. When asked what he would do if he couldn't pull together a study group, he answered matter-of-factly, "I'd drop the class."

Other gifted ADD students develop systems of cheating. Sometimes this begins in high school, sometimes not until college. The fact that they had to resort to cheating usually brings with it a great deal shame. However, they were desperate – nothing they tried had worked. Grades were low. Test scores were low. They felt they had no other alternative.

It is not unusual for our gifted ADD adults to have completed doctoral or even post-doctoral programs. However, there seem to be two common threads among this particular population that are interesting. One thread is that they feel that they have somehow "faked" their way through their doctoral programs. They perceive their colleagues as much, much more intelligent and don't feel that they can even compete with them. One of our undiagnosed ADD adults had a position in one of the most prestigious postdoctoral programs in the United States. It is obvious to the academic world that you are not given this particular post unless you are genuinely talented. However, this ADD adult didn't feel that way at all. In fact, he lived in constant fear that he would be given a research project that would be beyond his capabilities (which in reality wouldn't happen). At that point he was afraid he would be found out for the fake that he thought he was.

The second thread among this particular population is the feeling that everyone else is doing much better than they are in terms of recognition, promotions, and even awards. One of our more interesting cases was an older adult who was professor emeritus of mathematics from a midwestern university. After he was evaluated, it was apparent that he did have difficulty with processing of information. It took him two or three times before he could grasp an idea that was being presented. Since he was so bright he had protected himself from the cutthroat political environment of the large university by developing excellent coping skills. To mask his difficulty processing information, he had developed a gruff exterior that his graduate students were not about to attempt to penetrate.

At the conclusion of the evaluation we asked what was the single most thing that he felt had impacted his life as an ADD adult. His reply was unexpected, but certainly made sense. He said, "All my life my friends have gotten Nobel awards, and I have never gotten one and never understood why." Too far above most of us, but an award that might have been his if he had been identified and had treatment earlier.

Another ADD adult who was identified as functioning well into the gifted range was a top producer in his company. His job required him to travel extensively, as he had numerous overseas accounts. He admitted that he never felt he was capable of doing well on the job, even though his performance was excellent. He lived in constant fear that the myriad of details he worked with on a day-to-day basis would prove to be too much, and he would forget something crucial. He stated that he was absolutely certain that if the company gave him even one more account, he would be totally overwhelmed. At that point he was afraid that he wouldn't be able to keep track of anything, and he would lose his job in disgrace.

With our gifted ADD adults, the deep-seated fear that they are "fakes" or not doing as well as everyone else sometimes is manifested by stress disorders such as Irritable Bowel Syndrome, migraine headaches, ulcers or diarrhea.

Summary

As an ADD adult you may have had a horrible time in school. The very sight or smell of a school corridor may be enough to bring back disastrous memories. Although your early report cards may have been filled with comments indicating "problems with attention," "difficulty remaining on task," or "not working up to potential," the diagnosis of ADD most probably had never been considered. If you were very bright or an exceptionally motivated student there is an even greater chance that your ADD was never identified.

In adulthood you may feel that you never achieved success in your career. If you have your own company, you may be aware that you have always been just short of reaching what you would consider success.

This chapter gives you some understanding of ADD children in elementary school through college. It may help you understand what has happened in your own life and also to pinpoint any specific spots in which you became stuck.

As an ADD adult you need to realize that there is a good deal of assistance out there waiting for you. Look at your history and decide just where you need to re-enter the educational system. Do you need to get your GED? Community colleges or contract independent study programs at the high schools are there to help you. Have you made it through high school but are afraid to try college? Go for it. Start at a community college and learn to ask for help from the Learning Disability Center. They are there to support you. Sometimes they are even capable of providing an ADD diagnosis. You may need to request note takers, books on tape, modified assignments or other accommodations, but you are entitled to this help. If you have always dreamed of a master's degree or Ph.D., but never felt you were smart enough, think again. Assistance is available for students at those levels too. There is help available. There are lots of ways that an ADD adult can enter or re-enter the educational system. Go for it!

Chapter 5

Memory and Study Skills
for ADD Adults

Part 1: ADD and Memory

The topic of memory is a touchy one with most people. The ones who have great memories want to tell us about it, and the ones who have terrible memories (or have been told they do) squirm uncomfortably when the subject comes up. With the ADD adult, the issue of memory can be difficult to pin down (like the rest of the diagnosis) because we vary widely from one person to another; however, our hope is that this chapter will shed some light on memory and provide some useful tips for memory concerns.

There are so many deep, wrenching and worried emotions associated with memory for people who are diagnosed with ADD. Often people are even more upset with their memories prior to an actual ADD diagnosis because at least once their problems have a name, there might be some kind of solution available out there! There are worries such as:

> *If my memory is poor at twenty-five, will it get worse with age?*
> *What will I be like at sixty or seventy?*
> *Does my poor memory mean that I'm stupid?*
> *If I concentrated harder, would I be able to remember better?*

There is often the fear that our sketchy memories may be early signs of Alzheimer's or some other dreaded disease that robs us of our dignity – these memory concerns are truly scary stuff!

The reality for those of us with ADD is that difficulties with memory often increase with stress. We might be functioning just fine at the beginning of our work day but notice that, after a day of answering phones, interacting with people and fielding many things at once, we just can't seem to remember all of the details that we "should." We might notice that at the beginning of our week, we can juggle many details. By Wednesday or Thursday, forget it! We had better write everything down if we expect ourselves to remember it and get it all done.

It is clear that being under pressure, having to perform and feeling stressed combine to create overload and an inability to think clearly and rapidly. Whether in academics or in sports, stress affects an ability to think and remember. Increasing amounts of research show that peak memory and performance actually occur when we are more relaxed and "flowing" with the activity at hand. It would make sense then, as ADD folks, that we should turn our attention to relaxing (breathing) and using our coping strategies to help our memories, rather than tensing up and perpetuating the stress. Once you relax and the stress level drops, your memory functions will come back.

One of the confusing aspects of an ADD person's memory is that it can be razor sharp when remembering certain phone numbers, special events or significant names. At the same time it can be completely fuzzy about what happened five minutes ago, how to navigate a familiar street, or which points were made in an important conversation about the future of a significant relationship! It's this very "Swiss cheese" quality of solid memory one minute and a complete hole in the next that can really leave us puzzled as to why and how our memories work best (and worst).

For many ADD adults, the subject of memory is an even more painful one because of that phenomenon we call "the black hole" of memory. Often we have been misdiagnosed as being amnesiac or having a not-yet-remembered traumatic event in childhood because of this inability to recall significant chunks of our childhood, adolescence and/or parts of our adult life. It literally feels as though our past is similar to a game of hide and seek – parts of our memories are visible and solid, but then there are these giant hiding places where entire events, days or even years are completely blanked (or blacked) out!

Why is this? Are some people just born with great memories? Is a "good" memory a sign of intelligence? Is it genetic? Is something wrong with my memory? Is something wrong with me as a person? Other people seem to be able to remember an incredible amount – are they gifted?

The truth is, there is a definite difference between intelligence and memory. *Intelligence* tests measure a person's ability to form concepts, solve problems, acquire information and reason; *memory* is the recollection of past experience or information. Enhancing memory is a *skill*, and there are many coping strategies available to help you build that skill.

The truth is, only a tiny percentage of human beings are born with photographic (what we call "perfect") memories. The rest of us have as much capacity to improve our techniques to compensate for memory problems as the non-ADD adult. In the ADD adult the questions of "Will my memory improve?" and "Will it get worse?" are often asked with great concern. The answers are that your memory will become temporarily worse with stress and that, while your memory doesn't necessarily improve with treatment, you will get much better at focusing and using your learned coping skills.

Often an ADD person's memory skills (and certainly forgetfulness) are worse than those of the general population, but, through practice, the ADD adult can learn to deal with the issues of stress and memory and learn to cope successfully. To describe and understand how memory works, we first have to know that humans basically have two kinds of memory – short- and long-term.

Short-Term Memory

Research is currently being conducted to determine whether chemical imbalances can affect our short-term memory. This has exciting implications for the ADD adult in understanding why we might have memory problems in the first place. Short-term memory lasts twenty seconds or less. If you don't use the information within fifteen to twenty seconds, it's gone forever. Short-term memory is the type of memory we use when we call information for a phone number, hang up, dial the number we were just given, hear a busy signal and can't remember the number we just finished dialing to dial it again. Sometimes the ADD adult reports "I can't even remember the number as it's being spoken by the information computer because there are too many distractions!" The poor auditory processing of numbers that often accompanies ADD exacerbates problems with memory.

So, here we are. Our thoughts come and go at their own will (not ours). We have brilliant ideas in the shower, while changing lanes in traffic or preparing a meal, and, if we don't log those ideas somewhere, they are gone in twenty seconds or less. In order to reduce the chances of forgetting that great idea, person's name or a solution to a problem that's been bugging you, you have to jot it down or it's gone, gone, gone!

A bit more on memory in general – we human beings take in tremendous amounts of information (called stimuli) from our environment at one time. We are constantly bombarded by what we see, hear, touch, taste and smell. For ADD adults, this bombardment is even more challenging because our filters are not very consistent. We can't screen out stimuli with the same apparent ease as the non-ADD person. We hear a waiter talking at the next table, we see a fly buzzing around at the window, we feel the texture of the carpet under our feet or shoes, we smell someone's perfume from across the room – all at the same time we're supposed to be listening to our mate share a serious concern. Clearly this inability to screen out stimuli causes many problems in our lives. Although we are all designed with a short-term memory for quick input, evaluation and discard of unneeded information (which can cause its own problems), the ADD person's difficulties are compounded by problems with the other type of memory – the long-term memory which will be explored later in the chapter.

Quick Coping Techniques for Short-Term Memory

For the short-term memory, there is a real need for quick coping techniques or adaptation, because it is a twenty-second-or-less, packaged deal, by nature's design. Here are some suggested coping skills to enhance your short-term memory (and remember to make these your own by adapting them in any way you want or need to):

- Keep sticky pads or Post-it® pads in every room of your home, in your car, in your pocket or wallet to jot down your thoughts as they come (the fluorescent ones that come in hot pink, lime green, bright orange, bold blue, etc., are even more attention-grabbing – try them!)

- Keep a small tape recorder under the seat of your car, in your briefcase, in your purse. Once you get over your hesitation of listening to your own voice, know that you will listen to yourself with a lot more attention than you can give to another person's voice; it's in *your* perfect sound and pitch range!

- Investigate computer equipment and software that makes life *easy* for the ADD person. There are small, interactive computers and computer software that help you organize your thoughts and your necessary routines. Try before you buy – if they're not ADD user-friendly, don't spend the money and watch it collect dust.

- Use your answering machine as your memory ally. When you are out and discover that you've used the last check, run out of business cards or need to send a note to Aunt Mabel thanking her for your birthday gift (which you keep forgetting to do), call yourself and leave a message that reminds you to take care of the item.

- Use the small press dots in bright, compelling colors to remind you of a certain phone call, errand or habit that you are trying to remember to build into your schedule – let the small dot remind you, instead of relying on your memory.

- When you jot a note to yourself, *hold* the paper in your hand for a moment and anchor the words or picture on your note in your memory for thirty to sixty seconds – it really helps!

- Place items you will need for the next day – keys, shoes, briefcase – in a line or row by the door the night before. That way, as you walk past them you collect them one by one and remember all the pieces!

- Establish specific places for keys, income tax paperwork, etc., and don't vary them – for example, a key "home" might be a basket directly inside your door, so that *all* keys are deposited in the *same* place every day.

- Use out-of-place cues that help you remember things; for example, leave your car keys in the refrigerator so that you remember to grab that lunch you prepared, or place your shoes on top of your organizer so that as you put them on, you remember to pick up the organizer too!

- When memorizing phone numbers, place the first three numbers in your mind on automatic pilot and just concentrate on the final four numbers until you can dial.

- When you pick up an item or piece of paper that you are supposed to *do* something with, keep the item in your hand until you actually *do* what you are supposed to do with it!

Remember – if you don't try these, you will never know if they work! Challenge yourself to try a couple of techniques a week and keep the ones that work for you as a part of coping with your ADD!

Long-Term Memory

Long-term memory comes into play in this way: all stimuli come in and bombard the brain; the brain decides what to keep and use for twenty seconds or less (short-term memory) and what it wants to hold onto more permanently (long-term memory). There is a third part of the memory process that has to do with long-term memory which is called *recall* or *retrieval*. You see, if we store information in long-term memory and need it again, we will have to recall it. If we stored it incorrectly, then the memory problem we have is that of remembering what we once learned and want to know again.

Long-term memory and *recall* work hand in hand; if we store information correctly, we can retrieve it accurately. If, on the other hand, we store it improperly, it's hard to predict what we will and will not get back. It's kind of like putting your belongings into boxes in a storage unit and forgetting to mark the boxes . . . when it comes time to locate something you need, figuring out which box it's in can be a tough and time-consuming project!

The long-term memory can be enhanced by any combination of the formulas that will be outlined for you to learn and begin to practice. As a note to each of you – if you read or hear about certain coping skills that sound workable for you but you never try them out, you won't be much farther along in your growth and mastery of the challenges of ADD. If, however, you try even parts of our ideas and others you come across, you are much closer to your goal of coping, succeeding and adapting to your ADD.

The idea behind any of these memory formulas is one of *rehearsal*. If we rehearse information in one or more different ways, we are far more likely to store that information in long-term memory. For any of you who have ever played or sung a piece from sheet music, or who have acted in a school or community play, think of the first time you ever saw your music or script. Think of how awkward the music sounded or how stilted the lines came out. Now think about how much improvement occurred after several rehearsals of the same music or script. The same thing happens when we begin to use the memory formulas to assist our long-term memory.

As we begin to explore our ADD, we often feel overwhelmed by so much reading that it is difficult to stay focused or to really take in what we've read. Because of this, the ten memory formulas will be listed, and you can then decide which one you want to read about first, second, third, and so on, by locating the heading before the following paragraphs.

The formulas are:

- Decide to Remember
- Making Sense
- Visualization
- Chaining
- Consolidate
- Memory Tricks
- Enhancing the Concept
- Refreshing Your Memory
- Study Period vs. Cramming
- Grouping and Titling

Decide to Remember

One of the first formulas to be aware of is *deciding to remember*. This means that we should establish ahead of time that something is worth remembering, or that it is important enough for us to need it in the future (from our long-term memory storage banks). When we decide our intention ahead of time, it puts the memory and the body on red alert to pay special attention. An example would be going into a class you're taking and beginning to think about the course content, your notes and your textbook before the teacher even begins lecturing, rather than talking to classmates, eating a doughnut or just spacing out. In the first situation, your mind is already open and receptive to the topic before the teacher even begins, and the probability of long-term memory storage is increased dramatically because of your *deciding to remember*.

Making Sense

Another of the formulas to know is that of *making sense*. Despite what the words might mean to us in everyday language, in the world of memory it means that information that makes sense to us is far more likely to be stored in long-term memory than information that we can't really put into order or that doesn't make sense. Usually the information is either too disconnected, or we've never been exposed to it before. Our ADD adults often report that the material just seems jumbled.

An example of this would be reviewing a list of spelling words or business terms important to our grade or job. Words that we have some familiarity with or that we can make sense of have a better chance of being stored in our long-term memory than a word we've never seen before. Therefore, for ADD adults to increase the chances of long-term memory storage, it would benefit us to find ways of talking about or reading about a subject until we at least have some background knowledge and can make sense out of it before we try to memorize it. Once we have some background and can make sense of what we're trying to memorize, we have handled the concept of *making sense*.

Visualization

Yet another important formula of memory, and one that is receiving a lot of press and research attention, is that of *visualization*. Visualization is a formula that states that *as you are able to make something real by picturing it in your mind, you are enhancing your ability to make it real to your long-term memory storage*.

The concept behind visualization is that most information we want to memorize comes to us in the form of words and letters and symbols. These symbols are handled primarily by the left brain – our logic center. When we begin to use visualization by picturing things in our minds, we activate the right side of our brain – our creative and abstract center. By engaging both sides of our brain, we maximize our ability to memorize and store long-term memory information. When you begin to picture something you want to memorize or commit to long-term memory, it's important to include as many of the five senses as you can so that the picture reflects reality as much as possible.

An example of this would be memorizing your responses to an athletic performance; the more closely you are able to visualize that tennis court or baseball field or chessboard, with all of its sights, smells, your temperature, body state and reactions, the closer you will be to perfecting that performance in real life. Your responses to specific situations will be stored in long-term memory and retrieved when you need them, just the way you rehearsed them.

Picture yourself outlining a football field in your mind's eye, placing the players on that football field, giving color to their uniforms, the field, the referees, the sky, feeling the air temperature, sensing the excitement of the game, and then setting that football game in motion. It can feel as real to us as the actual event if we're careful in putting together our *visualizations*. When we rehearse in this way, we are much more likely to perform that same way in real life.

Chaining

Chaining is the next formula. Chaining is when we chain together knowledge or information that we previously had with new information that we want to store in our long-term memory. Chaining says that we can link together old information as an *anchor* for the new facts as they hook together for better long-term memory retention.

A great example of this is when we learn a language. First, we learn a few basic words; then, once we have those rehearsed into our long-term memory, we add a few more until we have a complete sentence! Another example is cooking. When we first learn to cook, we have to use a recipe or cookbook, even for the basics. Once we have the basics memorized, we can begin to *chain* certain herbs and spices with certain dishes until we're well on our way to advanced gourmet cooking!

Consolidate

Consolidating means *condensing* things into a nutshell; it means taking a lot of material to be memorized and boiling it down to simplified key words or concepts. ADD adults often have difficulty with consolidating because as we begin to speak or write, we might have the tendency to go on and on while our listener is saying, "Will you get to the point?"

Practicing consolidation is best done with written material in the beginning. Practice reading only one paragraph at a time. Then try to find one key word or *very small* phrase that describes that passage in a nutshell. Write the word or phrase in the margin of the paragraph (in pencil until you feel more confident about your ability to condense). You can test your consolidating abilities by going back and re-reading *only* the margin cues – can you remember what that paragraph was about by reading just your key word?

As you get better at consolidating, you can practice in your personal and business relationships as well. Imagine writing out everything you want to say to your mate about particular issues you have with him or her. Now go back and look at your paragraphs. See if you can boil your points down to certain key words or phrases that can later steer the whole conversation.

Don't hesitate to put those key words on a card or note for you to have in front of you when the real discussion takes place – cue cards can enhance a discussion (often a welcome relief for the non-ADD listener who gets lost in our wandering stories). Once again, *consolidating* things into a nutshell helps us by condensing our information into a more manageable package of short key words or phrases.

Memory Tricks

Next, we will discuss what happens when we develop *memory tricks* (sometimes known as *mnemonic devices*) to help us learn and remember. Some of these memory tricks have become so common for us that we don't even remember how we know them! Some examples are CIA (Central Intelligence Agency), NOW (National Organization of Women), BLT (bacon, lettuce and tomato sandwich), USC (University of Southern California) – even ADD (Attention Deficit Disorder)! Most of the memory tricks were created by using the *first letter* of *each* word in a phrase or title enough times that these letters created a memory trigger of the longer version of the phrase.

Imagine yourself needing to run three errands. Your first stop is the bicycle shop to pick up your son or daughter's repaired bike, next is the cleaners for your business suits, and finally the auto parts store for new windshield wiper blades. You might try arranging the first letters into a word to trigger your memory about your errands, i.e., **C**leaners, **A**uto parts store, **B**ike shop. The word **CAB** could serve as your memory cue for the three separate errands you have to complete. Please remember that tips on improving your memory are best used in combination with other tips, so don't hesitate to jot yourself a note in addition to creating a *memory trick* to remember things!

Enhancing the Concept

Enhancing the concept is the formula that states that when we put a bit more energy into information we want to remember by elaborating or expanding on it, we are much more likely to remember it. *Enhancing* is defined by the *American Heritage Dictionary* as "to increase or make greater, as in value, beauty or reputation; augment," so it follows that if we provide increased value and rich detail to what we are memorizing, it will become enhanced for us in our long-term memories.

For example, let's say you're practicing your job interviewing skills. Imagine yourself at a job interview, feeling a bit nervous, watching the clock as the time ticks by until the interview begins. Now, to practice enhancing, begin to provide greater detail about the office and your upcoming experience – go ahead and expand on the furniture, picture yourself in a certain suit that feels and looks great, notice you're feeling calmer inside. Now take the enhancement even further and imagine yourself being called into the interviewer's office, sitting calmly and answering the interview questions. Practice everything you know about the company, the job, your qualifications – go ahead and enhance to your heart's content, because what this will do is commit your solid answers and interviewing style into long-term memory for even easier execution when you are actually in the interview situation.

Does this sound a lot like visualization? It is very close, and when the two of these principles are used at the same time, they're a winning combination! Visualizing brings the picture to your mind and enhancing makes it so real it can't be forgotten!

Refreshing Your Memory

This seems like a good time to bring up the subject of *refreshing your memory* (also known as review!). It might seem silly or self-evident that we would need to periodically refresh our memories about our learning material, but we sometimes have the mistaken idea that once we commit something to long-term memory, we never have to pay attention to it again and it will always be there. This is an incorrect assumption.

The truth is, noted study skills author Kathleen McWhorter talks about a "forgetting curve" that takes place where certain things we've memorized fade into the background. There are simply too many things to learn and know and too much to pay attention to in this world. If we want certain things to stay "front and center" with our attention, we have to review them every now and again.

An excellent way to both learn and refresh information is to make flash cards. Flash cards are a wonderful tool for the ADD adult (and children, too!) because they are portable, can be done with brightly colored pens and/or paper, and because they are created with no more than one fact or concept on each card – keep it simple!

The single word or concept should be on one side of the card and the definition or concept description should be on the other. Experts in memory say that if we get that same flash card correct four times in a row, we have committed it to long-term memory and now just have to periodically refresh our memories to keep the information close at hand.

✔X✔✔✔✔

ONE FACT OR CONCEPT PER CARD

Flash card example:
1. No more than one fact per card.
2. Work with stacks of ten at a time.

3. When you get it right, place a check mark in the upper right-hand corner.
4. When you don't get it right, place an "X" in the upper right-hand corner.
5. When you have four check marks in a row, with no "X's" in between, move that card to your periodic review pile(s).

Study Period vs. Cramming

Along the same lines as refreshing your memory is a formula that states *periodic study periods are much more effective than cramming.* We have all had to cram information into our memories at one time or another – when we ran out of time to study for all of our classes at once; when we had a huge business meeting to attend on short notice with a lot of new facts to present; when we were asked to speak at a PTA meeting at the last minute after a scheduled speaker cancelled – recognize any of those scenarios? It isn't that cramming is a complete waste of time. After all, a certain amount of that crammed information stays with us (at least for a while). It's just that study periods at regular intervals have been proven to be a much better way to keep more information in our long-term memories across time. The formula works like this: when we learn new information, we haven't had time to really make sense out of it or assimilate it into our previous knowledge. We often feel overloaded.

When we give ourselves a breather before taking in *more* new stuff, we give our minds a chance to sift and sort, to organize and question, to settle in before being ready to accept more. It's very much like the paper towel commercial where the cheap brand and the heavier expensive brand are side by side over two puddles of water. Think of *cramming* as the cheap brand and *regular study periods* as the more expensive brand. Now picture those towels trying to wipe up the puddles – which is most effective? That's right, the thicker one is, as is maintaining regular study periods to sort out your learning of new information.

There is also some speculation by brain researchers who study sleep patterns that a great deal of our learning takes place during our rapid eye movement (REM), or dream state, sleep. It's one of the reasons that infants need so much sleep – they have a lot to learn! If this research is accurate, then we need our dream sleep to mull over what we are learning and trying to memorize in between intensive study times. Remember, just a little at a time goes a long way in terms of memorizing. Remember to leave *time* between your learning *practice* sessions – check it out!

Grouping and Titling

The last formula to be experimented with is *grouping and titling.* The idea with this one is that human beings naturally and quickly put people, places and things into *groups* and then *title* those groups to both learn and remember important things about them.

An example of grouping and titling is learning the bones of the body in an anatomy class. If all we have is a list of the bones and they're not in any order (or groups), it would take us a long time to memorize the information because it would be random and disconnected. If, however, we title an area "bones of the arm," then we can pick from our list only bones that belong with the arm, and our grouping makes them much easier to commit to memory.

Supermarkets have taken this formula and used it to make sense out of their stores. Picture the signs in each of the aisles that label what you can find there – all of the goods are grouped by product, and you can use the title overhead to find those products. Now imagine this is your shopping list:

eggs   celery   coffee   margarine   crackers   chicken   soap

Do you notice yourself grouping certain items together to save yourself time and energy when you go into the store (instead of wandering and backtracking through the aisles)? Usually we can go right to the titled aisle and pick up several things in that area that are grouped together.

Now think of how confusing and frustrating it is for the ADD person who has to go into a different store than she is used to – she spends twice the time trying to figure out which groupings go with which title. This can also be confusing and disorienting when your favorite grocery store decides to move some of its items or displays around. Cat food used to be with household supplies; now it shares the aisle with baby goods! It can take several trips to that familiar store to relearn the groupings and their titles – be patient with yourself and realize that this can be very tension-producing.

While we're on the subject of tension, imagine how much stress is produced where *grouping and titling* is concerned in a place like Southern California. As creatures of habit, we begin to lump together (or group) our favorite dry cleaners, grocery store, accountant, baby-sitter, etc., in a certain area known by a certain title (perhaps a city's name or a neighborhood term), or label. Well, we live in a fast-paced society that is constantly moving, changing, "earthquaking," being torn down and built back up somewhere else. The best thing you can do for yourself is to identify when your groupings and their titles (your familiar neighborhood) have been broken down, grieve the loss of the familiar, and begin to re-group and re-title for your own sanity and sense of security in the rebuilding process. This is particularly important for ADD adults who can find change upsetting and confusing to their established routines.

Memory Summary

In most cases of adults with ADD, there is some variation of memory impairment. This is often reflected in our test scores, as well as in problems dealing with our real life experiences. The most important thing to remember about your memory is that it is a *skill* and can be *built upon*, regardless of your method of treatment for ADD. Although our memories are often frustrating to us, by using the coping techniques discussed (and creating some of our own), we can experience more mastery of memory than at any other time in our lives.

Part 2: ADD and Studying

ADD adults and studying seem to come in two versions – there is either a strong ability to focus and drive hard to a positive study result, or there is so much interference from the ADD characteristics, even with medication, that the distractibility factor makes studying nearly impossible. For those of you who have been *Study Successes*, this part of the book is designed to give you some new ideas for that extra edge; for those of you who have been *Study Strugglers*, this part of the book will give you practical, useful ideas to try out. As you sort through the tips, you will be able to create your own sharper edge to studying.

Whether you're a *Study Success* or a *Study Struggler*, ask yourself these questions to figure out what kind of information you need on how to study better.

- Do you want to skip classes or meetings because what they're talking about doesn't seem to make any sense?

- Do you find a million other things more important to do than studying (like putting the clothes from the washer into the dryer)?

- Do you doze off to sleep after a page or two of heavy reading, even though you've got three chapters to cover?

- Do letters and numbers seem to blur, wiggle or breathe on the page?

- Are you absolutely sure you did well on a test, only to find out that you bombed it?

- Do you read your notes over after class or a meeting and can't make sense out of them? (if you've even been able to take notes?)

- Do you suffer from what we call highlighting overdose? This means that after you highlight your reading, is your entire page yellow?

- Have you bought into the myth that "some folks have it and some folks don't" when it comes to studying or getting good grades?

If any of these apply to you, read on for some hot tips on how to make studying work *for* you instead of against you.

Setting the Stage by Managing Our Time

Some of us have trouble studying because we are better distracters than we are time managers. We have good intentions of studying, but time just slips away while we pay attention to other situations that pop into our lives and distract us. The first step in studying and learning is to decide that it's a priority – that what you'll get out of studying will serve you far beyond what you'll get out of moving that pile of clothes or catching that TV commercial.

This can be a hard one for ADD adults, as the payoff can seem too far in the future to hold onto for the present, or the payoff for studying has been one big headache for no great gain. Please keep in mind, while you read this chapter, that experts state that by the year 2000, a college degree will be required in order to apply for and get a decent job. Sometimes a statistic like this from the Department of Labor has to serve as our incentive or payoff. Any education you get will give you that extra edge that you'll need as we move more and more toward an "Information Society."

Once you've decided that studying is a priority – whether for yourself, your family or the changing job market – remember this: every minute you spend studying is a minute you *don't* have to spend later on the same material. No matter how it feels, we never go over the same material the same way twice. This means that every paragraph you get out of the way by reading, highlighting and using the study tips that follow is a paragraph off your chest when you open that book again for another study session. You can't lose!

Lots of times we don't even want to get started studying, or we say that we have no time to study because we think we have to study for hours at a stretch. For an ADD person, an hour of concentration can feel like a week! Instead, picture approaching your studies with the thought of "every five or ten minutes I give to studying now, I will be that much further ahead next time."

Getting Started

One thing we need to do for starters is to analyze how much we have in our lives and assess whether everything we do fits into the time we have available. Don't laugh now. We know that the ADD adult has trouble with time management or we wouldn't include it in our book. *Reality Check*: We have twenty-four hours a day, times seven days in a week = one hundred sixty-eight hours per week – that's it, per person, per week, every week.

There are Only So Many Hours in a Week – A Fun Exercise About Reality

1. Take out a sheet of paper and write a list of everything you do in a week's time. Include activities like sleeping, grooming (showering, shaving, hair), working, being in class, studying, commuting, clubs or organizations, church commitments, chores, child care, exercise, etc.

2. Now to the right of each activity, in column two, write down the approximate number of hours you spend doing that activity in one day. For example, if it

takes you one hour a day to groom yourself, you would have a total of one hour in column two directly across from *Grooming* on the list.

3. Multiply the number of hours you do an activity each day by the number of hours you would do that activity in one week. Place that number in column three.

4. Now total column three and see how close your grand total comes to the one hundred sixty-eight hours per week that we have available as human beings. Are you over or under?
   Example:

Column One (Activity)	Column Two (Hours/Day Average)	Column Three (Hours per Week)
Grooming	1	7
Sleep	8	56
Commute	1	5
Work	8	40
Class	3/5	15
Studying	3/7	21
	Grand Total	**144**

Get the picture? If we have a lot of "free time" hours, we will get lost in whatever catches our attention. We may never feel like we are accomplishing our goals. If we have no free time or, like many of us, even exceed the one hundred sixty-eight hours per week available, we are so overloaded that there is no way to come out ahead. This will increase our feelings of tension, pressure and hopelessness. These feelings compound into a feeling of being overwhelmed, which makes studying look even less appealing.

Tips for Better Time Use

The following tips are designed to help you get the most out of your time, whether you are a *Study Success* or a *Study Struggler*:

- **Use peak periods of attention.** If you know you are a night owl, save your most complicated tasks for the evening when your mind is sharper and more focused. During the day, do more routine tasks like laundry, errands and returning simple phone messages. On the other side, if you are a day lark, use your morning hours to attack your most complicated tasks, and save your routine tasks for later in the day or evening when you don't need to concentrate as much. This is the idea of using your brain power to your best advantage – using your edge.

- **Study your most difficult subjects first.** Our tendency as ADD adults is to avoid or put off our most difficult tasks or subjects for later, often promising ourselves that we'll make time to come back to them. The problem is that we don't usually make time to come back to them and then we are buried beneath the mountain of procrastination. If we study our most difficult subjects or complete our most difficult tasks first, we have maximum brain power and concentration available. Then, as our fatigue level increases, we can slack off a bit to our easier subjects where our full attention may not be as crucial. An example would be if you found writing to be a difficult task and math to be easier to do. While the tendency would be to finish math first, writing would be a better use of your initial energy.

We can often get ourselves started by setting a timer or clock for fifteen, twenty, or twenty-five minutes, telling ourselves that we *only* have to study for that amount of time. Once that time is up, a short break to move around, get that cup of coffee, etc., is important. Set the timer for break, too, or else the tendency is to get involved or lost in what we're doing during our break time. You can use the timer to get you back to studying, then restart the timer for the next study period.

- **Be generous when estimating how much time you will need.** As ADD adults, we have a tendency to underestimate how much time a project or paper will take, or how much time we'll need to study for an upcoming exam. We often have an unrealistic or idealistic view of how long something will take, only to find out that we may need twice as long to do the task. This can foul up our schedules and lead to complete frustration and disappointment. It is better for us to leave some padding – a safety zone – than to program ourselves so tightly that there is no room to shift or alter plans. We have a therapist friend who says, "You have to leave room for the universe to burp." "Burps" in our lives may be a traffic jam on our way to an exam, a broken copy machine when we have a paper due, a busy signal on the phone or a sick child who seems to be conspiring to make our studies a struggle. No matter what the burp is, it can get in the way. Once it does, we can feel completely thrown off track. See the coping skill of *Clearing* in Chapter 14 for tips on scheduling time better.

- **Use the A-B-C system of priority.** Frequently, ADD folks have trouble with time management and priorities because we take care of things as they come up, rather than having a system to decide what should be taken care of first, second, third. The A-B-C system of priority is designed to help you look at your list of things to do and assign a priority status to each item or activity. We may sit down to chemistry, only to be distracted by a loose pile of papers threatening to fall off our desks, then to be drawn toward the bookshelves to re-organize them, then to be driven to make that call to a study buddy to ask for his notes. Using the A-B-B system allows you to look at all of the things you could or want to do, and then to realistically assess how crucial each activity is in the overall set of goals you have toward *Study Success*.

The A-B-C System: An Exercise:

1. Make a list of *all* the things you need to do right now. Don't worry about the order of them, just get them on paper. Include study items, chores – anything you need to do that's been clogging up your head with worry.

2. Make a copy or photocopy of this system to post at your desk or on the refrigerator:

   A = Top Priority, Red Alert, Must Take Care of as Soon as Possible

   B = Very Important, Has Impact on My Life, But Isn't a Red Alert

   C = Not That Important. May Wait Until I Have Some Extra Time to Do It

3. Now, using the A-B-C system, assign a letter to each one of your items on the list of things to do – don't spend too much time on any one item. If you are confused about something on the list, go to the next item and give it a letter. You can come back to the confusing ones later. Somehow, after you've put everything in its place, it becomes easier to see which letter should be assigned to the confusing ones.

   IMPORTANT! When using the A-B-C method, *you must complete at least one "A" priority every day* or you will not respect your new system.

- **Set up cues for yourself that mean something specific to you.** It helps to structure and manage your time when you set up specific anchors as your cues to begin work or study. When you get home, dropping your backpack next to your desk or taking your suit coat off is the cue to get studying, even for five minutes. One client we know can only study once her shoes are off, cueing her to get down to the business of studying since she won't be leaving her immediate study area or home without her shoes!

   It might be that a specific desk area, study corner or drafting table is the one place you associate with studying, and when you sit or stand there, it's time to take care of study business. There is a documented scientific advantage to using the same place over and over again for a specific activity like studying. This helps the brain be clear about what we're supposed to do in that place – study.

- **Use the phone to check on scheduled dates, activities, comparison shopping and everyday needs.** Because ADD affects concentration and task completion, it would be very easy for us to get lost running around town looking for that special deal, that calendar we saw once for organizing our studies, and any number of actions that work like wheels spinning in the sand – we get nowhere fast and feel discouraged just as quickly. At least if we get off track in our phone-calling at home or the office, we're in a safer environment that supports us with other tasks to take care of if we get distracted, rather than being halfway across town, frustrated in our cars.

Tips for Reading and Highlighting Books and Textbooks

The following tips are designed to help you get the most out of your study reading, whether you are a *Study Success* or a *Study Struggler*:

- **Set a reasonable goal.** If you only have a half an hour to do the reading, make a pact with yourself that you will read two or three pages and take notes on that reading – not the usual ADD sand trap of saying, "I can get through this twenty-page chapter in thirty minutes!" and then belittling yourself when you can't do the undoable.

- **Break the reading into paragraphs.** Focus is a problem. When you expand your focus to include too much material, you risk losing the comprehension of what you read. A paragraph at a time is a reasonable focus. Some ADD adults we work with cut a paragraph-sized window in a sheet of paper to isolate *just* that paragraph on which to concentrate.

- **Read first before you highlight.** The first time you read through something, it either looks like everything is important and you should highlight the whole thing, or nothing looks important enough to highlight. You then have nothing to show for your reading attempt, except the sinking feeling that you have to do it over. Read the paragraph first, *then* go back and highlight the main idea of that paragraph.

- **Consider using different highlighting colors.** Sometimes it helps to use one color for the main idea of the paragraph, another color for supporting details of the main idea, and yet another color for any examples that make the material real for you. It may sound like a lot of color, but your brain will adapt to the system. *You have to be consistent in your system or you'll blow it!*

- **Use margin notes.** This one takes some practice, but we have found that if you place a key word or two in the margin next to the paragraph you've read which sums up what the paragraph was about, you can use those key words later to review for a test or to look up specific information quickly. Remember to keep margin notes short and to the point. To test yourself, try using margin notes in one chapter or section, then go back and reread just your margin notes. Can you track the material? If so, then your margin note is the flag that points to the paragraph, and the highlighting expands on the subject it covers.

- **Consider colored overlays.** There is an entire field of study that focuses on how poorly the human eye can respond to black print on a white page. This focus problem can get worse if the pages are glossy white and create even more glare. In any art supply or stationery store you can locate clear plastic sheets in varying colors – some with a non-glare finish and some without it. Take one of your textbooks into the store (or use one of their books) and test out your eye comfort as you place a plastic colored sheet in rose, blue, green, brown, etc. over the text print and begin to read. We have found this tool increases reading comfort time, decreases eye strain and therefore reduces reading stress. Take your time in color selection. We're an impulsive group overall and will often grab the first color that brings relief, when a different color may improve our reading power even more dramatically.

- **Use a buddy system.** If using any kind of a study system is new to you and you feel uncertain as to how well you're highlighting, using margin notes and covering the material, do not hesitate to have someone whose study skills you respect look over your system and make helpful observations or confirm your *Study Success* path. Better to have a friend look things over and point out possible improvements than to have your test grade point out the problem when it's too late.

Tips for Note Taking

Note taking can be a particularly frustrating experience for the ADD adult. The very act of taking notes requires a variety of skills to be working in top order, all at the same time: thinking, organizing notes on a page, condensing the lecture or meeting content into a nutshell, maintaining fine motor control to write out the words, maintaining focus on the lecture for a sustained period of time. Is it any wonder that we often have difficulty in the art of note taking? The following tips are designed to help you minimize your note taking frustration and to become a note taking *Study Success*.

- **Learn about note taking systems.** If we learned to take notes at all, we usually learned the outline system that looks like this:

Topic (at top of page)

    A. Main idea #1
       1. Supporting detail of main idea #1
       2. Supporting detail of main idea #1
          a. Concrete example of supporting detail of main idea #1
    B. Main idea #2
       1. Supporting detail of main idea #2

and on and on and on . . .

While this system works very well for clear, orderly thinking and professors who lecture in logical sequence, it's easy to get lost trying to figure out which are the main ideas, which supporting details I should note, and so on.

An alternative to the outline system of note taking was generated at Cornell University and is therefore called the *Cornell System*. The Cornell System looks like this:

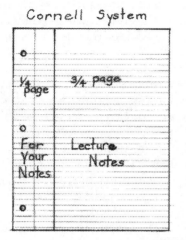

The paper is divided into three-quarter/one-quarter segments. On the three-quarter, larger side, the main lecture notes are placed. On the one-quarter, smaller side, there is ample room for drawings that explain the lecture, your own notes and questions about the material to clarify later. You can also include the listing of page numbers in your textbook that correspond to the lecture material so you don't have to waste time finding the page numbers when you're studying later. Cue words in the margins that function a lot like we talked about in study reading to guide your review are also helpful.

The Cornell System is very useful for professors who digress – you know, the wandering professor who lectures on one thing, then goes off on a tangent (and so do your notes), and then returns to the original point. Instead of having a page full of arrows that connect your notes, you can use the one-quarter side of your note sheet to write the digressed information directly opposite the original subject – voila!

Yet a third system for note taking is called the *mind-mapping system*. This system is especially helpful for visual learners. The topic or key concept is placed at the center of the diagram. The supporting details radiate from the key concept and the concrete examples radiate from the supporting details. Our clients have shared many delightful adaptations of the mind-mapping system, which we illustrate below:

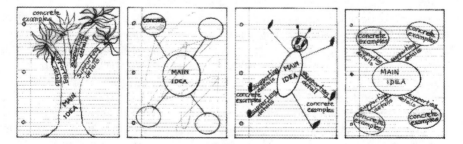

- **Consider tape-recording the lectures.** When your notes keep looking like incomprehensible chicken scratches and note taking seems impossible, consider tape-recording the lecture. Be sure to obtain your instructor's permission to tape in advance. *Warning: We live in a busy, busy era. If you will not have time to listen to the taped lecture, this method may not work for you.* Also, don't forget to label the tape with its contents and a date. There is nothing more frustrating than a box of unmarked tapes to decipher before a test.

- **Tape-record your notes in your own voice.** As we talked about in the short-term memory tips, we respond to our own voices far better than anyone else's. Once we get over the discomfort of hearing our voices on tape, we find that we listen to ourselves with rapt attention, since the voice tones, vocabulary and ways of explaining are perfect for us! Consider putting notes you have taken onto a tape recorder in your own voice and listening back to the tape when it's time to review.

- **Reduce the amount of handwriting required.** Writing by hand requires concentration, fine motor control, and the ability to keep on writing for periods of time, regardless of how frustrated you may be. Often the ADD adult has difficulty with legible, planned, orderly handwriting. This can result in words placed too closely together and/or misspelled. Our sentences are often too lengthy or too brief. Instructors will sometimes allow the use of a computer or word processor for written work and note taking, which will give the ADD learner an advantage.

- **Use a note taker.** In many settings note takers and/or tape recording equipment for student use are available for ADD-diagnosed adults. Sometimes a classmate may be willing to take notes and share them or to become your study buddy. Consult our chapter on ADD and Education (Chapter 4) for more details. An old friend of ours used to say, "If you don't ask, you don't know!"

Tips for Test Taking

Test taking is a skill – a skill not often taught in school when ADD adults were kids. Under a time limit one must give one's full, immediate attention, demonstrate competence with the test material, have complete recall of what was studied, show information recognition, move through the test rapidly, and complete it on time. Sounds like a pressure cooker, right? You bet! The following are some test taking tips to help you to become a *Study Success* with tests:

- **Ask about the test format.** There are two types of test formats – objective and subjective. These types of tests require different ways of study and preparation. You have the right as a student in a class to know what type of format the test will follow, how many points it involves, and how much weight it carries in your overall grade.

  Objective tests include true-false, multiple choice, matching and fill-in-the-blank. With objective tests you are required to recognize the correct information/answer from the possible choices. The best way to study for objective tests is to use flash cards as discussed earlier in this chapter. Flash cards require you to recognize one fact, word, concept or definition on sight, just like the test will. They encourage the student to recognize correct information.

  Subjective tests include short answer and/or essay questions. With subjective tests you are required to have complete recall of the topic (uh-oh!) and be able to elaborate on it in your answer. The best ways to study for subjective tests include making up sample test questions and answering them thoroughly, and to practice answering questions in outline form. Students can convert the outlined answer into essay form easily. *Note: Often professors have test banks on file in their offices or in the library so that you can familiarize yourself with their testing style. You can also use a study buddy and exchange made-up test questions for variety.*

- **Have all necessary supplies with you.** Be sure you bring everything you might remotely need on the day of the test. Extra pencils, pens, paper, whiteout, scratch paper, calculator, slide rule, Kleenex®, good luck charm(s), Scantron forms, blue book, floppy disk – these are *vital* for your test taking adventures. There is nothing more unsettling than to get to the test site without the proper materials and then trying to scramble to locate what is needed. This increases test anxiety unnecessarily, so make it easy on yourself and have a "test emergency kit."

- **Preview the entire exam.** A cross-country or marathon runner would never dream of starting a race without previewing the course. If he didn't, he'd risk a sprained ankle from potholes or pacing problems with steep hills. Why you immediately start answering questions on a test before you look the whole thing over is a mystery! After you put your name on the test, but before you start answering, have a look at what you're up against. Is the test five pages or two? Are the points distributed evenly, or are the higher point value questions at the end? Is the test divided into parts? What format(s) did the instructor actually use? How do you need to pace yourself to have sufficient time? Previewing the test allows you to make decisions about points, pacing and content that maximizes your testing success.

- **Read the directions.** Impulsivity is a problem for ADD adults. Too often as ADD adults we read a word or two of the directions and infer the rest (if we read the directions at all). This can be a disaster if we misinterpret the directions or miss directions that are presented in more than one part (i.e., list and define). On the next page is a list of terms most commonly presented in test instructions. It benefits you enormously as a *Study Success* to learn them and to learn what these words are actually directing you to do on the test. Many test grades have dropped for ADD adults who too hastily think they already "know" the directions.

When the Directions Say:	You Should:
Compare	Examine two or more things; identify similarities.
Contrast	Show how items are different; include details or examples.
Criticize	Make judgments about quality or comparative worth.
Define	Give an accurate meaning of a term to show you understand it.

Describe	Tell how something looks or happened; include who, what, when, where, why and how.
Discuss	Consider important characteristics and main points.
Enumerate	List ideas, aspects, reasons, etc., one by one.
Evaluate	React to the topic in a logical way, including strengths and weaknesses of the topic.
Explain	Give the facts and details that make the concept clear and understandable.
Illustrate	Show clearly, explain or use examples to demonstrate.
Justify	Give reasons that support an action, event or policy.
Prove	Establish that a concept or theory is logical or correct.
Summarize	Cover major points in brief paragraph form.
Trace	Describe the development or progress of a particular trend, event or process in chronological order.

- **If you're stuck, mark it and move on.** We can paralyze ourselves so easily, can't we? We'll often get stuck on a question and then tie ourselves in knots trying to come up with the answer, which blocks memory skills and wastes valuable test time. Force yourself to move on and then come back to the ones you were stuck on if there's time.

- **Review your test before handing it in to the instructor.** Save a little bit of time at the end to briefly go over your test. Check that you put your name on the test (a basic fatal error), that your answers on the Scantron match up with the questions (a fatal mechanical error), and that you at least provided your outline notes if you ran out of time on an essay question (in case the instructor gives partial points for work attempted). Change your answers *only* if a question somewhere in the test jogs your memory for a previous question.

- **Review the graded test when it's returned to you.** The usual tendency when getting a test back is to look at the grade and then file the test away some-where (if not in the trash!). Looking at the test closely is an excellent oppor-tunity for the ADD student to investigate strengths and weaknesses to improve performance on the next test. Did you run out of time? Did you have problems with one type of format as opposed to another? Did you study incor-rect material that wasn't on the test? Did you misinterpret the directions? By approaching our graded tests with a spirit of noncritical investigation of what to improve for next time, the ADD student plays an active role in becoming a *Study Success.*

- **Consult with the instructor.** If your test performance continues to be a disaster, consider consulting directly with your instructor. Perhaps a portion of the test can be done orally if writing is a problem; perhaps the instructor will allow the use of a word processor rather than requiring handwritten work; perhaps your instructor would benefit from some information on ADD.

- **Use special testing options.** As a diagnosed adult with Attention Deficit Disorder, you are entitled to special testing considerations. These include, but are not limited to, extended time for taking tests, proctored tests in a non-distracting environment, or the use of a reader. Your options are covered more extensively in Chapter 4 – Education: ADD's Impact. The important thing to know are your options for these accommodations. Check with your campus for the services that are available.

- **Remember to use *visualization* as your ally.** Visualizing a successful test situation is a powerful ally in utilizing long-term memory. Find a comfortable, quiet place in your home, such as a favorite chair in the den, where you can build your visualization. A test-day visualization might go like this:

> Picture yourself arriving at your test site well-rested, with all of your test supplies in your backpack or briefcase. See yourself locating a familiar desk and arranging your things the way you like them. Now take a moment, close your eyes and *breathe*. See yourself feeling confident in the studying you've done and ready to tackle the exam. (Breathe.)
>
> Picture the instructor walking in with the exams. (Breathe.) He or she passes them out, and, as soon as you receive yours, you write your name on it and begin to pre-read the exam. (Breathe.) You observe the format(s), the distribution of points, and the broad overview of the material covered. You begin answering questions confidently, marking the ones that aren't clear so you can come back to them if time permits. Before the end of the test, you review your answers to make sure you haven't left anything out. You turn in your test, gather your belongings and leave the classroom, leaving stress and tension behind you as well. You use each testing opportunity as a chance to gain an even sharper edge for the next exam.

Summary

Study skills for ADD adults must start with your ability to manage time. The focus of this part of the chapter is to bring your attention to the reality of how much time you have available, how to prioritize your tasks, how to read and highlight more effectively, how to take notes more efficiently and some invaluable tips on how to master test taking. Use whichever ideas in this chapter seem helpful, and don't hesitate to invent your own. No matter how quirky, colorful or unique they may be, they all work together to make you a *Study Success*.

Chapter 6

The Silent Killer of Relationships:
Mating and Relating with ADD

One of the most challenging and difficult areas of an ADD adult's life is that of personal relationships. We want a relationship with a special someone, we want to share our lives, we want to be happy and in love, but we just seem to blow it over and over again as a result of our ADD characteristics. There are often complaints about us as partners because of situations caused by our time management problems (you *said* you would be here two hours ago!), memory problems (you did *not* tell me about that dinner engagement with your boss!), concentration and overload problems (are you even listening to me? You look like you're in outer space instead of here with me!), and mood problems (you're like a yo-yo – one minute you're happy and bubbly and the next you're completely down in the dumps!).

This chapter will explore how relationships are impacted by the ADD condition, provide a compassionate note to the ADD spouse or partner, and look at the patterns and pitfalls that often occur. We would also like to point out that many ADD adults marry other ADD adults. Whether this is because they are attracted to traits similar to their own, whether impulse drives them together, or whether their individual ADD fingerprints seem different enough that they feel like opposites attracting, it is our experience that many ADD adults marry and mate with others who have ADD.

Couples typically come to our office after trying to solve their problems via magazine article suggestions, self-help books, the advice of well-meaning friends and relatives or just trying to talk things out. They are often embarrassed that they couldn't solve their own problems, disappointed in each other and the relationship, and frustrated that they can't understand what's wrong. One or both partners may not have been diagnosed, and even if an ADD diagnosis has been given, professionals often forget to tell us what to do about the ADD traits and how to work with them successfully.

Our first goal is to reassure a couple that what they have been going through is understandable, explainable and typical for a couple dealing with ADD. The *diagnosed* ADD person has been wrestling with his own physical state, lack of attention, or mood swings, and the spouse or partner has been at the mercy of these characteristics – often at her wit's end about what to do or how to survive. Having someone listen carefully and comprehend both sides without judgment greatly relieves a couple, who at last feel there are people who understand the struggle.

A special note about responsibility: The ADD condition is not a fad, it is a real phenomena. However, it is not a blanket excuse for participating half-heartedly in your relationship or blaming the ADD for behavior that is irresponsible to your partner. Each of us has a responsibility to learn everything we can about the ADD condition and then to make changes and adjustments wherever possible for the good of the relationship – whether ADD partner or spouse. Many times we have seen the diagnosis of ADD take the blame for forgotten dates, rude outbursts and silent treatment that lasts for days or even weeks – it is not okay to use ADD as a scapegoat for poor behavior.

A great deal of this book focuses on the ADD person, but the dilemma of the spouse or partner cannot be ignored. Often the partner feels anger and despair over the problems between them and a sense of hopelessness about the success of the relationship. He may feel disrespected and disconfirmed after having poured his energy and ideas into the relationship, often for very little gain. He may also feel he's had to co-dependently wrap himself around his partner instead of having his own needs met in the relationship.

When the relationship is in good shape, it's easy to remember why they chose each other, but when it's being tested by the ADD person's mood swings, hyper- or hypoactivity or inattentiveness, the spouse's anger fuse gets shorter and shorter. The spouse may look around at other friends' and neighbors' relationships and wonder if working so hard on his own is worth it.

On the one hand, we have the ADD person feeling awful about behaviors and quirks that can't seem to be controlled. On the other hand we have the spouse who feels like a nag, a scapegoat or a parent to his mate. All intimate relationships have cycles – ups and downs – it's just that the cycles are often worse when the ADD condition is added to the relationship stew. A further complication occurs when we consider the fact that many ADD partners are likewise attracted to someone who *also* has ADD. Now we have two people with two sets of characteristics feeling twice as frustrated, while neither is getting his or her needs met!

Common Relationship Problems

Let us give you some extra tidbits about relationship patterns which come into play in every relationship, yet are heightened in the ADD connection. They will be divided into subsections with headings.

Just Like Mom and Dad

Often our attractions are based on the "fit" of each of our early childhood patterns in the first place. Certain events and interactions formed our early childhood experiences, and we are deeply imprinted by these experiences – they can become the basis for all of our interactions from that point forward.

For example, each day as children, we watched Mom have a hard time getting out of bed, dragging through the chores and leaving them only halfway done, and interacting with us and with Dad in a halfhearted way – as if she didn't really care.

As children, we had a hard time getting out of bed, dragging through our teeth brushing and schoolbook gathering, leaving important books or papers behind, and hugging Mom good-bye with a halfhearted embrace – as if we didn't really care. The pattern is copied, repeated and extended into adulthood without a second thought to its impact or message to the other people around us.

Another example is that of a mom or dad who constantly interrupts our and other peoples' conversations. That parent might chatter away a mile a minute, not letting the other person talk at all, and get irritated when someone else has an idea or thought to bring up that demands attention. Even though we may hate that characteristic in our folks because we remember what it's like to get cut off every time we start a conversation, or to feel like what we have to say is unimportant, we replicate the pattern. We find ourselves cutting into our friends' conversations, trying to monopolize everyone's attention and getting irritated when someone brings up a thought or idea instead of us.

It's like we are little audiences for our parents who are up on stage, modeling for us the ways we should be, the things we should do and the way we should treat each other. If one or both parents are ADD, they are modeling the ADD behavior for us! We often select a mate who treats us just like Mom or Dad did. We unconsciously begin to act out our parents' patterns over and over again – sometimes with mate after mate.

By the way, these characteristics aren't strictly bound by the gender of your parent. You can just as easily be attracted to a guy who acts just like your mom and/or a woman who acts like the spitting image of your father!

Take the example of Maria and Gabriel. Maria swore she would never marry anyone who acted like her father. He was rude, self-centered, angry, loud and interrupted conversations continually. When she first met Gabriel, he seemed quiet, soft-spoken and dedicated to his work – all qualities she had been looking for in a partner. Six months after they began dating, Gabriel was laid off from his job due to a company reorganization. Within one month he was argumentative, harsh, angry and demanding with Maria. It seems that his ADD energy had been tunneled into his job, and without it, he was unable to control his biochemistry. This resulted in his reverting to the very behavior Maria had sworn to avoid – that which was like her father's. Careful investigation into their individual childhoods revealed that Gabriel's father had been much the same as Maria's, and Gabriel had sworn never to echo *his* dad's traits. Without meaning to be, both were trapped in their own pattern of *Just Like Mom and Dad.*

These patterns of behavior that we learned from our early caregivers are almost set in stone for us. These early patterns feel right, even if they're terribly unhealthy, because that's just the way things have always been done! There's a very subtle message that gets communicated (through modeling) for you to act in certain ways, say things in a certain way and conduct your relationships in a certain way. This message is *so* strong that you'd rather get into a screaming argument or refuse to speak to each other for days at a time, than examine and change your behavior(s); as the old commercial stated, you'd rather "Fight than Switch."

This creates a whole host of problems in intimate relationships, because we often fight for the sake of fighting or for some behavior that we're not sure was really ours in the first place. It was just something we watched over and over again in childhood. We stubbornly hold on to the familiar, rather than trying to see each other's perspectives and early childhood patterns, and seeking solutions and harmony together despite our differences in upbringing.

Breaking out of some of the patterns is possible, but sometimes the "mis-fit" just becomes stronger and more obvious than that original, romantic "fit," and a break-up is likely to occur. Fortunately, this can be worked out within a couple's counseling setting, often with surprising and satisfying results.

Water Under the Bridge

An area that causes major problems for an already committed couple is called the *Water Under the Bridge* syndrome. Often partners in the relationship have suffered repeated hurt, broken promises, perceived (unintended) lies, unkept commitments and empty apologies. It is common to hear one spouse or partner start in on a list of complaints such as "You never listen to me," "You forgot our second anniversary," "You were one-and-a-half hours late for our date," "You promised me you would pick up milk and eggs at the store on your way home," "You forgot the Little League awards ceremony that we discussed just last week," "Sally waited at the bus stop for forty minutes – where were you?" "You're always depressed – why don't you lighten up?" "Stop fiddling with the channel changer and listen to me!" The litany goes on and on. After so many years of battling every inch of the way, there is often just too much *Water Under the Bridge* to heal the hurt – or even the energy or the will to do so. Often one or both partners will have just given up.

We often see this in interactions between couples who have been together for years, but are obviously unhappy – the wife who bitterly snaps at her husband in the grocery store, "Don't you dare pick up that can of peas! How many times do I have to tell you that we only buy Del Monte? You'd think you'd get that into your thick head after all these years!"

Restaurants are another fascinating place to study how little a couple can say to each other when their relationship has so much *Water Under the Bridge*. Even requests such as "pass the salt" or "move the chips closer" are delivered with such sarcasm that each word drips with seeming hatred for the other person. These real-life accounts of interactions are filled with the bitterness and disappointments stored, unhealed, in each partner, and this stored venom often triggers ugly behavior that demeans, demoralizes and eventually destroys the relationship.

This behavior may range from verbal abuse to physical assault and from insults to complete silence for days and even weeks. Whatever form it takes, this behavior is unhealthy and toxic to intimate relationships. If you have never sought help for relationship problems, please know that *Water Under the Bridge* issues are often triggered by *Just Like Mom and Dad* behaviors – whether intended or perceived. We often can't see the problem or the way out without some mediation or feedback from someone outside of the relationship who can see the patterns more clearly than we. After all, we're right in the middle of the relationship stew!

It takes mutual commitment to some form of counseling or mediation to get through the *Water Under the Bridge* stuff. We recommend an empathetic and skilled counselor who is familiar with the ADD condition and can help a couple work through the hurt, the tears, the deep resentments, and the collected list of wrongdoings.

A combination of education about ADD and short- or long-term counseling focusing on solutions for past problems and tools for the future are vital to the resolving of relationship conflicts within ADD couples.

ADD-Specific Problems

Disorganization

We're putting this first because it is by far the most complained-about problem in ADD relationships. "Stacks, stacks, stacks and more stacks" often seems to be the concern. No matter how many times ADD adults sort or try to organize their briefcases, desks, cars, garages or homes, the avalanche of disorganization always seems to win in the end.

At the other end of the spectrum are the ADD adults who know there's a tendency to fall into a disorganized mess and who put one hundred percent of their energy into keeping things compulsively neat – so much so that there's a place for everything, and when something's not in its place, the adult may fly into a rage.

Somewhere in the middle are the ADD adults whose homes may appear immaculate, but there's this one room that no one is allowed into – mostly because it's so filled with stuff that you can barely edge your way in to see it! Then there's the partner who is neat and organized at work, but can't keep it together anywhere at home. This is enough to make the spouse or significant other want to tear his or her hair out!

Take, for example, Helena and Gregg. Gregg is a non-ADD partner of an ADD spouse with disorganization as the major complaint. It seems that Gregg could locate Helena anywhere in the house by following the newest paper trail. He constantly asked where she put that bill or this coupon or the phone number of the new client referral who called. Helena's response was usually, "I know right where I put it! Let me see, it was over here the last time I saw it. Just give me a minute." Well, that minute usually stretched into twenty, ending with Gregg saying that he couldn't trust her to keep anything in a safe place and Helena in tears because she expected so much more from herself and just couldn't get organized.

Often the partner may feel that the disorganized mess is a sign of marital problems or a lack of interest in home or family matters. This is especially true when the spouse sees the ADD partner hold it together in another area, i.e. work, but never sees the partner translate that organization to their mutual home.

Anger and Rage Attacks

If an ADD adult tends to fly off the handle with the slightest provocation at home, at the office or on the freeway, you can bet that the relationship is in trouble. ADD adults who experience anger and rage are so unpredictable in relationships that their spouses or significant others often live on the edge of fear a good deal of the time. If children are present in the family, this sense of danger and fear often accelerates.

Some ADD adults have an extremely difficult time controlling anger and rage. Without medication, they are often unable to predict their quick escalation into rage. Instead, their systems are telling them that what they are feeling is perfectly valid. It is only after the explosion that they can step back and realize what they have done. Beyond that, they often realize the dangerous position in which they have placed their families and suffer a terrible sense of remorse.

Many ADD adults express their anger and rage only at home. Perhaps this is because the pressure of behaving all day culminates in an explosion at home; perhaps it's because our homes are the safest domains in which to express ourselves, no matter what. Perhaps it's a facet of the "boss-yelled-at-me,-I-yell-at-my-wife-and-kids-when-I-get-home-and-can't-help-myself" syndrome; perhaps it's a combination of these.

To illustrate the devastation that can be caused by rage attacks, let us tell you the story of Larry. While driving on the freeway with his wife in the front seat beside him, and his two daughters, ages three and five, in the back seat, he was cut off by a young man in his twenties. "He cut me off! I'll show him! How can he do that to me?" This was the dialogue (with a few more colorful words added) that exploded out of Larry's mouth just before he took off down the fast lane of the freeway after the Toyota pick up. The speedometer hit fifty miles per hour, then sixty, seventy, eighty and finally ninety miles an hour. Obviously, this combination of rage and high speed can be deadly. His wife began pleading with Larry to slow down. His daughters were crying hysterically in the back seat. Larry was oblivious to all of this. He was totally absorbed in catching the offending driver.

Finally, he pushed the driver off on the shoulder, jumped out of his car, popped open the trunk and grabbed the tire iron. He stalked over to the truck and beat the windshield to pieces. At about the same time, a CHP officer arrived – summoned by a passing motorist. He wasn't about to listen to Larry's reasons for the chase or the windshield bashing. He took Larry into custody, leaving Jan and the girls to drive home alone, shaken and upset. Jan had to appear at the police station, hire a bail bondsman and phone an attorney. She knew what she was facing, since this wasn't the first time that he had blown up with no provocation.

At home the girls were left with a neighbor, and they were both weepy and in tears for hours. Sarah, the three-year-old, began to have episodes of wetting her pants at school, which lasted the next two months until her system calmed down from the trauma. Her older sister, Mary, took out her fear with aggressive acts and was frequently in the time-out corner at school.

Hyperactive vs. Hypoactive

With couples, there are distinct differences in behavior, depending on whether the ADD individual's physical makeup is hyperactive or hypoactive. Just how do hyperactive ADD adults differ from hypoactive ADD adults in relationships? Both types face challenges which will pop up whether or not the ADD person marries or mates with someone who also has ADD.

The *hyperactive* adult may feel very slowed down by a mate who doesn't move around or talk a mile a minute and follow everything the hyperactive mate is talking about (even though there may be four or five topics at one time!).

Pete, an ADD adult with hyperactivity, was extremely disappointed after he married Jan, who did not have ADD. While they were courting, they were both excited to see each other, talking about everything under the sun and organizing ongoing, fun-filled activities. The disappointing reality set in when Jan finally stated, after three months of marriage, that she was exhausted by the pace, suggesting Pete do more by himself or with friends, rather than dragging her along everywhere. She stated that he wore her out, that she couldn't keep up anymore and that he'd better find something to do with all that energy. Pete felt that he had made a poor choice in Jan after all, and they came to our office for marital counseling to decide whether or not the marriage could be modified in some way for them to stay together.

Conversely, the *hypoactive* ADD adult may feel extremely hurt and frustrated at being labeled as lazy or unproductive. Actually, that adult has the same capacity to be alive and active but just can't seem to pull it together to get started, especially not on the average time line. This was the case for Robert and Krista, who came to our office for premarital counseling with serious issues to discuss. Robert used three alarm clocks to wake him in the morning, placed strategically well away from the bed to get him up and moving. This habit in itself drove Krista crazy.

Complications went on from there. Once Robert finally got out the door and on to work, his activity level and tunnel vision surfaced. He dedicated himself to his job as a planning engineer and poured all of his available energy into his work, with outstanding results. After a hard day at work, his energy gave out and he could barely keep himself awake driving home on the freeway. Once he got home, he used all his remaining energy to pull together a frozen dinner and plop on the couch in front of the television, channel changer in hand. It was too much effort to make a phone call to Krista to talk about the day and wish her sweet dreams.

He couldn't pull his thoughts together for ideas about what they should do on a Friday or Saturday night, so they usually had to rely on her planning skills. Krista was fed up with Robert's lack of initiative where their relationship was concerned, especially since she had attended several social functions at his work and heard what an incredibly productive employee he was. By the time they came into our office, they were both frustrated and overwhelmed by the problems in their relationship.

The Extroversion vs. Introversion Factor

There are also individual differences between someone who is more introverted (or inner world-oriented) versus someone who is more extroverted (or more outer world-oriented). In his book, *Please Understand Me*, Keirsey writes, "the person who chooses people as a source of energy probably prefers extroversion, while the person who prefers solitude to recover energy may tend toward introversion."

Another way to picture an extroverted person is to think of people you know who strike up a conversation with the grocery clerk, the bank teller, someone waiting at the bus stop with them – anyone – whether they are talking to a friend or a stranger. The extrovert has a *need* to connect with people verbally – talking is her way to making social contact and animate her world. When we extend this to include ADD adults, we are also talking about patterns of frequent interrupting, outbursts of anger or high emotion, and the possibility of hyperactivity which turns up both the speed and the noise of the person involved. The introvert, on the other hand, has a *need* to have some alone time to sort out the thousands of events, thoughts and feelings of the day, to come to some of his own conclusions, and then maybe share a part of those conclusions with his mate, usually in many fewer words.

These aspects add another wrinkle to the picture of an ADD adult in a successful relationship. It can be very difficult for an introverted person to understand that his extroverted mate *needs* to talk through her thoughts, feelings and line of reasoning with her mate in order to feel validated and complete; conversely, it is very difficult for the extroverted person to understand that her non-stop chatter overwhelms her introverted mate, who *needs* some quiet time to process and untangle the various incidences and conversations of the day.

A thorough discussion of understanding and appreciating differences is vital to the life of the ADD relationship. Additionally, and apart from extroversion or introversion, many ADD people have a need for *alone* time in order to settle down internally or to back off from the overstimulation often felt as a result of the ADD. It's as if too many demands have been met, too many conversations fielded, too much stimulation came in, and the person just needs to shut down for awhile – it has little or nothing to do with the mate, and everything to do with the ADD condition.

One couple we know has learned to cope with these differences by what we call the "angel and the elephant" story. She is a highly extroverted, hyperactive ADD adult who holds multiple jobs and comes home filled with news that she's dying to share with her mate. He is a rather quiet, introverted, hypoactive ADD adult who really values his alone time to just sit and think about the day, his life or just to space out in his quiet zone. For years she drove him crazy by chattering about everything that had happened in her day and then by being hurt when he only answered in one or two words or didn't answer at all – in fact, it seemed like he couldn't wait to get away from her!

He, on the other hand, loved her dearly, but couldn't seem to get the words put together to let her know how desperately he needed her to shut up sometimes, just so he could think! Their solution (with the help of a competent therapist who understood ADD) was to select an object in the house that would represent each person.

She selected a clay angel, and he selected a carved wood elephant. When he experienced a day where he just needed peace and quiet, he was instructed to place the elephant on its side in a prominent place on their dining room table. When the elephant was upright, she was free to chat with him and share her day; when it was on its side, he really needed that time to be private, and she learned (over time) to do other things around the house, call friends or read until he was available again.

Conversely, when she desperately needed her mate to share and to listen and to be particularly attentive to her, she turned her angel on its side in the same prominent place on the dining room table. This was his signal to override his natural tendency to be quiet and to be available to her as much as possible. Time limits for each partner were established in counseling in order to honor their responsibility to each other not to use the ADD or absence of it as an excuse to be hurtful.

The Black Hole of Memory

Difficulty with memory is very common among ADD adults. In a relationship, this can cause problems both for the adult with the poor memory and the spouse or significant other on the receiving end of the poor memory.

For the ADD adult with a poor memory, it seems as though she is always being questioned about something she promised to do or reminded about something she said. The problem is that she typically has no recollection at all about her promises or commitments. Many ADD adults are constantly fighting the black hole of memory. Entire chunks of time or entire events simply drop out. An ADD adult may not remember promising to be home for dinner by 5:30. This in itself is bad enough, but to make matters worse, she may not remember anything from the conversation in question. When asked, in her own defense, she often becomes righteously indignant.

The ADD spouse or significant other typically feels as though he is caught in a revolving door. He is constantly in a hopeless circle with no resolution in sight. He tends to feel that his spouse is deliberately lying to him, going back on her word to escape work or trying to drive him crazy.

Since both adults typically feel strongly that what they perceive and what they remember is correct, the difficulty with memory causes incidents that are almost impossible to resolve – that is, until the ADD adult finally realizes that her memory is poor and is causing the majority of the trouble.

For an example of just how frustrating problems with memory can be, meet Alice and Stanley. Stanley was a successful attorney with a busy practice and a secretary who constantly ran interference for him by keeping track of his appointments and obligations. Her efficiency caused some of his problems in his relationship with Alice. His secretary was not about to tell him he *ever* forgot anything, so Stanley had no reality check. In the business world he was made to feel he was always right.

His new wife, Alice, was a bright and assertive lady who was very dynamic and direct. Soon after their marriage they moved into a new house and agreed that new carpet was needed. They agreed on the style and color of carpet; however, they hit a roadblock when they began discussing whether the closets should be carpeted. For some reason, Stanley felt strongly that the closets should *not* be carpeted. Not surprisingly, Alice felt just the opposite. With a good deal of effort, Alice finally wore Stanley down, until one night he agreed that the closets could be carpeted. The carpet layers came and Alice, with a clear conscience, had them lay carpet in all the closets, including the huge walk-in closet in the master bedroom.

When Stanley came home from work, he was pleased with the carpet selection but hit the roof when he saw the closets. "I told you I didn't want carpet in the closets! How can you just ignore me like that? Don't you care about my feelings?" Alice tried to tell him that he had agreed to have carpeting in the closet after a long discussion the previous evening.

Stanley truly didn't remember the conversation or the agreement. Furthermore, he wasn't willing to entertain the idea that he had a poor memory. He adamantly held to his position that she had pulled something over on him. This disagreement grew until it was a major incident in their marriage.

Fortunately, an ADD/therapist was able to ferret out other incidents where memory had been a problem for Stanley. He begrudgingly began to consider the notion that, just possibly, he had forgotten the conversation.

North, South, East, West?

Hopelessly lost! One of the weird quirks of ADD, that is almost impossible to understand unless you yourself are affected, is a problem with directionality. Very simply, this means that an ADD adult often has no clue where she is as she drives down a freeway offramp. If she has learned to protect herself by writing down clear directions to her destination and tracing a map as a visual aid, she feels secure until she finds that she cannot reverse the directions to find her way home.

To compound this, ADD adults often have problems with memory. That means that even if an ADD adult has successfully found one particular building six times in a row, if a few weeks or months elapse, she won't have a clue as to how to find it on that particular occasion. One of your authors worked at a local elementary school for nine years. This means that she drove to the school approximately one thousand eighty times (working there three days a week). She left that job. Only two years had elapsed when she needed to return to her old school. Could she find it? Not on your life.

The problems with directionality often make an ADD adult feel quite stupid. After all, how inept must you be to be unable to reverse directions or to get lost on the very same stretch of freeway time after time? As it does with all of us, this sense of shame makes us even more adamant and set on holding on to our dignity. Thus the ADD adult with a directionality problem will often never admit that she is lost, much to the anger, dismay and frustration of her spouse or significant other.

The story of Lisa, a well-established educator, is a good case in point. Before she was diagnosed with ADD in her late twenties, Lisa recounts a time when her father had had a spinal fusion at St. Joseph's Hospital in a local city. Lisa's family made it a point to gather at the hospital before any member's surgery to exchange support and wish the patient well. Lisa daily traveled the freeway off of which this hospital was located and, in fact, had been to the hospital several times in years past.

On the day of the surgery, Lisa left work and headed for the hospital on the familiar route. About a half an hour later, she found herself in *another* city at St. Jude's Hospital, asking for her father's room. She became frustrated at the hospital's apparent lack of cooperation when she suddenly remembered that she was supposed to be at St. Joseph's! Embarrassed and ashamed at being lost (again), Lisa spent another twenty minutes trying to locate the route back before she finally asked for directions. Often the experience of being lost or late due to directional problems is so persistent that the ADD person's personality traits are expanded to include, "Oh, you know that Lisa. She can get turned around in her own driveway. What a ditz!" This can make it difficult to ask for directions as a matter of shame and pride for both men and women.

Impulsivity

Over and over we've heard stories from couples where impulsivity has nearly cost them their homes, their credit, their jobs and their life savings. The promise is almost always "Of course, I'll consult with you before I buy X or do X," but the reality is often an impulsive shopping spree, a trip booked and partially paid for (non-refundable, of course), a new puppy or a one-week notice at work because another job looked more appealing.

Over and over, our ADD adults give their word that they have turned over a new leaf, that they've now learned self-control via this book or that tape or this fail-safe system. Over and over again, in the flash of a neurotransmitter skip, they've purchased that new car, invested in a high-risk business venture, or spent the mortgage money. This tendency has disastrous consequences in a marriage or significant other partnership.

Michael was immediately drawn to Sophia. She was cute, fun-loving, active and always seemed to live life with zest. As their relationship deepened, he noticed that she seemed to have little control over whether she spent her money impulsively or over what she bought. She liked cooking, so she had impulsively bought every kitchen gadget that showed up on a TV commercial – many of which she never used. She liked clothes, so she had several pairs of everything – many with the tags still on. She liked the smell of new cars, so she bought herself at least one per year, always trading up, of course.

Although Sophia had a great job with a steady income, Michael worried about how she could possibly keep up with the bills. When he questioned Sophia, she was offended that he would even imply that she wasn't handling her money, her purchases or her life well. In fact, she was so offended that she went out and bought herself an expensive piece of exercise equipment so she could work off her frustration with Michael.

We saw Michael and Sophia for premarital counseling (fortunately). With a combination of education, role-playing, coping skills and a neutral money manager, we were able to negotiate to have both Michael's need to feel financially solid and secure and Sophia's need to impulsively spend worked out to a happier compromise.

Flooding

"Flooding," or feeling overwhelmed, is a common theme in many ADD relationships. The on-again, off-again, light switch effect of ADD provides much puzzlement between partners. The ADD partner may be able to juggle several things on one day, smoothly meshing all the activities together and showing up with a marvelous memory for details. The very next day this same partner may stand slack-jawed in front of his clothes closet, not even being able to think clearly enough to match colors or put something together to wear to work! This is very confusing for both the mate of an ADD adult and the adult himself.

Sometimes flooding envelops the ADD person and feels like a way of life. It may begin with the alarm clock and end when the person falls into bed at night without accomplishing a heck of a lot in between. She may have been simply frozen by the feeling of flooding, and then the stress of worrying about the consequences of being overwhelmed further aggravates the ADD symptoms. We have heard statements like "I can't count on her to do anything. As soon as the project gets complicated, she throws up her hands and quits! I can't always be here to rescue her."

To illustrate flooding, let's look in on Carla and Steve. They've been together for three years, but frustration is what brought them into our office. Carla has ADD. She gets overwhelmed regularly and can't seem to follow through on goals in her own life, much less the goals she and Steve had agreed upon as a couple. She has been trying to run her own business from home, caring for her aging mother and working toward some home improvements that she and Steve listed on the refrigerator. Each day for the past few years she sets daily personal goals to make progress in each of these important areas. Each day she has great intentions of getting things done. Sometimes she even promises Steve she'll have something handled *today*. Each day she gets about one-fourth of the way through her goals before flooding makes her stick in one place like cold molasses.

Never Reaching Potential in Life

Many ADD adults show great promise in early childhood. They may be functioning in the gifted range intellectually and making straight A's. They may be star athletes and lead their Little League or AYSO (American Youth Soccer Organization) team to smashing victories. However, as they move ahead into junior high and high school their potential never seems to be reached. They fall short of their parents' expectations, but most importantly, they fall short of their own expectations. Possibly they graduated from college, but never reached the heights they were told they *could* achieve.

Other ADD adults may do exceptionally well in high school and college and come away from their school experiences with astounding grade point averages. However, once an ADD adult leaves the relative structure of college, he finds his career path is pockmarked with rough stretches of road. He is hired by one company, but doesn't like his boss. After a year on the job, he looks elsewhere and is hired by another company. After a span of two more years, he complains about the politics within the company and decides to quit. Soon there is a third company, and he does well for an entire year before he complains about the vacation schedule and pay scale. This pattern of changing jobs every one-and-a-half to two years often continues for the next ten or fifteen years.

Finally, he decides that he is truly, in his heart, an entrepreneur. He explains to his wife that he has the answer. He knows he will finally reach his ultimate destiny by starting his own company. He rents office space, arranges for phone lines to be installed and hires a secretary. He starts off like a ball of fire, but is unable to sustain this amount of effort. Soon he is going out for coffee at the neighborhood Deidrich's at 10:00 a.m., meeting a so-called "client" for lunch at noon, and finishing the afternoon with a quick nine holes of golf – of course, with a potential client. He is unable to continue the amount of effort needed to bring a business out of the red. Everything he does is done in short bursts. Any type of continuity is impossible. This type of start-and-stop pacing is death to any type of business, and he ultimately fails. ADD adults often are able to rationalize this to himself by saying, "The economic climate is poor. My advertising was targeted at the wrong population. My secretary simply couldn't take messages and we lost a lot of clients due to her ineptitude." The real truth is that the ADD adult was unable to prolong the amount of consistent effort needed to make a business successful.

To illustrate this point, meet Sean. Sean had a degree in industrial design and had done very well working for two or three large companies. His job required him to design products and then oversee the tooling and production. His salary was in the six-figure range and Sean, his wife and children had a nice house, living the very typical Southern California lifestyle with lots of vacations in Hawaii and a new car every year. However, Sean got itchy feet. He decided that he didn't like working within a corporate structure and told his wife that he was sure he could be tremendously successful in his own company. He quit his job, cleared out one of the bedrooms in his house, and bought second-hand office furniture and a computer.

Sean began contacting old clients and telling them of his new business. At first, he pulled in one or two jobs. However, the initial wellspring of work dried up, and Sean was faced with the necessity of making cold calls and publicizing his business. This is when he fell apart. When Sean became stressed he began to experience a low but persistent level of depression. He began avoiding phone calls and took an extra day or two to return calls, even from previous clients. He had difficulty completing the projects that were already in the works. He had trouble with deadlines.

Soon the calls to Sean became less and less frequent, and no new projects were on the horizon. His wife began to complain about his lack of ability to follow through. She became quite fearful because Sean's steady source of comfortable income had disappeared. The more she questioned and complained, the more Sean became adamant that his business *would* work and that he was never going to return to a corporate structure ever again. After three years of this pattern it was obvious even to Sean that he could not put food on the table, pay the mortgage and feed the kids. In fact, the family was in danger of losing their home. His wife finally issued an ultimatum to Sean, saying, "You either find a job or I am out of here. You decide. I can't live this way."

Along the way, Sean had been diagnosed with ADD and, with the help of a counselor, began to examine his pattern of life. He was finally able to see that his wife's requests were realistic. He soon found employment in another large company as a designer and once again moved up to his six-figure salary. Although he still had dreams of his very own company, he was able to see that the dream could not be reality, at least at this time.

The Value of Couples Counseling

Now that we've explored some specific problems that affect ADD adults in relationships, it's time to look at some solutions. We often feel that being diagnosed with ADD, or having our loved one identified as ADD, will be the answer to our problems.

Our relationship (if we have one) will magically heal because of a pill or a technique. Our dating partner (if we don't already have a relationship) will show up and have no problem dealing with us, since we now have something that explains our difficulties. We have a condition that so affects us that we may forget to follow through on commitments, space out in the middle of a conversation, get lost on a completely familiar street, lose our temper or our energy in a split second, and more. The other person should understand perfectly, right?

Unfortunately, this is not so. Research and couples' interviews indicate that if there were irritating to severe problems in the relationship *before* an ADD diagnosis, there will be irritating to severe problems *after* a diagnosis. Just having the diagnosis, reading a book on ADD or going to a single counseling session isn't enough. The problems are often longstanding, and the diagnosis itself isn't magic. Let's also remember that ADD adults often marry other ADD adults. This can mean problems times two. Each couple needs to evaluate the extent of their commitment to each other, the amount of energy available to put toward resolving issues that come from patterns such as *Just Like Mom and Dad* and *Water Under the Bridge*, and the interest they have in seeing the relationship through to a new level, in spite of the ADD.

People often ask, "Can couples counseling really help?" Absolutely! At the very least, counseling can help you identify certain behavior patterns that belong to each of you, and you can decide whether or not you are willing to live with them (even *with* the treatment of the ADD through coping skills and/or medication). At best, counseling can help you find alternative methods and new behaviors that give you hope for resolving and appreciating your differences. Counseling also provides tools for use out in your real world, such as the couple using the angel and elephant figurines to communicate their needs.

Chapter 7

ADD and Domestic Violence

What disturbing words! Why are we talking about abuse in a book about ADD adults? Sadly, some ADD adults are guilty of verbal and emotional abuse when dealing with their spouses or children. They can also be guilty of physical abuse – another name for domestic violence. The saddest part is that ADD adults often don't know that they are being abusive. Several of the personality characteristics that are part and parcel of the ADD condition put ADD adults at great risk for abusive behavior.

To show you what we mean, let us introduce Charlie. Charlie has a wife and two children whom he loves very much. However, Charlie is one of those ADD people who is driven nuts by clutter. Guess what? Charlie's wife is a clutterer. When Charlie comes home from work at night, the first thing he does is check the house to see if the kids' toys are put away from that afternoon, and then he checks that the kitchen is clean. He does this even if the kids are in the middle of their homework and his wife is cooking dinner. If things are not to his specifications, he takes it as a personal affront and launches into a rage. The dialogue usually takes the form of "Can't you kids do anything? What slobs! Don't you have any respect for your things? Don't you know you live in a nice house and should appreciate it?"

Leaving the children near tears, Charlie moves to the kitchen and begins his tirade at his wife. "Can't you cook without getting every pot in the kitchen dirty? Why don't you wash each pot as you use it, so that the kitchen stays clean when you cook? What, have you been on the phone again? That is all you women do, talk all the time! Dinner isn't ready, and the laundry is still in the washing machine! You are so lazy, what do you do all day? Nothing!"

After months or years of this, Charlie's wife and kids begin to get resentful and, in their own defense, they argue. Now Charlie's anger escalates into a rage. There is a great deal of agitation and an increase in volume in his voice. Soon he is shouting. If the kids tune him out, he will push them up against a wall so that he is sure that they hear him. If his wife decides to ignore his anger, he becomes more angry. If she tries to go upstairs, he follows her up the stairs so that he is sure he is making his point. If she uses the ultimate retreat – the bathroom – he beats on the door until she comes out. Once he took the bathroom door off the hinges and threw a glass of cold water on her.

Eventually the children began to act out the abuse that was going on in the family. Charlie's junior high son began to pick fights before and after school. Ultimately, as a payback, he planted a knife in another kid's locker and was expelled. Charlie's seventeen-year-old daughter began body piercing as her revenge against her father. To date, she has had ten body piercings and a small rose tattooed on her ankle – finally she found something that her father couldn't control.

Charlie's wife became more and more upset with her husband's behavior as she saw her children deteriorate. She began drinking "just a little more wine" to get through the evenings. To escape her husband's caustic comments she occasionally hid the wine bottle in the coat closet for easy access. One night her husband happened upon the bottle and accused her of being a raving alcoholic. The violence escalated.

So that we don't appear sexist, let's be clear that abuse can happen on either the male or female end of the marriage or relationship. To illustrate this, let us introduce Sally.

Sally has always had a fun-loving streak and a mildly wild personality which made her loads of fun when she was in her twenties. She loved to scuba dive, ski, and even tried her hand at skydiving. As long as she was excited and moving, she was up and happy. If, however, things got too dull or minor details got snagged, she'd blow up. If she wasn't happy with something as petty as a particular room in a hotel that didn't exactly suit her – look out! She'd throw things, yell, storm down to the desk and obnoxiously demand a change.

On the surface, she represented the typical fun-loving, exciting ADD adult profile. Underneath, she had a temper. By the time she was twenty-six years old, she had fallen in love. She was very clear with her fiancé that her personality was "just that way and a package deal." She saw her temper outbursts as a part of her personality.

After having three children, Sally had fewer outlets for fun. The ski vacations were few and far between. She had married a man who was stable and hard-working. There wasn't much fun coming from his end of the marriage either.

Over the years she became resentful of her lot in life. The fun-loving part of her personality turned into an abusive streak. She began to insist on controlling everything in the house. If the towels weren't folded perfectly, if the kids left anything on the floor, if things didn't go her way, she would become enraged. Her way was the right way – period. Anyone who tried to establish a sense of individuality was simply shouted down.

As her three children reached adolescence, they began to distance themselves from her more and more. They found excuses to stay away from their house and their mother's wrath that awaited them there. One of her children got a job working nights, delivering pizzas. Another child put his energy into sports and participated in every sports activity possible. The third child, the youngest, began using marijuana to get away from it all, and the marijuana use quickly turned into a full-blown addiction.

What about Sally's husband? He was CEO of his own company, respected in the business community, and doing well. He wasn't faring as well at home. When he and Sally would have a difference of opinion, the first few minutes of the conversation remained civil. As he attempted to stand his ground, Sally's irritation grew, and soon she was enraged. No matter how calm and rational her husband remained, he found that it didn't stop Sally's escalation of anger – if anything, his calmness fueled her rage. In any discussion, within a few minutes the conversation moved into verbal abuse. The crowning blow was an argument that occurred in their bedroom as he was dressing for work one morning. Sally was so enraged that she went beyond yelling. She grabbed his testicles in one hand and squeezed. Practically spitting venom she said, "You're not really a man. I might as well rip these off."

Sally's husband, not surprisingly, began to pull away from Sally just as the kids had. He spent more and more time at work. He seemed to have important errands to do on the weekends, which kept him out of the house all day. He became involved in church activities. Every Sunday he would usher for the morning service, help during the fellowship time, and lead the senior citizens' prayer group in the evening. When he arrived home at 9:00 at night, Sally fumed, but he had an excuse. After all, he was at church. Eventually, Sally's husband found a soft-spoken, gentle woman at church and made a new life with her.

Come on. You mean to tell me that this qualifies as abuse? Yes, it does. Too many times, however, the spouse and kids have lived with this pattern so long that it begins to feel normal to them. They don't see it as abusive because they have lost their sense of perspective. The damage is being done, whether it is by words or by actions. Abuse takes its toll.

Let's Define Abuse

Verbal Abuse

Verbal abuse is spoken words that are intended to demoralize, embarrass or shame a person. Verbal abuse is a parent or spouse who says things such as: "You are stupid," "Can't you do anything right?" "What is the matter with you?" "If I've told you once, I've told you a million times, do it this way!" "You are a slob!" "I can hardly wait to go to work and get away from you." "I can't stand the sight of you!" "I had a lot better sex with my last partner!"

Emotional Abuse

Emotional abuse is considered to be one of the most damaging forms of abuse. It continues over time, is usually subtle, doesn't leave bruises on the body and is much more difficult to pin down. Emotional abuse can be nonverbal and is the *action* that says to a spouse or child, "You are stupid," or "I don't like you." It can be a shrug of the shoulders, a walling-off of emotions, a coldness or a rolling of the eyes. People receiving emotional abuse constantly ask themselves, "Am I imagining all this? Maybe I really *am* wrong or stupid."

Physical Abuse

This is the parent or spouse who pushes, shoves or hits. We are going to broaden the concept of physical abuse to include the person who threatens violence, bullies or moves into someone's physical space so that the *threat* of bodily harm is there, even if the blow is not actually delivered.

It is important to understand that the potential for abuse increases if the parent or spouse comes from a home where the mother, father or siblings have actually shown physical violence. This particular individual may have never laid a hand on anyone. However, if there is a history and a pattern in the family, it makes the potential for violence a distinct possibility, *Just Like Mom and Dad.*

Are Abusive ADD Adults Bad People?

No. Absolutely not. In fact, many times they are extremely sensitive. Often they are aware of their own level of pain and are hurting deeply. If this is true, why are they abusive?

Please Hear Me!

Sometimes, the ADD adult can't find the words to tell anyone how he truly feels, so his feelings stay hidden deep inside. There are three reasons why this may occur.

First, as children many ADD adults found that their teachers and their parents didn't listen to them. They may have had "behavior problems" in school, they may have run around with a questionable crowd, or they may have had a bad reputation. Eventually, their teachers and parents let them know loudly and clearly that they couldn't be trusted. They were automatically wrong, no matter how they tried to explain their thoughts or actions.

The second reason is that many ADD children lie to protect themselves. They cannot explain that it was a biochemical imbalance that interfered with the neural pathways in their brain that caused them to throw the baseball through the window. They lie and swear on their oath that Jack, who lives down the street, did it. Or they may lie because they don't want to do what their parents tell them to do. They don't want to brush their teeth or take a shower. They lie that yes, they did shower, and they explain that the tile is not wet because they carefully wiped it down with a towel. When asked why the towel is not wet, they explain that they blew it dry with a hair dryer or hung it out the window.

Even when it is crystal clear that they are lying, they continue with their fabrications. Often the lying becomes such a habit that lies pop out of their mouths as a conditioned response. No matter what they are asked, they lie. They even lie about things that couldn't possibly get them in trouble. Soon the ADD child realizes the adults in his world don't believe a word that he is saying.

The third reason has to do with the ADD biochemical imbalance. There are some ADD adults who have a great deal of difficulty expressing themselves verbally. There is a technical term for this – Expressive Language Disability. This means that there is a blockage in their ability to speak and explain what they feel inside. They may know what they feel inside and what is so hurtful or frustrating, but they can't translate these feelings into words. In any argument, they are left tongue-tied and frustrated. This leads to anger and rage.

Back Off! Explosion Imminent!

Hurt and pain are two of the most basic human emotions. However, our society doesn't train us how to express hurt and pain appropriately. Especially for many males, the message from their parents and society is to simply hold hurt and pain inside. Just to remind you, the biochemical imbalance of ADD prevents the adult from controlling the quick trigger, so he moves almost immediately from the difficult feelings of hurt and pain into rage. Society has not given him any outlets or automatic response except anger.

For the ADD adult, this sequence of events is compounded by the surge of feeling that explodes before she can count to three – before she has any chance to think about what she is feeling, or why she is feeling it. After the explosion, she is sorry. However, her own ADD biochemistry functions as a trigger to action.

Misunderstood

Why are many ADD adults abusive? The answer lies partly in the biochemical imbalance that may make them move quickly into anger or rage. The answer also lies partly in the build-up of emotions caused by the pain and suffering that many ADD adults have experienced from early childhood into adulthood. By the time they are adults, their experience has taught them that the people in their world will automatically judge what they are saying. The judgment will come back that they are either wrong, stupid or lying.

For all of these reasons, ADD adults often present a picture of prickly sharpness on the outside. This is the exterior. This is what people see. Really, they are more like a porcupine with its sharp quills for protection, but soft, tender and vulnerable on the inside.

Specific Traits That Make the ADD Adult at Risk to Abuse Others

Temper

ADD adults often have a short fuse and explosive temper. Something small can push them over the edge. Often they will explode before they even realize it is happening. It is only *after* the fact that they realize they have lost their tempers. After the explosion they are remorseful, but it is too late.

Impulsivity

ADD adults act first and then ask themselves, "Why did I do that?" Due to the biochemical imbalance of ADD, they often have little control over impulsive actions. As we've said before, the sequence for the impulsive ADD adult is *Ready, fire, aim.* The words are said and the act is done before she is aware she has opened her mouth. She apologizes and feels terrible for her actions, but the behavior happens again and again.

Poor Self-Esteem

Many ADD adults have poor self-esteem. If there has been difficulty at home with rebellion or acting out, or in school with reading, writing or math, the ADD adult's whole life feels like it has been filled with obstacles. Through twelve years of school, or sixteen years of school (if he went to college), he was constantly aware that he had to work harder than other students. What did that mean to him? It meant he was dumb. What does this do to self-esteem? It sends it crashing. Lifelong self-esteem issues take their toll.

If, on a certain day, a non-ADD adult feels rotten about herself, she can get very thin-skinned. This is even more likely for the ADD adult. It doesn't take much to be sure that the woman he sees laughing on the stairs is really laughing at him. He is sure that the boss gave him a funny look as he dropped off that paperwork. This makes the ADD adult more fragile, more apt to react in anger.

Living in an Abusive Family

The apple doesn't fall far from the tree. If you grew up in a home where people yelled, shouted and were abusive, you learned that type of behavior at an early age. ADD families are especially vulnerable to this type of pattern. Once the behaviors are entrenched, it takes a conscious awareness to have hope of change.

The biggest problem with growing up in an abusive family is that abusive behavior feels "instinctively" right to us, *Just Like Mom and Dad*. At some level, it becomes part of the way we think people behave. This is true even if we swear that we will *never* be like our parents. In moments of stress, lo and behold, we shout or yell the same way our parents yelled at us when we were young. Their behavior has become imprinted on our behavior.

Difficulty Reading Social Cues

As we wrote in Chapter 3, the non-ADD child learns at an early age to "read" other children's non-verbal cues. If he walks across Sally's sand castle in the preschool sandbox, he can see by her face and body language that she is angry. Because he recognizes how she feels, he has control over his actions. He can crush her sand castle again and choose to make her angry. Or, he can avoid her sand castle and hope to make her a friend.

Many ADD adults have never learned to "read" other people's cues. In that same sandbox, an ADD child may crush Sally's sand castle for the third time, and be in total shock when Sally cries and runs to the teacher, which results in a stern lecture and a time out. If ADD adults don't learn to read body language and social cues as children, they still don't know how to read them as adults. Many ADD adults truly don't understand that their behavior is abusive to their spouses or children.

Filling the Day to the Brim

ADD adults typically like to move toward a feeling of energy or excitement. Thus ADD adults always have too many things to jam into their days. It is certainly more exciting to have five things going on at once, instead of working on just one boring task. ADD adults thrive on juggling the phone, the boss, the huge sale that is pending – all at once. Actually, there are positives when the ADD adult is in this mode. Typically, she finds she can produce a better product or write a more dynamic sales presentation. She experiences a higher degree of creativity when she is in an energized mode, so she often plans her life this way. At times, planning is conscious, but most of the time it is unconscious. Friends and family certainly don't understand the rationale for this behavior, and the ADD adult is labeled a "workaholic."

If this technique of overcommitting works for her, what is wrong with that? The problem with this level of activity is that it eventually drains the ADD adult's reserves. If you are pouring water out of a pitcher, and you don't stop to refill it, it will become empty. The ADD adult often pours out so much energy on a daily basis that her reserves become drained and she feels empty. With the press of life going on around her, this creates tension. If she has the feeling that there are never enough hours in the day and life is closing in on her, tensions escalate.

Depression

Many ADD adults are like chameleons who change their color in seconds. ADD adults can experience a change of mood from hour to hour. If their body chemistries are really out of balance, their moods can change from minute to minute. They can feel up and happy one minute, and the next minute they feel depressed. Depression is often so uncomfortable or frightening that, rather than allowing it to linger, the adult moves towards irritability or prickliness. In this stage, every little thing feels like fingernails on a blackboard. Finally, the depression can accelerate into anger or a rage that leads to abuse.

Does Abuse Only Happen Within the Family??

"Is my partner only nasty to me?" Most often it seems that way. Why? The heart of the family is where we can let our real selves show, even if that part of us is not very nice. It is impossible to keep up a façade in every part of our lives; it is too exhausting. We often see the spouses of ADD adults in our practices who truly believe they are going crazy. Their ADD spouses can be the most charming, delightful, even-tempered people to the outside world. Feedback from friends, neighbors and acquaintances may revolve around how lucky he/she is to be married to these people, how ideal their relationships must be.

In reality, once the facade drops, these same people can become cruel, harsh and abusive. They can even go as far as saying, "Go ahead and tell people how awful I am! They won't believe you anyway." Abusive adults are often upstanding members of the community. No one but the family and intimate circle of friends may have any idea of their abusiveness. Part of our interventions with people is to validate the experience of the abused spouse while treating the ADD adult.

Why does it seem that some ADD adults are different at work than at home? Perhaps they have had to develop coping techniques at work. Maybe the ADD adult has been fired from one or two jobs for exploding at co-workers. The adult must learn to stuff or repress the anger and control the explosion, or risk being fired again. The anger may simply simmer until it can be released in the safety of the home.

Sometimes ADD adults only *think* that their behavior is not abusive at work. They say, "Everyone in the office loves me. I work well with my employees." Thus they carry a distorted picture of themselves into the workplace. The truth may be very different. One CEO was adamant that he was not abusive at work. The truth was that he only hired people who would do as he said, *immediately*. If he made a mistake and hired the wrong person, he or she didn't last long. He was surrounded by people who simply asked, "How high?" when he said, "Jump." His wife wasn't about to do that at home, which triggered an abusive pattern.

Excuses. Excuses. Excuses.

So, what are we saying? Are we saying that the ADD adult has a biochemical imbalance that makes her prone to certain traits, such as temper and impulsivity?

Yes. Are we saying that she can't help it, and therefore it is perfectly okay for her to be abusive? Of course not.

However, ADD adults do have a special set of problems. If you are an ADD adult and you have been accused of being abusive by your spouse or children, what can you do? Listen to the people who love and care about you. Of course, this is easier said than done.

If you feel that you have been misunderstood for many years, you have spent those years building walls for protection. Those walls have been a necessary and important protection to you when you have a lot of pain and hurt inside. It is both difficult and frightening to even think about lowering the walls. But, if you suspect that you are abusive, you have a lot to lose if you don't change your behavior. To be able to change your behavior, you must first be able to recognize it. You must be aware of what you are doing. The question that you must be prepared to ask is, "Am I abusive?" More important than asking, you must be prepared to receive an honest answer.

What about asking your birth family? Do you have a sister or brother who has said repeatedly that you have a terrible temper? Or do you have a sister or brother who has simply withdrawn after your last explosion? Maybe you haven't seen them for a month or two? Ask them how they feel about your explosions or temper. They might tell you that your temper is so explosive that any response at all on their part simply escalates the argument. Ask them how they feel about you. When you are angry, are you verbally abusive to those around you?

What about asking your spouse? Has your spouse accused you of being abusive for years? Or has he or she finally retreated into silence? Is there more and more distance developing in your relationship? What about asking your adult children?

What about asking any friends who know you well, perhaps even from high school? Unfortunately, friends are often unwilling to be direct and confrontive, but typically there will be a history of them kidding you about your temper or the way you talk to people.

Let us tell you about Lee, a prominent dentist. He has a thriving practice and is known for being exceptionally kind to children and older clients in his office. His patients love him. He can be totally charming and personable.

Lee grew up in a close-knit family with four sisters. Throughout his life, his behavior had been explosive. As he moved into adulthood, he became even more outrageous. Whenever he exploded or became verbally abusive at a family function, his sisters left the event and his parents turned their backs. Unfortunately, as soon as enough time passed, his behavior was forgiven. It was as if it had never happened and the incident was never brought up again. The family excused it by saying, "Well, that's just Lee. He'll cool off soon."

He has been married three times. He has two sons by his first wife, two sons by his second wife, and a stepson from his third marriage. He and his first wife were in their early twenties when they married. He told her she was stupid, a terrible housekeeper and couldn't do anything right. He made her feel worthless. His explosiveness and abuse was unpredictable and increased over the five years of their marriage. She finally divorced him because of the abuse.

After nine months of being single, Lee met his second wife, who was very intelligent and had definite career plans of her own. In this marriage, there was an even greater chance for conflict. With conflict there was also a great chance for anger and abuse due to Lee's pattern. Three days before the wedding his abusive nature surfaced for the first time in the relationship. His wife-to-be had two large dogs, and he became angry because they had dug a hole in the yard. She came home to find him beating them with a rubber hose. But she was in love, and had been swept off her feet by his charms. Wedding plans had been set, family members were already on their way, and the wedding occurred.

Over the four years of this marriage, the abuse escalated. He criticized her parenting skills. He criticized her for letting the dogs in the house. He criticized her for anything and everything. As his sons grew up, he was verbally abusive to them as well. When they would fall down he'd comment, "What the hell is wrong with you? Get up! You're no wuss." He'd often make them feel insecure about their abilities to measure up to him as men, saying, "Real men don't do that."

For a long time, his wife tried to understand what she was doing wrong. Why was he continually upset with her? Why was he so explosive and unpredictable? Why was he abusive not only to her, but to their sons? As often happens, she was able to see the abuse more clearly when it was directed away from her. She was better able to evaluate what was happening with the children. She began to defend herself and the children because she instinctively knew that they had to be protected. This only escalated the abuse. Lee bullied, threatened, raged and moved well into the range of physical intimidation.

Ultimately, her only choice was to divorce him, but the abuse didn't end there. He would come into the house at two or three in the morning and demand to talk to her. He would call and yell at her on the phone. He told his oldest son that if he lived with his mother, he'd never grow up to be a man. Finally, she and the children moved to another state.

Lee is currently in his third marriage . . . anyone want to guess how long this marriage will last?

What we are suggesting is certainly not easy. ADD adults need to find the courage to talk to people who they know, deep down, love and support them. This includes family and friends who have been there for them over the years. They need to let their loved ones know that they want some straight answers about their behavior. ADD adults need to assure family and friends that if the truth is given about behavior, it won't be used as ammunition in future arguments. ADD adults need to admit they really *want* to change. They must be prepared to sit down, sit still, and *really and truly* listen. Beyond that, they must be prepared to listen with no arguments and no defensiveness.

Don't Wait Until the Situation is Critical

Too often the ADD adult will absolutely refuse to believe that there is a problem with his behavior. At times this happens because in the public sector of his life he has a reputation for consideration and kindness, and is generally thought of as being a nice person. It is often only within the intimate circle of family or close friends that the abusive behavior is apparent. In his mind there is always a valid reason for his complaints about his current spouse, or for the fact that he has already had two or three marriages.

To illustrate the lack of awareness, let's look at one couple, James and Myra. Myra was verbally abusive. She continually demeaned James with sarcastic comments about his inability to provide sufficient income for the family, his manhood and his performance as a father.

For years, James continued to alternate between telling Myra that she couldn't talk to him like that and moving out of the house for a day or two until she cooled down. When he was forty-two, James suffered his first heart attack. He was told emphatically by his physician that it was directly caused by stress in his life. His physician insisted that he seek some counseling. James was afraid for his life, and he finally went to a counselor for some help with stress only (not for "real" counseling).

Fortunately, he had been referred to an excellent therapist who helped him realize that he had been burying his feelings about his wife's abusive comments for years. Finally, he had enough strength to ask Myra to join him in counseling. She readily agreed. In her own mind, she was planning to tell *her* side of the story and to straighten the therapist out on some issues. The therapist recognized her strategy and skillfully allowed the session to develop so that James could confront Myra with the abuse. Myra wasn't happy with the outcome and began to sabotage the counseling. She complained that the therapist, who was a male, sided with her husband, and that both ganged up on her because they hated women.

Next, Myra and James tried a female therapist. By the second session, the therapist confronted Myra with her behavior. Myra accused the therapist of being a career woman who didn't understand marriages, and she refused to return. The third attempt at counseling was with a Christian counselor – that was not successful either.

Finally, James filed for divorce and moved out of the house permanently. Myra suddenly discovered that she was very alone. Not only had James left her, but over the years she had alienated her children and friends. The isolation finally brought her to a dead stop in life. She began to feel depressed and spent a good portion of her days crying. Finally, after six months of misery, she started listening to James when he would stop by the house occasionally to drop off an alimony check. Looking back over her life, she realized that her parents had tried to tell her about her sarcastic nature for years, but she had refused to listen. Finally she began to realize that her behavior was abusive, and she needed to change. In this case, it was too late for her marriage.

Do You Need Medication?

ADD is a biochemical disorder, not a psychological condition. At times medication is necessary to correct the biochemical imbalance that it causes in the brain.

For all ADD adults, the severity of their individual ADD symptoms will fall somewhere on a continuum from mild to severe. An ADD adult may have severe learning problems caused by ADD, but mild problems with temper or moods. Another ADD adult may have had no problems in school at all, and may even be a physician or have a Ph.D., but have severe mood swings and a clear pattern of abusive behavior.

An ADD adult who experiences severe mood swings, depression or anger often fights a daily battle to remain level and avoid sudden plunges into the depths. It is rather like the shifting floors of a Fun House. One minute you are walking along on a level floor – suddenly, a section falls out from underneath you with no warning. You find yourself rushing down a fifteen-foot slide to the floor below, with no control over your body or the situation.

The severity of each individual's ADD symptoms do not necessarily remain static through life. Stress increases the severity of ADD symptoms. Thus a trauma in life such as a divorce, a death, or being out of work may trigger an increase in symptoms. These symptoms may have been uncomfortable before, yet manageable. With the added trauma, he or she suddenly escalate into rage or abuse.

ADD adults may have moods and episodes of temper that escalate so quickly there is little chance for control. Their flash points may be almost instantaneous. Other ADD adults may find they are continually irritable. The world irritates them, not to mention their families and children. For these adults, this irritability feels as though it is the way life is. For them, it is reality. Because they are continually in the grip of moods or anger, they have no periods of feeling normal, so they have no ability for a reality check. They can't say to themselves, "I felt happy yesterday. Nothing has changed. The fact that I am irritable today has no basis." Instead, they will blame their irritability on those around them.

To illustrate, Ted is an ADD adult who grew up in a middle-income, hard-working family. From the time he was a toddler, his parents described him as being "high strung" to excuse his episodes of temper. His behavior was unpredictable. At typical childhood functions, such as birthday parties, he would suddenly be in tears or explode in a fit of anger when he felt that something didn't go his way.

Ted was also exceptionally neat. At age seven, he had lined up his books from tall to short in his room. All of his toy soldiers were placed in a certain spot. He became upset when anything was moved from its special place whenever his mother cleaned.

When Ted was in junior high school, he and his friends began using alcohol. He found that the alcohol gave him some peace and calmness in his life. After six or seven beers, he could cope with life and actually tolerate people. Ted's alcohol use continued through high school and college, and he describes being in an alcoholic haze for many of those years.

In his middle twenties Ted fell in love with Mary, and they became engaged. Both he and Mary realized that his drinking was excessive. He agreed to stop drinking completely, and he kept his word for the first two years of their marriage. During those years, the relationship was fresh and new, and Amy, their daughter, was born. During this time their neighbor, who was an avid mountain biker, invited Ted to try the sport. Ted fell in love with the excitement of the ride. He also realized that the amount of exercise that he got on a three- or four-hour bike ride seemed to make him much calmer and more centered than usual.

Ted was hired in a small, slow-paced, family-oriented company that was very supportive of its employees. He was offered an interesting job with a promising opportunity for career advancement. For a long time, Ted had recognized that he was unable to think clearly, much less produce work, if his work space was disorganized. Fortunately, he was given an office, and his work space was totally his own. He was able to arrange his papers, books and desktop with the precision that he required.

Ted was excelling in his career, and he decided that, after two years of training, it was time to go out on his own. He began his own business and was tremendously successful. His business grew from one employee to five, and eventually to thirty-five. It took more and more of his energy to manage his employees and his customers. Although the stress was a result of business success, and in that sense positive, it was still stress. Ted was so busy at work he realized that if he was going to spend any time with Mary and Amy, he must give up his mountain bike riding, which he did.

In contrast to the stress at work, Ted looked forward to coming home to a clean and quiet house each night. But as caring for a house, a baby and working twenty hours a week outside of the home put stress on his wife, some of her natural personality traits began to emerge. Ted realized that his wife wasn't bothered by clutter. Worse than that, she didn't even notice it. When Ted straightened the living room, he insisted that the magazines and pictures be completely ruler-straight, or it drove him crazy. Mary truly didn't notice when the coffee table was littered with eight magazines, three cookbooks and two baby bottles. Amy took after her mother and had toys and books strewn over most of the house.

With the stress of business, the sudden decrease in exercise, and the clutter at home, Ted found that his old moods and irritability were back. From his early pattern of being calm and understanding, he changed to being irritable. His employees saw this Dr. Jekyll and Mr. Hyde transformation, certainly not understanding the cause. They weren't tolerant of his behavior. One employee told him off and walked out the door. Two other employees told him they had been offered other jobs and left rather suddenly.

At home he began to criticize Mary and asked her to change. But, no matter what he said to her, the house remained cluttered, bills occasionally weren't paid, and Amy's toys continued to spill over into most of the rooms of the house. He became frustrated, and his criticism grew stronger. Finally, he became abusive. His comments ranged from telling Mary, "You are a total slob! What is wrong with you?" to telling her, "You are a terrible mother! Amy will grow up to be a complete pig!" This was a side of Ted that Mary had never seen. At first, she thought it was her fault. She did her best to keep things neat. She finally realized that her level of neatness would never reach the ruler-perfect level that Ted demanded. Mary began to argue with Ted, and his verbal abuse increased.

Ultimately, this story has a happy ending. Ted was diagnosed with adult ADD and placed on Ritalin. He found that the Ritalin did a great deal to improve his moods and ability to control his temper when using the medication. Unfortunately, during periods when Ritalin was out of his system, he was still volatile. These were the times that he was at home with Mary and Amy. As he learned more about adult ADD he discovered that many ADD adults benefit from a second medication that increases serotonin levels. For ADD adults, the psychostimulant alone does not alter body chemistry enough to soften aggressive traits. Ted, like many ADD adults, initially rejected the idea of a second medication. We often hear clients say things like, "This is just going too far! How many more pills will I have to take?" "If one isn't working all the time, why will two help?" "Won't I be considered a drug addict?" "Do you think I'm crazy? Is that why you want me to take a second medication?" The reality is that often a second medication is highly beneficial because it more directly affects serotonin levels in the brain. This cooperates with the stimulant medication that more directly affects dopamine levels. It's a carefully monitored sort of hydraulic system, not a symbol of craziness or drug addiction.

The marriage deteriorated until Mary was fed up and threatened divorce. Ted finally agreed to get some marriage counseling, and Mary insisted that it be with a therapist familiar with ADD. After Ted and Mary explained the persistent pattern, the therapist also encouraged Ted to try a second medication. He was asked to set a specific period of time for a trial and evaluate the effects for himself. To his great surprise, the medication made a remarkable difference in his ability to control his temper and verbal abuse. He was amazed that he felt much calmer and often didn't have to work at controlling his temper. It simply wasn't a problem. After years of Ted's pattern of verbal abuse, Mary and Ted still had a tremendous amount of work to do on their marriage. But, with the medication, at least they had a fair chance to talk, discuss issues and find a common ground.

If you are an ADD adult with significant mood swings and depression, especially if these feelings lead into episodes of temper or rage, you might need medication. This might be a difficult truth to hear, but it is very important. There truly are ADD adults whose body chemistry is so variable or whose moods are so drastic that there is little hope of a happy life without medication.

Why the Reluctance to Medicate?

For some, the idea of medication is very difficult. Why is this the case? We are living in a society that talks about the dangers of drugs and alcohol. Many ADD adults must move past the feeling that they are doing something wrong if they consider medication. Often they can deal with the idea of one medication, but if a second medication is suggested, they get very upset.

Remember, we are still at the beginning stages of understanding how the brain works and, beyond that, how to correct its biochemical imbalances. At this time many ADD adults seem to benefit from two different medications to correct both the dopamine and serotonin imbalances in their brains. This does not mean they are drug addicts. This does not mean they are crazy. It simply means that our scientific understanding of treatment is still very limited. One day – hopefully in the near future – we may find a way to correct the genetic imbalances of ADD before birth, and medication won't be necessary.

Because ADD is not life-threatening, many ADD adults question if they truly need medication or if it is just a crutch. They feel they should be able to control their moods by willpower. Often these feelings are confirmed by friends or parents who say, "You don't really need a drug." After all, it is true that they won't suffer any physical symptoms or die if they don't take medication.

But, for the ADD adult, the use of medication is very much like the use of contact lenses or glasses. When your vision is corrected with glasses, you can see much better. When you don't wear your glasses, life is much more difficult but you don't die. Since science has advanced to the point that contact lenses and glasses are available, why not use them? Why go through life not being able to see to the end of an aisle in the grocery store, or be denied a driver's license because you can't pass the vision test? Sounds rather silly when it is put that way, doesn't it? The use of medication for the diagnosed ADD adult falls into exactly the same category. It assists in the temporary correction of a condition. Why not use the medical technology available to us, especially if it means the prevention of domestic violence?

This is a Hard Truth

The fact that body chemistry, family background and school history sets some ADD adults up for a pattern of abusive behavior is a hard truth. But, once this truth is understood, there is light at the end of the tunnel. With knowledge and understanding, ADD adults can find their ways out of the maze.

Domestic Violence Checklist

Do you or the person you love:

YES   **NO**

_____ _____ Embarrass, humiliate or shame you in front of others?

_____ _____ Create feelings of being stupid or inadequate, even though the words might sound "normal" to the outside world?

_____ _____ Push, shove, slap, kick, bite or hit?

_____ _____ Have a family history where verbal, emotional or physical abuse was present?

_____ _____ Seem to fly into a rage quickly or have a very short fuse, even if the trigger seems minor?

_____ _____ Seem to have little or no impulse control when in a discussion or argument, resulting in anger outbursts?

_____ _____ Over-commit time, energy and/or money, then erupt and take the pressure out on those around?

_____ _____ Seem to live on an emotional roller coaster between highs and lows and blow up when the stress increases?

_____ _____ Have difficulty identifying and dealing with feelings, often resorting to rage when the feelings become too overwhelming?

_____ _____ Blame the ADD condition for the mood swings, rages and outbursts?

_____ _____ Use sex, alcohol or drugs to alter moods, only to erupt into rage after using the numbing substance?

_____ _____ Get easily overwhelmed in a discussion and resort to attacking the partner rather than admitting feeling helpless and/or out of control?

If you find yourself answering "yes" to these questions pertaining to you or your partner, you may need help. Please turn to our hotline reference in the appendix or contact a therapist or local group in the area for help.

Chapter 8

ADD and Addiction:

What is Controlling My Life??

The ADD adult constantly fights a biochemical imbalance. Her system doesn't feel right. It's off kilter (at some basic level, she is aware of this). If she happens to encounter something – anything at all – that makes her body feel *right* for a period of time, she wants to return again and again to that feeling. She is forever seeking the feeling of being *normal*.

In her need to return to that feeling of being normal, the ADD adult sometimes becomes addicted. The addictions are not always harmful, negative or abusive substances, but they are addictions because the ADD adult must continue the use of these acts or substances to function *normally*.

Let's look at the range of addictions that ADD adults typically choose. These addictions fall into five distinct categories:

- *Category 1*   *Positive Addictions (Exercise)*
- *Category 2*   *Non-Life-Threatening Addictions (Coffee)*
- *Category 3*   *Dangerous Substances – Non-Life-Threatening (Diet Pills)*
- *Category 4*   *Life-Threatening Addictions (Cocaine, Amphetamines)*
- *Category 5*   *Less Recognized Addictions*

Category 1 – Positive Addictions (Exercise)

In high school or college, the ADD adult often decides to run cross-country, try out for the track team or join the swimming team. A steady, strenuous level of exercise seems to make him achieve better grades, concentrate in class and feel happier. His parents may joke about the effects of exercise and say something like, "Boy, swimming sure helps Sam burn off his excess energy. He has less time to party and drink, and, unbelievably, he wants to stay home and study once in a while!"

For many ADD adults, neither their parents nor they themselves put two and two together and realize that exercise normalizes their brain chemistries. A certain level of exercise changes the endorphins in the brain which shoot adrenaline through the system, ultimately resulting in a normalization of brain chemistry. Many times the ADD adult continues to participate in sports throughout college, and often she does well. Then, after college, she runs five or six miles a day or remains involved in some regular cardiovascular exercise. As long as exercise remains constant, she functions normally.

Is exercise a positive addiction? Absolutely. The danger comes when the ADD adult uses exercise to correct her biochemical imbalance without realizing what she is doing. When problems arise, it is usually because the exercise has stopped abruptly.

The College Athlete

Devastated because his wife told him that their marriage was finally over, Jeff came in for a counseling appointment. He told how his marriage had disintegrated over the last three years. He could not understand what happened. He said she accused him of becoming more and more moody and being lazy and unmotivated in his work. We asked Jeff to think about what changed in his life three years ago, and he stated with absolute certainty that nothing had changed. Nothing at all! When pressed to think back, he remembered a knee injury that, three years ago, ended his daily runs.

An ADD adult, Jeff used his daily runs to change and normalize his body chemistry and correct an undiagnosed ADD condition. Once he stopped exercising, his ADD characteristics began to surface. He began having difficulty at work; the tasks facing him were just too much. He often felt overwhelmed, and when he arrived home each night, he retreated to the den to play on his computer. When his wife wanted to talk, he became irritated.

Jeff's problem was his lack of awareness. He had no idea he was an ADD adult, and he had no clue as to the part exercise played in his life. Again, his trouble didn't arise *because* he exercised, but because he *stopped* abruptly.

A High School Senior's Transition to College

Kathy was a bright high school student with a GPA of 4.0 who had been in gifted and accelerated classes through high school. She was happy, loved life and loved her dancing. In fact, she danced four or five hours a day, in addition to being on the drill team. She applied to several colleges and was delighted when she was accepted by UCLA. Once she arrived as a freshman, she promised herself she was going to take her education seriously and stop all unnecessary extracurricular activities, so she stopped dancing.

Kathy did quite well throughout her freshman year at UCLA and continued to make A's in her classes. However, we received a panicky call the first semester of her sophomore year. She was getting C's and D's on her tests even though she was studying twice as hard as before. She had never *ever* received a C, much less a D, and she couldn't understand what was happening.

After an evaluation, it was clear that she was an ADD college student. In addition to being brilliant, it was apparent that through dancing in high school, she had self-corrected her ADD condition. Her self-corrected body chemistry had maintained through her freshman year, but her body chemistry switched back in her sophomore year. Once she was diagnosed and placed on medication, within two or three months her grades were back in the A range. A year later she called the office and asked us to write fifteen letters of reference. She had decided to apply to medical school.

Category 2 – Non-Life-Threatening Addictions (Coffee, Etc.)

Many ADD adults describe their brains as being fuzzy. They feel as though they are in the middle of a fog. They often find that coffee, cola, tea and other caffeinated substances make a difference. After two or three cups of coffee, they can think better. Their mornings always start with caffeine. Sometimes the need for coffee or tea increases to a substantial level; for example, one father of an ADD adolescent admitted to drinking thirty cups of coffee a day.

An ADD adult's body chemistry can be very particular in the way it uses a non-life threatening substance. One ADD adult found that just any type of coffee wasn't a help. She had happened upon a special espresso shop that sold a certain type of coffee bean and which made espresso with a specific type of espresso machine. A cup of *that* particular espresso helped clear up her thinking for four to five hours – no other coffee seemed to make a difference. She bought an identical espresso machine and coffee beans from that shop and made her own espresso. However, her body system's requirement was so specific that if she kept the beans longer than a week, she felt little stimulant effect. If she attempted to take the coffee with her in a thermos, the effect was nonexistent.

Other ADD adults decide to get their caffeine through pills. Often they take Excedrin® or Vivarin® in progressively larger doses. Initially one or two Excedrin® a day may meet their needs. Over time, they find they must use more and more to get the same effect. The use of these substances depletes body reserves and does damage, particularly when they are used over time. (By the way, the speculation is that those substances are ineffective and don't produce the brain chemistry response needed.)

Category 3 – Dangerous Substances/Non-Life-Threatening (Diet Pills)

ADD adults often find that coffee, exercise or Excedrin® just don't work – at least not enough for them to succeed in their careers. They may find that something like a diet pill makes an amazing difference in their lives. On amphetamine-based diet pills, they can think and function at a level that was impossible before. For non-ADD adults, diet pills typically cause a depression of appetite, which aids in weight loss (interestingly, ADD adults seldom find that they lose weight or experience the typical appetite loss on diet pills. Instead, they comment that they are able to concentrate and generally think more effectively).

Although amphetamines (dextroamphetamines belong to this class of drugs) are addictive and even life-threatening at certain levels, we have placed all diet pills in this non-life-threatening category for a couple of reasons. First, when used as diet pills, low doses of amphetamines or non-amphetamine stimulants are prescribed. An inordinate amount would have to be ingested on a regular basis for an adult to become addicted. (There are also a number of prescription appetite suppressants that are non-amphetamine and have a lower potential for abuse, but we have not found this class of drugs to be effective in dealing with ADD symptoms.)

Secondly, diet pills are prescribed by a physician and are regulated in that way. There are certainly cases where an adult has been known to visit two or three physicians, falsifying the situation and obtaining diet pills from each one – admittedly, if an adult is determined and successful in getting large quantities she can become addicted, especially to the amphetamine class of drugs. We find, however, that if an adult is that committed to the search for amphetamines, she most probably turns to street drugs as an easier source. For these reasons, we have placed diet pills in the non-life-threatening category.

For the ADD adult, using diet pills brings danger from an unexpected direction. Often the addiction makes him feel dirty, no better than an addict on the street. He is dependent on diet pills to do well at work or at home, having taken them far longer than he should have. He may have moved from physician to physician to find someone else to prescribe the pills for him. The danger in this is the loss of self-esteem. In his mind, he is abusing the diet pills, and he begins to feel guilt and shame.

He hides this secret from the world. Actually, many ADD adults successfully use diet pills (in moderate doses) over many years to treat their ADD condition. They have no idea their problem lies with their biochemical imbalance; therefore, they don't understand that in taking diet pills, they are attempting to self-correct their imbalance.

One Attorney's Story

Camille, a very successful and sharp attorney, called the office for an ADD evaluation. Camille told of attending law school at a university that also had a medical school. (As one of our senior citizen ADD adults, she attended law school in the late fifties). During midterms and finals, the medical school put out a bulletin that it would supply any student who so desired with Dexedrine (the brand name for dextroamphetamine).

With the Dexedrine, Camille found she was able to concentrate and study. She experienced a clarity of thought unusual for her. Although she was extremely intelligent, she had realized in high school that she had to study twice as long and three times as hard as her classmates to be competitive. This changed dramatically with the Dexedrine. She used up her supply of Dexedrine and then bought additional supplies from her non-ADD classmates, who saw little benefit in it beyond being able to pull all-nighters while studying.

She used Dexedrine judiciously through law school and early in her practice. When she ran out, she began to use diet pills for much the same effect. During periods of time when they were not available, she had problems with her partner, didn't complete work for her clients, and wasn't as successful.

Like many ADD adults, Camille was caught in a dilemma. She realized that the Dexedrine helped a great deal, but she felt she was abusing drugs. She lived with guilt and shame for many years until she read about ADD in adults. She finally realized that her pattern was normal for the ADD population, and was soon diagnosed with ADD.

Category 4 – Life-Threatening Addictions (Cocaine & Amphetamines)

The search by ADD adults for substances to correct their body chemistries is an instinctive one that happens without thought or planning. Occasionally, they can hold the addiction to a low level and correct their body chemistries. Often, however, they cannot hold these addictions in check.

Certain addictions are considered life-threatening because, unchecked, the ultimate outcome is death. Drug abuse is a horrifying fact of life. Individuals and their families' lives are often ruined. Abusers cause accidents that kill and maim. Sometimes they are in jail for years, or are poisoned by street drugs or overdoses. Here, we are focusing specifically on the role that drug use plays in the ADD adult population. We don't claim to be discussing the full range of drug abuse and its related problems.

Some ADD adults who use cocaine or speed fall into a different category than many drug users. They report that "just a little" makes them feel normal for the first time in their lives, and they can think while under the influence of these substances. Often they do better at work – at least for a while – until the addiction becomes full-blown. This places them in a unique dilemma. Society says drugs are bad. While they see danger in the drugs (or in using too much), they also know they experience positive effects from the drugs.

This reasoning, of course, is faulty. Just try to tell a police officer who is busting you for cocaine possession that "just a little" actually makes you a safer driver. If ADD adults are not totally addicted, they are afraid to use the drug at all, for fear of what will happen next. Yet, at the beginning stages of self-medicating they are much more functional on drugs than off. What a dilemma.

On the other hand, some ADD adults quickly move past any careful or judicious use of a drug. They move hard and fast into addiction. They often lose their jobs, homes and families. They bankrupt their businesses, alienate their friends and exhaust their bodies. They may have been in and out of a multitude of recovery programs. They get clean and sober, only to start using again. For this ADD adult population, the yo-yo effect, or the pull of the addiction, has a special hook because of their body chemistries.

Even when they are in recovery programs, or are maintaining sobriety, this population faces one additional problem – once off their drug of choice, they don't feel better. They feel worse. Their ADD body chemistry is still off-kilter. Recovery programs are often unaware of the dilemma faced by the ADD adult because they don't understand the biochemical imbalance and its contribution to drug use. The next chapter deals with the problems the ADD adult faces in an alcohol or drug recovery program.

Other Addictions

As we get to know and work with our ADD adults, we are finding certain addictions popping up more and more. These addictions may not have been previously linked to ADD, but their repetitive nature and compulsive aspect of the addictions indicate it's a body chemistry problem. Plus, they are considered problematic because they result in negative consequences in our society.

Sex Addicts

Today, sexual addiction is considered problematic; in another culture or era, it might have been a sign of virility or strength and highly prized.

In Chapter 1, we described the ADD characteristics as falling on one end of a continuum or the other, with normal being in the middle. With ADD adults, sex also appears on the continuum. ADD adults often report being oversexed or undersexed. Although this has been more obvious in the male ADD population, this may be because of a reporting bias on the part of ADD females.

On the undersexed side, ADD adults may report almost no interest in sex, even during their adolescence. There doesn't seem to be any connection with sexual preference; there is just a lack of interest in sex.

On the other side of the continuum, some ADD adults report feeling oversexed, just as they did during adolescence. They may want sex daily, or even several times a day. In certain adults, sex is a true addiction. These adults often report being happily married and committed to their families, yet find themselves drawn to topless bars, prostitutes on the street corner, or involved in dangerous liaisons with the boss or a close family friend. Not only are they unable to walk away from sex they realize is risky, they are often consumed by thinking about it to the point that it interferes with their daily lives. They often seek help from a group such as Sex Addicts Anonymous, or they go into therapy.

Sex addiction is particularly problematic for ADD adults because the risk of discovery and the completion of the sexual act function together to stimulate and alter brain chemistry. This produces the same effect as does adrenaline in a dangerous situation. For the ADD adult, this results in a feeling of calmness.

Danger Addicts

Some ADD adults love the adrenaline rush of danger. They live for thrills. They drive fast. They take chances on the road. They skydive or bungee jump. Some ADD adults say they need danger on a regular basis. Sometimes it is once a month, sometimes once a week and sometimes once a day. Danger produces an adrenaline surge that causes a change in body chemistry. The adrenaline surge takes people over the hump and allows a calming effect. They say they feel more "normal" after such an experience. Without that release, they are agitated, angry and talk about feeling crazy.

Danger Addicts to the Extreme

Carry out the need for danger and the adrenaline rush of living on the edge to the nth degree, and what do you have? A gun in your hand during a robbery. There is fascinating new research being published on our prison population that indicates a significant percentage are ADD adults. (This will be examined in detail in Chapter 10 – The ADD and Crime Connection).

Food Addictions

It is common knowledge that people with eating disorders have difficulty because of psychological factors of which they may not be aware. For example, someone may eat whenever he is upset because when he was a child, his mother gave him a cookie to make him feel better. He may overeat because his father always told him he was fat, and now he is living out a self-fulfilling prophecy.

Professionals working in the area of eating disorders, including compulsive overeating, anorexia and bulimia, estimate that a *third* of their population are ADD adults. Although ADD adults are also caught in the psychological realm of the disorder, for them the addiction goes beyond this. Food produces a very real chemical change in the ADD adult body. One ADD CPA said that for her, any type of wheat product, such as bread and pasta, produced a tranquilizing effect on her system. Although research certainly indicates that pasta and other wheat products produce a calming effect on all people, the ADD adult has a biochemical imbalance with which most of the population doesn't contend. Thus the ADD adult may need greater amounts of a certain food to correct her biochemical imbalance. The non-ADD adult may need only one plate of pasta to produce a feeling of calm, while our ADD accountant needs three or four plates of pasta to change her body chemistry and make her brain take notice.

An ADD adult may also find that one food in particular makes a marked difference on her unique chemical balance. Thus she tends to "specialize" in certain foods. One ADD secretary is addicted to chocolate. Her boss gave her Belgium chocolate as a gift, and she ate five pounds in one sitting. She is an example of an ADD adult with an addiction to a specific substance, and also one who has a high need for a large quantity of that substance.

Gambling

Two dollars on the nose or, for some people, two thousand dollars on the nose! The ADD gambler experiences a tremendous adrenaline surge as he places his bet and anticipates the result. He experiences another adrenaline surge as he waits for the outcome, and a final surge as he realizes he has won . . . or lost. This scenario holds true whether it is a horse race, a crap table in Las Vegas or a poker game. For the ADD gambler, it is this adrenaline surge that alters his body chemistry and makes him feel "right."

There's Hope

On a positive note, more is known now on the subject of addiction and ADD than ever before. The biochemical component of ADD has opened the door to new treatment and rehabilitation methods, offering hope and success for ADD adults.

Chapter 9

ADD Adults in Recovery:

Why a New Approach is Needed

Why does the ADD adult have so much difficulty in alcohol and drug recovery programs as we know them today? Simple. Most recovery programs don't consider that an addicted adult may be suffering from a biochemical imbalance that may *cause* the addiction or require a different approach to recovery.

We are grateful to Dr. Frank R. Zelarney, MFCC and Certified Alcohol and Drug Counselor, for his insights and experiences with the world of ADD Adults and recovery.

The Search for Recovery

We wish we had a nickel for every time we have heard a spouse or parent say, "Let's put John (Mary) in a rehabilitation program." They think these programs are magical. If they can just convince their spouses or adult children to step through the doors of rehabilitation units, the recovery is assured. Unfortunately, there is an eighty percent recidivism rate in these programs. This means that about eighty percent of the people who enter rehabilitation or recovery programs will drink or use drugs again. These odds are not encouraging.

Before we examine how this impacts our ADD adults, let's take a broader look at the process many people go through. We have titled this process *the endless search for recovery*. After the first "slip," or relapse, and the realization that the twelve-step program alone may not be enough to maintain sobriety, adults tend to look about for other answers to their recovery problems. For some, this begins a long, time-consuming process which results in the endless search for recovery.

While this endless search is a tribute to their persistence, it often yields a distinct pattern. First, there is a cycle of excitement where it seems that the answers are finally there. This is soon followed by a period of questioning whether this approach will work. The final phase of the cycle is the intense disappointment of yet another approach that has fallen short.

There are several resources and philosophies circulating in the world of recovery, any one of which may serve as a starting point for the endless search. Claudia

Black's pioneering research in alcoholism and children of alcoholics for the first time brought the ideas of dysfunctional family, roles of each family member and talking feelings out of the closet and into the light of day. We certainly recognize her outstanding and ongoing contributions to the field. However, Black's work, in and of itself, has not dramatically affected the recidivism rate. Therefore, adults working with the ACA philosophy alone often find themselves with a feeling that something is still missing. What to do next? Their endless search must continue.

Many adults in recovery are struck by John Bradshaw's warm and charismatic approach in books and seminars and are drawn to begin their "inner child" journeys. His contributions to inner child work, as well as to the roles of guilt and shame in alcoholism and recovery, are important contributions to this body of research. However, it is commonly said among professionals in the field of recovery that once the adult is launched with her inner child, it is as though she is in a boat with this inner child, paddling continuously but never reaching the opposite shore. Of course, the metaphor of reaching the opposite shore represents an adult who accomplishes the inner child journey, pulls his life together and becomes an adult once more. While there is certainly validity to Bradshaw's approach, it is one in which we have seen numerous clients spend thousands of dollars in books, tapes, seminars and therapy – all over a period of many years. Still, the feeling continues that there are pieces to the recovery puzzle missing.

Another entry point to our adult's quest is that of religion. We in no way mean to suggest that religion is not a valuable, vital cornerstone in people's lives. However people in recovery do not approach religion to seek a balance in their lives; instead, they often take a rather dogmatic approach and become zealots who have replaced one addiction with another. In this culture we would often expect the focus to be Christianity or Judaism; however, this also extends into a more recent upsurging of Buddhism and New Age philosophies, such as those of Deepak Chopra. Again, while we recognize the invaluable contributions of each of these philosophies, they are often not the final answer The endless search continues . . .

Since the recidivism rate sits at about eighty percent, it is clear that something is still missing. If this is true for adults in recovery, it is doubly true for our ADD adults in recovery with their biochemical imbalances which making their search even more difficult.

With our broader perspective fleshed out, let's return to our discussion of twelve-step programs.

Before people who are staunch AA or NA members throw this book across the room, let us say a few additional words. AA, NA and other anonymous programs have filled a definite need. The concept of people who are recovering helping and supporting other people in recovery is valid and useful. AA, NA and other anonymous programs use a twelve-step program that requires the abuser to systematically work through a sequence of steps in his or her recovery. This structured program gives a framework for many people who are lost at sea in their addictions. The support and acceptance that is felt from the group when an alcoholic or addict comes forward in a meeting and says, "Hi, I'm Jane, I'm an alcoholic/addict," is tremendously important. Over the last months we've become aware of several twelve-step programs especially for ADD adults. However, these are geared to the ADD adult population as a whole, not just for individuals who have substance abuse issues. These programs will be discussed in more detail in Chapter 14.

For many people, recovery and twelve-step programs work. For some people, they work the very first time and are vitally important. Realistically, they don't work all of the time for all people. Now is the time to honestly ask, "Why not?"

Basic Beliefs of Recovery Programs

From the first AA meeting led by Bill (even the founder is anonymous), members of AA have strongly stated that alcoholism is a disease over which the alcoholic is powerless. Their position has been that alcoholics (and drug addicts) *are never recovered*, they are always in recovery or recovering. Why the distinction? AA and NA believe alcoholics or addicts can slip back into abuse at any time, With just one drink or one hit of speed, the addiction will reappear. Furthermore, they contend that it won't just reappear but come back with even more force and devastation.

This philosophy has made people in AA and NA wary of dangers of any substance that might in some way lead the person in recovery back into addiction. For a long time the use of medication, even aspirin, was resisted. For years an adult who was in recovery who had been diagnosed as depressed or bipolar had a long, hard road ahead with fellow AA members if medication was prescribed by a psychiatrist to treat the condition. The belief is that the alcoholic/addict must remain vigilant and aware of the "cunning, baffling and powerful" nature of substances at all times or risk being pushed back into addiction before they even know what happened.

The Fear of Relapse

Both AA and NA members realize that their population has a definite tendency toward relapse. These programs feel that, once the member is in a recovery program, relapse begins well before the first drink is taken or the first line of cocaine is snorted. AA and NA members feel that relapse is a slide that begins slowly and insidiously. Members are warned to be aware of changes in thought patterns, an increase in stress or a tendency to isolate themselves.

The potential of relapse is also evaluated by a person's life success. If a person in recovery has lost a second and third job, her sponsor is quick to ask if she is on the verge of relapse. She is told to work her program. If she is working a program, she is told to attend more meetings, make more calls, maintain closer contact with her sponsor. If these interventions continue to be ineffective, she is finally told to get some counseling.

In AA and NA work there is a great deal of emphasis placed on these signs of relapse. Several authors have written extensively on this particular subject. One of the best-known writers in the field of alcohol and relapse is Terry Gorsky. He is well-known for his published work listing the thirty-seven signs of relapse. These thirty-seven signs of relapse are typically used to indicate whether a person is in trouble in his or her recovery. People in AA and NA use these signs as indicators of how well they are "working the program" and avoiding relapse.

This poses a real problem for the ADD adult. Twenty-eight of Gorsky's signs of relapse relate directly to an ADD adult's profile. For the ADD adult, these may not be signs of relapse at all, but definite signs of the ADD condition.

Unless the ADD adult is properly diagnosed and possibly placed on medication to correct the biochemical imbalance, he will forever feel (and be reinforced to feel by well-meaning sponsors and fellow members) on the verge of relapse. No matter how hard he is trying to work his program, he is failing. On the heels of this realization comes both the guilt and the shame that he is not doing better. This is a vicious cycle that must be addressed for the ADD adult.

The following list contains Gorsky's thirty-six of the thirty-seven signs of relapse. The indicators of relapse that typically apply to ADD adults have been printed in **bold** type. The authors' comments that apply to ADD will appear in ***bold italics***.

Relapse Prevention Training
The 37 Warning Signs

1. <u>Concern About Well-Being</u>: **The alcoholic feels uneasy, afraid, and anxious. At times s/he is afraid of not being able to stay sober. This uneasiness comes and goes and usually lasts only a short time.**

    Talk about uneasy – when our body chemistry plays hide-and-seek and we are up one day and can't think straight the next, of course we are concerned with our well-being.

2. <u>Denial of the Concern</u>: In order to tolerate these periods of worry, fear, and anxiety, the alcoholic ignores or denies these feelings in the same way s/he had at one time denied alcoholism. The denial may be so strong that there is no awareness of it while it is happening. Even when there is awareness of the feelings, they are often forgotten as soon as the feelings are gone. It is only when the alcoholic thinks back about the situation at a later time that s/he is able to recognize the feelings of anxiety and the denial of those feelings.

3. <u>Believing "I'll Never Drink Again"</u>: The alcoholic convinces self that s/he will never drink again and sometimes will tell this to others, but usually keeps it to self. Many are afraid to tell their counselors or other AA members of this belief. When the alcoholic firmly believes s/he will never drink again, the need for a daily recovery program seems less important.

4. <u>Worrying About Others Instead of Self</u>: The alcoholic becomes more concerned about the sobriety of others than about personal recovery. S/he doesn't talk directly about these concerns but privately judges the drinking of friends and spouse and the recovery programs of other recovering persons. In AA this is called "working the other guy's program."

5. <u>Defensiveness</u>: The alcoholic has a tendency to defend self when talking about personal problems or his/her recovery program even when no defense is necessary.

   ADD adults have learned every trick in the book to defend themselves. How many times can you lock your keys in your car, take the wrong freeway exit or forget what someone has just said to you without developing a heck of a defensiveness?

6. <u>Compulsive Behavior</u>: The alcoholic becomes compulsive ("stuck" or "fixed" or "rigid") in the way s/he thinks and behaves. There is a tendency to do the same things over and over again without a good reason. There is a tendency to control conversations either by talking too much or not talking at all. S/he tends to work more than is needed, becomes involved in many activities and may appear to be the model of recovery because of heavy involvement in AA 12-Step work and chairing AA meetings. S/he is often a leader in counseling groups by "playing therapist." Casual or informal involvement with people, however, is avoided.

   This is often the hallmark of the ADD person. Whether it is interrupting, talking too much, working too much or obsessing too much about his/her ADD, this is pretty typical behavior.

7. <u>Impulsive Behavior</u>: Sometimes the rigid behavior is interrupted by actions taken without thought or self-control. This usually happens at times of high stress. Sometimes these impulsive actions cause the alcoholic to make decisions that seriously damage his/her life and recovery program.

   Impulsive? As we write this, one of the authors is taking off for a week backpacking in the Mayan empire with no travel arrangements beyond an airline ticket. Impulsive? You bet. Frequently ADD adults are well known for their impulsivity.

8. <u>Tendencies Toward Loneliness</u>: The alcoholic begins to spend more time alone. S/he usually has good reasons and excuses for staying away from other people. These periods of being alone begin to occur more often and the alcoholic beings to feel more and more lonely. Instead of dealing with the loneliness by trying to meet and be around other people, he or she becomes more compulsive and impulsive.

   If you couldn't control what came out of your mouth, would you be in public a lot? ADD adults are so accustomed to living undercover, they often avoid social contact and report being lonely as a result.

9. <u>Tunnel Vision</u>: Tunnel vision is seeing only one small part of life and not being able to get "the big picture." The alcoholic looks at life as being made up of separate, unrelated parts. S/he focuses on one part without looking at the other parts or how they are related. Sometimes this creates the mistaken belief that everything is secure and going well. At other times this results in seeing only what is going wrong. Small problems are blown up out of proportion. When this happens, the alcoholic comes to believe s/he is being treated unfairly and has no power to do anything about it.

    For ADD adults, tunnel vision is sometimes the only way to focus and to keep from feeling so fragmented. If they saw all the bits and pieces of "the big picture" they would be totally over-whelmed and not be able to get anything done. Tunnel vision is often the other end of the spectrum from the scattered attention of ADD.

10. <u>Minor Depression</u>: Symptoms of depression begin to appear and to persist. The person feels down, blue, listless, empty of feelings. Oversleeping becomes common. S/he is able to distract self from these moods by getting busy with other things and not talking about the depression.

    When the body chemistry is continually off balance, we often feel blue and out of sorts. It is extremely common for the ADD person to feel minor to major depression.

11. <u>Loss of Constructive Planning</u>: The alcoholic stops planning each day and the future. S/he often mistakes the AA slogan, "One day at a time" to mean that one shouldn't plan or think about what s/he is going to do. Less and less attention is paid to details. S/he becomes listless. Plans are based more on wishful thinking (how the alcoholic wishes things would be) than reality (how things really are).

    Do nine thousands lists make a difference? Sometimes wishful thinking is more constructive than the frustration an ADD adult feels for never completing plans.

12. <u>Plans Begin to Fail</u>: Because s/he makes plans that are not realistic and does not pay attention to details, plans begin to fail. Each failure causes new life problems. Some of these problems

are similar to the problems that had occurred during drinking. S/he often feels guilty and remorseful when the problems occur.

For an ADD adult, plans fail all the time! It's more of a surprise when the plans succeed!

13. <u>Daydreaming and Wishful Thinking</u>: It becomes more difficult to concentrate. The "if only" syndrome becomes more common in conversation. The alcoholic begins to have fantasies of escaping or "being rescued from it all" by an event unlikely to happen.

"If only I didn't have ADD! Everything would be so much easier and I would feel more okay." This isn't just a sense of failure, it's true!

14. <u>Feelings That Nothing Can Be Solved</u>: A sense of failure begins to develop. The failure may be real, or it may be imagined. Small failures are exaggerated and blown out of proportion. The belief that, "I've tried my best and sobriety isn't working out" begins to develop.

No matter how many times I clean out my drawers and organize or try to solve problems in my relationships, the papers multiply as though they have lives of their own and my relationships are still in a tangle. It doesn't feel like anything can be solved.

15. <u>Immature Wish To Be Happy</u>: A vague desire to "[sic] be happy" or to have "things work out" develops without the person identifying what is necessary to be happy or have things work out. "Magical thinking" is used: wanting things to get better without doing anything to make them better.

16. <u>Periods Of Confusion</u>: Periods of confusion become more frequent, last longer, and cause more problems. The alcoholic often feels angry with self because of the inability to figure things out.

Confusion? Confusion is often the ADD person's middle name and is experienced as ongoing, rather than just periodic.

17. <u>Irritation with Friends</u>: Relationships become strained with friends, family, counselors, and AA members. The alcoholic feels threatened when these people talk about the changes in behavior and mood that are becoming apparent. The conflicts continue to increase in spite of the alcoholic's efforts to resolve

them. The alcoholic begins to feel guilty and remorseful about his/her role in these conflicts.

Are you irritated that your friends are irritated that you've never been on time to anything yet? How unreasonable of them! Are you irritated that your spouse is irritated that you can't remember anything they've said? Totally unreasonable as well!

18. Easily Angered: The alcoholic experiences episodes of anger, frustration, resentment, and irritability for no real reason. Overreaction to small things becomes more frequent. Stress and anxiety increase because of the fear that overreaction might result in violence. The efforts to control self adds to the stress and tension.

What about a sign that says "Handle with care, neurotransmitters on quick trigger?"

19. Irregular Eating Habits: The alcoholic begins overeating or undereating. There is weight gain or loss. S/he stops having meals at regular times and replaces a well-balanced, nourishing diet with "junk food."

Meals at regular times? Is that possible? You mean the drive-thru at Del Taco doesn't comply with the food pyramid? Regular eating habits require discipline and pre-planning – not the ADD adult's forte.

20. Lack of Desire to Take Action: There are periods when the alcoholic is unable to get started or to get anything done. At those times s/he is unable to concentrate, feels anxious, fearful, and uneasy, and often feels trapped with no way out.

Can't get started? Can't get anything done? Yep, that's ADD to a "T." This especially plagues the hypoactive ADD adult.

21. Irregular Sleeping Habits: The alcoholic has difficulty sleeping and is restless and fitful when sleep does occur. Sleep is often marked by strange and frightening dreams. Because of exhaustion, s/he may sleep for twelve to twenty hours at a time. These "sleeping marathons" may happen as often as every six to fifteen days.

This one is easy. Just work the night shift along with the day shift! The ADD adult's sleep patterns are often disturbed.

22. <u>Loss of Daily Structure</u>: Daily routine becomes haphazard. The alcoholic stops getting up and going to bed at regular times. Sometimes s/he is unable to sleep, and this results in oversleeping at other times. Regular mealtimes are discontinued. It becomes more difficult to keep appointments and plan social events. The alcoholic feels rushed and overburdened at times and then has nothing to do at other times. S/he is unable to follow through on plans and decisions and experiences tension, frustration, fear, or anxiety that keep [*sic*] him/her from doing what should be done.

    Even if you posted a calendar in every room of the house and in the car(s), the concept of daily structure would still be foreign to the ADD adult.

23. <u>Periods of Deep Depression</u>: The alcoholic feels depressed more often. The depression becomes worse, lasts longer, and interferes with living. The depression is so bad that it is noticed by others and cannot be easily denied. The depression is most severe during unplanned or unstructured periods of time. Fatigue, hunger, and loneliness make the depression worse. When the alcoholic feels depressed, s/he separates from other people, becomes irritable and angry with others, and often complains that nobody cares or understands what s/he is going through.

    If you failed in school, changed jobs every three months and had relationships that were like revolving doors, wouldn't you feel deeply depressed?

24. <u>Irregular Attendance at AA and Treatment Meetings</u>: The alcoholic stops attending AA regularly and begins to miss scheduled appointments for counseling or treatment. S/he finds excuses to justify this and doesn't recognize the importance of AA and treatment. S/he develops the attitude that "AA and counseling aren't making me feel better, so why should I make it a number one priority? Other things are more important."

    ADD adults are a slippery population. They can't be held to a schedule. We've tried to run ADD groups for ten years, and we just can't get people to attend regularly!

25. <u>Development of an "I Don't Care" Attitude</u>: The alcoholic tries to act as if s/he doesn't care about the problems that are occurring. This is to hide feelings of helplessness and a growing loss of self-respect and self-confidence.

26. Open Rejection of Help: The alcoholic cuts self off from people who can help. S/he does this by having fits of anger that drive other away, by criticizing and putting others down, or by quietly withdrawing from others.

27. Dissatisfaction with Life: Things seem so bad that the alcoholic begins to think that s/he might as well drink because things couldn't get worse. Life seems to have become unmanageable since drinking has stopped.

28. **Feelings of Powerlessness and Helplessness: The alcoholic develops difficulty in "getting started;" [sic] has trouble thinking clearly, concentrating, and thinking abstractly; and feels that s/he can't do anything and begins to believe that there is no way out.**

   If you were at the mercy of your biochemistry, would you feel empowered?

29. **Self-Pity: The alcoholic begins to feel sorry for self and often uses self-pity to get attention at AA or from family members.**

   Remember Eeyore in Winnie the Pooh? *The dark cloud stayed directly over him, even at his own birthday party!*

30. Thoughts of Social Drinking: The alcoholic realizes that drinking or using drugs would help him/her to feel better and begins to hope that she s/he [sic] can drink normally again and be able to control it. Sometimes these thoughts are so strong that they can't be stopped or put out of mind. There is a feeling that drinking is the only alternative to going crazy or committing suicide. Drinking actually looks like a sane and rational alternative.

31. **Conscious Lying: The alcoholic begins to recognize the lying and the denial and the excuses but is unable to interrupt them.**

   Who, me? Did I finish that last report? Of course I did. I left it in my briefcase in the car – I can't help it that my car was stolen so now I can't turn the report in. I'll need some extra time.

32. **Complete Loss of Self-Confidence: The alcoholic feels trapped and overwhelmed by the inability to think clearly and take action. This feeling of powerlessness causes the belief that s/he is useless and incompetent. As a result, there is the belief that life is unmanageable.**

So, I'm only eighty-two years old. Maybe next year I'll be able to stay in a relationship, finish painting my house, or have a plan that works. Maybe?

33. <u>Unreasonable Resentment</u>: The alcoholic feels angry because of the inability to behave the way s/he wants to. Sometimes the anger is with the world in general, sometimes with someone in particular, and sometimes with self.

    My biochemistry is messed up. Of course I'm resentful when somebody else is on time, organized, coherent and perfect. S/he really ticks me off.

34. <u>Discontinue All Treatment and AA</u>: The alcoholic stops attending all AA meetings. Those who are taking Antabuse forget to take it or deliberately avoid taking it regularly. When a helping person is part of treatment, tension and conflict develop and becomes so severe that the relationship usually ends. The alcoholic drops out of professional counseling even though s/he needs help and knows it.

    Yes, I found the answer. But wait! It's been a whole week of trying and my life still hasn't turned around. I'm outta here!

35. <u>Overwhelming Loneliness, Frustration, Anger, and Tension</u>: The alcoholic feels completely overwhelmed. S/he believes that there is no way out except drinking, suicide, or insanity. There are intense fears of insanity and feelings of helplessness and desperation.

    Ever feel like the "Ty-D-Bol®" man about to get flushed?

36. <u>Loss of Behavioral Control</u>: The alcoholic experiences more and more difficulty in controlling thoughts, emotions, judgments, and behaviors. This progressive and disabling loss of control begins to cause serious problems in all areas of life. It begins to affect health and well-being. No matter how hard s/he tries to regain control it is impossible to do so.

Recovery in the Nineties

As we look at recovery programs in the nineties, we need to be very clear that we are dealing with two completely different factions with very different philosophies within these programs. These two factions are made up of the "old-timers" and the professional administrators.

Old-Timers

The old-timers are people who have been in recovery and religiously attended AA or NA meetings for years. They are typically vocal and adamant about the danger of using any "mind-altering" or pain-reducing substances. Often the old-timers have been in recovery for twenty or thirty years. They feel a real sense of responsibility about the twelve-step program and what is right and wrong. Furthermore, they feel it is their duty to strongly warn a newcomer about the potential danger of using medication.

This sense of duty is certainly well-meaning, but it is hard to counteract because it tends to have a righteous overtone. It is as if the old-timers are the only ones with the straight scoop, the ones who really know recovery. They are often much better at giving advice than at being willing to listen to any new ideas on recovery. However the *A.A. member – Medications and other Drugs* [*sic*] pamphlet copyrighted in 1984 by the Alcoholics Anonymous World Services, Inc. states an important perspective on medication and AA members. This section is represented below (bold type ours):

However, some alcoholics require medication . . .

At the same time that we recognize this dangerous tendency to re-addiction, we also recognize that alcoholics are *not immune* to other diseases. Some of us have had to cope with depressions that can be suicidal; schizophrenia that sometimes requires hospitalization; manic depression [bipolar disorder]; and other mental and biological illnesses [*sic*]. Also among us are epileptics, members with heart trouble, cancer, allergies, hypertension, and many other serious physical conditions.

Because of the difficulties that many alcoholics have with drugs, some members have taken the position that no one in A.A. should take any medication. **While this position has undoubtedly prevented relapses for some, it has meant disaster for others.**

A.A. members and many of their physicians have described situations in which depressed patients have been told by A.A.s [*sic*] to throw away the pills, only to have depression return with all its difficulties, sometimes resulting in suicide. We have heard, too, from schizophrenics, manic depressives, epileptics, and others requiring medication that well-meaning A.A. friends often discourage them from taking prescribed medication. **Unfortunately, by following a layman's advice, the sufferers find that their conditions can return with all their previous intensity. On top of that, they feel guilty because they are convinced that "A.A. is against pills."**

It becomes clear that just as it is wrong to enable or support any alcoholic to become re-addicted to any drug, **it's equally wrong to deprive any alcoholic of medication which can alleviate or control other disabling physical and/or emotional problems.**

This medication vs. no medication controversy puts an ADD adult who is in a twelve-step recovery program into a dilemma. The AA or NA program puts forth the belief that the person is in the grip of a disease and needs to surrender in order to remain clean and sober. The twelve-step program sets forth a prescribed system that he must move through in sequence. This format places an ADD adult in a mind-set of compliance. He is told that he must follow the program or a relapse is almost certain.

What is the dilemma? The ADD adult is being told on the one hand that he has a biochemical imbalance that was instrumental in causing the addiction. Furthermore, the ADD condition often needs to be medicated so that he will experience a more normal biochemical balance. On the other hand, he is being told that he must be compliant and not question the AA or NA perspective about substance use. He is caught in the middle of two opposing camps – at least it feels that way.

The Other Camp – Administrators

Professionals who are administering recovery programs and who are trained in alcohol and substance abuse recovery typically seem to be very much aware of the ADD adult and the part that correcting a biochemical imbalance plays in recovery. With education and training, they are more open-minded and see the understanding and treatment of biochemistry as the wave of the future in successful recovery programs. They are willing to combine the traditional AA or NA programs *with* medication in order to meet the needs of ADD adults.

This enlightened view has certainly not yet permeated traditional AA and NA meetings. How long will it take before they understand that cooperation between the medical and spiritual communities creates the strongest potential for successful recovery? How long before this filters down to the level of local AA and NA meetings? Hopefully not too long, for the sake of the ADD adult caught in the middle.

The ADD Adult in Recovery

There are two different ADD populations who find themselves in recovery programs – the undiagnosed ADD adult and the diagnosed ADD adult. Are these populations different? Yes, they are, and the difference is their understanding of the role of their biochemistry in their addiction.

The Undiagnosed ADD Adult in Recovery

Let's track the path of an undiagnosed ADD adult who eventually becomes addicted to alcohol and enters a recovery program.

Fred began using marijuana and drinking when he was twelve. He was always an active kid, and when he became an adolescent, sitting in a classroom for longer than twenty minutes made him feel as though he was going to jump out of his skin. He found that smoking a joint before school relaxed him just enough so that he could sit in class. He didn't learn much, but he attended class and didn't spend his days in the principal's office.

His parents didn't know that he was drinking or using; he was great at covering it up. At night, he had always had trouble going to sleep. In elementary school, his folks had insisted that he be in bed at 8:30 p.m. He spent what felt like hours each night staring at the ceiling and hating every minute of it. In high school he began drinking at night – just a beer or two – so he could fall asleep.

Fred graduated from high school and was hired as a salesman in a computer store. This was a fast-paced environment, and Fred was constantly on the go. Fred found that after eight hours at work, he was wound up tighter than a drum. He tried to relax when he got home, but it was impossible. He continued using marijuana for about four months but got scared when two of his friends were tagged by police due to their marijuana use. Instead of marijuana, he began drinking two or three beers to help him relax once he got home. He still had trouble falling asleep, so he increased his nightly beers to four, then to five, and finally to a six-pack. Soon he was drinking at lunch and during his days off. Finally, Fred developed full-blown alcoholism.

Fred's alcohol use eventually caused him to be fired from his job. He returned home to live with his parents, and they eventually confronted him about his pattern of substance use. Fred was a good person. He genuinely wanted to work and do well. He was willing to listen to his parents and signed up for an outpatient rehabilitation program. Fred was able to stop using alcohol. He religiously attended his AA meetings four or five times a week, and he worked his program. In short, he followed the recommendations to the letter.

Things still weren't right. He was jittery. He was short-tempered. He began feeling depressed. Soon he was fired from his job for inconsistent performance. He talked to his sponsor in AA and was advised to attend even more meetings each week, which he did, but his life didn't get better. When he talked to his sponsor again about still feeling the same way, he was told he wasn't working the program seriously enough. He was warned that he was on the verge of relapse and that he should seek some counseling. Fred had really tried. What was wrong with him? He began to feel shame and guilt that he wasn't doing better – after all, it must be his fault!

In desperation, Fred sought help from his sponsor once again. His sponsor pulled out Gorsky's thirty-seven signs of relapse and went through the list with Fred. To Fred's horror, he fit about twenty-eight of the categories. He now knew he was doomed and heading right toward relapse. He had done his best, but it wasn't enough. Ultimately, he gave up and began drinking again.

What is the moral of our story? *The ADD adult who has never been diagnosed or treated for ADD will continue to experience the ADD symptoms, even in recovery. The problem is that he will attribute them solely to the substance abuse.* To make matters worse, these symptoms often become even more pronounced when the person is clean and sober and the ADD is experienced in its unmedicated, unadulterated form. The ADD person becomes excruciatingly aware of his ADD patterns.

What's the answer? In recovery programs, the biochemical imbalance of the ADD adult must be considered, evaluated and dealt with as part of the recovery process.

The Diagnosed ADD Adult in Recovery

The path of any ADD adult as he moves into addiction is similar to Fred's path. Typically, a substance is used in order to correct or to get away from a problem in life, such as not being able to sleep, feeling depressed, not being able to sit still, etc. Soon, the ADD adult finds that he is addicted to the substance and dependent upon it to alter his physical state or moods.

Whether diagnosed or undiagnosed, participating in recovery programs and attending AA or NA meetings is a viable path for the ADD adult. The camaraderie, the structure of the program and regular meetings offer a framework that is often helpful; however, the ADD adult must join the recovery program with a full understanding of how his body chemistry makes him different from the non-ADD or typical AA or NA population. The ADD adult must make the crucial decision whether medication will be used to normalize his unique body chemistry in the face of opposition from hard-line "old-timers."

Medication in Recovery

If the adult feels that the impact of ADD on her life requires medication to correct the condition, she needs sufficient education and support. She will need to combat some of the resistance she will most likely encounter in a recovery program or in a group home. As recovery programs are staffed by professionals, the physician responsible for the program is often aware of ADD and understands that medication may be a necessary intervention. It has been our experience that recovery programs don't present any special problems for our population.

Group homes or halfway houses are a somewhat different situation. Although administrators who own the group homes are licensed individuals, the houses themselves are usually overseen by an ex-addict or a recovering alcoholic who functions as a houseparent. Thus there is quite a variation in response from each group home. We have recently run into homes where an ADD adult is not allowed to remain if he is taking any medication to treat his ADD symptoms. There are other homes that take a softer approach and will "allow" medication, but only in small quantities and with great reluctance.

In most homes the houseparent keeps the medication and the resident must ask for it on a regular basis. There is certainly nothing wrong with this approach. Unfortunately, the houseparent too often makes the resident feel that, even though the medication has been prescribed by a physician, it isn't really necessary or that he is doing something wrong by taking it. Add to this a strict code of behavior present in most group homes, along with a good deal of peer confrontation, and you set up a sensitive situation which places an additional burden on ADD adults in recovery. Fortunately, there are a few group homes with an enlightened administration and houseparents who work well with ADD adults, including administrating medication.

Either in a recovery program or in a group home, adults in recovery are almost always required to attend AA or NA on a regular (typically a daily) basis. They will need to develop coping strategies to combat the resistance they will undoubtedly encounter in AA or NA meetings. They need not only an understanding of ADD, but also additional insight on how to deal with the AA or NA philosophy and tools on how to maintain their participation in AA or NA in spite of resistance they may encounter. They need techniques on how and when to inform their peer groups in AA or NA about the biochemical component of ADD, and their decision to use medication or keep silent. Will they share what they know about adult ADD and possibly provide information to others in the same situation? Will they keep the information to themselves, take the necessary medication and not raise the medication issue in their group? Again, this is a very personal decision.

After hearing stories from clients in our office, we find that there are basically three positions that are taken. The first position is that of maintaining a low profile by not discussing the fact that medication is being used. The problem with this is that it runs counter to the AA philosophy of honesty. This places the adult in the double bind of how to be honest in recovery, yet make a medication choice that improves the quality of life. The second position we see is that of an adult who decides to talk about the decision to use medication with her sponsor but chooses not to share it with the group. The third position is that of an adult who decides to talk about his decision to use medication with the sponsor as well as openly sharing in group meetings. All three positions are difficult.

The first position requires that an individual must have the strength of conviction to remain apart from the group in this one area. The second and third positions are tricky because they invite feedback from people who may view the use of any medications as a sign that the person is in denial or on the verge of relapse. The use of the word "denial" immediately engages the adult and the sponsor or group members in a circular argument. "You are in denial." "I'm not in denial." "See? You are in denial." And, that's how it goes. The more the adult tries to defend or convince others he is not in denial, the worse the situation becomes.

The ADD adult needs to have enough education about ADD, as well as a sufficient support group, that he is well-informed and well-armed and can withstand the pressure of others who may have no respect for his position. The ADD adult's position should encompass the knowledge that medication is right for him.

Without Medication

If the ADD adult decides that medication is not necessary or not an option in her recovery, then she must be absolutely clear how the ADD impacts her life. Just being in recovery alone won't change her ADD patterns. She needs to be aware that, for her, difficulty with concentration, depression, etc., is not a sign of relapse or a dry drunk, but a manifestation of her ADD condition. She needs to be able to separate her own personal ADD profile from the non-ADD person's signs of relapse.

Does Medication Cause a Return to Addiction? What is the Truth?

It is true that addictions are dangerous and can be life-threatening. It is also true that the ADD adult is more prone to addictions due to the biochemical imbalance of his condition. The body of published research on this issue is limited, perhaps because of the many factors that need to be taken into account. These factors include the emotional component of addiction (such as self-destructive tendencies), the severity of addiction as it relates to individual body chemistry, and the role of medication in treatment.

It is currently true that recovery programs vary in their understanding that a biochemical imbalance must be considered in the process of successful recovery. It is true that the ADD adult in a recovery program must make a personal decision whether to use medication or not. If the choice of the adult is that medication is not needed, the ADD adult must be very clear in his own mind how the ADD symptoms appear in his life. He must be able to separate ADD symptoms from symptoms of relapse. If the ADD adult chooses to use medication, he must be clear that everyone in his AA or NA support group may not understand his use of medication to treat the symptoms of adult ADD.

It is true that it is possible to successfully bridge the chasm of being an ADD adult in a recovery program. With information and education, the ADD adult is empowered to decide for himself how he can best deal with recovery. We look forward to exciting future developments as the research questions noted above begin to be translated into successful outcomes for the ADD adult battling addictions.

Chapter 10

The ADD and Crime Connection

How often do ADD adults find themselves in jail? Too often, according to some rather alarming statistics that are beginning to come out of our prisons.

If adult ADD represents nine to eleven percent of the population, as stated by Drs. Sallee and Leventhal at the 1996 U.S. Psychiatric and Mental Health Congress, it seems that ADD adults in jail should reflect that same percentage. Prison research regarding the ADD population is still an extremely new field; however, research studies are beginning to emerge that conservatively estimate that about one-quarter of the men in prison are ADD adults. The proportion of ADD men in any given prison population increases as the number of violent crimes increase.

We know that many of the ADD population have accompanying difficulties ,such as addictions or depression. There is a particular prison in California that houses men who have been identified as Axis I offenders (the designation "Axis I" refers to a code indicating some mental problem as defined in the *Diagnostic and Statistical Manual*, which is used by psychiatrists and psychologists when they classify different mental disorders). In this particular prison, the prison psychiatrist became very interested in the new research on the adult ADD population. He did a study of his prison population, and, to his amazement (and the amazement of everyone else), his population was made up of seventy-five percent ADD adults.

Another factor that must be considered in the ADD prison population is the incidence of Tourette Syndrome (TS), which we talked about in Chapter 3. Remember, in its most severe form, adults with TS manifest obvious behaviors such as motor or vocal tics, which may appear as a convulsive jerking or twitching; they may swear or spit uncontrollably, or they may erupt into violent rages with little provocation at all. Even though these symptoms are obvious, TS is probably the diagnosis that is most often missed. This is truly unfortunate, because their swearing or violent outbursts are seen as antisocial behavior, rather than as a manifestation of a biochemical condition beyond their control.

To make the diagnosis of TS even more difficult, it can appear with symptoms that are less blatant, but still problematic. Again, some individuals with TS may be fascinated with fire or knives. It is easy to see why a proportion of these individuals also end up in prison.

TS can also appear in a much milder form, where motor or vocal tics are almost imperceptible. While overt physical symptoms may not be present, the swings of rage and violence may still occur. In adults with mild TS, a diagnosis of TS is rarely ever made, and many of these individuals are condemned to life in prison. Even if they serve time and are released, if untreated, their symptoms will reoccur and they will be back in prison once again.

Why Do We Find a Disproportionately High Number of ADD Adults in Prison?

To begin to explain this, we'd like you to meet three men. These three men are all in jail or prison. These men are all ADD adults – a common thread in their lives. In each case, a variation of the ADD condition was responsible for their running afoul of the law. However, their stories and the reasons why each one ended up in jail are very, very different.

Tom

Tom is a real charmer. He is intelligent, good-looking and a smooth talker. He lives on thrills – if it isn't fast cars, it's women. Tom never did well in high school – not for lack of intellect, but because the classes were boring. He found it hard to sit in class, and he blew off his studies. Finally, school got to be too much work, and he became truant more and more.

To support his need for thrills and excitement, Tom began dealing drugs. Drugs gave him fast, easy money. He knew that anyone who dealt drugs and used them was a fool. Tom was no fool. He was a dealer, not a user. Tom also got a rush from fighting and danger. If there was a fight in town, Tom was typically in the middle of it, so police started watching him. Tom began to get even more of a rush from baiting the police. He knew the law and knew just how far they could go. He swore and cussed at the police and dared them to touch him. The police got fed up and began an all-out campaign to arrest him for dealing.

After two years, they were successful. Tom was arrested and sent to jail on a felony charge. Once he had served his time he was released, but his ego didn't let him take parole seriously. He ran around with the same friends. He delayed doing community service, and he lost one job after another. The police continued to watch and harass him at every chance. He continued to be rude and obnoxious when he was stopped by the police. He continued to look for thrills and excitement.

Tom had another characteristic often found in ADD adults – he was egocentric (focused on himself) and tended to think of himself not only as a leader, but as a champion of those who were younger or weaker. As the champion, he would often join fights as a follower's protector and felt it was his duty to do so. One night he was out with his friends and a scuffle erupted. Unbeknownst to him, a young (fifteen-year-old) follower had a knife and stabbed his assailant. Tom's impulsivity was high. Without a second thought, he rushed into the fight, kicked the assailant, threw his friend in the car and drove away.

Once in the car, speeding away from the scene, his young follower said, "I have a knife, and I think I stabbed him." Tom was in it too deep to turn around and wait for the police. His follower threw the knife out of the car window. The police were waiting at Tom's house. He was charged with a felony assault and ultimately convicted of that charge – not because he used the knife himself, but because he kicked the assailant, was involved in the incident and then fled the scene.

Tom had actually been diagnosed with ADD in high school. Like many ADD adolescents, he flatly refused to take any medication. He also refused to take the ADD diagnosis and its implications seriously. He was "just fine" and in perfect control of his life. After being released from jail on his first felony charge, he still refused to take medication; however, after the second felony conviction he began to recognize that he was impulsive and did tend to make bad choices. He also realized that he often jumped into dangerous situations to help a young friend without even thinking of the implications for himself, such as a possible parole violation.

What are the odds that this pattern will continue? For Tom, the prognosis is good. He has been encouraged by his parents, who have provided strong emotional support, hired skilled attorneys and continued to stress the importance of medication and counseling in Tom's life. Tom's safety net is still intact. He was supported until life experiences and maturity combined and allowed him to grasp a much clearer picture of his own brand of ADD, the havoc it had caused in his life and the steps he needed to take toward responsibility for his actions.

Jake

Jake is currently up on his third felony charge and is in danger of spending his life in jail due to the "Three Strikes" law. Jake had a terrible time in school. He had severe learning disabilities, and in fact, spent his entire time in school in a Special Day Class (this kind of class is reserved for students who are having major trouble learning). When he graduated from high school he was reading at a third grade level, his math was at a fourth grade level, and his spelling was at about a second grade level.

Over and above the low academic levels, Jake had a difficult time processing information. Even though his IQ was average, he had no common sense. He couldn't see that his actions had consequences. He cut school and wrote himself excuse notes. He printed the note and misspelled several words, so the attendance office spotted the note as a fake quite easily. He served detention. Did he learn from this experience? No. He wrote himself notes on several other occasions as well, even though each time he was caught.

He never really understood jokes told by his classmates. He was easily led by a bigger boy in his class and was often put up to things such as minor shoplifting or stealing pencils from the teacher's desk.

The school had talked to his parents about Jake being ADD when he was in fourth grade. His parents were frightened by the thought of medication, however, and decided not to pursue the issue of ADD any further.

After Jake graduated from high school, he couldn't keep a job. His parents became more and more worried about him, but they had less and less control. He fell in love and often stayed with his new girlfriend. He was visiting a neighbor whom he had known all of his life and found himself alone in the house. He loved his girlfriend very much, so he decided to take a pair of earrings and give them to her. The neighbors filed a police report, and his attorney recommended that he plead guilty – this is how he got his first felony conviction. After he was released from jail, his parents, having read more about adult ADD, arranged for an evaluation. Jake was still resistant to medication, and at this age his parents had even less control over his behavior.

His parents urged him to get a job, and he finally found work in a used car lot. He needed a car, so he forged his mother's name on a check and bought himself one. He wasn't caught right away. He forged a second check and bought one of his friends a car. Finally he was caught and charged with his second felony. After being released from jail a second time, his parents were more and more aware that he wasn't functional or able to support himself by holding down a job. He lived at home, unless he was spending a night or two with his girlfriend.

His parents rented a storage unit for him so he would have somewhere to go and putter. They felt that would give him something to do, and it would also get him away from the house so they could have some peace occasionally. Soon he broke into a neighbor's storage unit and took four boxes that contained small items of little or no value. He gave two or three items to his girlfriend but didn't even open two of the boxes. He had taken them out of sheer impulsivity. Once again the police were called. This time he was charged with his third felony. He now faces the possibility of life in prison due to the "Three Strikes" law.

The combination of a young adult with Attention Deficit Disorder and learning disabilities is a deadly one. Not only do adults experience the typical ADD characteristics of impulsivity, temper and mood swings, but they have difficulty understanding the consequences of the actions of their lives. Thus they often repeat the same type of offense over and over again. The following letter was received from Jake in jail and has been reproduced as it was received:

> Dear   ,
> Will Hello There Young Lady. How you doing? Hope everything is will will you for one It Could Be better. I guess well I Just Wanted to Say Thank You for Comming to Court for Me that was Very nice. Will I will make Sure I Get the Help I need and I will Keep on Getting the Help So I can Be a Better Person Will I have until Oct 95 until I get Release from Jail I will see you soon. Do you Know what kind of Medcation I wil be Taken Will Thank You Again.
>
> >   Love, Jake

What is the prognosis for Jake? It's hard to believe, but the prognosis is actually good. Jake is extremely fortunate because he, too, has a supportive family that has continued to provide a safety net for him. Finally, the experiences with the police and jail have gotten his attention. Jake is saying that he is ready to listen to his parents. He is willing to give the medication a try and is willing to receive some help. To make all of this work, the individual pieces of the safety net must be strengthened and put in place as he comes out of jail. This means some vocational training, a job, structure and regular counseling until he is more stable in life.

Barry

Finally, let's meet Barry. Barry really did okay in school. He managed to make C's in his classes and was never in any learning disability classes. Barry had twitches, or tics. These tics were beyond his control. His eye would blink, and half of his face would contort. His arm would often move in a circle. He would hum incessantly without knowing he was doing it. These movements were all beyond his control. Kids thought Barry was strange and would tease him. In elementary school they would follow him home, calling him names. Barry also had a bad temper. When his classmates teased him at recess he would explode and often be in a full-blown rage. In elementary school his mother was often called to the school to calm him down.

Barry had Tourette Syndrome; however, the fact that he had a medical condition was never diagnosed. As we said before, TS is a condition found in a percentage of the ADD population. Children, adolescents and adults with TS experience all of the ADD symptoms, but in a more violent form. In a way, Tourette Syndrome can be thought of as ADD with tics. According to Comings, et al. and Tourette Syndrome Association literature, up to sixty-five percent or more of people with TS also have ADD, and the ADD diagnosis may precede the diagnosis of TS by an average of two-and-a-half years.

An ADD person can become angry, but a person with TS can become enraged, out of control and likely to hurt someone. When Barry entered adolescence, his symptoms became more pronounced; his temper was wild and instantaneous. He seemed unable to control his violent reactions. His parents took him to several counselors, but nothing seemed to help. Finally, they admitted that they just didn't know what to do with him.

In high school he was frequently teased by his classmates, so he finally exploded and hurt a classmate one day in his English class. He was expelled from school. He enrolled in another high school, but was soon expelled for the same reason. His parents thought he was doing it on purpose – after all, they had *tried* counselors. The school was telling them it was their son's fault (or possibly their fault due to poor parenting). His parents were fed up. They agreed that he must be getting in trouble intentionally and asked him to move out.

By fifteen or sixteen, he had begun living under the Hermosa Beach pier (in California). He was able to steal small items from a nearby junkyard and make enough money selling them to buy food. He learned which restaurants would give him a free handout. Barry couldn't understand what was happening to him. He knew he wasn't really a bad person. On the other hand, he couldn't seem to stop himself from exploding. He decided to try school again but was subjected to more teasing. This time he seriously hurt a classmate and was put in jail for assault.

What is the prognosis for Barry? Unfortunately, it is not good. The fact is that Barry had a medical problem had been overlooked by the professionals in his life. The schools never identified the presence of TS. The counselors who his parents approached for help never identified the TS condition. Barry was identified as an adolescent with a terrible temper and was labeled a danger to others. Due to the nature of TS, this type of behavior will continue unless the condition is diagnosed and treated. If Barry's TS is diagnosed and he is placed on medication, does the prognosis change? You bet! At times the correct medication for a Tourette Syndrome adolescent or adult produces an almost miraculous change in his ability to control his behavior and live within the context of society. Unfortunately, the medications often stop working after a while, and the trial-and-error quest for the "right" medication begins yet again.

Are ADD Adults at Risk?

The biochemical imbalance caused by ADD tends to cause difficulty in certain areas. Several of these areas can lead to behaviors which result in law-breaking activity and ultimately result in jail time.

Impulsivity

Many ADD researchers feel that impulsivity is the very cornerstone of most ADD adults' behavior. Because of the biochemical imbalance, when an impulse hits, the section of the brain that normally allows an adult to *control* the impulsivity does not function, so the ADD adult simply acts on that impulse.

This can range from impulsively shoplifting – even when the adult has money and credit cards in his or her purse or wallet – to stealing money from a cash register on the job. Impulsivity can spill over into acts which harm others, such as shoving, hitting or pushing when anger flares. Impulsivity can include things such as grabbing a handy gun to rob the corner liquor store, or killing someone with no immediate thought of the consequences.

Temper

Many ADD adults have tempers with extremely short fuses. These adults are quick to blow up with the slightest provocation. Drivers changing lanes in front of them on the freeway may be enough to cause them to chase down the offending cars and drivers. People accidentally pushing or shoving past them in crowded stores might be enough to bring forth swearing or a push or shove back in retaliation.

ADD adults often have not only a short fuse but a violent and explosive temper once it is triggered. These ADD adults don't just get mildly angry or even just mad – they become furious. Their rage starts at their center and explodes outward. They describe the sensation as white hot rage or "seeing red." In the middle of this rage they are incapable of thinking rationally; they just react.

Low Self-Esteem

Many ADD adults have had a terribly hard time in life. Often they had problems with reading or math through all their years in school. Classmates teased them unmercifully, and they felt as if they were on the outside looking in for most of their younger years. As adults they still carry many of these scars. They simply don't feel good about themselves. When we don't feel good about ourselves, we have much less resilience and are much more easily moved to anger. Our tolerance level for the stressful things in life is much lower, and we don't know what to do about it.

Living for Thrills

Some ADD adults report a building of tension or agitation that can only be released when they experience danger. As teenagers they have driven their cars down winding roads at full speed. At the bottom of the hill the adrenaline surge produced from the fear of the event caused a period of calm. As we discussed in Chapter 8, some ADD adults require this sort of dangerous activity as often as monthly for the less severe, to hourly for the more severe. Some require this feeling once a week. For some ADD adults, nothing beats the thrill of holding a gun and rushing into a liquor store. Their body chemistries dictate how often they may need to do this to be satisfied. They are being driven by their bodies' craving for danger, and they are calmed by the feeling of release it provides.

Survival Mode

If an ADD adult didn't do well in school, even the thought of a trade school or, heaven forbid, college, is beyond consideration. If the ADD adult has a lot of impulsivity or difficulty with people, he may not be able to keep a job. For many ADD adults with the need for instant gratification, the idea of a minimum wage job, with its constraints of a forty-hour rigid schedule and the resulting boredom, is impossible. Even if the job has potential for the future, the idea of starting at the very bottom of the ladder and working up in the company year after year has little appeal; thus there is a conflict.

The need for immediate gratification battles with the need to have a roof over their heads, food on their tables, and clothes on their backs. Some look for an easy way out – they may begin to deal drugs or to steal. Both avenues provide fast and easy money. It makes them feel important to have five hundred dollars in their pockets. Once they begin getting their money in this way and they experience how having lots and lots of money feels, it is hard for them to change.

Learning Disabilities

The words "learning disability" often bring to mind a child or adolescent in school who has trouble reading, spelling or doing math. Adolescents who have severe learning disabilities still have severe learning disabilities as adults. They will still have problems reading, spelling or doing math. This often makes them settle for minimum wage jobs. It also makes them feel stupid and generally terrible about themselves. This is bad enough in itself, but we need to broaden the concept of a learning disability in order to understand just how devastating it can be to an ADD person's ability to cope with life. The following three categories apply specifically to ADD adults with learning disabilities.

Processing Problems – An ADD adult with learning disabilities often doesn't understand things that go on around her to the extent you would expect, or to the extent that the rest of the population expects. She may have trouble understanding something verbally told to her by another person. On the job, she may not understand directions or instructions the first, second or even the third time they are given by the boss. If she is told to check the storage room and stock the shelves, she may not understand exactly how to do a task that would seem simple to most adults. Since it seems such a simple request to the boss, the request is not broken down into step one, step two, etc. Ultimately, the boss may feel that the ADD adult has "blown off" his request.

She may have trouble reading directions from an employee manual. Even if she can read the words, she may have trouble understanding the instructions. Something that often causes as much or more difficulty is the ADD adult's difficulty in understanding or processing social situations at work. A co-worker may make a comment that is not meant to be offensive, only to have the comment totally misunderstood by the ADD adult. Another co-worker may tell a joke. The ADD adult may miss the point of the joke and become offended.

Cause and Effect Reasoning – Some learning disabled ADD adults simply don't understand that a particular action will inevitably lead to a certain consequence. They can't project ahead in their minds and see the consequences coming. Even worse, they must often have the consequence repeated two or three times before they finally realize deep within themselves that, "Yes, by gosh, I will get in trouble if I do this again." For example, most adults – even ADD adults – understand that if you shoplift, get caught and go to jail, this same sequence will occur again if you shoplift again. The ADD adult with severe learning disabilities often misses this fact. He just doesn't get it. He will repeat the same offense over and over and be truly surprised when he once again finds himself in jail.

He may have trouble interacting with salespeople in a store when he is trying to return merchandise. Often he doesn't understand the system and becomes angry. Our world is made up of one system after another. We must understand how to maneuver within these systems. If we choose not to move within the systems, we must understand the consequences of our decisions. The learning disabled ADD adult does not understand this principle.

Applying One Situation to Another – ADD adults with severe learning disabilities do not have the ability to hold on to a set of information over time. For example, if they shoplift in Southern California in 1995, they don't feel it is the same thing if they shoplift in Northern California in 1996. They have difficulty with abstract thinking. If two events are not identical, they have trouble seeing that there is any similarity at all. If they shoplift and take a cassette recorder, they feel that this is different than "borrowing" a neighbor's bike and riding it away. They are very concrete and literal in their understanding. Too often, we assume that they get the connection. Too often, they don't.

Special Considerations

Are More Men Than Women at Risk?
Although no formal studies have been done on ADD female versus male jail populations, it appears that ADD males are more at risk. It may be because the male hormone testosterone plays a part in this scenario. With excess testosterone comes aggression and anger. Although both males and females carry testosterone, it tends to be found in much higher quantities in the male. However, there are certainly some ADD women who do have strong components of anger and rage, as well as a high degree of impulsivity and a pressing need for danger. Thus far, sufficient studies have not been done in this area and more research is certainly neces-

sary. *Because of the seeming preponderance of ADD males versus females in the prison population, the ADD person will be referred to with the male gender designation in this chapter.*

A Special Word About ADD Adolescence

Our legal system designates eighteen as the age of adulthood. After that time any offender is tried in the adult justice system. In fact, in certain crimes, younger offenders may be tried in the adult justice system if their crimes are sufficiently severe, such as in the case of murder.

The ADD adolescent is particularly at risk in our present justice system. Why? The ADD adolescent typically experiences a developmental delay of somewhere between two and three years. That means an ADD adolescent may have a chronological age of eighteen, but emotionally and developmentally be only fifteen or sixteen. If there is a severe learning disability, the gap may be even wider. Often these youngsters, at eighteen, think and operate more as if they were thirteen or fourteen. They don't have the maturity or reasoning power of an adult, due to the biochemical problems caused by ADD.

Because of the release of hormones in the adolescent period, the symptoms of the ADD condition usually are at their peak during the years of puberty. The hormones don't settle down until the ADD male is about twenty-two or twenty-three, so during the years between eighteen and twenty-three, he is still battling his hormones, which make the ADD condition even more rampant. This is certainly the time when the potential for trouble is highest.

Should ADD Adolescents and Adults Get Special Treatment?

Before answering that question, let's look at the bigger picture that is facing society. We are truly in trouble. We are building more and more prisons, and they are quickly becoming overcrowded. Violence and violent crimes are increasing across the country. The current system has not been able to stem the flow of violence. The bigger question is, what can be done to stabilize society and reduce the number of violent crimes?

No one is suggesting that an ADD adolescent or adult should do anything that is against the law. No one is suggesting that an ADD adolescent or adult shouldn't be brought to trial or put in prison for his actions. Time in jail, however, is only a small part of the entire puzzle that faces us. Let's look at what happens to our adult before, during and after prison. Then let's talk about what can be done.

What is the Prognosis for an ADD Adult in Jail?

The prognosis is poor. The ADD adult has trouble due to the biochemical imbalance in his system; added to that, there may be a learning disability. A problem with impulsivity or rage further complicates the picture. With this population, just placing them in jail does nothing to correct the reason that they are in trouble in the first place. For the ADD adult, jail is merely a holding pattern. Once the ADD adult is released, the very same areas of dysfunction are still present. Often he has even more difficulty than the normal population getting and keeping a job, so it is much more difficult for him to pay off court costs and fines.

He probably doesn't make friends easily, so he tends to revert to his old circle of friends, who have also often done jail time. Even though violence in America is listed as the number one concern of the government at this time, in actuality prison rehabilitation programs have not yet begun to address the ADD population.

In order to make changes, we must have a clear understanding of the situation for the ADD adult in prison at this moment in time. What has happened to our ADD adults before they were sentenced, during the time they are in prison, and after they are released? Where can changes be made? What is the most effective way to approach this problem?

Before Prison

What Is – Although we are talking about ADD adults, the path to prison begins in adolescence. Thus our story must begin there.

Currently a great many ADD adults have never identified as having ADD in childhood or in adolescence. If Tourette Syndrome is present, this condition is even less likely to be diagnosed. Even if by some chance ADD was diagnosed in childhood, too often the medication is discontinued at the onset of adolescence. This leaves the ADD adolescent unmedicated during the same time that hormones are raging through his body and accelerating the effects of the ADD symptoms.

In high school, behavior problems are typically dealt with in a disciplinary mode. In fact, if an ADD adolescent in junior high or high school once enters the disciplinary track at a given school, he is almost never evaluated for ADD or learning difficulties. Unfortunately, school officials and even licensed counselors do not understand the broad range of behaviors that are associated with ADD. Beyond that, they do not understand how to properly manage treatment using a blend of medication and specific counseling techniques.

We are in the midst of a change in society that is adding to the problem. Our society is moving away from a sense of individual responsibility for our actions and the idea of consequences for our behaviors. In the past we had a system of checks and balances which is no longer present today. If a teenager damaged property or ran away from home he could be placed in juvenile hall for a night or two. This often acted as a deterrent, since he soon got a sense that society did have rules that could be enforced. If the teenager acted up in school, disciplinary measures were evoked and, most importantly, enforced. It seems more and more that individuals have the right to do whatever they please and neither school, parents nor police have the ability, or even the right, to stop them and say "No, this is not appropriate behavior."

Without realizing the damage they are doing, parents themselves often make matters much worse. Often they will step in and protect the offending adolescent rather than allowing the natural consequences to occur. This makes the situation swing to the other side of the pendulum, and the adolescent gets the idea that whatever he did was really okay. Beyond that he begins to feel that he is being unfairly harassed by the authorities, including parents, school personnel and police. This sets up a pattern of disregard for the rules in society that make the path to prison inevitable. ADD adolescents began to get the feeling that, with enough money, they are able to manipulate the system or are simply above the law.

To compound matters, ADD is usually genetic. If you have an ADD adolescent, you often have an ADD adult with the same patterns of temper and volatility. The school, as well as the police, view these parents as uncooperative and hostile rather than understanding their actions as ADD symptoms. Parents and police often find themselves at war rather than trying to work together to find a common solution.

What Should Be – Obviously, early identification and treatment of every ADD youngster is imperative. A great deal of education and training is necessary for school personnel and professional counselors who work with children and adolescents. Treatment should always carefully consider the appropriateness of medication, counseling and academic remediation.

ADD families need help and are often chaotic. You can never treat an ADD adolescent without taking into consideration the ADD parents. ADD parents need education and support as they, too, are being required to make significant changes in their methods of operating.

In Prison

What Is – Attorneys are seldom aware of the ADD condition. They don't understand how a diagnosis of ADD might be used in their clients' defenses. Judges seem to be more aware but certainly don't want to excuse criminal behavior just because there is an ADD diagnosis. Once the judge pronounces the sentence, the ADD adult is whisked away by the bailiff. Once he enters the closed system of jail or prison, he is, for all intents and purposes, beyond the reach of anyone on the outside. Even if a perceptive judge is aware of ADD and orders that medication be prescribed while the adult is in jail, too often the orders regarding medication are lost or ignored.

What Should Be – Just think for a minute – what if all adults who were convicted received a routine ADD screening? What if a positive diagnosis of ADD from the simple screening resulted in a more thorough evaluation? What if a diagnosed ADD adult could be started on medication while in jail and monitored closely? Just think – once he was released, he would have his body chemistry stabilized on medication.

Is that enough? No, not by a long shot. Prisoners would need education and coping techniques. They would need information about how ADD impacted their lives, and coping techniques to modify some of the symptoms. Many need academic remediation, as they are seriously deficient in reading, math or writing. One of our local therapists works in the county jail and has begun a group for ADD adults who are doing jail time. These men come together as a group to learn about ADD and, equally as important, to share their stories and learn from each other, preventing the feeling of being alone with their symptoms. This program is an unqualified success.

Upon Release

What Is – Do most of us know what faces a prisoner who is released? No. If he is lucky, he can go home to his family and have a place to stay and food to eat while he looks for work. If he is not lucky, he may be out on the streets. He must check in regularly with his parole officer. He must pay the state or federal government money, sometimes huge sums, in retribution. To make money, the assumption is that he needs a job. Will most employers hire a felon? What do you think? How does this prisoner get a job? At best, he is looking for a minimum wage job. Often he is fired when an employer checks his past history and finds that he has a felony behind his name.

If the released prisoner has a learning disability or severe ADD, he is under a significant handicap. However, there are no county, state or federal services available to help this prisoner. He is not considered to have a condition that is sufficiently severe to qualify him for support, such as SSI. Vocational Rehabilitation Services were, at one time, a possibility for help. However, registration and testing to qualify often took six to nine months, and that process must have been completed before any job training could begin. Recently Vocational Rehabilitation Services have been cut back along with other services, so this avenue has been drastically curtailed.

An ADD adult has often had such a terrible time during his school years that he is too frightened to even consider returning to a community college for job training. He has no information about learning disability programs or any possible help that might be available. Even if training is a possibility, the reality is different. How can he take the time to train for a better job if he is working forty hours a week at a minimum wage job? If there is no hope, it is easy to return to crime. If the ADD condition is untreated, he is still dealing with the same impulse problems and the same problems with anger that caused him to be in jail in the first place.

As a nation we are worried about the increase of violent crimes and the recidivism of prisoners. The key word to understand is *recidivism*. Recidivism means that someone returns to the same place as before. In short, he relapses to the old behavior, which returns him to jail. Our recidivism rate as a nation is high. Much of our concern with violent crimes and our crowded prisons would be solved if we could dramatically reduce the recidivism of prisoners.

What Should Be – If we don't want ADD adults to return to jail, we need rehabilitation programs that first will evaluate and diagnose ADD and then treat it.

Rehabilitation Programs That Work

Rehabilitation programs must be developed that will address a multitude of areas:

1. **Diagnosis**: A thoroughly trained team of professionals should be involved in the diagnosis of ADD/Tourette Syndrome.

2. **Treatment**: The treatment of each person's ADD needs to be individually determined by the team making the diagnosis. Various aspects of treatment may include:

   a) *Medication:* Not only must the appropriate medication be found for each individual's system, but medication must be made available. Too often, the best medication is prohibitively expensive. Medication must also be monitored and controlled over time.

b) *Job Skills:* Once on medication, the impulsivity or temper problems that prohibited ADD adults from acquiring job skills are hopefully under control. They are facing a new lease on life. However, most of our high schools long ago abandoned their vocational training programs. Long gone are most of the auto shops or woodworking classes. If an adolescent has had accompanying learning disabilities, the government has attempted to insure that some job skills are in place. Under California Education Code 56460-63, IEPs must address this issue (contact your state's Department of Education for its applicable special education laws). In reality, many school districts' personnel are either unaware of the laws or are reluctant to authorize the services, regardless of the educational code. Parents are not actively being educated by the school districts about special education laws, so they may not even know to ask for the help. Some parents are so tired of dealing with their child's handicaps and fighting for services that they don't bother to ask – it's just one more battle to fight.

By the time our ADD adult graduates from high school, he is so tired of studying and so embittered by his school experiences that the last thing he wants to do is go on to higher education, or even real vocational training. Since our ADD adult didn't receive adequate vocational training in public school, he didn't learn the skills to be employable. Now he is out of prison and should have a new lease on life, but he is able to get only a minimum wage job.

The community colleges do offer excellent occupational programs which provide training in specific skills in areas such as auto mechanics, plumbing, etc. Upon completion of the program a certificate is awarded that certifies a skill level. However, these programs are not as easy to access as would seem. If an ADD adult is released from prison in September, he would probably need to wait until the beginning of the next semester (probably January) to even begin to receive any training. These programs typically last from six to eighteen months. Even so, how does our ADD adult feed and clothe himself while waiting for the program to begin? How does he work and participate in the training program at the same time?

Training programs may require a certain level of academic performance. Many of our ADD adults have difficulty in reading comprehension or problems with spelling and writing. While they are protected under the Americans with Disabilities Act, they often do not want to tell anyone they are having trouble or even know how to ask for help. Feelings of embarrassment or hopelessness may set in and they may drop out of the program.

c) **Academic Remediation:** If the ADD has been severe, the ADD adult may not be able to read or write. He may not understand money or how to handle a checkbook or even a credit card. Some ADD adults need basic life skills. For the ADD adult who is able to function in society, he may need the opportunity to improve his ability to read or write. If this is not done, the feeling that he is stupid, and the shame that this brings, will forever cause a serious problem with self-esteem.

d) **Academic Accommodation:** This would include smaller satellite schools so that ADD students would be able to attend classes in a less distracting facility, extended time during testing, proctored alternative test sites, tutoring, other accommodations as noted in both Chapters 4 and 5 that are shown to be vital to academic success.

e) **Education About ADD:** To most ADD adults, the condition that has severely impacted their lives is a total unknown. They need information about how their biochemical imbalance has caused problems for them in school, in relationships, on the job and with life.

f) **Coping Techniques:** Beyond education about ADD, they need training in the specific coping techniques that will work for them. These techniques are specifically designed to assist in the areas of temper, poor memory, impulse control and getting along with people.

g) **Counseling:** Prisoners with ADD have had a miserable time in life. Not only have they been in prison, but they have alienated their families. They have been unable to keep relationships. They may have a son or daughter who they haven't seen for years. They haven't been able to get and keep a job. There is a lot of despair. The adult needs some assistance with the despair so that he will feel that there is hope after all.

h) **Support System:** It is a lonely world out there. If you think you are the only ADD adult in the world, it is even lonelier. Are there really other people who have ADD? Are there really other people who are as messed up as you feel? Do these people really get better? Do they really stay out of prison? Do they really find jobs? Do they really ever lead happy lives? ADD adults out of prison would benefit greatly from a support system of other ADD adults, possibly set up along the lines of AA or NA.

3. **Long Range Intervention:** Rehabilitation programs must address the need for early identification of ADD. Schools and professional counselors must be trained in the appropriate diagnosis and treatment of ADD youngsters.

The Picture is Not Pretty! Is There Hope?

There is always hope. Humans have an incredible way of bucking up and finding solutions when things seem the darkest. Our prisons are overcrowded. There is an undeniable escalation of violence in our cities. Obviously, right at this moment, we *are* facing our darkest hour.

The first step that will move people to finding a solution is awareness. This has occurred. We are aware that there is a terrible problem that is facing all of us. We are afraid for ourselves, and we are afraid for our children. We are told that the top priority of our government is to fund research projects and grants that will address ways to stem the tide of violence in our cities. The government is aware! Good! Now we have everyone's attention. It's obvious there is a problem, but out of the awareness comes the drive to find solutions.

The solutions will come partly from understanding the role that ADD plays in violence and prisons. Our prison system needs to be revamped. We need to provide screening and identification of the ADD condition while ADD adults are still in prison. Treatment must include medication as well as education. We need to revise our rehabilitation programs so that the ADD adults have a very real chance of success in life. We must think ahead and provide early identification of ADD while children are still in school. We must begin to prepare now, so that the youngsters in elementary school will have a chance and won't need to serve time in jail because of an undiagnosed biochemical imbalance.

We would like to conclude this chapter with a story of hope about a little boy who could have fit our ADD criminal profile and instead emerged a success, all because of early detection of his ADD and learning disabilities.

Jim's mom died when he was seven, and he was sent to an orphanage (as was often done when the remaining parent couldn't adequately care for the child). When Jim was nine, his dad died and he was sent to a foster home. Although the foster parents were less than kind, Jim was never abusive or malicious. He did, however, get into one thing after another, with failing grades and "poor citizenship" comments galore. The school principal once asked, "I say don't do it again, you say okay and you don't, but then you come up with something else. When are you going to run out of new things?"

Back when Jim was ejected from the orphanage, he overheard another "goody two shoes" sister of his best friend say, "You'll never see him again; he's destined for jail." In the tiny country country school he went to there were no special education teachers to analyze the gap between his ability and performance. He was falsely accused of cheating on his very first day of class, and his reputation worsened from there.

How many other undiagnosed ADD kids grow up bitter and turn to paying the world back for the many times they've felt betrayed, falsely accused and voiceless? How often is a kid without the "typical educational profile" sent to the principal's office for cheating, only to have it proven later that it *was* the truth being told? The damage done is often nearly irreparable.

Fortunately for our story, Jim is one of the kids who beat the odds. To everyone's surprise he made honor roll once and received nearly the highest ACT and SAT scores in his class. He went to a community college, took a full semester of remedial English, reading and writing, and got a bachelor's degree in engineering in five years. He earned his master's degree before the class valedictorian (the "good" Johnny Doe back in seventh grade). He was always "near the top" with his peers at work and way ahead on points, but never at the top.

Twenty years later, he found out more about adult ADD and worked for three years getting the medicines right. His life moved up four notches, he does two times the work in one tenth of the time, and spends the other ninety percent telling people that ADD is invisible, illogical and awful! Jim is currently a consultant with an investment and advisory firm and organizes conferences on both the West and East coasts dedicated to providing the latest information on research, diagnostics and treatment of Attention Deficit Disorder in adults.

Yes, there is hope!

Chapter 11

Understanding ADD
in the Workplace:
For Employers, Employees
and Co-Workers

ADD adults make up a very special and talented segment of our work force. They are often not only intelligent, but highly creative. Their enthusiasm for life and continued quest for fresh approaches to mundane tasks often enables them to envision dynamic ideas which may lead to the success of their companies. Many of our ADD adults are our greatest thinkers, including Einstein, J.F. Kennedy and Edison. Typically, ADD adults are divergent thinkers. One small idea leads them down a path to another idea and then another.

We must recognize that many of our ADD adults do extremely well in the workplace. They may have long histories with one company and may have enjoyed regular promotions. In these cases the ADD characteristics may have not presented problems in the workplace. Or, they may have become masters of coping strategies. Other ADD adults may have their own businesses and enjoy the status of entrepreneur. This leaves them free to follow their own interests without worrying about fitting into a corporate structure. ADD adults can be in careers that are very specialized and require a high degree of training as well as physical skill, such as firefighters and paramedics. Other ADD people can be dentists and physicians who are able to structure their days so that they are always on the move and routine tasks are kept to a minimum.

Now for the flip side of the coin. Obviously many ADD adults have difficulty in the workplace or we wouldn't be writing this chapter.

Problems in the workplace are twofold. Understanding ADD and its implications is often lacking on the part of the ADD employee and his or her employer. This is compounded if a formal ADD diagnosis has not been made.

ADD Employees

If an ADD adult has not been diagnosed and trouble erupts on the job, there is a lot of self-criticism. He doesn't understand what is wrong. He doesn't understand why he can't complete his expense report on time or why he can't get his stacks of paperwork organized. He doesn't know why the thought of writing ten performance reviews for his group keeps him awake for nights on end. He can't comprehend why his brain seems to function one day, then the next day he is operating in a gray fog, a mental vacuum. On those days he can't get anything done and the guilt mounts.

Even if his ADD is diagnosed, it takes time to get medication adjusted properly. It takes time to develop coping strategies that will solve some of his difficulties. ADD adults are terribly hard on themselves. They want to do the best job possible. Deep inside they know that they are capable, but they face a constant struggle on the job.

Even on medication and with coping techniques in place, some of the ADD characteristics improve only slightly and still present real problems on the job. Perhaps the ADD adult is so distractible that he will *never* be able to work in the middle of a bustling work space.

Trouble in the workplace is often compounded by problems at home. He may have a wife who doesn't understand his struggle and may be applying pressure to "change, or else!" implying a possible threat to end the marriage. If our ADD adult has children, you can bet that they are ADD as well. Thus, in addition to the work and family problems, he may be fielding calls from the vice principal at his child's school at the same time he is worrying about his own job performance.

Employers

Many employers have little information about ADD. In fact, many, if not most, don't have a clue about ADD in adults and the problems that it can cause. Beyond that, they have a hard time understanding that many of the problems are correctable. If their ADD employees exhibit many of the typical ADD characteristics such as distractibility, it is seen as resistance. Worse, it may indicate to the employer that the ADD adult doesn't care about the quality of her work and her relationships with other workers, or that the ADD adult is not willing to put effort, energy and thought into her job.

The truth is that our ADD adult is often struggling desperately to do a good job. She is motivated and sincere in her desire to succeed, but because of the combination of ADD characteristics, she simply can't pull it off. The end result is that an ADD adult often bombs out in the workplace.

We are fortunate to be living today, rather than in an earlier century. People with disabilities or handicaps are now recognized as a population with special needs which are protected by the law. This protection began with the physically handicapped, which resulted in such accommodations as wheelchair access to buildings. The definition of disabilities was broadened and soon encompassed all people with special needs. This population includes adults with Attention Deficit Disorder.

ADD is one of those disabilities that is considered a "silent disability," meaning it is harder to spot. An ADD adult does not wear braces, does not speak with a lisp or have red spots on his or her skin. It is a much less obvious problem with the biochemistry of the brain. Even so, ADD is now recognized as a true disability, and there is protection under the law.

To get a sense of the types of problems encountered on the job, let's look at several ADD adults.

Tim: *ADD Computer Genius*

In front of a computer keyboard, Tim's genius is apparent. He can write programs with ease. He is able to maneuver within the most convoluted of programs. At *times* he is absolutely brilliant. However, this is the key to his difficulty. He is only able to function *at times*.

Tim was definitely a hyperactive kid in elementary school and high school. It took all of his energy just to remain in his seat through an entire class period. Once the bell sounded at the end of the period, he would bolt for the door and freedom. He hated the confinement of his classes so much that the idea of college was impossible to even consider.

When Tim was seventeen, he found a job in a small computer company. His boss appreciated his expertise on the computer and was happy with whatever programs he was able to develop. For the first five years of his job, he was left pretty much on his own. He would typically arrive for work at 1:00 in the afternoon and work into the wee hours of the morning. For him, there were no deadlines. His co-workers viewed him as something of an oddity, an eccentric genius, and they tended to leave him alone. This was just as well, since Tim had difficulty with social relationships and covered up his discomfort and fear with a gruff and sullen attitude.

Finally, the company became very successful and acquired a contract with the federal government to plan events requiring security, such as a Presidential visit or a visit from other dignitaries. Suddenly, the pressure was on, and Tim was on a time schedule with deadlines. If an important visit was scheduled, Tim had to plan alternate security routes, program the entire visit, and the work had to be done *on time*. Not surprisingly, Tim didn't do well with deadlines. He was usually two or three hours late with a project. As the pressure mounted, he would often be as late as a day or two.

Soon Tim's boss changed his opinion of Tim, from being a valued (although unique) individual to a real pain. The boss no longer had patience with Tim's quirks. Pressure was applied. Tim fell apart and eventually quit.

Samantha: *ADD And Overwhelmed*

Samantha was very bright and in gifted classes through high school. As a straight-A student her parents and teachers told her that she was bound to be very successful. Once she reached college, to her horror she found that she couldn't force herself to study. She was caught between two realizations. On the one hand ,she felt that she didn't have enough time to do the endless reading and papers that were required. On the other hand, she realized that an entire semester stretched out in front of her, giving her a sense that a great deal of time was available. In college there was too little structure, and she often went skiing instead of attending class. She was not accountable in her classes until the end of the semester, and by then it was too late. After six years, she finally managed to graduate.

Samantha began her career in a sales position, but a divorce, as well as a disastrous child custody battle, sent her into a tailspin of depression. She was out of work for some time, re-entered the work force as a temp and finally found a full-time job with a food distributing company. Her job required her to visit the local markets, set up sales promotions and complete paperwork. This job was manageable for one or two years, but her responsibilities grew. She was still hanging on, until her children, who were now teenagers, began to go through their turbulent adolescent period. She was called to the high school at least once a week because of truancies or poor grades. Her daughter became involved with a boyfriend, and suddenly a pregnancy added to her burden. The pressure of her children and her work combined to lead her into another depression. She was unable to concentrate at work and tasks were left undone. Her boss was extremely critical and began to drop in unannounced on her at work to check up on her daily progress. Finally, everything became too much and she was unable to function. She tried to ask for a stress disability leave but was rejected. She had no choice but to return to a temp job with less pressure, but also much less money.

Jess: *ADD and Obnoxious*

Jess is a handsome, smooth-talking ADD adult who works in high-end retail sales and can outsell anyone else in the store. He is the quintessential salesman. Jess has been fired from several managerial positions over the years because he has difficulty working with his co-workers. He is abrupt, abrasive, cuts co-workers off in midsentence and is generally hated for his arrogance. This is sad because Jess is very sensitive. He is unable to keep himself from blurting out his ideas or opinions to his co-workers. He often makes cutting or unkind statements without realizing what he is saying. He often interrupts because if he doesn't, he is afraid he won't remember what he was going to say. He senses that his co-workers don't like him, but he doesn't understand why. He doesn't know what else to do, so he isolates himself and is considered aloof.

When Jess is working with a customer, he has realized that he must learn to curb his impulsive speech and habit of blurting things out. He found a way to check himself, but only with a great deal of difficulty. He has managed to develop a tactile cue for himself as a reminder that he must keep his mouth shut when approaching clients. Jess always buys a pair of shoes that are one half size too large. As he approaches a new customer in the store, he curls the toes on his left foot. This produces enough discomfort that he is able to focus part of his mind on his hidden signal to himself, and it serves as a constant reminder to monitor what is coming out of his mouth. This takes tremendous effort and he can't maintain this level of vigilance throughout his entire day, so his co-workers receive the brunt of his abrasiveness. What a dilemma! Jess is the best salesman in the store, but a thorn in the side of his co-workers.

Obviously, Jess will be a salesman forever. Promotion is not in the cards. If the pressure from his co-workers increases sufficiently, he may get fired – again.

Common Pitfalls in the Workplace

ADD adults have several tendencies that are part and parcel of the ADD condition that wreak havoc in the workplace. They often have no clue that they are exhibiting these traits and tend to go merrily on their way, never understanding why they are having difficulty on the job.

Impulsivity

The impulsiveness of the ADD condition often causes adults to blurt out what they are thinking or feeling at any given moment. Unfortunately, these comments are often inappropriate. In a business meeting the ADD adult tends to say exactly what is on his mind instead of thinking first and phrasing the statement in a more socially acceptable way. He may blurt out, "Your idea is stupid," instead of using a more gentle, "Let's look at this another way."

This same impulsivity causes ADD adults to interrupt in the middle of conversations and cut co-workers off in midsentence. This is certainly not meant to be rude; they don't even realize that they are doing this. When their habit of interrupting is brought to their attention, they are often surprised. After thinking it over, they realize if they don't say something at the moment it occurs to them, they are afraid they will forget it completely. They don't see any other choice but to interrupt.

This same impulsivity may cause our ADD adult to abruptly walk off a job without thinking of the consequences. The impulsivity may keep our adult hopping from one job to another or moving from company to company. Several of our ADD adults were comparing their job histories. In our experience, two years at any given job is fairly typical for ADD adults. Recently, one ADD adult shared with us that his length of time on a job was only nine to twelve months. Another ADD adult had had twenty-seven different jobs in nineteen years.

Rough Around the Edges

An ADD adult often uses defense mechanisms to hide her confusion about her performance on the job or to hide her discomfort with people. She may be bristly and unapproachable and may even have a reputation as the office grouch. She may not see herself this way at all. If she begins to sense that people don't like her, she often withdraws even more, thus reinforcing her negative image.

Late Again!

ADD adults often misjudge time. They are usually late – often exactly ten or twenty minutes late. If they are criticized for this trait and they vow to be on time, they cannot seem to be exactly on time. Instead they are early, and this overcompensation never lasts long (one article links this time distortion to a lack of dopamine. Whatever the reason, it is a problem). Sometimes they are late because they simply cannot get up in the morning or don't hear the alarm (or two or three alarms) ring. More often, it is simply one of those unexplained ADD traits.

Rigidity

If something gets out of control, whether it is paperwork or employees, the ADD adult often fears that he can never regain control. Sometimes this causes him to clamp down and become rigid. ADD employees who feel "I must do it my way" typically don't last long on the job because they are quickly fired.

The ADD boss who demands a rigid standard of performance and insists that things be done exactly to his specifications is another matter. Anyone who questions or deviates is quickly terminated and the workplace contains only compliant workers. The boss' viewpoint is distorted. From his vantage point, everyone agrees with him. Yes, that's true, but he has fired everyone who would have a different opinion.

Where is Your Brain?

With the chemical imbalance of ADD and its over- or underarousal of the brain, information may just not be able to work its way in to be processed by the ADD adult (especially the first time.).

Even though an ADD adult may be brilliant in her particular field, she may have problems understanding concepts as they are presented. In a meeting she may need to ask a million questions or have someone repeat information again, but in a different way. To the boss this often looks as though the ADD adult is not very intelligent, or worse, not listening.

The reality is that understanding concepts and new information requires the ability to process accurately and on the spot. While the ADD adult may have the ability to do this some of the time, it is not reasonable to expect that it can be done consistently. We want to reiterate that there is no correlation between intelligence levels and memory or processing difficulties. It's the intermittent biochemistry that holds the key.

Socially Inept

As young children, many ADD adults never understood the meaning of social cues. They never realized that there was a subtle message in the shrug of a shoulder or a facial movement and this skill never improved in adulthood. ADD adults have problems realizing when someone is irritated with them. They often miss body language cues altogether or misinterpret the cues. This also applies to being unaware of their *own* body language and cues. Instead of recognizing, "I'm on dangerous ground," they plunge blindly ahead and typically make matters worse. If they are finally confronted by co-workers and told that they hurt someone's feelings, they are caught by surprise. "What did I say?" and "I certainly didn't mean to sound that way," are all typical comments. Obviously, the inability to recognize social cues puts someone at a definite disadvantage in the workplace.

Memory

"I never said that!" "Where is it?" "You never gave me that piece of paper!" Universally, ADD adults have a terrible memory. Often entire chunks of memory will simply drop out of their minds, and they will forget entire business meetings or even fun-filled events such as the company picnic. They are also prone to forget details such as the location of a specific piece of paper they filed just yesterday. ADD executives who have good secretaries are fortunate because it is the secretary who takes over the memory function. Our executives sheepishly admit that their secretaries *never* give them original copies of anything because they are notorious

for losing papers, contracts, and bills. They are also well-known for filing information away and then forgetting what they filed it under, resulting in hours of
searching. (As a reminder, one of the solutions for filing problems and lost papers
is to file information in more than one way. An example would be to file
Executive Report under **E** and **R**.) To others, this lack of memory looks as though
the ADD adult simply is not paying attention to work – he just doesn't care. A
non-ADD co-worker or employer cannot understand how in the world an adult
can totally forget a statement, a promise, a business meeting or lose an important
piece of paper.

Organization

"The stacks of papers you see on the floor, on the desk, on the filing cabinet do
not mean I am disorganized. I can find anything I need at any time," or so says the
ADD adult. To someone walking into an ADD adult's office, the first picture is
often one of total disarray or, to be even more blunt, messiness. There are papers
all over, swatches of samples thrown in the corner and six coffee cups on the desk
– one with a good growth of mold. It is true, the ADD adult can, at times, put his
hands on a specific file. But more often it requires a thorough search, which takes
time and often produces a lot of frustration before the lost file is retrieved. Again,
it looks as though our ADD adult is not putting the time and energy into work
that is required.

Start That Project!

Procrastination is the middle name of many ADD adults. The energy required
to jump into projects often seems insurmountable to the ADD adult, although she
knows she is capable of actually doing the task that is involved. What does she do?
She waits for the inevitable deadline to creep closer and closer. She is up all night
before the project is due. Sometimes she can't make the deadline, and she is late
again. To the boss this can be terribly confusing. On one hand, it looks as if she
doesn't care about her work, but on the other hand, although it may be late, her
work is brilliant.

Finish That Project!

ADD adults often experience a great burst of enthusiasm and creative spark
that literally explodes them into a new project. However, when it comes to the follow-through required to actually complete the project – the nitty gritty, step-by-
step process of dealing with details and bringing a project to completion – they can
be a dismal failure. To co-workers and their bosses they are often viewed as total
flakes. They are full of hot air, with a lot of talk but no action. The reality may be
that once the ADD adult has launched himself and is deep within the project, it
may be difficult to focus on the next set of sequences to complete it. The ADD
adult may have had a clear vision of the project, only to lose focus and become
overwhelmed by too many details. Often the ADD adult has completed outstanding work up to a point and may be too embarrassed to show it or to ask for help in
redirection.

Mistakes: *Again and Again and Again*

If an ADD adult must copy a line of numbers or tally receipts, she will often make extremely simple mistakes, but these mistakes will be enough to throw off a tally or stop a computer program. The mistake is usually so simple or so elementary in nature that it looks as though the ADD adult doesn't care about the job. In actuality, the prolonged effort that is required to concentrate on a tedious task is very difficult for this population. Once again, the ADD adult is misunderstood by boss and co-workers alike.

At All Levels of Business

Whether our ADD adult is a employee, supervisor or owner of the company, the ADD traits can present real obstacles. At every level they can not only prevent good working relationships within the workplace, but interfere with success.

Yes, There are Problems. What About Solutions?

As with all aspects of the ADD condition, solutions can be developed in the workplace as well. The first step is to review your stance on the two fundamental parts of treatment for any ADD adult: medication and coping techniques.

Are you taking medication? Is it effective or does the dose need to be adjusted by your physician? If you are not taking medication, do you need to reconsider this question?

What about your knowledge of coping techniques? Do you need to seek alternatives? Remember, coping techniques are techniques or methods that ADD adults can use to moderate and change many of the troublesome ADD characteristics. Have you developed coping techniques to begin tasks, to remain organized, to begin projects and to complete projects? Just for you, we have written Chapter 14 entitled "Help! Even with Medication I Still Have Problems: Learning to Cope." This chapter explains coping techniques, gives specific examples and is a chapter the ADD adult should read carefully. If coping techniques are not enough, proceed to the next step, which is to consider the protection afforded ADD adults by the Americans with Disabilities Act.

Some ADD adults experience symptoms that are so severe that even with coping techniques and proper medication, they still have difficulty functioning. They may be unable to concentrate in a crowded work station. No matter how hard they try, they may be confused by directions coming from too many different people. The difficulties caused by their own particular brand of ADD create insurmountable obstacles on the job.

If you fall into this category and you are an ADD adult with significant disabilities, you do have protection under the Americans with Disabilities Act.

Americans with Disabilities Act

Americans have a strong work ethic and take great pride in a job well done. The Americans with Disabilities Act (ADA) is designed to protect the rights of individuals with disabilities and to insure that they have an equal chance to experience the pride of a job well done. In order to accomplish this, the ADA recognizes that modifications or special accommodations may be necessary.

We have taken the Americans with Disabilities Act and attempted to make the law very clear. Other help is available as well. The U.S. Government has a great deal of information about the ADA in the form of pamphlets, brochures and phone numbers, which provide even more information (see bibliography).

The Americans with Disabilities Act states "a qualified individual with a disability is an individual who, with or without reasonable accommodation, can perform the essential functions of the job in question." Reasonable accommodations may include, but are not limited to:

- Making existing facilities used by employees readily accessible to and usable by persons with disabilities.

- Job restructuring, modifying work schedules, reassignment to a vacant position.

- Acquiring or modifying equipment or devices; adjusting or modifying examinations, training materials or policies; and providing qualified readers or interpreters.

Translation Please!

If an ADD adult has trouble doing well on the job *because* of the difficulties or limitations that the disability (the ADD condition) causes, the employer must provide help. This help could include a change in working conditions, a different way of giving instructions to the employee or other modifications. The intent of this law is to allow the ADD adult to be successful and work to his or her full potential.

How to Make the ADA Work for You

If an ADD adult feels she needs to use the protection offered by the Americans with Disabilities Act, it is important that she do her homework and learn *exactly* what the law says. To make this task a little easier we have reviewed the ADA and broken it down into four different segments. This is one time that the typical ADD pattern of reading just bits and pieces of information will not work. Consider the information in the next four sections as a homework assignment in a class. **Read the entire four sections from start to finish so you don't miss any crucial points!**

1. *Exactly* what protection does the ADA provide?
2. *Exactly* what protection does the ADA *not* provide?
3. *How to approach* your boss, supervisor or HR person
4. *What to do if nothing works* and you are still on probation or in danger of being fired

Exactly What Protection Does the ADA Provide?

Applying for a Job

The ADA is designed to offer protection to the ADD adult applying for a job. It says that the employer cannot ask you about the presence of any disability during the hiring process. This means that you cannot be asked questions about a disability on a form you are filling out or in an oral employment interview.

The ADA states that you are under no obligation to disclose any disability *before* you are hired. Thus, if you think you are capable of performing the tasks required on the job, you cannot be penalized because you did not disclose your ADD condition.

During the Interviewing Process

The employer cannot ask you if you have a disability or illness that it should know about, or if you've had any diseases. (It *can*, however, ask these questions after an offer of employment is made and if *all* candidates are asked the same questions). It cannot ask you if you ever filed a worker's compensation claim, except after an offer of employment is made and the same questions are asked of all candidates. It cannot ask if you are taking any prescribed drugs. It cannot ask you if you have any problems or defects that prevent you from performing certain kinds of work or that may affect your performance in the specific position. The employer cannot ask how many days you were absent from work for illness last year. It cannot state, "To do this job you will obviously need accommodations. Which ones will you need?"

What if you have no idea that you are an ADD adult? If you experience difficulty at work and *then* are diagnosed as an ADD adult, you are still protected under the ADA.

Difficulties on the Job

Just Hired? – It is the first day on the job and our ADD adult discovers that the actual job of data entry is no problem, but the distractions in the noisy work center make concentration impossible. In this situation an ADD adult would qualify for protection under the ADA.

Promotion with More Responsibilities – Our ADD adult has done an excellent job in the warehouse and has just been elevated to warehouse supervisor. In this capacity our adult must keep track of all time cards, evaluate subordinates and route all packages in and out of the facility. This is a big step up, not only in responsibility, but in organizational skill. If our ADD adult finds that new systems need to be put in place, this comes under the protection of the ADA. If our ADD adult needs help in structuring the process of communicating and evaluating of subordinates, this comes under the ADA's protection.

Change of Physical Job Space – Our ADD adult has had a job in a growing microcomputer plant for the last five years and has done well. Suddenly, business explodes and the company moves into a larger building. Our employee is surrounded by ringing phones, a dozen new employees and a desk located under fluorescent lights that hum all day long. Our ADD adult is feeling crazy and certainly is functioning at a lower capacity. This situation also comes under the protection of the ADA.

Hated by Co-Workers – Our ADD adult is a caring, sensitive person who desperately wants to be accepted by colleagues at work. However, our adult often leaps into the middle of personal conversations and is considered intrusive and, more than that, a real pain in the neck. More employees are fired because of difficulty with co-workers and inability to function within an office setting than an actual inability to get the work done. Where does this leave our ADD adult? Fortunately, our adult falls under the protection of the ADA.

Exactly What Protection Does the ADA Not Provide?

The ADA is meant to protect individuals with disabilities, but it also protects the rights of employers. The ADA does *not* say that any disabled individual can have whatever he or she wants, whenever he or she wants it, at the expense of the company.

Although this statement sounds rather harsh, it is extremely important that the ADD adult recognize that many employers have felt taken advantage of by employees who used the umbrella of the ADA as a mask for laziness or their unwillingness to put in a full day's work.

So the ADD adult can get a glimpse of the ADA from an employer's perspective, here is a true story of one ADD adult who worked as a nurse's assistant in a busy hospital. He was written up for being abrasive and downright nasty with the nurses who gave him instructions. He was also written up for his inability to follow through with directions. Our ADD adult used the umbrella of the ADA to ask for compensations on the job. He requested that only one nurse give him directions and that they be written. This was done. Next, he began to come in late for work, stating that because of his ADD he couldn't wake up in the morning. His work hours were adjusted and he was given a later shift. Next he complained that he was being given too much work.

The employer became concerned and called an ADA mediator. A hearing was set, but the employee never appeared; however, he continued to come in to work intermittently and remained caustic to his co-workers. A second hearing and then a third was scheduled, but he never attended either one. Even though the company was more than willing to provide accommodations, this particular adult apparently wanted a free ride. Although he eventually left town, he also left an extremely bad taste in his employer's mouth.

As an ADD adult you need to be prepared to be calm, organized and know the ADA as you present your case. This is important for two reasons. First, you are representing all the other ADD and disabled adults who will come after you. You are setting an example. Secondly, you may be called upon to undo some negative images left by a previous petitioner.

Employer Cannot be Made to Lower Standards of Quality or Production Standards

What does this mean? If a company produces electronic pumps and is intent on maintaining a certain standard of quality, it will not be made to produce an inferior product just to accommodate an ADD adult's disability.

Employee Must Possess Skills Required for Job

To understand this, think about a job such as a secretarial position, which requires letters, memos and manuals to be typed. If our ADD adult has no computer skills or keyboarding skills she cannot claim that she should be allowed to do this particular job. It is not her disability that prevents her from applying, it is the fact that she doesn't have the correct skills needed.

If a particular job requires certain abilities or skills, it does not automatically mean that an individual with a disability should be hired. To make this even more concrete, take the example of a telephone repair person. If an individual is in a wheelchair, he cannot apply for this particular job claiming that the telephone company should lower all the poles to wheelchair height. Sounds silly when it is put this way, doesn't it?

The ADD adult needs to be sure that he has the training and qualifications to do the particular job. Over and above that, he is certainly entitled to accommodations.

Company Size

The ADA covers only companies of twenty-five employees or more. Technically, if you are employed by a small two- or three-person company, you do not fall under the umbrella of the ADA. This is an important point because it will affect how you present your case. In a small company your request will need to be phrased as just that – a request, not as a demand with full protection of the law.

Not Intended to Bankrupt Companies

The ADA is intended to be fair to both the disabled person and the company. The ADA will not require that a company make large and expensive modifications in the plant in operating procedures to accommodate an individual if it will bankrupt the company. However, there is a loophole in this aspect of the law. Small divisions of the state or federal government are part of much larger institutions with huge budgets. There have been cases where a particular department has been required to make modifications, even though the cost of the modifications exceeded its individual budget. This is because it falls under the umbrella of a much larger structure.

How to Approach the Boss, Supervisor or Human Resources Person

Stop. Take a deep breath. Consider the five points listed below and then carefully plan your approach. This is one time that the ADD adult simply cannot afford to allow impulsivity to erupt. Words once spoken cannot be retracted. Think about the old proverb, "Engage brain before putting mouth in gear."

1. Have your ADD diagnosis substantiated on paper.
2. Remain as positive as possible.
3. Don't wait until it is too late.
4. Be prepared to educate.
5. Consider your co-workers.

The Diagnosis

Before you attempt to present your case to your supervisor, be sure that you have your diagnosis substantiated on paper. To many, the notion of ADD is still very suspiciously dismissed as the yuppie disease of the nineties.

Wait. Don't skip this section because a psychiatrist has told you verbally you are ADD and may have even prescribed medication. Unfortunately, getting the ADD documented on paper is not as easy as it seems. We have had many clients in the office with sad tales of their experiences. There are some psychiatrists who become elusive when asked for documentation. They promise they will write a letter but somehow never get around to it. Other psychiatrists initially provide a diagnosis of ADD, but later in the treatment suddenly change their diagnosis to a bipolar disorder or depression, and refuse to document their original diagnosis of ADD. Sometimes move to another state and records are unavailable. Sometimes psychiatrists die.

If you haven't been diagnosed, but are under treatment for ADD, ask whatever professional you are consulting to provide a diagnosis *on paper* that documents your condition. You might even go as far as withholding final payment until the document is in your hands.

Remain Positive

When we are frightened we all tend to become defensive. If we feel that we are backed into a corner, we will attack. Jobs put food on the table and roofs over our heads. If our job is threatened, the world becomes a scary place.

Take a step back and think long and hard about a positive approach to use with your supervisor. Your task is to inform that person about your diagnosis of ADD, be able to explain exactly why it has caused difficulties on the job and, if at all possible, offer some ideas for solutions and information about the ADA in a non-confrontive manner.

Don't Wait Until it is Too Late

If trouble looms on the horizon, our tendency is to stick our heads in the sand. We often deny the extent of our problems with ADD in our jobs, hoping that the problems will resolve themselves (magically) or just go away. If our coping strategies aren't working and we're deeper and deeper in a mess at work, if our piles just get shuttled from one place to another but never get smaller, then it's time to take action. The key phrase here is *don't wait until it is too late*. If you begin to feel overwhelmed or if your job performance is slipping, the best approach is to go to your supervisor early in the game. Don't keep quiet and hope that trouble will evaporate. Often there are accommodations that can be made that bring relief *and* boost productivity for the ADD worker.

Be Prepared to Educate

Most large companies, especially if they receive state or federal funds, are knowledgeable about the ADA. (Other companies, even if they are of a decent size, may not be aware of the ADA.) Our ADD adult may find it is necessary to educate the supervisor or even the human resources (HR) person about the law. Come prepared with pamphlets, handouts and flyers that are listed in our bibliography and can be obtained from the government at no cost.

Our experience has been that many supervisors or HR people respond positively to the information about ADD and the fact that there are solutions to difficulties on the job. If you approach your supervisor as a potential ally, not a potential enemy, he or she will be more apt to help.

If the company is large or has state or federal contracts, it will have had inservices about the ADA and how to deal with employees who have disabilities. If the company is small, there may be more resistance.

How to Handle Co-Workers

What about the people who work side by side with our ADD adults? What happens if they begin to feel that these adults are getting special treatment? Are there stirrings of jealousy in the ranks? What happens if they begin to hear talk of a separate office with a door? They might begin to wonder what the phrase "special accommodations" means.

Whether to tell co-workers or not to tell co-workers about an adult's ADD diagnosis and the accommodations that are being requested is a very personal decision for each adult. However, the attitudes and feelings of co-workers need to be taken into account and a plan of action or non-action clearly decided upon to alleviate potential hard feelings or problems.

Particularly when the ADD adult has had difficulty on the job for lengthy periods of time, co-workers certainly have expressed resentment of the special accommodations. Even if they are educated about ADD they may question the diagnosis by saying, "Oh, come on. That's just an excuse." Or they may say, "You are too intelligent. With a Ph.D. you simply can't have ADD. You are just trying to get off the hook. The truth is you have been a jerk all these months."

At other times co-workers have been tremendously supportive and helpful. One ADD adult was going to be provided a separate office to minimize distractibility. He took the time to explain his own particular brand of ADD in short and simple terms to each and every co-worker and also to ask if they had a problem with his separate office. They all thanked him for sharing the information and were extremely supportive. This is certainly an ideal scenario but not one that we consistently hear.

A Case History: *Best Possible Scenario Using ADA*

Dave, an undiagnosed ADD adult, worked as an information liaison officer in the library of a large hospital for four years. His workplace was isolated in a corner of the old library building, and he was so far off the beaten path he didn't even need to contend with foot traffic. He was highly respected for his ability to retrieve and disseminate needed information quickly. Suddenly, the hospital received state funds and remodeled the facility, including the library. Dave's work station was now at the hub of the library, and he was surrounded by noise and activity. He was constantly interrupted and also distracted. He was unable to concentrate on his work, much less think. Suddenly he was unable to do his job.

What Did Happen?

Fortunately, Dave had read some information about adult ADD and was diagnosed. He approached his supervisor and, with the assistance of an advocate, was successful in working with the hospital administration. A new work setting with walls and a door was provided, and he happily returned to his usual standard of excellence.

In this case, the hospital's human resources department had received a good deal of inservice about the ADA and was well-prepared not only to deal with Dave's concerns, but to understand his plight. This is an extremely positive example and shows how the protection offered by the ADA should work.

Another Case History: *Worst Possible Scenario Using ADA*

Max was an ADD adult who was socially inept. He was a loner, hated people and was generally gruff and abrasive, but he wasn't afraid of hard work. He had worked for a local funeral home for seven years, and his job was to drive the hearse and to keep the hearse and limousines spotless. What a perfect job for him. The corpse didn't care if there was dead silence.

All went well for a year. Max was considered a valued employee. This changed when a female housekeeper was hired to clean and dust the coffins and urns in the basement where Max kept his auto polish and clean rags. Although no smoking was allowed on the grounds, the housekeeper constantly smoked in the basement. Max hated smoking and told her in no uncertain terms to stop. He complained to his immediate supervisor, who did nothing. After three or four months of conflict, Max finally exploded into a rage. The housekeeper ran screaming from the basement, yelling that he was a madman and dangerous. She threatened to sue the funeral home if Max wasn't fired. His supervisor recognized that Max had always had difficulty working with people and decided that the incident must have been Max's fault. Max was fired.

What Should Happen?

Under the ADA Max's ADD should have been identified. Once that was done, the supervisor should have worked with Max to establish his rights on the job. His co-worker should not have been allowed to smoke. Co-workers would have benefited from an inservice regarding Max's difficulty in talking to and relating to people. Handled correctly, the situation should have been a win-win all around. The funeral home would have kept a valuable employee and Max would still have his job.

Special Section for the Supervisor and the Human Resources Person

One of your employees has just told you that he or she is ADD and, furthermore, is protected by the ADA. You have done a little research and found that the ADA is a real law with teeth. In fact, if a legitimate case gets as far as court, it is most likely that you will be at fault and the company will lose big-time, paying substantial damages.

You have thought for a few months that this employee was a complete flake. Projects haven't been turned in on time, he's been late for work, and he is obnoxious and often interrupts in business meetings.

As a supervisor you have been concerned about performance and have written his performance reviews carefully. You have attempted to provide extra help for him or spent more of your own time with him to make him successful, but nothing has worked. Now suddenly he is telling you there is a reason for poor performance. What's more, he is talking to you about "accommodations." What is that?

As a supervisor, we encourage you to follow the following guidelines:

1. Ask your employee to provide his or her ADD diagnosis on paper to substantiate it.
2. Remain as positive as possible – there are several ways to tackle and resolve work problems with your ADD employee. If one way doesn't work, try another angle.
3. Have your employee help you problem-solve alternative ways to get the job done. Just because the employee has come to you with his or her condition, this doesn't mean it rests solely with you to provide solutions (or else risk an ADA challenge). Your ADD employee has been living with this condition all or most of his or her life and may have brilliant tips or suggestions to maximize job performance.
4. Don't hesitate to ask for more information on ADD. If it's unfamiliar, educating yourself about all of its facets is extremely helpful.
5. Carefully determine whether the employee should be encouraged to share his or her diagnosis with co-workers, especially ones with whom he or she must work closely. Do not break confidentiality, but discuss this aspect with your ADD employee.

As a supervisor, you need to know that the law protects you as well. It specifically states that you do not need to relax your standards or quality of product. It should not make the company any less successful or decrease profit.

What the law does require you to do is talk to the employee and discuss modifications that would make a difference in the quality of performance. The concept is that a person with a handicap should not be prevented from doing the job he is able to do because of the handicap.

You are caught in a bind as a supervisor. How can you do your job? What can you do? The following are checklists provided by IAM Cares, a division of the International Association of Machinists and Aerospace Workers. They are authorized and funded by the U.S. Department of Education to provide information and materials to individuals covered by the ADA. To obtain copies or more information, you can contact their Technical Assistance Centers at 800-949-4232.

Checklist Related to Job Descriptions and Qualifications

	Yes	No
1. For jobs that are vacant or soon to be vacant, we have a record of the essential functions.	_____	_____
2. Functions characterized as essential have been judged against the EEOC criteria regarding reasons for and evidence of essential functions.	_____	_____
3. Job information is phrased in terms of what each job is to accomplish, not in terms of how it is to be performed.	_____	_____
4. The information is accurate and complete, and reflects work currently being done in those jobs or similar jobs.	_____	_____
5. We evaluate an individual in terms of his or her ability to perform essential functions of the job for which the person is applying or in which the person is assigned.	_____	_____
6. When a need for reasonable accommodation arises, we have a procedure to follow that will permit us to provide such accommodation in a timely manner.	_____	_____
7. Anyone with responsibility for screening or evaluating applicants or employees is aware of ADA requirements, including those connected to medical examinations, and complies with them.	_____	_____
8. We have posted and otherwise made available notices about ADA requirements in print and non-print formats.	_____	_____

Checklist for Interviewing

	Yes	No
1. We have deleted all questions related to disability from applications and in interviews.	_____	_____
2. We have posted notices on the provisions of the ADA.	_____	_____
3. We have notified applicants of our obligation to provide reasonable accommodation on applications, job announcements, and/or during interviews.	_____	_____
4. Interviewers have been briefed on appropriate ways of interacting with applicants with disabilities.	_____	_____
5. Interviewers have been informed about and observe the pre-employment restrictions on questions related to disability.	_____	_____
6. We hold interviews in accessible locations.	_____	_____
7. Before an interview, we provide detailed directions and accessibility information on interview locations to applicants.	_____	_____
8. We provide detailed information to applicants on job functions.	_____	_____
9. When requested we provide interpreters or other forms of accommodation during interviews.	_____	_____
10. Interview questions focus on eliciting information about an applicants [sic] ability to do the job.	_____	_____
11. Before interviews, interviewers know and prepare questions concerning the applicants [sic] ability to perform functions of the job.	_____	_____
12. We have a procedure for addressing requests for accommodation.	_____	_____
13. During interviews interviewers are willing to discuss and consider how any job function may be performed in an alternative manner.	_____	_____
14. We ask all applicants the same questions.	_____	_____
15. We maintain information associated with requests for accommodation and disability in a confidential manner.	_____	_____

Tips on Working with an ADD Adult

As a supervisor, you suddenly find yourself face-to-face with an employee who has a disability; however, you can't see this disability. Furthermore, you are not sure that you understand this disability. The situation can quickly become critical. As a supervisor, the last thing you want is conflict in the workplace, or worse than that, the hassle of a lawsuit.

Empowerment and understanding are the two key words to remember. For the supervisor, both of these words may put fear in your heart. You may suggest that if you are understanding and, beyond that, if you empower the ADD individual, you will be negotiating from a position of weakness, a one-down position. Nothing could be farther from the truth. The truth is, the employee desperately wants to keep the job. It took a good deal of courage for the employee to come forward and ask for special considerations. If you can remain understanding, there is hope for a positive resolution.

Let's take a closer look at both of the concepts that these words imply.

Understanding

This needs to be taken two ways. First, it will be important for you, the supervisor, to have a thorough understanding of Attention Deficit Disorder. You will need to read a book or two. You need to understand the Americans with Disabilities Act and how ADD pertains to that law. You will need to become familiar with the employee's unique brand of ADD and *exactly* how the ADD affects his performance.

Secondly, you will need to understand the plight of the ADD individual. Although ADD is often called the silent disability, it is still a very real disability, and more than that, it can be devastating. Often the ADD diagnosis has been made only after the employee began to experience difficulty on the job. The notion of ADD may be new to him as well, and the idea that he has something that is classified as a disability may be troublesome in itself. Suddenly the employee is faced with telling you, the supervisor, that he has a disability. Beyond that, he is faced with concerns about the reactions of his co-workers.

Empowerment

What? You are going to give power to an employee who is asking for special considerations? Are you nuts? Let's back up and look at the larger picture. In this day and age jobs are not easy to come by. Job performance is in question. The employee may be on the verge of getting fired, so her self-esteem is shot. She desperately wants to keep her job or she wouldn't be asking for help from you under the ADA. Even though your own research may have indicated to you that the ADA is a powerful law, the employee may have some doubts about its ability to protect her as an individual with a handicap. She is depending on you for fair treatment and help.

Use the tactic of empowering the ADD employee so she functions as an ally. Don't try to mandate solutions that you feel will work. You are not in that person's skin. Instead, work *with* her to create solutions to the problems. Allow a working relationship between you and the employee to develop.

Help, Nothing is Working!

Okay, even though you have been understanding and attempted to empower the employee, the employee and you are at an impasse. You feel that the employee is asking for impossible or unfair accommodations. The employee feels that you are rigid and unyielding. What can you do?

Find a Mediator

There is a small but growing number of professionals who function as mediators. These mediators will typically be clinical psychologists, Licensed Clinical Social Workers or MFCCs who have a thorough knowledge of ADD and also the ADA. The mediator is usually hired by the company to find a solution that will be acceptable to both the company and the employee. Although mediators are hired by the company, they are actually working as advocates for employees. The goal of the mediator is to engineer a win-win situation for both parties.

Keep It Out of Court at All Costs

The regulations contained in the ADA are very specific. If the employee meets the criteria and the company is not willing to provide accommodations, there is good reason to believe that the company will lose in court. If this happens, actually it becomes a lose-lose situation. The company will be required to pay damages. The employee will lose also because it typically takes three to five years to have a case heard in court, to say nothing of the hard feelings that persist if the employee should stay with the company.

Dry, Uninteresting Technical Information
(Note: Read this section only if you are desperate)

If ADD adults are thoughtful in their approaches to supervisors regarding the ADA, most likely they won't need to read this section. If, by some chance, your supervisor or HR person is not responsive and you need legal counsel, it is **imperative** that you read and understand this section.

The laws surrounding the ADA are clear. They are not in question. What you will be called upon to do is to defend the fact that *the diagnosis of ADD is included as a handicapping condition under the ADA.*

To make an airtight case for ADD being included under the ADA, we need to use two pre-existing laws (the Rehabilitation Act of 1973 and the IDEA) to support this position. The information has been simplified for you in this chapter. If you need a more detailed explanation, refer to *Attention Deficit Disorder and the Law: A Guide for Advocates* (see bibliography).

The Rehabilitation Act of 1973

Section 504 of the Rehabilitation Act is the crucial piece of legislation that directly states that ADD is considered a handicapping condition.

In the mid-seventies Congress adopted legislation whose purpose was to end discrimination against the handicapped and to improve education, as well as other services available to them. This is the law that insisted there would be wheelchair access in restrooms and ramps into buildings.

The important piece of legislation to remember is a Letter of Findings in OCR Case No. 04-90-1617 (September 17, 1990). In this case the U.S. Department of Education's Office of Civil Rights found that a school district in North Carolina failed to provide an ADD child with appropriate education. This forever documents ADD as a recognized handicapping *condition under the law.*

You are probably asking, what do the findings of a school district have to do with my job? The law takes many twists and turns. In this case, an older piece of legislation provides documentation that the ADA covers ADD, but it is by a circuitous route.

The Letter of Findings and Memorandum establishes:

1. The right of an ADD individual to equal education under the Rehabilitation Act,

2. The right is independently conferred by the IDEA (the next law we'll be discussing) and

3. The Rehabilitation Act's definition of a handicapped individual has been utilized in the Americans with Disabilities Act, which was passed in July, 1990, and is broader than the definition in the IDEA.

The Individuals with Disabilities Education Act (IDEA)

In 1975, Congress enacted the Individuals with Disabilities Education Act (IDEA). The main focus of this act is to insure that children with disabilities have a free and appropriate education available to them. This act emphasizes special education and related services designed to meet the unique needs of children with learning disabilities.

Here is the catch. The term "Attention Deficit Disorder" does not appear in the IDEA. *It is important to understand why this particular name (ADD) was not used.* It was not meant to exclude this population. In fact, the term Attention Deficit Disorder was first used in the *Diagnostic and Statistical Manual of Mental Disorders (DSM-III)*, which was published in 1980 (after Congress had enacted the law). Previously, ADD children had been identified as "hyperactive" and, earlier than that, as having "minimal brain dysfunction."

There has been much controversy whether individuals with ADD, but with no accompanying learning disability, are covered under the law. A memorandum issued by the U.S. Department of Education's Office of Special Education and Rehabilitative Services on September 16, 1991, confirms that ADD can be considered within the scope of the IDEA. This depends on the circumstances as (1) an "other" health impairment, (2) a "serious emotional disturbance" or (3) a "specific learning disability."

This particular law focused mainly on children in school. There has been continued disagreement whether ADD is covered. According to our references, *ADD and the Law*, the clearest acknowledgment that ADD is covered by the IDEA, is found in *Valerie J. and Michael J. individually and as Parents and Next Friends of Casey v. Derry Cooperative School District* (771 F. Supp. 483; D.N.H., 1991).

Americans with Disabilities Act (ADA)

The Americans with Disabilities Act was passed in July, 1990, and extends the provisions of the Rehabilitation Act of 1973. In this act ADD is not specifically mentioned as a handicapping condition. The important thing to note is that *ADD is also not excluded as a handicapping condition.* The U.S. Department of Justice states, "Finally, it would not be possible to guarantee comprehensiveness by providing a list of specific disabilities, especially because new disorders may be recognized in the future, as they have been since the definition was first established in 1974." Thus, although ADD is not specifically mentioned, *it is not excluded.*

Here comes the important link between the Rehabilitation Act and the ADA. The Department of Justice goes on to state that *the list of disabilities used in the ADA closely tracks the one used in the regulations for Section 504 of the Rehabilitation Act of 1973.* Bingo! Here is the validation under the law that documents Attention Deficit Disorder as a handicapping condition under the ADA.

Summary

In this chapter we have looked carefully at ADD in the workplace. We have examined common pitfalls and looked at solutions and coping strategies. We have presented the Americans with Disabilities Act (ADA), what it provides for the ADD employee and what protection it cannot provide. We have included a section on how to approach your employer, as well as a section for the employer or supervisor on how to approach you as the ADD adult. We have also included a technical section which guides you to the specific laws, acts and sections that combine to establish ADD as a valid condition subject to the protection of the ADA. If you or someone you work with appears to have ADD-like symptoms, use the checklist that follows to further determine whether ADD is a factor in your workplace.

ADD and the Workplace Checklist

Use this list as an employer or employee to determine whether ADD is a factor in performance.

Yes	No	
_____	_____	Do you constantly move from one task to another on the job, rarely completing any one task?
_____	_____	Do you find yourself blanking out as you listen to detailed instructions, then hesitating to ask for clarification because you might appear stupid or slow?
_____	_____	Do you put off meeting deadlines, trusting that the adrenaline surge at the last minute will pull you through?
_____	_____	Do you tend to interrupt clients, co-workers or employees frequently, often breaking the rhythm of a meeting, project or plan?
_____	_____	Are you bright but feel stupid when you have to ask a million questions regarding how, when and why a project is to be done?
_____	_____	Do you frequently forget where you filed an important document, wrote down a crucial meeting, or left your briefcase or cellular phone?
_____	_____	Do you constantly arrive late to work meetings, even evaluations?
_____	_____	Do you rigidly demand a standard of performance or organization of files, expecting super-human efforts that cannot be lived up to?
_____	_____	Do you get easily distracted by any movement in the office – phones, air conditioning kicking on, papers rustling, a co-worker sniffling?
_____	_____	Do you have a reputation for having brilliant business ideas, only to have them disappear completely unless you write them down?
_____	_____	Do you maintain your office space so that it is (dis)organized into messy piles or (to compensate) make sure it is ultra neat and tidy, with everything in its place?
_____	_____	Do you find that you operate beautifully with written instructions but fail miserably with verbal (spoken) instructions, or vice versa?

If you answered "yes" to several of the above questions, you may be dealing with ADD in yourself, a co-worker or a boss. Remember that you have the right to job protection/modifications and that many of the coping skills can be easily adapted to the workplace.

Chapter 12

I'm Convinced!

Where Can I Get a Diagnosis?

If you have read this book on ADD and perhaps several others, you may be absolutely convinced that you are an ADD adult. However, obtaining a diagnosis may present some problems until you know the ropes.

Self-Diagnosis

First of all, some of the new ADD authors are stating that ADD seems to be one condition that does lend itself to self-diagnosis. This is true in our experience as well. Many ADD adults read a checklist or complete a self-rating scale, such as we've included in Chapter 1 of this book, or the checklist found in the book *Driven to Distraction*, and are astonished at how many ADD symptoms are present in their profiles. They may find themselves crying in relief because the ADD symptoms hit so close to home. The ADD description is right on for them. They'll say to us, "That article mentioned things about me that I've never told anyone. I always thought I was stupid or crazy."

If you have read this book or other ADD books and find that you fit many of the symptoms, don't be afraid to pursue your convictions, even in the face of family who thinks you are looking for an easy answer or an excuse for your problems. Pursue your conviction even in the face of professionals who say that ADD doesn't exist in your case and, in fact, doesn't exist at all, or who say, "You can't be ADD – you're too smart, too successful, too old."

Remember that in this book we have painted a picture of ADD as being a broad descriptor for a biochemical disorder which is multifaceted. We have used some general broad descriptors of ADD, such as problems with attention or impulsivity. But we have also made the analogy that ADD is as individual as a fingerprint, so your ADD symptoms might not look like another person's at all. The first step is to reach way down inside and ask yourself if there has always been something that has puzzled you. Is there something that hasn't seemed quite right? As we've said in our title, is there something in your life that has made you feel stupid or crazy?

The first thing to do in the diagnostic process is to learn enough about ADD so that you can take the first steps to make a self-diagnosis.

Spousal Diagnosis

What if the potential ADD adult is your spouse who is very reluctant to look at the possibility of ADD? Sometimes we all have our heads in the sand. This is equally true for ADD folks. Sometimes an ADD adult will be having trouble performing on the job due to a lack of concentration or organization or problems with temper. Often the spouse will be the one who comes across information about ADD in adults. Not too surprisingly, spouses are pretty accurate at diagnosing.

When the spouse makes the diagnosis, he or she will be the one who brings the ADD adult along to an informational lecture or the first evaluation session.

Professional Diagnosis

Even though we are saying self-diagnosis is often accurate, most ADD adults need additional input or verification that they are on the right track. After reading the ADD symptoms, it seems as though ADD is simply too easy an answer and only an excuse for troubles that have occurred in their lives. Most adults need confirmation of their own opinions regarding ADD.

There are also many, many ADD adults who have suffered all of their lives, but who simply don't have a clue that there is a name for their malady. Many of these adults have been from therapist to therapist, some for most of their adult lives. Many have been from psychiatrist to psychiatrist, each time trying another course of medication, but to no avail. These adults are lost. Sometimes they will run into a therapist with some knowledge of ADD who will either tentatively or with authority (depending on that therapist's own knowledge of ADD) put out a suggestion that there seems to be something going on that is not responding to traditional therapy. The therapist may question whether the adult has ever considered the possibility of ADD. Often a knowing therapist is the catalyst that sends the ADD adult out into the professional community for an evaluation.

Since ADD is a biochemical imbalance in the brain, medication is often needed as part of the treatment. This in itself demands that a medical doctor of some sort be involved in the diagnosis or treatment.

Professionals Who Diagnose ADD

The Medical Field

Psychiatrists – ADD is often confusing because it seems to fall between a medical problem and a psychological problem. Thus the first place many people turn is to a psychiatrist.

A psychiatrist who is knowledgeable about ADD typically takes a thorough background history about school performance, family patterns and early health and developmental issues. After that they typically use various checklists (self-rating scales) that the potential ADD adult and, very often, one other adult must complete. The use of an additional adult (spouse, sibling, good friend) is to provide a little more objectivity than is often provided by the client himself.

If all the factors are in place, the psychiatrist makes a diagnosis of ADD and then is able to prescribe medication if it is warranted. Should all potential ADD adults head for a psychiatrist? The answer to that blanket question is "No!" Unfortunately, finding a psychiatrist who says he or she knows about or treats ADD does not guarantee an accurate diagnosis.

In fact, there can be definite negatives if the ADD adult turns to a psychiatrist for a diagnosis. Many psychiatrists have been in practice for quite a while. While they were in their residencies, nothing was known about adult ADD. They were trained to treat heavy-duty disorders, such as schizophrenia and severe depression. Too often psychiatrists don't really believe that ADD exists. It wasn't there in medical school, and it still isn't commonly written up in psychiatric journals. In addition, many ADD adults need extremely small doses of medication. To the psychiatrists, these doses are at the subclinical level and seem so ridiculously low they believe they can't possibly work. Too often the ADD adult is placed in the position of justifying his symptoms of ADD and his response to medication to the psychiatrist.

The need to justify anything to a psychiatrist presents problems in itself. Not all, but certainly many, psychiatrists have definite egos. If what the client is saying is not in their own experiential base, they are often unwilling to listen. ADD adults see a psychiatrist, only to be told there is no such thing as ADD, or else they are placed on the wrong medications.

In fairness, we must be clear that we do know extremely competent and knowledgeable psychiatrists who are invaluable to us in the office when we must treat an ADD adult who has a difficult body chemistry. We consider these psychiatrists to be an absolute necessity.

Neurologists – The neurologist is skilled in the brain and its influence throughout the body. Neurologists typically use the EEG and other medical tests to assist them in their diagnoses. Unfortunately, most fall into the same category as psychiatrists. If ADD hasn't been presented in medical school and doesn't show up on tests (which are not sufficiently sophisticated to identify ADD), it doesn't exist. Of course, as with psychiatrists, there are exceptions. There is a very small handful of neurologists across the country who have specialized in ADD and are very helpful in making a difficult diagnosis.

Pediatricians – Pediatricians are probably the only medical specialty area who receive education in ADD as part of their basic training. The catch is that their training deals with children and adolescents. Often a pediatrician who has seen a potential ADD adult in her practice as a youngster will be willing to treat him as an adult.

A pediatrician will usually make her diagnosis of ADD by using checklists that are completed by the child's parents and teachers, as well as some neurological tests administered in the office. A few pediatricians have broadened their practices and are willing to deal with adults even if they didn't treat them as children.

Family Practitioners – The family practitioner is a generalist trained in knowing when to refer to a specialist. Family practitioners usually are not willing to diagnose and also prescribe medication for ADD adults. Typically, they don't feel that they have sufficient training in adult ADD to make such a diagnosis. In addition, they usually feel much more comfortable prescribing medication for ADD (which typically requires a triplicate form) if there is documentation in the patients' files from other professionals that an ADD diagnosis has been made.

However, family practitioners are excellent at overseeing medication for the ADD adult once the requirement of a written diagnosis is fulfilled. In fact, in our opinion, the family practitioner is the best person to be involved in treatment for many ADD adults because she sees the "whole" adult. She will typically draw blood, check all the vital systems and keep an eye on overall health. She continues to monitor the adult as medication is being prescribed. Most family practitioners are part of medical plans, so the ADD adult can receive excellent, all-around service and pay a great deal less than he would if he were seeing a psychiatrist.

The Psychological Field

This field tends to become lumped into one category by most people. If people are having problems that require counseling, they tend to seek some sort of psychologist for assistance, without really understanding the distinction between the different aspects of the profession. If a potential ADD adult is looking for assistance with an ADD diagnosis, it becomes vital to understand the differences in skills and licensing requirements of this population. Let's see if we can break the huge field of psychology into manageable segments for you.

Clinical Psychologists – This specialty area has a broad base of training in a wide assortment of counseling techniques. They also have a basic knowledge of psychological tests, which include the WAIS-R, Rorshach and many others. If the clinical psychologist has training in diagnosing and treating adult ADD, he or she is often an excellent choice.

Neuropsychologists – Neuropsychologists are trained to use a multitude of diagnostic tests to assist in diagnosing difficulty within the cognitive systems of the brain. They are specifically trained in the area of brain dysfunction, such as may be caused by an injury or a brain tumor. Neuropsychologists have a wide and valuable area of expertise that is often very helpful. If they have been trained in ADD and how to diagnose it in adults, they are often excellent professionals to assist you in your search for a diagnosis.

Marriage, Family and Child Counselors – MFCCs have extensive training in counseling individuals, couples and families, but seldom in any actual test administration. MFCCs are often at the "front line" of recognizing the potential for ADD within the individual or family. They are useful as a referral source to send the ADD adult to someone with more formal diagnostic expertise.

Educational Psychologists – Educational psychologists are trained to diagnose learning disabilities and Attention Deficit Disorder in children. They must have served at least three years in a public school system before they can obtain the designation of Licensed Educational Psychologist (LEP) from the state. Educational psychologists probably have the broadest area of expertise in the ADD field. However, most educational psychologists work with children and many may not have made the transition to evaluating adults. Once again, you need to ask questions about his or her expertise with ADD.

The Different Facets of an ADD Diagnosis

After reviewing the ADD literature, as well as attending workshops across the United States, we find that most professionals agree that there are three facets that must be in place to ensure a comprehensive ADD diagnosis. 1. The clinical history, 2. Test data, and 3. Rating scales specifically designed for use by ADD adults. These are explained below:

The Clinical History

The clinical history reviews family and relationship history, school and work history and developmental information. Under each section there are some specific indicators that are generally present in an ADD adult. The diagnosis of the ADD adult is made up of a number of different facets and is somewhat like putting a jigsaw puzzle together. The professional is looking for clues or for pieces to the puzzle. Factors included in the clinical history are listed below:

Family History – ADD is usually genetic, so it makes sense that the family history is reviewed. The adult is asked about his biological mother and father. Specific questions are asked about his parents' levels of education and if they were ever diagnosed with dyslexia or a learning disability as children. Most parents came from a time when there was no information about ADD in children or adults, so they certainly wouldn't have had an ADD diagnosis, but problems in their history are often apparent.

The adult is asked if there is a history of temper outbursts, depression, mood swings, drug use or alcoholism in the family. It is not unusual to find that the ADD adult has relatives on both sides of the family who have had what are labeled as "emotional problems." An aunt may have been depressed throughout her life. An uncle may have had such violent temper outbursts that he served some prison time. Possibly one or two relatives had problems with alcoholism or substance abuse.

Very often, a "dysfunctional" family system of some sort will be present, ranging from the alcoholic family pattern to a pattern of sexual or physical abuse. There are often stories about a "crazy" relative in the family. For example, they describe Aunt Sara, who took every medication in the world, finally needed electroshock treatments and is still not very functional.

Don't forget the ADD adult's children. At this time the identification of an ADD child in the family is often the first diagnosis that is made within the family system. From there, the father or mother begins to say, "I'm just like Johnny," or "I'm just like little Mary." If a child has been diagnosed with ADD, it usually verifies that there is a genetic strain of ADD in the family. Not only the adults but the other children need to be evaluated to make sure that ADD is not present. ADD has the potential to cause difficulty in school or relationships, even though the initial symptoms may be subtle.

Sometimes a child has not been diagnosed with ADD, but with ODD (Oppositional Defiant Disorder). Perhaps a problem adolescent has never been diagnosed with anything at all, but there are a multitude of truancies, defiance of authority, running away from home, moods or depression. Let's take the ODD child or adolescent first. There are a number of behaviorists working in the ADD field who attempt to differentiate the ADD child from the ODD child. Some studies seem to indicate that medication does not improve the behavior or learning patterns of the ODD child. It is our opinion that we are not far enough into the game to differentiate between ADD and ODD. Many ADD characteristics, such as a hot temper and impulsivity, could easily *look* like ODD. The other hard truth is that if a *problem* is not identified by adolescence and trouble starts, adolescents are almost *never* looked upon as people with the possibility of a disability or other condition by the school or even most professionals. Instead, they are placed on the discipline track in school and often make up a large portion of the population in any continuation school or independent study program. If this level of educational support is not enough, they often move on to activities which place them within the juvenile justice system.

If a potential ADD adult was adopted, an automatic red flag is raised. At first this statement seems strange. Why should adoption have any implications on ADD? But, when you realize that the most pervasive part of ADD condition is impulsivity, it begins to make sense. An impulsive ADD adult gets in a situation where pregnancy results. That child is put up for adoption. Thus our adopted child carries the ADD genetic structure that made his parents impulsive in the first place. Sometimes the adopted ADD adult was raised in a family system that had no ADD characteristics, so he may feel even more out of place. It seems as though there is no connection between his ADD characteristics and his family system. Actually that is correct, but there is a connection with his birth parents and the genetic structure in the birth family. Obviously, common sense is called for. We are certainly not suggesting that every child who is adopted is ADD. Just remember to use the red flag concept.

Relationship History – The ADD adult often has had a number of different relationships or even a number of different spouses. When questioned about this, the ADD adult often admits that the relationship ended because he soon became "bored" with his significant other. He felt a compelling need to move on to something more exciting, or he may have had a number of relationships which ended because he chose significant others who were exciting, adventurous and unstable. This partner provided the required excitement but was not able to maintain a long-lasting relationship. The ADD adult may have had difficulty reading social cues ever since childhood. He may be a loner, unable to maintain any type of long-lasting relationship or even friendship. The ADD adult with a great deal of impulsivity or episodes of temper also finds it difficult to maintain long-term relationships.

School History – Remember, the ADD adult may or may not have had difficulty in school. If the ADD adult was very bright, or simply didn't have difficulty in the processing area, academics may not have been a problem, especially through high school. In fact, the ADD adult may mention that she "breezed through school" until she entered graduate school She began to notice she was working much harder than her classmates, but without a great deal of difference in their grades. Thus, difficulty in school by itself is not a requisite for the ADD diagnosis, but merely one of the identifying factors.

If school problems are present, there are several transition points in school where an ADD child or adolescent will experience difficulty. The first danger point is kindergarten or first grade, depending on the academic requirements of the classroom. This is the first time that children are typically asked to sit still and attend. Poor fine motor control and difficulty with written language when copying from paper to paper or board to paper often creates immediate and severe problems. In addition, the child who transposes letters and numbers and/or reverses the same often has severe trouble with all beginning academic work.

Third grade is another difficult grade due to the increased demands on concentration and independent work skills. Obviously junior high and high school entrance, with their multitude of teachers and classes – each with its own separate system and requirements – can cause problems as well.

A pattern that, at first glance, seems very unusual is that of the ADD adult who describes a difficult history throughout high school, possibly having even dropped out to work for four or five years, or spending four or five years in the service. Upon deciding to return to college, he is amazed because, after a horrible experience in high school, he reports making A's in college and actually enjoying his classes. He can't explain this phenomenon, saying, "I guess work [or the service] really made me grow up." What actually seems to account for the change is the passage of time which allows him to have moved through the adolescent years that often made the academic difficulties caused by ADD much worse.

Another scenario that is commonly found is an ADD adult who does well *only* in areas that capture her interest. She may do poorly in most of her college courses, but have an A+ in computer science or graphic arts. She finds that course of study fascinating, and thus develop a hyperfocus on that one particular subject.

Another place to look for evidence of ADD is in the comments placed on report cards, particularly in elementary school. When an adult's report cards are lined up, from first grade to high school, the teachers' comments over the years often illustrate a clear pattern of ADD behavior. In fact, the ADD pattern is often so clear that the real question is, "How could it have been missed?" To protect a child's fragile self-esteem, comments from teachers are often couched in positive and flowery phrases, such as the illustration below from a fifth grader's report card:

> "…Outside of a teacher-directed activity, he often gets up to wander around the room. He rarely is a discipline problem, but is always active. He is quite social, and likes interaction with others for all classroom activities. Quieter activities, such as reading, writing, etc., are difficult for him, as are organizational skills. His attitude and heart are joyous and delightful. It's just that some classroom activities (and homework) for Ted are like teaching a rabbit to swim and/or a duck to climb trees."

Work History – We begin to look at the adult's work history in adolescence. Often ADD adolescents have problems with authority, not only moving from job to job, but being fired because they can't get along with supervisors.

An ADD adult's work history can vary greatly according to the work ethic in the family. An ADD adult will often continue the pattern that may have been present in adolescence and jump from job to job, saying that each job got boring. There may be continued difficulty with bosses or supervisors as well.

However, an ADD adult often has what looks like a very stable job history. Perhaps he has remained with the same company for twenty-five years. However, when you look at his employment history, you may find that every year or two, at his request, the company has moved him to a different section of the company, or changed the job description in some way. Thus, every year or two the ADD adult has the stimulation and challenge of an entirely new job situation.

Many ADD adults instinctively move into jobs that allow a degree of mobility, have built-in excitement or provide for a continual adrenaline rush. We have identified several ADD dentists and physicians in our practice. Both of these careers provide periods of intense concentration, challenge and excitement, and the ability to move from room to room. We see CEOs in our practice who thrive on existing on the cutting edge of finance. Stockbrokers also carry the same type of job description.

There is not just one career path for the ADD adult. Examine the reason that the ADD adult has moved into a particular career and how the challenges are handled to get a sense of the ADD adult in the workplace.

Health and Developmental History – ADD is a genetic condition. In the previous section we took great care to thoroughly explore the history of each family member. In this section we are continuing to look for certain patterns that are typically found in ADD children, such as difficulty falling asleep, being an extremely deep sleeper, or having more than the normal fears of the dark or monsters under the bed. However we must now broaden our focus beyond the genetic information. We must investigate evidence of any trauma that may have caused an injury to the brain, causing ADD-like symptoms without the genetic pattern being present. Injuries to the brain can range from oxygen deprivation at birth to a concussion at any age.

Birth Trauma – There are certainly genetic factors in ADD. However, if an infant, child, adolescent or adult has sustained damage that has affected the brain, symptoms that are identical to those found in the genetic ADD pattern may result. During birth, fetal distress, a difficult forceps delivery, birth with the cord wrapped around the neck – all may place the infant at "risk" as potential ADD. It is important to understand that the physician who assured the parents that everything is well with their child after such a delivery is only observing the "hard" neurological signs. The "soft" neurological signs are the ADD indicators, which may present problems in school and in life. Very often the early history will present clues, but the actual difficulty is not visible until much later, usually upon school entrance. Unfortunately, many ADD infants are so active *in utero* that they twist and turn and may increase the possibility of some fetal distress.

Let's stop here for a minute and say a kind word about mothers who carry ADD infants. Many of the mothers complain that since feeling the first signs of life in their babies, the activity never stops. One mother had an emergency C-section. After the delivery she heard the doctor move into the hall and call to a colleague to come and take a look. Her son had been so active that there was internal bruising, which amazed the doctor.

ADD Combined with Birth Trauma – If there is a mild strain of ADD that is obvious in the family, damage during birth may cause ADD symptoms in that one particular child to be much more severe than in his or her siblings. One family came to our office with a child with severe learning problems and clear ADD symptoms. There were some mild ADD indicators in the siblings, but nothing significant. This particular child had experienced difficulty breathing after birth and had been sent home without any sort of a monitor. The mother reported that she had found her daughter tinged blue on two or three occasions from a lack of oxygen. This type of situation does cause brain damage and can produce ADD-like symptoms more severe than the ADD genetic pattern in a family.

Trauma Past Infancy – A trauma at any age can result in ADD-like symptoms. The toddler who falls from a two-story window or the elementary age child who's knocked unconscious due to a skateboarding accident can both have ADD symptoms. This is important to understand because these ADD adults often do not follow the *DSM-IV* criteria rule of "ADD must be present in childhood." If the diagnosis is to be made with this population, you will see learning and behavioral differences before and after the accident. We evaluated a high school football coach who was sent in by his wife. He had a history of impulsivity, temper and difficulty with concentration that wasn't evident until his senior year in high school. In giving his history, he reported sustaining five concussions while playing football; three occurred in high school and two occurred in college. He fit the criteria for ADD in adulthood; apparently his ADD symptoms were caused by a series of head injuries.

ADD Infant with No Birth Trauma – Most of the information under this heading does not appear in the literature, but has emerged from our own practices as we talk with our ADD adults about their childhoods.

ADD infants are often colicky babies. Many ADD adults have a high degree of gastrointestinal upsets, and this is seen as colic in infants. The colic usually ceases at three months of age. Until then many nights are spent either rocking the infant or driving around in the family car in an attempt to soothe her digestive system and let everyone get some sleep.

Some ADD infants resist cuddling, and it is very common to hear that as infants they stiffened out straight as a board as their parents attempted to hold or cuddle them.

Next we need to assess the developmental milestones. Under this category we usually don't see ADD children falling into our nice, easy, normal middle range; instead, they typically fall on one side of the continuum or the other. They may crawl and walk early and be extremely coordinated. On the other hand, they may be slightly delayed and fall a lot or walk into furniture and walls. These ADD youngsters may be described as happy toddlers who played well by themselves or were hyperactive to the point that they drove their parents crazy. There are many funny stories from ADD adults as they tell of the trials and tribulations of their parents. One adult mentioned that his parents secured a net over the top of his crib to keep him in; another set of parents used a harness.

The ADD child is usually either a daredevil and accident prone, or extremely careful of his body. The daredevil also provides many funny stories. One adult told of his passion for tree climbing. This passion ultimately resulted in a fifteen-foot fall from a tree and a broken tailbone. After recovering, he again climbed the tree, threaded a length of chain through his belt loops, added a padlock and secured himself to the tree trunk. (His mother climbed a ladder to unlock the padlock and rescue her ADD child). ADD youngsters often have an unusual amount of cuts, scrapes and bruises and sometimes know the local ED staff on a first name basis.

Many ADD children have problems with fine motor control. Some learn to tie their shoes late or, even as adults, tie them in an odd manner. Teachers throughout the school years describe their printing or writing as illegible or messy. Our ADD adult has usually dropped any attempt at cursive writing and instead has taken to either printing or a combination of writing and printing. The research suggests that many ADD adults are left-handed. We have not found this to be true in our practice.

There seems to be little correlation between early language development and ADD. However, when an ADD child has experienced many ear infections, had tubes or an unnoticed loss of hearing, some difficulty with articulation of words may be present.

Medical Indicators – In our practice we find that almost all ADD adults have allergies. Even if they are not aware that allergies were present in childhood, when we then ask whether they had early ear infections, the answer is usually "Yes." Ear infections are often caused by undiagnosed allergies. ADD adults often have a mild strain of asthma or have someone in their extended family who is asthmatic.

Under this section, questions regarding any high fevers during childhood such as those caused by meningitis or the presence of concussions must also be asked. Were there problems with potty training? In the ADD population there doesn't seem to be much actual difficulty with the potty training itself, but many ADD adults were enuretic in childhood. They often have disturbances in body temperatures, noting that they tend to feel quite warm or are always cold. As infants, they often awakened from naps with their sheets damp from perspiration.

Sleep Problems – Many ADD adults experience a disturbance in their rhythm of sleep. Many are night owls, describing how their brains turn on about 10:00 or 11:00 at night, and they are unable to stop the multitude of ideas that swim through their minds. In elementary school, the ADD adults are often the kids who lay awake for an hour or more staring at the ceiling and hating the fact that their parents made them go to bed. After being put to bed as a child, one ADD adult spent every evening sneaking out, hiding behind the living room sofa and quietly watching TV. Even with warm milk and lots of activity during the day, bedtime was often the biggest trial of their lives.

Sometimes odd sleeping patterns emerge as well. One adolescent related that he had a great deal of difficulty falling asleep. He found a solution that worked well for him, but which was rejected by his skeptical stepfather. He found that if he covered himself with blankets, opened his window to the widest point, left his feet sticking out so they would be cold but placed a heater by his feet, he was able to go to sleep. It is hard to explain why this system worked, but it did. Many ADD adults find that they can sleep much easier if they have fans in their rooms. More sophisticated ADD adults have used white noise machines or tapes with the sounds of the ocean.

Once asleep, most ADD adults tend to fall into an extremely deep sleep and typically sleep through earthquakes or the sound of a smoke alarm going off in the bedroom. They also sleep through alarm clocks, to the constant irritation of their spouses or employers.

One of our favorite stories that illustrates just how serious this condition can be is of an ADD adult who was on the verge of getting fired from yet another job because she simply couldn't wake up in the morning. Obviously, this problem caused her to be continually late for work. In an effort to solve the problem she added a second alarm clock, but she slept right through that one too. She bought a third alarm clock, which she placed in a metal washpail, but that didn't wake her either. In desperation she contacted two wake-up services and arranged for them to call her after her alarms had gone off, in the hopes that the sound of the phone would get through to her sleepy brain. The service didn't do the trick and she slept right through the three alarm clocks and her two wake-up calls. She had been told that if she was late just one more time she was out the door. Her last strategy was to have the loudest home alarm she could buy installed and set to go off at 7:00 a.m. Finally, something worked. The shriek of the alarm woke her up. Her job was saved! Of course, one minor problem was that she lived in a condo and her neighbors were less than thrilled with her solution.

We also find ADD adults who are hypersensitive to any noise at all when they are asleep. We never realized just how sensitive some of these individuals were until one ADD adult shared that a single snail crawling up the sliding glass door by his bed was enough to wake him up. This seemed so bizarre that we thought he had exaggerated. His wife was with him, and she verified the story, except that in her case it was two snails crawling up his bedside window that awakened him!

Some of these adults often hit the snooze alarm for an hour or more until they get out of bed. Unfortunately, this habit can cause a good deal of irritation to the spouse. In the morning many ADD adults are absolute grouches. They are in foul moods and don't want to interact with anyone. One ADD adult describes herself as awakening by layers. She remarked that it takes her an hour or two to be functional in the morning.

During childhood some ADD adults have experienced many fears surrounding the dark and sleep. They often insisted in sleeping in the light or slept on the floor in their parents' rooms, even if they were not allowed in their parents' beds.

Now that we've looked at the clinical history, let's look at the actual objective test data.

Objective Tests

Objective tests may or may not be part of an assessment for ADD in adulthood. The inclusion of objective tests will depend on the background of the professional who is doing the evaluation. If the evaluation is being done by a clinical or educational psychologist, the following tests are commonly used in the evaluation process.

Wechsler Adult Intelligence Test – Revised (WAIS-R)

The WAIS-R provides information in two areas. If an adult has ADD, a particular profile should emerge on the various subtests of the WAIS-R. The tests that appear to be impacted by ADD are those dealing with memory and spatial relationships. In fact, the WAIS-R includes ratings from a "Freedom from Distractibility Scale," which is helpful in the diagnosis. If this particular profile emerges, it is a strong indication that the person is an ADD adult.

The second piece of information that is gleaned from the WAIS-R is some idea of intellectual capacity. It is important to understand that, although the WAIS-R is a standardized and well-regarded intelligence test, any test scores for a potential ADD adult must be interpreted with a great deal of caution. The presence of the ADD condition itself will depress some of the subtest scores. In turn, the entire IQ will be depressed, since the test is an average of all the scores. An "adjusted range" of mental ability must be interpreted from the various subtests. This range is then used as a comparison between IQ and level of academic performance as measured by an academic battery of tests.

As an interesting aside, this helps to explain why an unidentified ADD child may have been evaluated and rejected for GATE (Gifted And Talented Education) placement several times through elementary school. In many cases, her scores were artificially depressed by the ADD profile, but this fact was never recognized by the school personnel administering the test. She never qualified for GATE classes, and this inaccurately and unfairly made the ADD child feel somehow "less than" and not quite as bright as her peers.

Academic Tests

If there is no Attention Deficit Disorder present and the individual has completed high school or college, the level of academic performance on any academic battery should correspond with the level of intellectual ability.

However, the ADD adult population very often has a discrepancy between their IQs and their levels of processing information, particularly in reading comprehension. Another area that is often low for the ADD adult is that of written language. Although he is often highly verbal and has great ideas, he is faced with an almost impossible task when he is required to write those thoughts on paper. He has also often had trouble spelling throughout his life. Another area that emerges as an area of difficulty is that of the ability to use phonics. ADD adults typically learn to read using a sight method. They simply bypass any phonics instruction given in their first or second grade classes, and the teachers are unaware of this coping strategy.

The academic test most often used by public schools and Learning Disability Centers at the college level is the Woodcock-Johnson Psycho-Educational Battery. This test measures academic levels in reading, math and written language.

Computer Tests

There are an assortment of computer tests available that assist in diagnosing ADD. These are grouped under a category called *continuous performance tests*. That means that the ADD adult is required to pay attention to the test for a specified amount of time.

In our office we have been very pleased with the TOVA (Test of Variables of Attention). TOVA was developed by Dr. Larry Greenberg, a psychiatrist at the

University of Minnesota who has worked for years with the ADD population. Dr. Greenberg's test is helpful because results are provided which give standard deviations and standard scores on four variables – inattention, impulsivity, response time and variability. In addition, he has computerized a short narrative paragraph that interprets the TOVA results so the test results make sense to the client.

The TOVA is a series of squares that appear on the computer screen at different speeds. The test is designed to determine if the adult being tested can concentrate and focus for the time that a normal adult (without ADD) has been determined to be able to focus. The person being evaluated is required to sit through twenty-two-and-a-half minutes of intense focus. Our adults often describe the TOVA as the most torturous, boring and taxing part of our evaluation. Dr. Greenberg did his job well. He managed to design a test that truly drives ADD adults crazy.

The TOVA is helpful as a *part* of the diagnosis. However, Dr. Greenberg is clear that TOVA alone should not be the only test used in the diagnosis of ADD. He notes that there is a twenty-seven percent false negative on the TOVA, and results can be skewed if an adult has ingested a lot of caffeine (coffee or colas) or is a computer whiz.

The TOVA can also be used after the diagnostic process is completed to assist in determining correct levels of medication (Dr. Greenberg normed the TOVA so that it is sensitive to every 2.5 mg. adjustment in medication). We have found it very accurate and very helpful in adjusting medication levels.

Adult Rating Scales

There are a variety of adult ADD rating scales that are either found in books about adult ADD or are sold as separate rating scales. Some of them are normed and, at the completion of the rating scale, provide a percentile score that assists in determining if the adult fits the typical ADD profile. An example of a normed scale is found in Dr. Edna Copeland's *Attention Please!*. Other rating scales include the one listed in Chapter 1 of this book and the rating scale by Drs. Hallowell and Ratey in *Driven to Distraction*. These provide information that allows the adult to make up his or her own mind about the "fit."

It is very important that not only the potential ADD adult, but a spouse or significant other complete a rating scale. This provides a little more objectivity, as well as an additional dimension.

Medical Tests

Medical science is advancing by leaps and bounds. In years past we had to wait twenty-four hours to culture strep throat; now there is a blood test available in doctors' offices that can identify the presence of Streptococcus (the culprit in strep throat) while we wait in the icy examining room. We used to wait for three months to make sure of a pregnancy; now we pluck a neatly packed kit from a drug store shelf that will tell a woman if she is pregnant. We believe, however, that the most exciting, most mind-blowing scientific advances have come from the field of molecular biology.

Finally, science and technology have advanced to the point where scientists are beginning to understand DNA, which, of course, makes up each individual's unique blueprint. For example, we now have the technology to identify a specific gene that is responsible for a certain strain of cancer that runs in a family and thus predisposes other family members to the risk of cancer. Fortunately, this technology has allowed researchers to better understand ADD as well.

Researchers have identified specific genes that they feel are part of the larger ADD picture. Some of the genes are implicated in dopamine production, and some are implicated in addictive patterns in families. At this point, the consensus seems to be that ADD is a polygenetic disorder (polygenetic means many genes, so ADD would be caused by many genes). Until recently the testing procedure has involved analyzing either blood or tissue samples. However, research has made another leap forward which may ultimately provide us with the quick and easy test for ADD that we've been talking about for years. In *Overload, Attention Deficit Disorder and the Addictive Brain,* authors David Miller and Kenneth Blum describe a brand new breakthrough in genetic testing, which involves merely swabbing the inside of the mouth which extracts cheek cells to use in identifying the presence of specific genes.

Let's be clear where science stands right now. We have research that identifies at least *some* of the genes that are implicated in ADD. The catch is that we do not have the technology that allows us to clearly identify the presence of ADD or make a firm diagnosis. We can only predict that with a particular gene the person has a forty, fifty or even seventy percent likelihood of exhibiting some ADD characteristics. No one is saying that we are even close to having the entire genetic picture of what makes up ADD in any individual. We now have many pieces of the genetic puzzle of ADD out on the table in front of us, but we are not sure we have all of the pieces or, beyond that, if they will go together to make a whole.

At this time there is absolutely no simple, easy-to-administer medical test *of any kind* that will identify the presence of ADD. The most accurate diagnosis must be made from a comprehensive assessment. The information from these component parts must then be pieced together like a jigsaw puzzle to provide the ADD diagnosis.

Positron Emission Tomography (PET)

Where else is medical science in its research? Can it provide any new information on the workings of the brain? Of course.

The PET Scan is truly an awesome advance in medical technology, but it is still considered experimental in nature. Due to its tremendous size and even more tremendous cost, it is found at only a few locations in the United States – usually at university campuses. To further complicate the matter, radioactive material is required. This means that a cyclotron must also be on the premises (or that radioactive material be within a two-hour drive or flight). It requires a bank of technicians to run the scan and another bank of technicians to interpret the computer diagnosis.

The process involved in the testing is lengthy in itself. The subject is administered the radioactive soup, usually in a glucose base, by an I.V. The person is then asked to concentrate on a specific task for thirty minutes. During this time the brain is absorbing the radioactive material into its various parts. The subject is then slipped into the scanner, which takes three hundred and sixty-degree pictures of the brain. After the scan is completed and the technicians work on the complex images, the information is presented in visual images (colored pictures of slices of the brain) and in statistical values. The spectrum of colors moves from blue through green, yellow, orange, then red. The move of colors in the picture toward the red spectrum indicates the more activity that is present. The move toward the blue spectrum would indicate less energy present. There is a great deal of ongoing research with the PET scan, not just with ADD individuals, but also in its use in understanding depression, schizophrenia, stuttering and many more conditions.

The PET scan provided the ADD population with the first medical proof of the existence of ADD. This important study was done by Dr. Alan Zemetkin at the National Institute of Mental Health (NIMH) and indicated that ADD adults have two lobes in their brains that emit less energy when their glucose level is evaluated.

Is there anything else medical horizon? Brain Electrical Activity Mapping (BEAM) is a technique that measures the electrical waves in the brain. Work done by Eric Braverman and associates suggests that BEAM may be useful in predicting the possibility of ADD in young children. Dr. Daniel Amen, a psychiatrist practicing in Northern California and author of *Windows into the A.D.D. Mind*, is using Single Photon Emission Computed Tomography (SPECT) scan imaging in evaluating and treating ADD. Based on his research, Dr. Amen believes that he and his colleagues are seeing five different brain patterns associated with ADD. Both researchers believe that neither test can be used in isolation in a diagnosis. However, valuable information is provided by both the BEAM and SPECT scan, so additional research is sure to be forthcoming.

Summary

At this time the evaluation process to diagnose ADD in adults is far from an exact science. The accuracy of the evaluation depends on the information the ADD adult brings to the picture. It also depends on the skill of the professional making the diagnosis. If an adult was diagnosed as ADD in childhood and placed on medication until adolescence, the diagnosis is an easy one. Even if ADD was not diagnosed in childhood, when there was a string of comments from teachers noting that the then-child never paid attention in class, was spacy, couldn't sit still, or never worked to his or her potential, the diagnosis is still fairly clear-cut. When the ADD adult has a more complicated history, or the ADD symptoms are compounded by depression, addiction or compulsive behaviors, the diagnosis takes more skill. However, even in these cases the diagnostic process outlined in this chapter holds the most promise for an accurate diagnosis. With enough information, the psychologist, psychiatrist or other professional will be able to fit all the jigsaw pieces into one comprehensive whole.

Remember, this is one area where self-diagnosis appears to have much validity. This means that if you have attended lectures, read information about ADD in adulthood, and are convinced that you are an ADD adult, have faith in your convictions. If a Learning Disability Center at a college or university diagnoses you as dyslexic, but doesn't mention ADD, consult another professional. If a psychiatrist tells you, "You can't be ADD – you are too intelligent," don't hesitate to get a second opinion.

One day in the future, the diagnosis of ADD will be as easy and uncomplicated as walking through a scanner or providing a drop of blood. At least our children or our children's children will have an easier road.

Chapter 13

Treatment of Adult ADD:
Now That I Know What I Have,
What Do I Do About It?

Author's note: In an effort to bring you, the reader, the most accurate, up-to-date information about medications commonly used to treat ADD, we consulted with our resident expert, Dr. Joseph Wu, Associate Professor of Psychiatry in residence, Acting Director of the University of California, Irvine, Brain Imaging Center. Dr. Wu is in charge of the PET Scanning Program at UCI and, thus, is at the center of all the newest developments regarding brain research, including the field of ADD. We thank him for his time and the insights he lent to this chapter.

Low sugar diets, no caffeine, exercise, acupuncture, acupressure, Chinese herbal medicine, Ritalin, Dexedrine, Cylert, antidepressants, antihypertensives, biofeedback, mind-over-matter, Diet Pepsi®, Coca-Cola® – these are some of the treatments used for adult Attention Deficit Disorder. As we mentioned in the chapter on addictions, it is common for ADD adults to have a long history of attempts to self-medicate in order to correct their body chemistries. There is also a long history of debate as to whether Western medicine is more effective than Eastern medicine; whether transcendental meditation is more effective than exercise; whether your physician, your nutritionist or your counselor should be your primary resource.

For many ADD adults, just having someone clearly identify the ADD condition in their lives evokes several responses. First, they are validated. The difficulties that they have encountered are not a result of laziness or a lack of motivation; they are not stupid. The next feeling is often one of relief. If the ADD condition is identified, it is a defined disorder and can be treated. There is a possibility of help from some avenue of treatment. There is a feeling of comfort in knowing that not only do their symptoms have a name and a label, but there are other ADD adults out there who have experienced many of the same problems. For many ADD adults, there is also a feeling of being totally overwhelmed. They realize with startling clarity that the ADD condition is very real, and it is there for life.

This chapter will consider the various treatments of ADD that will affect the biochemical systems in the body. The next chapter will cover coping techniques.

The first subject to be tackled is Western medicine (medicine typically used in our culture) and its usefulness in treating adult ADD.

Medication

For many newly-diagnosed ADD adults, the question of medication looms like a huge cloud on the horizon. "Do I really need medication?" "Should I take medication?" "Are there side effects?" "What will people think?"

The purpose of this chapter is to pull the question of medication apart and look at each specific aspect. This chapter will discuss various medications commonly used to treat ADD and when medications should be used in combination. The chapter will also discuss some of our ADD adults with unusual biochemistry where medications were difficult to adjust. We will end with several case histories.

As therapists, we work on the front line with ADD adult clients day after day. Our understanding of ADD and the treatment of ADD comes from listening carefully to hundreds of clients and then distilling that information. We reach conclusions based on cases we see daily in our practices. Neither of us is a physician. Is it presumptuous to write a chapter on medications? No! In fact, our experience with our own practices parallels newest information on adult ADD published by experts such as Hallowell and Ratey, Copps, and Copeland.

There is agreement between information obtained from therapists working within a practice and physicians and researchers. You, the reader, are getting the distillation of both worlds in one easy chapter.

Let's look at the problems surrounding medication.

Do I Really Need Medication?

Let's go back to the understanding that ADD is a biochemical condition. For the ADD adult, the brain chemistry is incorrect. As medical science understands it, there appears to be a chemical deficiency in the frontal lobes of the brain. Researchers such as Dr. David Comings are beginning to identify defects in specific enzymes as well. The result is that normal functions of the frontal lobes (attention, planning, organization, long-term goals, self-criticism) are ineffective. This also translates into problems with inhibition and control and problems with stopping the flow of attention, thoughts, emotions and ideas. If you are dealing with a biochemical imbalance, you may need medication to adjust the biochemical system.

Another consideration is the severity of ADD in each individual. ADD ranges from mild to severe. If you have a mild case of ADD you may find that the initial diagnosis offers tremendous relief in terms of, "Oh, this is a real condition. I'm not crazy." Beyond that, if ADD is mild it may be controlled by exercise, coping skills, etc., and you may not need medication at all.

But, if the ADD adult has suffered from academic problems in school, been known as a space cadet all his life, or tagged with the label of "lazy," the ADD is impacting his life in a significant manner. If the ADD adult is so hyperactive he can't sit still, if he is so impulsive he continually interrupts business meetings or has had relationship after relationship fall apart, medication may be not only help-ful, but necessary.

What Will People Say?

We are in an era that is focused on the *Say No to Drugs* slogans. Certainly the concept is important, because indiscriminate use of drugs is not good and certainly is responsible for a great deal of heartache and misery, as well as violence in soci-ety. The drug most commonly used as the first drug of choice in treating ADD in children and adults is Ritalin, which is sold under the generic name of methyl-phenidate. Ritalin is a controlled substance and, as such, is subject to regulation by the FDA. The implication is that Ritalin is somehow "dangerous" or "addictive." For the ADD adult, this presents additional problems. For many ADD adults, if they use drugs they somehow feel like a drug addict committing an illicit act. When they go down to the corner pharmacy they feel as though they are cruising the streets for a drug buy.

For many, there is an element of shame in taking drugs to correct the chemical imbalance of ADD, possibly because they still confuse medications for ADD and medications for mental illness. Added to this problem is the reluctance of some physicians to prescribe Ritalin because it is a Class II drug issued on a triplicate prescription form. Some pharmacists refuse to honor prescriptions for Ritalin unless they have had personal conversations with the prescribing physicians.

Even with all the ADD adult publicity that is in the media today, there is still a mind-set within some of the medical community that ADD is merely a figment of someone's imagination and should disappear at the onset of adolescence. There is also a preconceived notion that the use of stimulant medication is merely a method used by ADD adults as a way to get their next high or experience a pleas-ant "buzz." While this couldn't be farther from the truth, it has caused some embarrassing and unpleasant incidents.

We would like to relate several incidents that have happened to our clients in pharmacies and physicians' offices. This is not done to be negative or to frighten our ADD adults, but rather to alert them to problems that other ADD adults have encountered.

One of our middle-aged ADD female clients walked into her pharmacy that was located in the center of her small, but upscale, beach community. She encountered several friends and neighbors on her way to the pharmacist's area. When she handed the pharmacist the prescription, he said, loudly enough for the entire drugstore to hear, "Why, this stuff is addictive. Why in the world would you want to take it?" She was mortified, yanked the prescription out of his hand and scurried out of the pharmacy. It took two office visits plus a personal phone call to a new pharmacy before she would even attempt to get another pre-scription filled.

Another ADD adult, this time a young professional woman, had her pharma-cist refuse to fill her prescription for Ritalin. The prescription was printed by the physician, but was signed in cursive writing. The pharmacist accused her of illegal-ly obtaining the prescription and forging the physician's signature, which was understandably humiliating to her.

Another client, after his diagnosis, decided to return to his long-time family practitioner to discuss ADD and obtain a trial of medication. With disdain the doctor said, "You are too smart to have ADD. Look how successful you are. This is a bunch of hogwash, and all the medication will do is make you an addict."

A psychologist, who was a rather severe ADD adult himself, was part of a panel of speakers giving a lecture on ADD in children, adolescents and adults to a group of school teachers and administrators. The psychologist spoke clearly on the use of medication in adults with ADD, as well as his own experience of feeling "normal" for the first time in his life once he began medication. The next speaker was a pediatrician who hadn't been listening. In front of the entire group, the pediatrician remarked to the psychologist, "Ritalin in adults . . . I'm sure you get a nice buzz from the Ritalin."

Even in the face of our current medication research, the ADD adult will often face the implication that the medications used to treat ADD are addictive, harmful or merely provide pleasure. When these types of incidents occur, it takes an incredibly strong ADD adult to withstand the barrage, stand firm and try the medication.

Common Criticisms of Medication

The Ritalin Controversy – On May 15, 1996 the *New York Times* carried an article with the headline "Boom in Ritalin Sales Raises Ethical Issues." Included in the article was the graph reproduced below.

This statement raised an incredible amount of furor for a period of time. Additional newspaper and television coverage added to the hysteria. Since this statement has been put out there for the general public to read, let's hit the issue head-on and see what is really occurring.

Personal Bias – Not surprisingly, specialists within the ADD field present a considerable division of opinion, depending on their own bias regarding ADD treatment. Dr. David Velokoff, of the Drake Institute, specializes in treating ADD with biofeedback techniques. A transcript from the January 12, 1996 airing of CNN's *The World Today* quotes Dr. Velokoff as saying, "I am very concerned about how many children are medicated so aggressively today for this disorder, and everything in my medical intuition tells me it's wrong, that we don't have long-term studies on the effectiveness and safety of these drugs." In contrast, Dr. Joseph Biederman, Director of Pediatric Psychopharmacology at Massachusetts General Hospital in Boston, was quoted in the *New York Times* (May 15, 1996) as saying that he

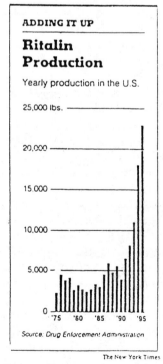

ADDING IT UP

Ritalin Production

Yearly production in the U.S.

Source: Drug Enforcement Administration

The New York Times

believed the recent surge in Ritalin prescriptions meant only that "the treatment is catching up with the illness."

Misdiagnosis – Another allegation is that ADD is being misdiagnosed and, thus, overdiagnosed in both children and adults. We have no doubt that this is occurring, but in our experience, the misdiagnosis leads to underdiagnosis. Let's take a look at why we are making this statement.

Our understanding of ADD has gone through several different phases over the years. In the 1950s we thought ADD pertained only to children. At that time ADD was a hot topic because Ritalin had just been released by Ciba Pharmaceuticals, and there was a huge amount of promotional material supplied to physicians, as well as to school personnel. As we've mentioned previously, the medication was overused and misused, and the entire area of the diagnosis and treatment of ADD fell into a dark period where it wasn't discussed at all. During this time, ADD was deleted from programs that trained psychologists, educators and physicians.

To illustrate just how thorough this blackout was, let us tell you a personal story. In the 1980s one of the authors completed a master's program, then specialized in the field of school psychology. In the state of California, a school psychologist is an individual who is responsible for identifying, diagnosing and setting up treatment plans for children and adolescents with learning disabilities and/or ADD, so the program certainly should encompass a good deal of training about ADD. That, however, was not the case. Even though this particular master's program was at a state university best known for its advanced work in treating learning problems, the subject of ADD was mentioned once, and that was only in passing.

If we extend this lack of training to other professionals, which include psychologists and psychiatrists, it is obvious that professionals being trained during the "blackout" years had no information about ADD in their coursework. Thus, ADD is very often *overlooked* as a diagnosis simply because there is a lack of knowledge about the condition on the part of the professionals.

In the 1980s Dr. Paul Wender's research began to indicate that ADD continues into adolescence and adulthood. This was supported by a host of additional researchers. However, information about ADD in adults was buried in academic and medical journals which were not easily accessible to the public. There were no huge pharmaceutical companies advertising any new product to treat ADD, but bits and pieces of information about ADD in adults emerged and began to be passed on. One national newsletter emerged, then a second and a third. The Ch.A.D.D. groups began to include ADD adults in their populations. The ADD adult movement is truly a grassroots movement that began slowly but, once it reached a certain momentum, spread like wildfire. Today we have numerous books on ADD in adults, as well as a multitude of newsletters and conferences that have come about as a result of this groundswell.

Another allegation is that children are being misdiagnosed so that Ritalin can be used as a behavioral control for children who may have other biological or emotional difficulties. This statement is difficult to understand. If a non-ADD child is given too much Ritalin, he or she will process it as a stimulant, and there will be an *increase* in activity level. Thus, if a non-ADD child is given Ritalin, there should be a negative effect from the medication that is very evident.

In summary, it is true that Ritalin prescriptions have tripled. However, we are no longer diagnosing only children with ADD, but also adolescents and adults. Adding those two additional categories alone would account for the increase in prescriptions. Furthermore, in the case of adults, medication is often continued through the life span, which would also increase the amount of Ritalin used. Thus, the increase in Ritalin certainly has a logical explanation and in no way indicates that there is a widespread misuse of the medication, or a great deal of misdiagnosis leading to overdiagnosis of the ADD condition.

The Abuse of Ritalin – The media, always busy, has also produced several articles and TV spots that indicate Ritalin is being widely abused among high school and college students. In fact, Ritalin has been called the new designer drug for our youth. In our own practices it's true we've heard stories about students selling their Ritalin to friends and classmates. We've also heard stories about teenagers crushing Ritalin with their heels and snorting it for a quick high. A news special on CNN exposed a pharmacist who not only snorted Ritalin but injected it as well. While abuse does occur, our own personal experiences in our practices indicate that this abuse is not as pronounced as the media would suggest. To take this allegation beyond the realm of our own clinical experiences, we've researched the literature for some answers.

It is accurate that Ritalin and cocaine, when taken nasally (or snorted), compete for the same binding sites in the brain. When Ritalin is snorted or injected, it is accurate that the initial "high" may seem parallel to cocaine. However, research noted in the *Archives of General Psychiatry* (1995) shows that methylphenidate clears the brain channels more slowly and, therefore, the "high" wears off significantly faster. Awareness of this response would suggest that Ritalin would not be preferred over cocaine in seeking a "high."

The warnings regarding strokes, hypertension and seizures noted in *Newsweek* (October, 1995) and *Seventeen* (February 1996) magazines, as well as the *20/20* coverage are valid. Since the energy burst received for the Ritalin abuser is short-lived, it drives that abuser to use more and more of the drug to try to equal the "high" achieved with cocaine. At such high doses of Ritalin, the risk of side effects such as strokes, hypertension and seizures *do* increase; however, most adolescents wouldn't choose Ritalin in the first place. It does not produce the same high over time and is not used as a major drug on the street.

But Ritalin is Addictive – When taken orally, no, it is not. But, information in the PDR doesn't help to clarify this question and, to make matters more obscure, Ritalin is on a triplicate prescription which, by its very nature, suggests that Ritalin is a dangerous drug. In actuality, Ritalin can be taken on an intermittent basis with no difficulty at all. It can be taken only when an ADD adult is in a college class and needs it to improve concentration, or only at work for the same reason. There is no psychological or physiological craving that occurs. However, ADD adults often do question if Ritalin is addictive because they suddenly realize that they are very careful never to let their supply of Ritalin run out, and they often keep a stash of several days' supply just for backup, in case their physicians are out of town when they need new prescriptions.

In fact, many of our clients are very concerned regarding the question of addiction, deciding to perform their own experiments and simply stop taking the medication. They always come back into the office saying, with amazement, "I didn't believe you, but you were right! There were absolutely no cravings for Ritalin once I stopped." What they experienced is exactly the same phenomenon that all of us experience when we stop using something as routine in our lives as wearing glasses or contact lenses. One of the authors is blind as a bat without her contacts. She is always very careful to keep a second set of lenses as a backup, particularly if she is on a trip. Without the lenses she could still function, but her performance in any work situation would surely suffer. On a trip, she wouldn't enjoy herself because she couldn't see beyond her nose. She is not addicted to glasses. She merely realizes they make life so much easier. That parallel holds true for Ritalin.

But we must also look at the other side of the coin. Unfortunately, humans who are addictive in nature are marvelously inventive. Both ADD adults and the regular population who abuse drugs have found that Ritalin does have an addictive quality. If Ritalin is crushed into powder and snorted or injected into the body it does produce a "high" and is addictive.

How Medication is Obtained

To obtain medication, a prescription is required. This necessitates an office visit to a physician, who should perform a complete physical examination. This exam will hopefully include laboratory tests that check levels of blood sugar, a complete thyroid panel, a complete blood count, and a liver function test if Cylert is prescribed. Many times blood sugar imbalances and thyroid or pituitary dysfunction will be manifested in symptoms similar to those of ADD. Providing there are no underlying illnesses or abnormalities, the physician may either prescribe a medication for ADD or refer the patient to a psychiatrist for the prescription.

A word to the wise is indicated at this time. Because of the recent understanding of ADD and the ever-growing pharmaceutical industry, many physicians are not able to adequately keep up with current trends and research. ADD is one of the fields with which many MDs are unfamiliar unless they have treated many ADD patients recently. It therefore becomes the responsibility of the patient to educate the physician, and the physician is often receptive to this education. Sometimes a therapist, counselor or a nurse will be able to assist the ADD adult in this task of educating the physician.

Another bit of advice – if you are obtaining your medication information from the *Physicians' Desk Reference* (PDR), don't. The *PDR* is written by pharmaceutical companies to aid the physician in writing a prescription and function as a quick reference. The description of Ritalin, for example, pertains to the normal or average person and is just the opposite for the person with ADD. Frequently, if ADD adults read the side effects of a medication, sure enough, those will be the ones they will exhibit.

As holds true for anyone prescribing or giving medication to a patient, the first question is which medication to prescribe, and then how much of the medication should be given and when. The amount of the drug may also be based on the patient's lifestyle and the individual relief of symptoms. The amount of specific psychostimulant, primarily Ritalin, varies widely between patients. When a combination of medications, such as psychostimulants, antidepressants and others, are prescribed, it is advisable to defer to a psychiatrist or someone with expertise in biochemical pharmacology.

Unique Considerations Regarding ADD Medication

Individuality

We have stated that ADD is no more than an umbrella descriptor for a bio-chemical imbalance. At this stage of medical research we are able to diagnose the overall ADD condition, but each individual with ADD exhibits his or her own unique set of symptoms. Adding to these unique symptoms, each individual also brings to the picture their own individual body chemistry. Each person's unique brand of ADD must be recognized as being as individual as a set of fingerprints.

Remember, there is no cookbook formula that we can follow. The same medica-tion or formula won't work for ADD adults across the board. The medication must be approached with each individual's unique brand of body chemistry in mind.

With this factor of individuality, the challenge in medicating ADD adults is finding the single drug, or combination of medications, that is most effective. To further complicate treatment, we have no simple blood test or any other method of calculating when the medication is absolutely correct and the brain chemistry falls within the "normal" range.

Due to this fact, ADD adults must be active participants in their treatment. This means that the physician administering the medication must be willing to lis-ten carefully to feedback from the patient and adjust the medication accordingly. The physician must also be willing to educate the patient about the various med-ications.

At times, ADD adults are precisely on target about the effects of medication on their lives; however, others have more trouble identifying changes in moods or levels of depression. Thus it is a good rule of thumb to have a spouse, sibling, par-ent or significant other involved in the regulation of medication. This means that another adult accompanies the ADD adult to the physician's office. People on the outside looking in are often extremely sensitive to changes in the ADD adult and can be surprisingly accurate in their descriptions of the changes. This feedback assists the physician in adjusting medication.

Systems Range from Sensitive to Resistant

While the systems of the ADD adult population are unique, according to Dr. Stephen Copps, there are some generally accepted guidelines in treatment. It is known that the very, very old and the very, very young appear to be physiologically sensitive to medication in some way. However, people after the age of six and before the age of sixty appear to react pretty much alike in their sensitivity. It does not appear that adults with ADD alone are any more sensitive to medication than the general population, although the ADD condition *is* unique, and we can expect there to be individual differences. Some ADD adults will be more sensitive to medication, others will be less. Only a trial of medication will tell.

With the sensitive end of the ADD population, it does not hold true that "If a little is good, more is better." If an ADD adult is extremely sensitive to medication, a dose of medication that would be considered subclinical (too small to produce any difference at all) makes a marked difference. Dr. Lawrence Greenberg, University of Michigan, who invented the Test of Variables of Attention (TOVA), reports that he often sees significant differences in the ADD adult population with just 1 mg. of Ritalin.

This very sensitivity can present problems for the ADD adult if the physician or psychiatrist is unaware of this tendency. If an ADD adult complains that a very small dose of medication causes negative effects, it could be interpreted as resistance on the part of the ADD adult, instead of an indication of extreme sensitivity. We have also seen a positive reaction to an extremely small dose of medication interpreted as only a "placebo effect."

Research done by Hallowell and Ratey agrees with the concept of sensitivity in the adult ADD population. In fact, they feel that perhaps one in ten ADD adults have an *extremely* sensitive brain chemistry. They also note that a history of brain injury, premature delivery or birth trauma may exacerbate this sensitivity.

However, ADD adults can also fall on the opposite end of the continuum and have systems that are extremely resistant to medication. In our practices, we have found that many ADD adults who have abused drugs as adolescents or into adulthood fall into this category. When a "normal" dose of a stimulant is prescribed, there is often no effect at all. It is only when doses are prescribed at higher levels that they begin to experience the ability to focus and concentrate, and hyperactivity is reduced and impulsivity curbed.

At this point we are not sure if these individuals became addicted in the first place because their brains had such a high tolerance for certain substances. The other possibility is that the normal sensitivity of the brain was altered because of the heavy substance abuse.

The difficulty in treating the ADD population is obvious. Pharmacists often question prescriptions that request high doses of controlled substances such as Dexedrine or Ritalin. The vast majority of physicians are reluctant to prescribe doses in excess of what is considered "normal" for fear of being audited by the DEA. Thus the prescribing of stimulants often tends to be very conservative by most physicians.

Respect

The ADD adult and the physician must develop a mutual respect and willingness to work together as medication is adjusted. It may be that the first medication is not successful. It may be that the ADD adult experiences an unusual effect or side effect from the medication. When he attempts to relay his experience with a particular medication, he may say something that the psychiatrist has never heard before and thus tends to disbelieve.

For example, some of our ADD adults have reported that on marijuana they tend to think much more clearly. They don't experience the relaxed, sleepy feeling that is the response experienced by most of the population. Their body chemistries are truly different from the norm. It is important that the psychiatrist listen carefully and be willing to catalogue the various responses. It may be that the ADD adult has an extremely sensitive body chemistry. On a normal dose of any given medication, she may experience bizarre side effects. However, on a tiny, tiny dose that would be considered a subclinical dose, she feels beneficial results. Psychiatrists often disregard these comments and tell the client she couldn't be feeling anything at all, that it must be only a placebo effect.

However, with ADD adults, due to an extremely sensitive body chemistry, minuscule doses of medication are often all that are needed. It may be that two, or even three, medications are needed to balance the body chemistry correctly. This inevitably means that there is a period of trial and error where one medication is administered and adjusted, and then a second, and often a third, medication is added. The client must respect how difficult this is for the psychiatrist and how much skill is required. At this level, the mixing and blending of medications is more an art form than a science. The psychiatrist must be willing to listen closely to the ADD adult and adjust medications according to the feedback received. The psychiatrist must understand how frustrating this period of adjustment is for the clients and be extremely sympathetic and supportive.

Comorbidity

We have been speaking of ADD as a totally separate and distinct condition up to this point. However, humans are rather complex creatures. It stands to reason that, at least in some of our ADD adults, ADD may be present along with another disorder. It is very common for ADD adults to also have a mild form of depression or a tendency to be compulsive about arranging paperwork or cleaning the house. As long as the ADD is the predominant condition (the condition that is causing the most distress), it remains the primary diagnosis.

However, it is also possible that our ADD adult may be suffering from a more serious condition, as well as ADD. They may have a bipolar disorder or have severe clinical depression. In those cases, the *Diagnostic and Statistical Manual – IV (DSM-IV)* has some very clear rules about how a diagnosis must be made. The *DSM* states that the condition that is the more severe (i.e., is causing the most problems in life) is the one that leads the diagnosis. Thus, if a person is clinically depressed, can't get out of bed, has lost his/her job, is nonfunctional and also ADD, depression would be the major diagnosis. In this case, ADD would be considered a comorbid condition. That word "comorbid" sounds pretty grim, but it's just medical jargon meaning that there are two or more conditions present that must be treated.

The 1996 U.S. Psychiatric and Mental Health Congress, held in San Diego, CA, cited the following statistics regarding comorbidity among the ADD adult population:

- Depressive disorders
  – Major depression (17 to 31%)
  – Bipolar (5 to 31%)
- Anxiety disorders
  – Generalized anxiety, panic attacks plus agoraphobia (20 to 43%)
- Substance dependence disorders
  – Alcohol (27 to 36%)
  – Drug (18 to 21%)
- Antisocial disorders (12 to 18%)

At this point you may be wondering why we are belaboring the subject of comorbidity or the way a diagnosis is made. It is an important piece of information because the diagnosis often dictates the type of medication that is prescribed. For example, let's take an individual who has been diagnosed as having both ADD and bipolar disorder. In that case, the diagnosis of bipolar disorder alone usually precludes the prescription of a psychostimulant, since stimulants often cause an acute episode of manic behavior. However, when an ADD adult has been diagnosed as ADD *and* bipolar, the ADD diagnosis indicates that her body chemistry is unique and often unlike that of an individual who has only a bipolar disorder and no ADD.

To a great degree, the diagnosis itself acts as a guideline for medication. We do see cases where stimulant medications work successfully with bipolar individuals and do not cause manic episodes, but rather treat both the bipolar condition and the ADD. The same premise holds true for other comorbid conditions as well. For example, if an ADD adult has had a substance abuse problem and has been on "speed," Dexedrine is often successfully used in treating the ADD symptoms without causing the addiction to continue.

Usual Sequence of Medication Prescribed – To continue with our promise of keeping the subject of medication simple, there is a formula to follow. The majority of the ADD adult population will notice significant benefits from one of the psychostimulants alone. This is typically the first medication that is prescribed. If the stimulant medication provides an improvement in concentration and processing, that is considered to be a positive sign, and the next step is to regulate the dosage. If compliance – or, in laymen's terms, "remembering to take the medication more than once a day" – is a problem, one of the time-release medications may be used. Some of these are more effective than others. For a more thorough discussion of the merits of each, read on to the descriptions of individual medications found in this chapter.

If the ADD adult continues to experience moods, depression or rage attacks, as soon as the first medication is stabilized and the correct dose is found, a second medication is added. The medication that seems to be the next choice is one of the newer antidepressants which fall under the category of the SSRIs (Specific Serotonin Reuptake Inhibitors). In our practice, we estimate that probably sixty-five percent of our clients are on this particular combination of medications, and the combination is working very successfully.

However, if one or the other of the medications does not work, if depression is still a problem or if there is a negative effect present, our ADD adult then falls into the category of having what we call (for lack of a scientific label) a "difficult body chemistry."

As we said before, at this level the adjustment of medication is more like an art form and must be done by a psychiatrist who is truly an expert in psychopharmacology. The psychiatrist must be able to adjust small quantities of various medications that interrelate to concoct that person's individual recipe. Once that is done, the dose of medication does not remain static but typically needs to be adjusted periodically.

The Medications Themselves

We are going to begin with the most simple treatment of ADD and move into the more complex. This goes with the old adage, "Keep it simple . . ."

Psychostimulants

Dr. Steve Copps, Medical Director, The National Professional Consortium in Attention Deficit Disorders, and a physician in Georgia, stated at an ADD workshop that there are "...only three to treat ADD." He was talking about Ritalin, Dexedrine and Cylert. In the treatment of adults, this is too simplistic an approach, but it does provide a starting place.

Due to the length of time psychostimulants have been used to treat ADD children, there is a huge body of research available on this subject. Because the adult field is still quite new, there is less research available. The consensus in the literature regarding medical treatment of children, adolescents and adults is that Ritalin is the first drug of choice. We are finding that to be true in our own work with ADD adults as well. Two of the most common complaints of this population are poor attention and impulsivity. The psychostimulants often treat these symptoms very effectively.

Finally, the response to both Ritalin and Dexedrine is rapid. The ADD adult will be able to determine whether it is effective in a short period of time. This is quite a contrast to the time required for an antidepressant to build up to an effective level in the system. Typically, the correct dosage of a psychostimulant can be ascertained within a two- or three-week period of time. As there is usually a marked effect on concentration and attention span when the medication is in the system, adults can usually give clear feedback on its effectiveness.

Ritalin – Isn't this the drug that makes zombies of children? When Ritalin was first developed in the 1950s it was overused by some practitioners and the dosages were quite high. With the ADD population, if too much of a psychostimulant is prescribed, it will often produce sleepiness – the drugged, zombie-like look. This is not the fault of the medication, it is the fault of an incorrect dose.

Ritalin has also been the subject of extremely negative publicity campaigns at various points in time by the Church of Scientology. Using pamphlets published under the title "Commission for Human Rights," the Church of Scientology has printed information about Ritalin that is not only misleading but incorrect.

According to information presented at the U.S. Psychiatric and Mental Health Congress (1996), as well as information in the majority of articles and books about ADD, Ritalin is the first-line choice in the treatment of ADD. In actuality, Ritalin is very safe. It has been around for over fifty years and has thus passed the test of time. The medical community seems to feel that if a medication has been used for fifty-plus years, there will be no surprises or unusual side effects noted after that time. There are longitudinal studies on children who have been placed on Ritalin in childhood and who are now in adulthood. For more information on this specific topic, read *Hyperactive Children Grown Up* (see bibliography).

As we discussed earlier in this chapter, if taken orally, Ritalin is not addictive. However, in some states it is still considered a controlled substance. This means that a prescription for Ritalin must be written on a special triplicate form and be filled within a specified number of days (somewhere between two to seven days, depending on the state). The prescribing physician may be audited at any time, which may make him or her reluctant to write a prescription for Ritalin at all.

At this point, our discerning ADD adults may be asking why Ritalin is *ever* a controlled substance if it is not addictive. According to Dr. Copps, Ritalin is an amphetamine and is actually derived from dextroamphetamine. Scientists attempting to synthesize ephedrine ended up with a product called amphetamine. The left-handed form of it is levo-amphetamine, or l-amphetamine; the right-handed form is dextroamphetamine, more commonly known by the brand name Dexedrine. Then a piperidine ring was attached, and they ended up with the product know as methylphenidate hydrochloride. This is passed out in the urine as an inactive metabolite, ritalinic acid, hence the name Ritalin.

Description – Ritalin is a small pill that can be obtained in 5, 10, and 20 mg. dosages. Although it is fairly tiny, it can be successfully cut in half or even quarters with a single-edge razor blade or one of the pill-cutters available at most pharmacies. Ritalin also comes in a 20 mg. sustained release form called Ritalin SR.

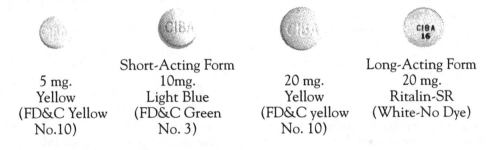

	Short-Acting Form		Long-Acting Form
5 mg.	10mg.	20 mg.	20 mg.
Yellow	Light Blue	Yellow	Ritalin-SR
(FD&C Yellow	(FD&C Green	(FD&C yellow	(White-No Dye)
No.10)	No. 3)	No. 10)	

Length and Type of Effect – Ritalin is a short-acting tablet which lasts three to five hours in the system, with the average being four hours, although the time factor can vary from adult to adult. It typically takes thirty minutes to take effect, and there is often a noticeable change in the ability to concentrate and focus at that time. It plateaus for three hours and then takes another thirty minutes to leave the system. Its half-life is very short – only two-and-a-half hours – so it is in and out of the system rapidly. Ritalin is typically taken at three- or four-hour intervals two or three times a day, depending on the span of time needed by the individual to focus and concentrate. With adults who have long work days, or with college students carrying heavy loads, sometimes four doses are used.

Ritalin SR is a long-acting form of Ritalin which lasts six to eight hours in the system – in fact, rarely does the dose last eight hours. Since the ADD adult population is made up of adults who are impulsive or have poor memories, the thought of needing to take a medication every four hours is formidable. So, Ciba decided to produce an eight-hour product. Sounds good – unfortunately, it doesn't work with most people. The eight-hour version is supposed to act like a tiny time capsule releasing carefully controlled amounts of medication – usually 10 to 12 mg. – on a regular basis throughout an eight-hour period. What often happens is that the medication is released in intermittent bursts, or the medication doesn't seem to be released at all due to the variations in individual metabolisms. Adults assume that they are on a medication when there is none circulating in their systems. The Ritalin-SR is very difficult to monitor for that reason.

Side Effects – With young children, one very typical side effect of Ritalin is a loss of appetite. Many ADD adults are delighted to hear of this particular side effect and hope it might reduce their appetites and they might lose some weight. With ADD adults, this almost never occurs. Darn! When Ritalin was first used people thought that it retarded growth. Even though this has little interest to our ADD adult population, this allegation should be explained.

As we mentioned, Ritalin often does depress appetite in children. If young children do not eat enough, they do not grow appropriately. As an example, instead of maintaining a forty-fifth percentile on the height curve in their pediatrician's office, after nine months on Ritalin they may have fallen to the thirtieth percentile. Their parents notice that their classmates seem to be getting taller and passing the ADD child in height. This phenomenon gave rise to the old concern that Ritalin causes retardation of growth. In research studies, when a child is taken off the medication (often over the summer) their appetites increase and, as a result, they grow. In fact, research studies indicate that each time the child is taken off the medication, the growth curve returns to the normal range for that particular child.

With ADD adults there are two very common side effects that seem to occur during the first week or two that the adult is taking medication. The adult often experiences a slight headache across the front of the forehead or some slight nausea, but these two symptoms are typically mild.

Generic Ritalin – Another specific word of advice on Ritalin is to be certain the medication dispensed by the pharmacist is Ritalin, manufactured by Ciba Pharmaceuticals, not the generic methylphenidate hydrochloride. "Do not substitute" must be specified on the original prescription by the physician in order to ensure that Ritalin is the medication you are receiving. Be aware that there is also a generic form of the sustained release form of Ritalin SR called methylphenidate HCl-ER (extended release). We have had problems with HMOs or specific physicians being unwilling to prescribe Ritalin, as opposed to methylphenidate. It is true there are no specific studies that validate the fact that methylphenidate is often not as effective as Ritalin.

There is actually a very good reason that no studies exist, since there is no financial reason for the companies that produce the generic methylphenidate to fund such a project. There is a good chance that the studies would show their products are inferior. On the other hand, there is no reason for Ciba (the producer of Ritalin) to fund a study, for the very same reason. However, the difficulty experienced with methylphenidate is among professionals working in the ADD field and is mentioned in many of the textbooks regarding the treatment of ADD children, as well as in many of the books published for ADD adults.

While the chemicals that make up Ritalin, as opposed to the generic form of the drug, should be identical, there are still some real differences that often affect the sensitive system of an ADD adult. Some pharmaceutical companies use colored dyes, or "binders" to hold the chemicals together. Because ADD adults often have sensitive body chemistries, they may be allergic or hypersensitive to the "binders" or colored dyes. Sometimes these additives alter the specific amounts of the drug that the body is receiving. In addition, the FDA allows a twenty percent variance of strength in generic medication.

How It Acts in the System – In very simplistic terms, Ritalin can be thought of as an energy source to the brain. Ritalin acts on the brain as a battery acts on a car.

In the brain, the complex chemicals that are produced come from a chain of events. To get an idea of the process, think of a series of dominos lined up in a long row, side by side. All it takes is one touch on the first domino to knock over the entire chain. The energy source – in this case the Ritalin – is that "touch" which allows the complex chemical reaction to occur. By activating this chain of events Ritalin assists the brain by increasing the concentration and activity of both dopamine and norepinephrine. By causing these chemicals to increase, reports indicate that attentiveness is increased, distractibility is reduced, concentration is improved, hyperactivity is reduced or hypoactivity is alleviated.

Because Ritalin is short-acting there is no therapeutic blood level that is maintained in the system. The dosage depends on observing the positive and negative side effects and the results obtained. The amount of medication needed to be effective depends upon body metabolism, the level of dopamine function, the balance of other neurotransmitters and, very likely, has nothing to do with the patient's body weight.

Fine-Tuning – For most ADD adults, it is possible to monitor the effectiveness of Ritalin by being conscious of what is occurring thirty minutes after it is taken. At that point, most ADD people experience a rather pronounced increase in concentration, ability to focus and decrease in moodiness. Occasionally, an ADD adult is not aware of the Ritalin entering the system. With those adults it is often helpful to look back over the day and gauge if they have been more productive or more able to complete tasks with Ritalin in their systems.

Ritalin is administered on a four-hour cycle in most ADD adults. However, some people find that taking the Ritalin every three-and-a-half hours produces a more even affect. If an individual's body chemistry metabolizes the medication quickly, he may need the medication every three hours.

Ritalin does produce a phenomenon called the "rebound effect." This means that for the thirty minutes wherein the medication is wearing off, there may be more difficulty with irritability or moodiness. If this occurs, it is helpful to take the medication every three-and-a-half-hours. As one dose is exiting the system, the other is already entering the system.

Many ADD adults worry that Ritalin will interfere with their sleep; however, for most ADD adults Ritalin is "normalizing" their body chemistries, so it is not a stimulant (if most ADD people take too much, they will feel sleepy) and should not interfere with their sleep. In fact, many adults report that their sleep is much more normal once they are taking Ritalin regularly. There are always exceptions. If an ADD adult finds that Ritalin taken after 4:00 p.m. keeps her up, she can experiment with a couple of alternatives. She can try taking a small dose of Ritalin an hour before she goes to bed. It is often the flight of ideas, the burst of exciting thoughts that magically appear and run through her head just as she is attempting to sleep, that cause the trouble. Often the Ritalin will allow adults to control, calm and focus their thoughts, thereby allowing them to fall asleep. A word to the wary – be sure Ritalin isn't taken so that the time intervals (rebound effect) are occurring as one falls asleep, or the rebound effect can prevent falling asleep.

Odd Notes

1. If you are covered by an HMO, fight to get the physician to insist that at least the first two or three prescriptions are Ritalin (not generic).
2. If you have a generic prescription, the vial will say methylphenidate.
3. Don't leave Ritalin in the glove compartment of your car in the summer. Extreme heat will make it lose its effectiveness.
4. Once your Ritalin dosage is established, with some insurance plans you can cut the pills and save money. For example, if your correct dose is 10 mg. you can save about fifty percent on medication by asking your physician to prescribe 20 mg. tablets and cutting the pills in half.
5. If the dose of Ritalin is high enough, you will feel some effect, either positive or negative. If you don't feel anything, don't simply stop and say the medication doesn't work. This only indicates that the dosage was never high enough to reach a therapeutic level.

What if it Doesn't Work? – If Ritalin doesn't work the typical next step in medication is Dexedrine, also known by its generic name, dextroamphetamine. While both medications are psychostimulants, they work differently in the brain. According to Hallowell and Ratey, the two drugs act upon separate neurotransmitter storage pools. Ritalin is a reuptake blocker of dopamine, leaving more dopamine available in the system. Dexedrine may exert some of its effect differently (Zemetkin, et al. 1985). For the ADD adult population who doesn't do well on Ritalin, Dexedrine may be very effective.

Dexedrine – If an ADD adult's body chemistry does not respond to Ritalin, Dexedrine is routinely considered the second drug of choice. Some physicians use Dexedrine as their first choice for an ADD adult without hyperactivity, particularly the slow-processing, sluggish individual. Dexedrine is more excitatory, while Ritalin is more calming.

According to Dr. Copps, Dexedrine appears to be no more addictive than Ritalin, which, in the oral form, is not addictive at all. It is the street drug methamphetamine (speed) which is addictive, not dextroamphetamine. Dexedrine is a very safe and effective medication for much of the ADD adult population. The dosage is kept to a low level and, of course, continually monitored.

Description

Tablet	5 mg.	Spansule	15mg.
5 mg.		10 mg.	
Orange		Clear/Brown	
(FD&C Yellow		(FD&C Yellow No. 5 and No. 6, FD&C	
Nos. 5 & 6)		Blue No. 1, and FD&C Red No. 40)	

Dexedrine is available in short-acting tablet form, but it only comes in a 5 mg. size. The tablet is triangular in shape and bright orange in color. Dexedrine also comes in a sustained release form, which is called a Dexedrine Spansule, and is available in 5, 10 or 15 mg.

Length and Type of Effect – Dexedrine tablets usually require about fifteen to thirty minutes to become effective in the system. It typically lasts between four to five hours and then the effects diminish. The time span seems to vary even more than with Ritalin. Each person must gauge for himself or herself the exact timing of the medication in his or her system.

Dexedrine Spansule – The spansule is a combination of long- and short-acting Dexedrine in the same capsule, and it is usually very effective. It typically requires forty-five to sixty minutes to become effective and lasts approximately five to six hours, depending upon the individual. Dexedrine, as with other psychostimulants, is initiated in small doses and increased gradually if needed.

How it Acts in the System – Dexedrine also acts as an energy source for the brain. Its action is slightly different than the action of Ritalin. Dexedrine is important as a releasing agent as it allows more dopamine to be released from the neurons.

Side Effects – The side effects of Dexedrine are very similar to those of Ritalin. It can decrease appetite and, in fact, is a substance commonly found in many weight reduction medications. It also stays in the system for a short time; however, the half life is longer than that of Ritalin. Dexedrine will come up positive on a drug test. There is a potential for addiction, and the dosage must be closely controlled.

Fine-Tuning – For many ADD adults, the Dexedrine Spansule produces a "softer," more even, feeling than does Ritalin, with its sharp in-and-out cycle. There is a more gradual release of medication into the system (even in the short-acting form). Although many adults find that this is a positive, it also makes it a little more difficult to monitor the medication when dosages are being adjusted. If an adult is being switched from Ritalin to Dexedrine, it is important to know that the medication does not equate straight across the board. Dr. Copeland, in her book *Medications for Attention Disorders*, states that the equivalent dose of Dexedrine is about one-half to two-thirds that of Ritalin.

A few adults have noticed excellent results on Dexedrine during the time the medication is operating in their systems; however, when they are off the medication or if they attempt to skip a day or two, they encounter a rather severe withdrawal effect which leaves them tremendously sleepy. This is a milder version of the withdrawal that someone on crystal methamphetamine ("crystal meth") feels. With a regular dosage of Dexedrine, the withdrawal is not harmful in itself, but can be annoying and may indicate that Dexedrine is not the best choice for that individual.

Odd Note – Orange or other citrus juices should not be taken with Dexedrine, since the acidity of the fruit or juice might interfere with the absorption of the Dexedrine. Different compounds have been formulated that are amphetamines that are marketed under different names. An ADD adult may respond differently to these various compounds. He may find that only one of the many variations of dextroamphetamine corrects his own particular biochemical imbalance and increases his ability to focus and concentrate. For example, one ADD adult experienced a negative effect from Ritalin. Dexedrine (both the short-acting and the Spansule) caused headaches. However, one of the lesser-known dextroamphetamine compounds, Desoxyn (which is true methamphetamine), seemed to fit the needs of his own biochemistry perfectly, and he reported a dramatic increase in his ability to focus and concentrate, even when taking small doses.

ADDerall – ADDerall comes under the general heading of Dexedrine because it is made up of dextroamphetamine salts. It was originally marketed under the name of Obitrol, a weight loss medication. ADDerall was released under its new name about two years ago and was quickly the hot topic in ADD lectures and support groups. The ADD population – children, adolescents and adults – often found this was very effective in decreasing their ADD symptoms.

Description

ADDerall is a 10 mg. tablet containing the following:

- 2.5 mg. dextroamphetamine saccharate
- 2.5 mg. dextroamphetamine sulfate
- 2.5 mg. amphetamine sulfate
- 2.5 mg. amphetamine aspartate

As a 20 mg. tablet these amounts would double.

Length and Type of Effect – According to the drug company that is producing ADDerall, the therapeutic effect often lasts up to eight hours.

Side Effects – The possible side effects parallel those noted with Dexedrine.

Fine-Tuning – This drug has not been on the market long enough as a treatment of ADD that we have much clinical information in the literature about fine-tuning. However, in our individual practices, we have had several clients and physicians who participated in the federal drug trial (described below). Thus, we are working with adults who have taken ADDerall for three to four years. They often report that the ADDerall provides a qualitatively different effect than either Ritalin or Dexedrine. Many clients describe a feeling of much greater clarity and improved ability to process information on ADDerall.

Odd Notes – We mentioned that ADDerall was an older weight loss medication, Obitrol, that was re-released. The first thing that comes to mind is a question regarding the safety of ADDerall. Was it taken off the market because it was not safe? Fortunately, no. It is actually an interesting story.

Years ago Obitrol (now ADDerall) was cleared for distribution by the FDA. When the new research about ADD existing in adolescence and adulthood began to emerge, the pharmaceutical company decided that Obitrol might be beneficial to the ADD community. To promote marketing of the medication, they changed the name to ADDerall. This name change was actually what caused all the difficulty.

The FDA became involved because of the name change and, upon checking the original clearance on Obitrol, found that some of the paperwork had been omitted. The FDA insisted that Obitrol (ADDerall) be removed from circulation and ordered new drug trials done to ensure its effectiveness and safety. For the last two years there were a few physicians who were participating in the ADDerall drug trials and were able to supply the medication to a very limited segment of the ADD patients who were participants in that trial. Finally, ADDerall was re-released with the FDA stamp of approval and is once again available.

Even though ADDerall is a dextroamphetamine compound, for many individuals it is much more effective than the standard dextroamphetamine. We asked our consulting psychiatrist, Dr. Wu, about this and found his explanation rather technical, but nonetheless extremely interesting. Apparently, ADDerall is the only product on the market that has a different optical orientation – that is to say, in both amphetamine sulfate and amphetamine aspartate, the light is twisted to the left in the crystalline pure form (technically speaking, it has a levo, or left, orientation). Richwood Pharmaceuticals, which produces ADDerall, contends that some ADD individuals respond well to ADDerall because they are responding to the "levo" orientation.

What if It Doesn't Work? – If you have been through Ritalin, Dexedrine and ADDerall is a bomb for you as well, don't despair. For whatever reason, the very individual body chemistry of ADD adults is simply acting up. The fourth drug of choice is the psychostimulant Cylert.

Cylert (pemoline) – Cylert is the fourth drug listed under psychostimulants. Does that mean that it is actually the fourth choice? Yes, it does, for two good reasons. The first reason is if Ritalin, Dexedrine or ADDerall work well in an ADD adult's system, Cylert is usually not as effective. Why not? This is another question that we can't answer. The second reason is that Cylert is the only psychostimulant that has the potential of causing liver damage, as it does build up in the system.

Description

| 18.75 mg. | 37.5 mg. | 75 mg. | 37.5 mg. |
| White | (FD&C Yellow No. 6) | White | Chewable (FD&C Yellow No. 6) |

Cylert comes in 18.75 mg. 37.5 mg. and 75 mg. doses. It is also available as chewable tablets containing 37.5 mg. of Cylert. There is no generic form available.

Length and Type of Effect – Cylert is administered only once a day and has a half-life of seven to eight hours. According to Dr. Copeland, it is rapidly absorbed from the gastrointestinal tract and achieves peak plasma levels in two or three hours. There has been wide variability reported in the metabolism of this medication; in fact, as much as two to three hundred percent variability in response has been reported. This means that one person may need a tiny amount of Cylert, and another person may need a large dose.

Although some effects of the drug can usually be seen in one to three hours of administration, the build-up of therapeutic effectiveness may take anywhere from two to three weeks. When it is discontinued, the medication requires several weeks to fully leave the bloodstream. Since it does have a build-up effect, it should be discontinued gradually.

Side Effects – A side effect commonly mentioned with Cylert is the potential for liver damage. Thus, when Cylert is prescribed, blood tests which include liver function tests are necessary on a routine basis. Blood tests are usually obtained before administration of Cylert begins and at six-month intervals during treatment. However, several sources, including Sallee and Leventhal (*Mastering Challenges with ADHD and Comorbid Conditions*) indicate that the chance of liver damage is really rather remote. They found that less than one-tenth of a percent of the population who take Cylert experience negative effects on their liver enzymes. Thus the fear of the damage seems to be much greater than the actual possibility of damage itself. Once the generally effective dose of 75 mg. a day is reached, it is often administered in two doses – two-thirds in the morning and one-third in the afternoon.

Seizures have been reported with the use of Cylert, so it is typically not indicated in those who have seizures disorders. However, for whatever reason, decreased seizure thresholds have been reported in patients taking Cylert as long as an anticonvulsant medication is prescribed at the same time (Copeland).

Fine-Tuning – If you are an ADD adult and Cylert is your fourth try at medication, the word is to be patient. Most adults will experience a much more subtle, hard-to-notice effect than with Ritalin and Dexedrine. Results are not as dramatic. Many ADD adults describe the action of Cylert as being similar to water dripping away at a rock, rather than a waterfall effect.

Odd Notes – There has been a recent change of heart regarding the first medication of choice among some of the top researchers who treat ADD. Dr. Dennis Cantwell, UCLA, spoke at a recent conference and stated he was finding that Cylert is an extremely effective medication. Other researchers disagree and maintain the position that Ritalin is the first drug of choice. In our own practices, our experience has been that Ritalin and Dexedrine are still the most effective medications. If an individual has not been able to take either Ritalin or Dexedrine successfully, they often do respond quite well to Cylert. However, if either Ritalin or Dexedrine have been effective, Cylert generally is not effective. The one thing we have run into again and again is physicians who prescribe Cylert due to convenience. They don't want to use the triplicate form required by the DEA when Ritalin or Dexedrine are prescribed.

What if It Doesn't Work? – Okay, you have run the gamut of psychostimulants. You have gone through Ritalin, Dexedrine, ADDerall and Cylert with no effect, or downright negative results. You unfortunately fall into that category of ADD adults that we clump under the term "tricky body chemistry." Don't despair – it happens. Read on.

Antidepressants

True to our promise of keeping everything as simple as possible, we'd like to move you to the next step in medications, the use of antidepressants.

Let's clarify that we are talking about a relatively new class of antidepressants called SSRIs (Specific Serotonin Reuptake Inhibitors). This class of antidepressants includes Prozac, Zoloft and Paxil. These medications are a breakthrough in treatment as they have fewer and less severe side effects than the older classes of antidepressants, the MAOIs (Monoamine Oxidase Inhibitors) and the tricyclics. Tricyclics often cause weight gain, constipation, blurred vision and have a tendency to block cardiac transmissions. The MAOIs can pose real dangers from an increase in blood pressure and a resulting stroke when they are taken in conjunction with certain foods. For example, something as innocuous as banana cream pie contains a chemical that, when combined with an MAOI, can cause a stroke.

Thus, the SSRIs are considered to be safer and a real boon in treating depression (with or without ADD). However, the widespread use of SSRIs, particularly Prozac, has caused concern that they are simply "cosmetic" or "feel good" drugs.

Although the drugs we will be discussing are marketed under the label of antidepressants, it is important to understand that they have a much broader function. The effectiveness of the SSRIs extends to any disorder which has as its base as a malfunction in the serotonin balance of the brain. The mechanism of the SSRIs prevents the reuptake of serotonin in the brain. In layman's terms, this allows more serotonin to remain available.

To visualize how SSRIs work, think of three household items: keys, locks and vacuums. Molecules of serotonin are the *keys* that float around in the neural pathways. The receptor sites along the pathways are the *locks* that turn the vacuum system on when the serotonin "keys" plug in. A process or action called "reuptake" is the *vacuum* cleaner that sucks up all the loose keys (serotonin) once the vacuum cleaner is activated. SSRI stands for Specific Serotonin Reuptake Inhibitor(s). They allow the keys to float around a longer time by blocking (inhibiting) the reuptake vacuums at the receptor sites. The SSRIs make sure that there is a readily available supply of serotonin at all times.

However, one of the first things that the ADD adult must get over is the label of "antidepressant." The application of antidepressants is quite extensive – try thinking of them as serotonin enhancers instead.

Let's look at some of the main functions of the SSRIs in the ADD adult population. ADD adults often have problems with anger control or rage attacks. The anger and rage attacks may be severe. Often the ADD adult describes the rage attack as a "white haze" or a "red haze" and is not conscious of its occurrence until after the event has passed. These violent and uncontrollable rage attacks are thought to be a result of too little serotonin in the brain. Obviously, the SSRIs would correct this imbalance and allow the individual to control his or her anger and rage.

ADD adults sometimes experience compulsions such as excessively checking the locks on the house when leaving or checking the controls on the stove six or seven times before retiring for the night. The SSRIs are routinely prescribed for individuals who check and re-check and who may have a mild form of Obsessive Compulsive Disorder.

ADD adults are prone to addictions of alcohol, drugs, food, even sex. A lack of serotonin is implicated in these difficulties as well, and the SSRIs often reduce the craving for various substances. With sex addicts, at times the SSRIs will provide some relief from the devastation that sexual preoccupation causes in their lives.

Finally, let's talk about depression. Many ADD adults suffer from a low level of depression that accompanies ADD. Perhaps they have never put a name to it, or they realized they were depressed because it has been present throughout their lives, even back to elementary school. It was so pervasive they thought that life was *just like that*. They can identify with the idea of depression if it is described as thinking the world is a shade of gray or somehow flat, without interest or color.

The SSRIs are often used in conjunction with Ritalin or Dexedrine. As they build up in the system they often provide an evenness and alleviate moods, depression, anger or addictions. One study indicated that the SSRIs might enhance the effectiveness of psychostimulants and suggests that the SSRIs be the *first* medication administered, with the psychostimulants added as a second medication.

It is sometimes appropriate to use the SSRIs alone. There are ADD adults who have no difficulty with concentration or focusing; instead, they are plagued with anger, depression or addictions. For some, the SSRIs alone will afford marked relief.

There is one word of caution concerning the use of SSRIs alone. Some ADD adults have been told that the use of SSRIs will improve concentration. In our experience, this is true only if concentration and the ability to focus have been impaired by the ADD adult's level of continuous depression. In these cases, the SSRIs alone are effective. However, if the difficulty with concentration is coupled with problems with reading (dyslexia), writing (dysgraphia), or math (dyscalculia), it is our experience that a psychostimulant is necessary in the treatment plan. The SSRI doesn't seem to cause improvement in these critical areas when used alone.

Prozac (fluoxetine hydrochloride) – Prozac! Here is another medication that has the potential of turning us all into mindless zombies or, even worse, ax murderers! Not true. Where does such drivel come from? Once again, it was the Church of Scientology that mounted an active advertising campaign against the use of this medication. In fact, they created such an uproar about Prozac that the FDA re-examined the medication and once again cleared it for release in the U. S.

Prozac was introduced in the United States in 1987. It was very effective and often produced dramatically positive results, so it quickly gained acceptance and became widely used. Because it has been so popular, the question has been asked whether the U. S. public is using it as a cosmetic drug, rather than as a drug needed to treat bona fide medical conditions. Peter Kramer, M.D., wrote *Listening to Prozac* in 1993, which hit the bestseller list and offered pros and cons on the subject of cosmetic pharmacology. While this maybe a legitimate concern regarding the non-ADD population, it is hard to understand that this type of medication could ever be considered cosmetic to an ADD adult who also has the depressive component of the disorder.

Description

Prozac is available in 10 mg. and 20 mg. capsules.

Length and Type of Effects – Prozac is one of those medications that needs to be taken only once a day. It is not considered to be fully effective until a therapeutic dose has been achieved in the bloodstream. The estimates vary widely as to the length of time this takes. The most commonly held belief is that there should be some positive response within a week or two, and certainly by the fourth week. After that length of time, if there is no response, it most probably will not be an effective medication. Prozac does need to build up to a therapeutic level in the body, so an ADD adult may notice a slight lifting of mood on one day and a gradual improvement on the following days until a therapeutic blood level has been reached.

The 20 mg. Prozac capsule is the strength typically prescribed. However, to an ADD adult who is extremely sensitive to medication, the 10 mg., or pediatric dose, is often sufficient. Many ADD adults find that they can take Prozac every other day and that an effective level is maintained in their systems.

One additional advantage to Prozac is that it has a long half-life (forty-eight to ninety hours). That means that if medication is missed on one day, it remains within the system for a longer period of time. There should be no abrupt cycles of moods if an ADD adult forgets medication for a day or two, since it leaves the system slowly.

Side Effects – If a person cannot tolerate Prozac, he or she will usually feel slightly more depressed, irritable, etc. If this occurs, the medication should be discontinued. One very common side effect of Prozac is a decrease in libido or sexual function. Both men and women have complained of this particular side effect, and at times it is sufficiently severe that the medication is discontinued.

Fine-Tuning – Prozac can make an ADD adult feel more alert or feel more sleepy. There is no way to predict this response. So, if you take Prozac in the morning and find that you are yawning throughout the day, take it before you go to bed. The reverse is also true, of course.

Suppose you are an extremely sensitive ADD adult and even the 10 mg. daily dose seems to be too high. There is a liquid form of the medication that would enable you to adjust your dosage easily. However, just to give you a "what if" scenario, what if your physician has prescribed the 10 mg. does of Prozac, but you feel that even that dose is too high? You have just picked up a two-month supply from the pharmacy, so you really don't want to request an additional prescription because of the expense. Here is the solution. Our resident psychiatrist verified that you can open the capsule and dissolve the powder in the water. Stir, pour off half of the solution into another glass and drink it. Cover and save the other half of the solution for the next day. Easy to do. No fuss, no muss.

What if It Doesn't Work? – Even though Prozac, Zoloft and Paxil are all SSRIs and similar in their actions, they are still separate and distinct medications. Very often, an individual will experience *different* responses on each medication. If Prozac doesn't work for you, Zoloft might be effective.

Zoloft
Description

50 mg.   100 mg.

Length and Type of Effects – Zoloft belongs to the same class of medications as Prozac. It is also taken only once a day and is not considered to be fully effective until a therapeutic dose has been released in the bloodstream. As with Prozac, ADD adults can often feel an alleviation of symptoms within a day or two, although this is not true for the non-ADD population. Zoloft has a shorter half-life than does Prozac – only twenty-four hours. This means that if a dose is missed, blood levels will change more quickly than they would on Prozac. The withdrawal symptoms experienced on Zoloft are often flu-like symptoms and can include nausea, vomiting and diarrhea.

Side Effects – If Zoloft is not going to work for an ADD adult, she will typically feel slightly more depressed, irritable, etc. As with Prozac, if this occurs, the medication should be discontinued.

Fine-Tuning – Zoloft doesn't seem to need as much fine-tuning as Prozac. Our experience has been that it either works or it doesn't. Period.

What if It Doesn't Work? – If an ADD adult has gone through a trial of Prozac and Zoloft, the third medication in the SSRI class is Paxil.

Paxil

Description

20 mg.   30 mg.

Length and Type of Effects – The information on Paxil is actually a repeat of the information given in the preceding paragraphs on Prozac and Zoloft, with the exception that Paxil is often more sedating than Prozac or Zoloft. Paxil is also taken once a day and typically needs a little time for the effectiveness to be noticed. Once again, however, an ADD adult may notice a positive change within a day or two.

Paxil is considered to have a more severe withdrawal effect than either Prozac or Zoloft. The half-life of Paxil is twenty-four hours, so once Paxil is taken, it must be taken regularly.

Side Effects – For whatever reason, clients report less sexual dysfunction with Paxil. For many it seems to be effective as an antidepressant.

What if It Doesn't Work? – If an ADD adult has been through Prozac, Zoloft and Paxil and he or she has no positive results in lessening of depression, reduction of compulsiveness, focusing/concentration or rage attacks, then it is time to move on to an entirely new category of medications.

Other Medications

Clonidine (Catapres) – Clonidine is actually a medication that was developed for the treatment of hypertension. However, it is often used to control the tics associated with Tourette Syndrome, and in children and adults with ADD, particularly when the component of aggression or overactivity is present. As far as medical science understands, aggression may be caused by too much norepinephrine being present in the system. The overabundance of norepinephrine also increases blood pressure. Clonidine slows the release of norepinephrine, which decreases blood pressure and decreases aggression. However, there is also an increase in sedation, and many children and adults on clonidine do experience lethargy or a feeling of fatigue.

Description

Catapres Tablets

01. mg.   0.2 mg.   0.3 mg.
light grey   melon   sand

Catapres Patches

(Transdermal Therapeutic System)

TTS-1   TTS-2   TTS-3

Clonidine is available in two forms – a pill and a transdermal skin patch. The clonidine pill comes in .1 mg., .2 mg. and .3 mg. strengths. The transdermal patch is not found in any other medications used for Attention Deficit Disorder. The patch is labeled TTS-1, TTS-2 and TTS-3 and represents doses of .1, .2 and .3 mg./per day respectively. The patches are worn on the skin and release the medication on an even basis throughout the day. They can be cut to achieve intermediate doses.

Length and Type of Effects – Let's talk about the pill form of clonidine first. Clonidine is usually begun in very low doses (.1 mg. two times a day) and increased gradually for maximum therapeutic benefit. One dose is recommended to be taken at night to aid sleep. Typically, the pill form of clonidine is used first because it is easier to monitor and adjust the dose. If the pill is successful, then the patch, which is often worn on the torso (out of reach of a child who is wearing it), is used. The effectiveness of the patch lasts from five to seven days, but there are some individual differences. Clonidine does need to build up in the system, and it may take one or two months for the full effect to be realized.

How It Acts in the System – Clonidine reduces the release of norepinephrine, which in turn reduces the state of overarousal. It affects the serotonin and dopamine neurotransmitter systems indirectly and thus calms down or modifies aggressive behavior. Its influence on that dopamine system also controls the tic movements common to adults with Tourette Syndrome.

Side Effect – The major side effect is drowsiness, which occurs approximately one hour after taking the medication.

Fine-Tuning – Oftentimes clonidine is extremely effective and acts almost as though it were a "miracle drug." As the person is becoming adjusted to the medication, it will often cause extreme sleepiness. This effect wears off over time, but with many adults seems to be a necessary effect that must be allowed to wear off. Decreasing the medication doesn't work.

Additional Medication

As a review, in this chapter we've indicated that the most commonly used medications to treat adult ADD are the psychostimulants, used alone or in combination with one of the SSRIs, such as Prozac or Zoloft. Clonidine is also a drug used to treat ADD, particularly if an ADD adult has rage attacks or Tourette Syndrome.

However, there is a wide range of pharmacology that does seem to have application in treating ADD symptoms. This is particularly true if a comorbid condition is present. A full description of the various medications that are less commonly used and their effectiveness can be found in Copeland's *Medications for Attention Disorders* (see bibliography).

What if Nothing Works?

For a small percentage of our adult ADD clients, finding the correct medication is a nightmare. They try one medication after another, each time with hope and the expectation of success. With many ADD adults, each new medication will work unbelievably well for a few days, up to months, then abruptly lose its effectiveness. During this time the ADD adult has been able to catch a glimmer of what medication can do to correct the biochemical imbalance. Sometimes, for the first time in his life, he is able to think clearly, concentrate and complete a task. The difference is remarkable, and there is a great relief and hope for a better and more productive life.

Then, for no known reason, the medication is ineffective. It is as if he is not taking medication at all. He may even begin to experience negative effects. What a disappointment! The ADD adult must return to the psychiatrist for a consultation and a trial of yet another medication. At this point, the ADD adult begins to wonder if the right medication even exists. The anxiety level begins to increase and, after several trials of medication, there is often real despair.

What is happening? Why is finding the right medication so difficult? We must keep returning to our earlier statement about our understanding of brain chemistry. Remember, medical science is still in its infancy, particularly where the brain is concerned. At some point in the future we will be able to scan our ADD adults with a beam that will tell us precisely which area of the brain is not functioning. Beyond that, we will understand medication in such a way that the specific chemical that is lacking can be prescribed; however, this is still in the realm of science fiction. The truth is, we don't fully understand how the brain operates, nor do we have the capability of making precise corrections in its chemistry. Simply stated, the brain is still a mystery.

If an ADD adult experiences difficulty with medications, he falls into two rough categories. He is considered either to have a "comorbid" condition, or he has what we loosely term as having a "difficult body chemistry."

Comorbid Conditions

Remember, a comorbid condition only means that an ADD adult has not only ADD but also another separate and distinct disorder(s), so the two or more conditions overlap. However, since they are both present in the system, they must both be attended to with medication. Obviously if two or more conditions are present, the adjustment of medication can be tricky.

Difficult Body Chemistry

This is our catchall term for an ADD adult who does not respond to the first or second line of medications for ADD. However, if an ADD adult falls into this category, it does not mean that the ADD is more severe or that the situation is impossible. In fact, the adult's body chemistry really may not be difficult at all, just very sensitive to medication. In these cases extremely low doses may be used. In some cases, the adult's brain may be very specific in its chemical needs.

Are There Times When Medication Doesn't Work?

Unfortunately, yes. Medical science only goes so far, and then it runs out of answers. However, there is usually one of the medications that will produce at least some benefit and give the adult at least partial relief from the ADD symptoms. If this is the case, the ADD adult must simply accept whatever benefit the medication can provide and supplement with behavioral techniques. If ADD adults find themselves in this position, our strong advice is to never lose hope. Medical science is advancing rapidly. If a particular medication hasn't been invented, it may be available next year, or the year after.

Other Approaches

Eastern Medication

The philosophy behind the Eastern treatment of illness is to treat the whole body with more of an emphasis on prevention. It is a gentle, non-invasive approach aimed at correcting the balance between parts.

With the biofeedback work, there is some indication that a change in brain waves does come from entering a meditative state. Meditation, acupuncture and Chinese herbal remedies have definitely made an improvement in some of our clients' lives.

Occasionally, one product or another does seem to help a segment of the ADD population. Our consulting psychiatrist mentioned that he had found that a product called Zyzixx (marketed by Pharmacotanixx in Irvine, California) produced a calming effect on some ADD adults when used in low doses during the day.

However, for Eastern medicine to be successful, the client must be willing to follow a given course of treatment and be patient and alert to subtle changes. One client didn't want to try Western medicine and sought out a holistic chiropractor who used a combination of massage and acupressure. Our client felt a good deal of relief from her ADD symptoms and experienced an increase in focus and the ability to concentrate.

Biofeedback

Very simplistically, biofeedback is a system of feedback from the person's brain to a computer that allows an adult to track his pattern of specific brain waves. Professionals involved in biofeedback believe very strongly that it is effective. In fact, they seem to have almost a "cult" approach to the subject.

An adult is usually diagnosed with ADD and then placed on a three- to four-month program of biofeedback. There does seem to be some benefit during this period of time. However, the question that has not been answered sufficiently is whether the treatment works for an extended period of time. Barkley, one of the foremost writers in ADD research, put out a position paper on biofeedback stating that there is simply not sufficient research at this time to document biofeedback's effectiveness.

Again, our consulting psychiatrist added his experience to our own. We all feel that, like anything, there are some people who do find biofeedback helpful; however, it is still considered to be controversial as a treatment approach. It is much more expensive than medical treatment and certainly more time-consuming. Although the biofeedback people claim that there is a persistent benefit from treatments over time, this has not been proven in any research. Some people may even need additional treatments, adding extra cost and an extra time commitment.

Information in psychiatric journals seems to indicate that there might be some new biofeedback techniques that will be helpful in the future.

Common Substances

Many ADD adults self-medicate with coffee, Coca Cola® or cigarettes. It is not unusual at all for an ADD adult to be on his fourth cup of coffee by 8:00 a.m. One client has a favorite coffee shop that produces double espressos in a special machine with a special coffee. One client who brought his son in for an evaluation routinely drank thirty to forty cups of coffee a day!

These substances do work, but only to a certain degree. The level of ADD must be considered. If ADD is mild, an adult might do fine with coffee or Coke® as a stimulant. However, if the ADD is severe, the adult must realize that she is doing more harm to her system with thirty or forty cups of coffee than by taking Ritalin. These substances don't work as well as either the psychostimulants or antidepressants.

Exercise

Let's clarify the level of exercise we are talking about. We are not talking about a twenty-minute jog four times a week or walking for an hour. This level of exercise is necessary for good health and is beneficial to everyone. The level of exercise that seems to impact the ADD adult population needs to be significant. What do we mean by significant? We mean the level of exercise that is necessary for running a marathon, training for a bike race or long distance swimming. Any cardiovascular exercise will do, as long as it's continuous and rigorous.

Our typical ADD adult often ran cross-country and track while in high school. He continued to run in college. After college he trained for marathons and perhaps attempted an "Iron Man" race or two. With this level of exercise, his ability to concentrate was increased. He was able to process information and there were no moods or depression. However, if he sustained an injury and was unable to train, he quickly found his symptoms returning.

Three Scenarios of Medication

James

James is a very successful businessman who was forty-five years of age at the time of his diagnosis. He found some information about adult ADD in a local newspaper and decided to pursue an evaluation. He explained that he had always worked inordinately hard in his business and often put in fourteen-hour days. He found it impossible to maintain any semblance of order on his own, so he typically had at least one employee whose sole responsibility was to organize his paperwork and remind him of appointments.

James had been married for thirty years and had three grown children. At the time of his evaluation, he had been in marital therapy for two years and his marriage was unstable. James had experienced rage attacks throughout most of the marriage, and his wife and children had suffered tremendous emotional abuse over the years, although he was never physically violent.

James was evaluated and ADD was diagnosed. The evaluation also indicated that James was extremely bright, but had problems understanding what he read. He was a slow reader and had problems with long-term memory as well. His tendency to rage attacks was apparent, but an underlying depression that had never been identified was also present.

James returned to his long-time family practitioner, who treated a number of ADD adults in his practice. The physician placed James on Ritalin, and his dose was adjusted every four or five days. Within three weeks James found that, for him, 10 mg. of Ritalin twice a day seemed to be the ideal dose. On that dose he reported that he could focus and concentrate, and he was able to maintain a semblance of order at work for the first time in his life. When the Ritalin was in his system he had much less difficulty with anger, and his depression had also lifted. Problems still existed, however. In the evening he did not take Ritalin. At home, with his wife, he was just like he had been before taking medication. He was disorganized, often floated off and didn't listen when his wife was talking to him. After consulting with his physician, he decided to add Prozac as a second medication. For James, Prozac didn't work – in fact, it made him feel more depressed. His physician next placed him on Zoloft. James began to notice that he simply was not angry at work or at home. His depression also lessened, and he described himself as feeling "even" throughout the day.

James is an example of what "should" occur and what usually occurs when most ADD adults are placed on medication. James was able to identify exactly what the medications did for him, and the symptoms of ADD were significantly reduced. In James' case, the combination of medications worked well and continued to be effective.

Lily

Lily is an engineer with a reputation on the job of being able to think through tough problems and come up with innovative solutions. However, she has had difficulties on her performance reviews problems organizing and prioritizing jobs, meeting deadlines and delegating work to her staff. A longstanding pattern of depression became even more problematic as the stress at work increased. This put a terrible strain on her marriage. In fact, her husband related that on any given day, he would never know just what kind of mood he would find her in when he came through the door.

Lily started school in a small private school and recalls only bits and pieces of her elementary years. In kindergarten, she recalls feeling that she was somehow different from her peers, that she was on the outside looking in. Because she was quite bright, she learned to read and do arithmetic quite easily, but learning to print so the teacher could read her work was almost her downfall. She did many papers over to please her teacher.

By second grade she had developed a reputation as the class clown. Her activity level had increased, and she found it almost impossible to sit still in class. She began looking for any excuse to leave the boredom of the classroom. When she asked permission to go to the bathroom, she would stay out of the room as long as possible and, to keep herself busy, would hang from the bathroom stalls. This type of activity, as well as her avid tree climbing after school, seemed to provide some release.

By fourth and fifth grade she was involved in some fights outside the classroom. In sixth grade many of her classmates were allowed to take advanced classes in English and reading. This opportunity was denied to her because of her poor handwriting. She saw this as tremendously, unfair and her competitive spirit was sparked. In junior high and high school she was almost a straight-A student and in advanced math and biology classes, although her handwriting was still illegible.

Through all those years she continued to feel like an outsider and began to hang out with the "druggies," although she never used drugs herself. She graduated from high school with a 4.0 GPA and desperately wanted to get away from her home town, to make a fresh start. She was accepted at college at the other end of the state, and she majored in engineering with a minor in math. Lily worked hard, and once she was past her general education courses with their writing requirements, her grades were A's.

However, she began to experience moods and periods of depression that caused her to stay in her room for two or three days at a time. In the evening she would often start crying and be unable to stop.

After graduation from college, she was hired by a high-powered engineering firm. At work she know her stuff and was great at looking at the big picture. Even so, she had trouble beginning her projects, staying on track and finishing things. Her reputation at work began to slip. What a dichotomy – she knew that she was very bright, but her overall performance at work certainly didn't show it. The depression she had felt in college returned with full force, and she called in sick so often that her boss began to question her. She pulled within herself, which distanced her from her husband. He was confused and didn't know how to help Lily, so his only recourse was to get angry. What a mess.

Finally, she happened to pick up Drs. Hallowell's and Ratey's book, *Driven to Distraction*, and, after reading their list of ADD characteristics, had an "Ah-ha!" experience. "This is me!" she thought, and she contacted our office for an evaluation. In her case, the ADD pattern was unmistakable. She began treatment with a psychostimulant, as well as doing some individual counseling specifically designed to work on coping strategies. The medication helped her to concentrate for long periods of time at work. The strategies enabled her to begin and complete tasks and improved her overall organizational ability. Because she was so bright, she picked up the coping skills quite easily, and work performance improved dramatically.

Next her physician added an antidepressant to curb her depression and moods. Lily reacted badly to Prozac and found that it made her even more depressed. Zoloft was then tried, but it decreased her sex drive, which wasn't acceptable. Finally, Paxil was prescribed and it seemed to work.

Slowly, and very cautiously, Lily learned to stop waiting for the other shoe to drop. This medication was truly working. Her moods and depression were greatly reduced, and even her PMS was better. Her husband was amazed at the change but understandably suspicious, since he had been on the receiving end of hostility for their entire marriage.

Between medication, counseling and coping techniques, Lily continued to improve at work. Her marriage problems smoothed out as well. Lily's story has a happy ending.

Richard

Richard is a tall, gruff adult who had had an incredible life in his early years. His wide assortment of jobs included working in construction, on the Alaska pipeline and as a mercenary. He finally settled in a small mountain community, and the town's residents feared him for his well-known erratic behavior and attacks of rage. At times he would be pleasant and able to operate in society. At other times, he would be extremely angry – almost as though there were coals smoldering inside him, ready to explode. Richard was fascinated by knives. Not only did he collect knives, but he made them as well.

Under his tough exterior Richard had a gentle streak and a romantic side to his personality, which he kept closely guarded. Eventually, a lovely and perceptive woman with two children moved into the community. He fell deeply in love and they married. In past times, his pattern of movement and types of jobs allowed him to exist with his erratic behavior and rough attitude; however, he couldn't maintain a relationship with this behavior. His wife found some information about adult ADD, and Richard came into the office for an evaluation.

Richard was evaluated and was diagnosed with ADD. However, Richard also had Tourette Syndrome (TS), which accounted for the erratic behavior, rage attacks and fascination with knives.

Due to the TS component, Richard was referred to a specialist. His case of TS was moderate to severe, and it took about six months before the right dose of medication and the right combination of medications were found. During that time he was in and out of the counseling office on a regular basis. At times he was pleasant, and at other times he would be agitated and angry. The office manager is truly kindhearted, and one day she had a friendly conversation with Richard as he wait-ed for his appointment. Unknowingly, she had made a statement that upset him. Richard was angered, but, instead of yelling or shouting in the office, he quickly turned around, mooned her and then left.

Finally, by working closely with our resident psychiatrist, Richard found the right combination of medications. His life settled down. He was able to work and bring in money for his family. His relationship with his wife improved. He had the ability to live a happy life. Most importantly, the medication gave him control over his life.

Summary

If an adult has ADD but the symptoms are mild, he or she might be able to use behavioral modification techniques alone. If the ADD is severe, the adult needs to consider some treatment that will correct the biochemical imbalance.

There are many avenues of treatment. The best course of action to determine the appropriate treatment for each individual is to do a lot of reading and research. If an ADD adult is athletic, a rigorous exercise program might fit the bill. If an ADD adult wants to experiment with Eastern medication, meditation, acupuncture and herbs might just be the answer. Biofeedback is certainly available in most com-munities. (This one needs to be examined closely as to price, as well as effective-ness). Or, a trial of medication might be the best course of action. No matter what avenue the ADD adult decides to take, it should be viewed as a trial only. The adult must continue to evaluate the effectiveness of the approach – "Is this working? Can I concentrate and focus more effectively? Is this correcting my symptoms?"

At this stage in medical science, constant monitoring of the effectiveness of any method of treatment is imperative. There is no one test or machine that will light up red or green when the body chemistry is "perfect." The search for bio-chemical balance must be done by trial and error, with active and knowledgeable participation on the part of the ADD adult.

So, what to do? Read, learn and ask questions until you understand your own brand of ADD and what works best for you.

Chapter 14

Help! Even with Medication
I Still Have Problems:
Learning to Cope

For many ADD adults, just having someone clearly identify the condition is both comforting and overwhelming. Adults describe a feeling of release when their ADD is identified. However, discovering that it is a condition that cannot be ignored or operated on causes yet another feeling – that of distress. Adults often report a strong fear reaction of "Now that I'm diagnosed, I'm close to being able to do something about me. What if this isn't *it*? What if treatment doesn't work? How will I know if it's working or not?"

As an ADD adult, you have a cycle of knowing something is wrong with how you feel or act. *You* want to know exactly what is causing the problems yet you *dread* hearing the diagnosis (What if I'm crazy?), and you want treatment to be *immediate and long-lasting* (which it often isn't).

Many diagnosticians of ADD administer the tests, type up the results and send them off to your physician or therapist, but they never clearly define how your ADD affects you or what you can do about it. Still others who offer an ADD diagnosis never allow you to see your results on paper, let alone explain them to you. You have the right to pin down the person who diagnoses you. You have the right to ask exactly how your ADD is likely to affect you. You have the right to ask which kinds of processing you will have trouble with and will need coping skills for, and the right to know the kinds of behavior triggers to which are most vulnerable and how to cope with them. You have a right to ask where you can get additional help and information about ADD. *You should ask for a written report and make sure you have one to take to your medical doctor (M.D.).*

Educate Yourself

The first step in really dealing with and accepting your ADD is to educate yourself. Read pamphlets, books, articles, and scan your newspaper for local lectures and seminars. Survey the various ADD newsletters and subscribe to one or two. Write or call the ADD Warehouse for their free catalog of ADD books and materials. Attend a local meeting of Ch.A.D.D. (Children and Adults with Attention Deficit Disorder). In the Appendix we have listed names and addresses of resources, as well as the national number to find the closest group in your area.

Remember that treatment of adult ADD is relatively new, so there are many differing and sometimes conflicting perspectives. These should all be weighed out before you take any one person's perspective as gospel truth. If you get totally overwhelmed, know that as you read and talk to others about ADD you'll find the information pointing in one direction – ADD is real, it affects people's lives and there *is* something you can do about it.

How to Cope

Using coping strategies is a vital part of surviving and enjoying life as an ADD adult. If you or someone you love has ADD, please give credit to the fact that many coping strategies have already been developed! In our classes we exchange survival strategies that work. These are often extremely creative! You didn't get to where you are today, reading this book, because you are (completely) incompetent. Survival strategies for remembering things, managing time, getting and keeping jobs, having friendships and relationships, and much more are tools of which you can be proud. We often stumble upon or generate ways of helping ourselves get through certain situations or moods after trial and error in daily living. Once again, give yourself *credit* for the strategies you've created that work in your life!

We've provided the following section to help expand your current coping strategies to include other proven tools with which you can experiment. Our coping strategies will be named for easy reference. We will talk about identifying and solving problem areas and setting reachable goals. We will also list tools for each of the three major categories: problems with attention, problems with mood and problems with physical state.

Identifying, Dissecting and Creating Solutions

• Identify

As ADD adults we need to look at our actions and thoughts clearly in order to figure out what to work on. We need to decide which general problem to work with and tackle one area at a time. It's important to look for the root of the problem.

We need to be very careful when identifying the root of the problem, because it often happens that what looks like the problem at first glance really isn't the problem. What we call "the problem" is often what is visible to the outside world and possibly to ourselves; the *real* problem is the origin of what happened to *create* the problem that became visible to the outside world.

One of our best examples of this phenomena occurred in the case of Stan. Stan came to our office as an ADD adult with a presenting complaint of difficulty firing bad employees. This had caused many headaches for Stan as the owner of his own business and resulted in a not-very-competent, non-cohesive staff to help him run his company. After careful questioning and exploration of the problem to help Stan clearly identify it, we became aware that the *origin* of the problem was Stan's impulsive hiring of people who were not qualified. As a side effect of his ADD, he jumped into the hiring process without checking references or qualifications. *Then* he was stuck with incompetent employees and was puzzled and angry at what he considered his poor managerial skills.

In Stan's case, we were able to brainstorm a solution that got to the origin of the problem by using a hiring committee with established guidelines and interview questions each time new positions came open.

Another example of identifying the root of the problem might be as follows: you always put off finishing a paper, painting a room, or writing a letter. Where is the root of the problem? It falls under procrastination – often a problem with attention. If you are never able to finish anything – your papers are half-graded, your house is half-cleaned, your car is half-waxed – then your main area of trouble is completing a task, which is another problem with attention.

If you lose your temper at co-workers or family, are accused of biting people's heads off, and if you feel depressed and moody a lot of the time – then your root may be a problem with mood.

If you feel nervous and restless when you sit in one place for too long, if you make impulsive lane changes while driving, your problem may be on the hyperactive side of physical state. If you just can't seem to get out of bed or off the couch, if any time you sit still you find that you can't get moving again, that you don't have the energy to budge, your problem may be on the hypoactive side of physical state.

Whichever problem area you choose, just tackle one at a time. Once you've decided which one to tackle, the next step is to dissect the problem.

- **Dissect**

It isn't enough for us just to say, "Oh well, I have a problem with finishing things, so I'll have to work on it." As ADD adults we need to, as *Webster's Dictionary* defines it, "separate (a thing, idea, etc.) into its parts so as to find out their nature, proportion, function, interrelationship, etc." We also need to know what to do about it. This may be to make a list of all of our behaviors that bug us or get in our way. We select a behavior on the list, really dissect it and determine exactly where the difficulty lies. If we're not sure about the problem, we can't design an effective solution – one that really works.

- **Create Solutions**

"What system can I use to tackle this problem each time it comes up?" "What can I do that is easy to remember and easy to apply?" "What system can I use to protect myself so my ADD behaviors don't get in my way?" Solutions for ADD behavior must be simple, make sense to us and be practical, which means they must fit into our lives easily. If a solution doesn't fit into your life, don't hesitate to change it, modify it or replace it with a system that works better for you. If it doesn't work, it doesn't solve anything.

An example of a very creative solution is a case of mothers chatting on the internet about a male ADD child who wouldn't urinate in the toilet, but instead sprayed the area, probably because of his inattention to the task at hand (no pun intended). One mother was sharing her absolute frustration when another said that she had had a similar problem with her ADD son and had created a game called "sink the Cheerios®." The mother explained that she would scatter some Cheerios® in the toilet and then challenge the son to sink them with his urine steam. This focused his attention, added incentive and solved the problem. Again, the solution was easy, practical and made sense, albeit very creative sense!

Summary

1. *Identify* the exact problem.

2. *Dissect* the problem so you know exactly where the glitch in your behavior lies.

3. *Create a solution* by asking yourself, "What system can I use to correct the problem?"

Anytime you face a problem, use this method to help. Consider copying the steps above and posting them on your refrigerator, desk or in your car.

Cleverly Named Coping Skills for Problems with Attention, Mood or Physical State

These are super-duper, but very specific, coping skills we've developed and named over the years of teaching and sharing.

Coping with Problems of Attention

Technique I: Clumping

Scenario: It's that time of month again. You need to pay bills. As you sit down to write them out, you realize your pen is running out of ink, the stamps are in the other room and your mortgage coupon is missing. As you get up to collect what you need, the phone rings and your spouse asks for a phone number you have posted on the refrigerator. You leave the stamps on the counter, go into the kitchen, repeat the number, hang up the phone, and walk back to the table where you were paying your bills. Where are the stamps? Where is the mortgage bill? You heave a big sigh of frustration as you get up to retrieve your missing things once again. Sound familiar?

Why not try **clumping**? Each task we need to do requires certain tools. For the ADD adult, our tools are often scattered in several places. This creates a problem because when we set a goal to complete a task, our wandering attention can take us all over the house, garage or office trying to collect the needed tools to complete the task. We end up starting many things and completing only parts. Our tendency is to give up in frustration, condemn ourselves and begin eroding our already fragile self-esteem with phrases like, "I can never do anything right," "I'm a disorganized mess," "I have such good intentions and I always get sidetracked." **Clumping** can help.

How to **Clump**:

- Identify the project.

- List items needed. Be complete and comprehensive. A brainstorming technique is often helpful.

- Make it a goal to gather all items needed in one place – do this quickly, using your list, and establish a single purpose of clumping everything in one place – hurry, hurry, hurry! If you stop to think about anything else but getting everything into one place you'll get sidetracked. We know from experience!

*Note: You may not have time to start your proposed project at that exact moment, but when you are ready to tackle it, you've removed the reasons to jump up and get distracted. If you don't have all the items you need for the project, this is a snag and you will have to brainstorm and **Clump** to run errands to get everything, i.e., stamps, envelopes, bank deposit slips.*

*Often ADD adults require specially marked boxes, baskets or cupboard areas for their clumped projects. While these may look like a disorganized mess to the outside eye, the ADD adult who begins to use or refine the coping skill of **Clumping** has a pretty solid idea of where that project's clump is located, how it is organized, and what needs to be done with it.*

Example of **Clumping**:

- Project: Pay bills

- Items needed: All bills (often spread throughout the house!)
                 Stamps
                 Return address labels
                 Stapler
                 Checkbook(s)or a computer program that issues checks
                     and maintains your account balance
                 Extra pens, pencils (in case of ink or boredom problems,
                     change colors!)
                 Calculator

- We recommend setting a timer and challenging yourself to gather all needed items within a shortened time frame. This serves as a challenge, an adrenaline rush and a feeling of accomplishment when achieved. If you need additional time, set the timer again – don't ever give up!

Technique 2: Clearing

Scenario: Your alarm is set for 6:10 a.m., you're due at the office at 7:30 for a meeting, have to drop the kids off at day care on your way, and stop at the Copy Center for the document you had bound for the meeting. You have another meeting with a client at 9:00 a.m. in another city, need to pick up something for dinner, and plan who will get the kids to a Scouts meeting since you won't be able to because you have to complete an important project for the next morning. Oh! Don't forget to pick up the dry-cleaning, dash off a thank-you note, and throw in a load of wash! Sound familiar?

Why not try **Clearing**? ADD people try to do too much. We try to do just one more thing before we leave the house or work. We are typically not great at estimating how long projects will take, how much travel time to leave ourselves or whether we'll have to wait in line. We often have so much crammed into our days (and nights) that there is no way we could complete all of it – it's doubtful that anyone could! Clients often come in saying "As soon as I get everything done, I'll be okay," "As soon as I finish my list, I'll be organized," "Once I get to the bottom of this file drawer, I'll feel more in control." Realistically, we may never finish our lists, our goals or our projects!

As ADD individuals, we have a tendency to fill up any open spaces in our calendars. We may eliminate one activity with the intention of keeping the time clear, then end up jamming three activities in the place where only one stood before! This is a difficult and challenging area for ADD adults. Time and lists are a really big deal. Lists? You will probably never get rid of your lists – there will always be more to add, but you will get better at getting more of your list items seen through to completion. **Clearing** can help.

How to **Clear**:

- Use a calendar, organizer or computer calendar – retaining your schedule in your head sets you up to forget what you need to remember.

- Identify what you want to accomplish – use a verb and a noun to keep it simple and concise, i.e. wash car, read two chapters, write memo to staff.

- Set a block of time *in your calendar* to accomplish the identified goal.

- Add at least thirty minutes to the time allotted for that goal. This allows for traffic, malfunctioning equipment and delays.

- If you fall off schedule while using clearing, give yourself five minutes to be upset with yourself, then analyze *why* it broke down. Was my system too complicated? Did I get distracted and lose track of time? Remember: *Identify, Dissect, Create Solutions*. Now start again!

Note: Everything takes time, absolutely everything. Do not leave out an activity just because you think you can handle it quickly or because it doesn't really matter. Everything matters, especially when we're talking about scheduling time and clearing schedules.

Examples of **Clearing**:

- Open your calendar – whether paper or electronic.

- Say to yourself, "Write memo to staff on evaluations."

- Create an island of time in your calendar for the sole purpose of writing that memo, i.e., Tuesday, 10:00-11:00 a.m.

- Add at least thirty minutes to the time allotted. It becomes Tuesday, 10:00-11:30 a.m. – Write Staff Memo.

- We recommend using brightly colored pens or highlighters to **Clear** your time. Try using red to line out your time so that it catches your eye and helps keep you on track. Make a deal with yourself that the block of time is non-negotiable – you can wander *after* you complete the goal for which you cleared the time.

Technique 3: Setting a Stop

Scenario: You can never get things done. Two months ago you painted the dining room but still haven't replaced the light switch covers; you started writing invitations to a party but got sidetracked by the phone, and the invitations are still sitting on the table; you bought computer software to make life easier, but it's still in the package on your desk. Sound familiar?

Why not try **Setting a Stop**? ADD adults often have trouble with deadlines. We miss them, renegotiate them, ignore them, try to meet them and set some that are impossible to meet! When the deadlines are set for us by others, we become resentful and feel out of control of our schedules. When we set our own deadlines, we are much more likely to meet them, but we need some tools for how to set them up. **Setting a Stop** can help.

How to **Set a Stop**:

- Identify the project or goal you have left undone or incomplete.

- Sit down and arrange an event or obligation that *requires* you to complete your project or goal before your arrangement can move forward.

- Make the initial phone call to cement your event or obligation. Be very specific about the exact day, time and nature of your commitment.

Example of **Setting a Stop**:

- You've painted your dining room but have not yet replaced all the hardware on the walls. This looks tacky compared to the new paint job and you feel badly about it every time it catches your eye, but nothing really motivates you to finish the job.

- Run through your list of people whom you respect and to whom you owe a dinner. Decide to ask them to dinner as a personal deadline to clean up your dining room.

- Call immediately and invite them to a special dinner next Friday night at 7:00 p.m. at your home. If you have to leave a message, ask them to RSVP before the day is over.

- Use your commitment to that dinner date as your motivation to complete the task before your guests arrive.

*Note: Other ways to **Set a Stop** include signing up and paying for a class you've been putting off, setting an appointment with your tax person, doctor, professor, counselor, or other professional to handle business you've been putting off forever, or asking a friend or spouse to accompany you to an event on a specific day/time (which then involves holding yourself more closely to the deadline than you would if you just had to monitor yourself). An example of involving a friend or mate might be inviting them to an investment/retirement seminar you've been putting off attending on your own. By calling in the RSVP for two and confirming the date, you are much more likely to actually go the seminar, rather than face the questions of your friend or mate as to why you're not going.*

These are examples of techniques we've come across that work. For the next two sections on coping with mood and physical state, our suggestions are listed for easy reading, but have not been named (yet).

Coping with Problems of Mood

Coping with problems of mood can be handled in many varying ways. In this section, techniques will be listed and should be experimented with – whether you are wrestling with depression, impulsivity, temper outbursts, rage, mood swings or feelings of helplessness and low self-esteem. In order to be sure of what works for you and what doesn't, we encourage you to try these techniques before you say to yourself, "Oh, this'll never work for me," "I'm not active enough," "I just can't see myself doing that," or "That's fine for some people, but not for me."

Following are some tips that really work for coping with problems of mood:

Coping with Anger:

- Pound a 4" x 4" board with a hammer (no nails – too much control needed for those, and the object is not to hurt yourself!)

- Pound a red brick into pieces with a hammer, then sweep up the pieces, thereby releasing your adrenaline surge.

- Use the local batting cages, gym equipment or handball courts as a focusing point for your anger, rather than your immediate peers or family.

- Go to your local beach and throw eggs at the breakwater jetty – the bottom dwellers will eat the shells and the sea gulls will eat the yolk and whites.

- Walk down the street, pretending to stomp on your adversary's face at each sidewalk crack.

Coping with Mood Swings and Depression:

- Learn to meditate using a book, group, tape or coach.

- Look into books that talk about "cognitive therapy." Examples of cognitive therapists are Dr. Albert Ellis, who wrote *The New Guide to Rational Living*, Dr. Donald Meichenbaum, Dr. Aaron Beck, and many more. Cognitive therapists focus on changing irrational thoughts and feelings into self-accepting, rational thoughts and feelings that make sense.

- Water, H_2O, agua – whether we are drinking lots of it; showering, bathing or sitting in a spa full of it; walking beside it on a beach, trail, or riverbed – water is a marvelous, restorative mood balancer. Perhaps it is because we are made of so much of it, perhaps it reminds us of our womb-like origins – whatever the reason, it works!

- Use support groups: There are many anonymous support groups available to us – AA, Packrats Anonymous, Adult Children of Alcoholics, and Narcotics Anonymous are just a few examples. These groups are in addition to the ADD support groups available in many areas. Most of these support groups are free, easy to locate in your community and open to participation at any time. Being able to talk about moods, feelings, events and memories can really lighten your load. Knowing that others share those feelings really cuts down the painful feelings of isolation – you are not in it alone. We'd also like to note that different meetings have different characteristics and personalities – please don't try just one and think they're all the same.

- Music, journaling or arts and crafts are means of self-expression and mood management – sometimes we can use our creative sides to help us manage mood.

- Medication – for some people, mood must be managed with medication. Because we cover this extensively in its own chapter, we recommend you consult Chapter 13 for details.

Coping with Problems of Physical State
Coping with problems of physical state can be an ongoing struggle as well as an ongoing challenge. Whether you experience hyperactivity and agitation or what we call hypoactivity and a feeling of sluggishness, or whether you fall somewhere in the middle of the continuum, we have found two groups of activities that help the ADD person cope.

Because ADD is biochemical in nature, we need to shift or change our biochemistry in order to feel differently and/or to cope better. These changes in biochemistry can be accomplished by *high intensity* or *low intensity* activities. Try activities from either group to become familiar with what works best for your unique chemistry. We have found no clear correlation between hyperactivity and high intensity activities, hypoactivity and low intensity activities, or vice versa. For example, some hyperactive ADD adults find needlepoint relaxing; others say it makes them crazy. Some hypoactive ADD adults do much better with large muscle group workouts; others prefer quiet meditation. Again, it seems to be as individual as a fingerprint.

High Intensity Activities *to Cope with the Physical State*:

- Physical activities – exercising, walking, cycling, jogging, Nordic Track®, dancing. For maximum benefit, intense use of exercise will be necessary to change the chemistry.

- Video games and interactive computer games that demand intense skill, concentration and focus

- Race car or go-cart course driving

- High-powered knitting (Really! One of our clients uses rapid-speed craft work to shift her physical state, and we would bet there are many more of you out there who haven't yet confessed!)

Low Intensity Activities *to Cope with Physical State*:

- Meditation or prayer

- Napping

- Seeing a movie (not action/adventure!)

- Taking a hot shower or a dip in a Jacuzzi®

- Painting, reading or soothing music

- Needlepoint

- Crossword puzzles

Note: Because of the nature of our biochemistry which changes according to our diet, exercise, sleep, stress patterns, etc., you may find yourself changing intensity activities from one day or week to the next. Don't be concerned about its "not working," but see it as an opportunity to do something different with your body state, rather than just feeling like you're at its mercy.

What About Counseling?

Now that we've looked at the ADD diagnosis, the importance of educating ourselves, whether or not to use medication, and how to cope with our ADD states and behaviors, the last dimension to consider is, "Would I benefit from counseling?" There are roughly three groups of ADD adults we encounter with respect to counseling.

Group 1

The first are the many ADD adults who are functioning in society and in their careers at the time of their diagnoses. With some education, possibly medication, and short-term supportive counseling for coping tools, they do quite well.

Group 2

The second group are the ADD adults who, along with the education and possible medication aspects of treatment, come from dysfunctional family backgrounds and feel the extra effects of the ADD on top of an already disturbing upbringing. Does this group benefit from counseling? Absolutely. With a qualified counselor or therapist (one who is very familiar with ADD), the ADD client and his or her family can safely explore the impact ADD has had on their lives. Specific behaviors or concerns the individual or family member has had and wishes to see changed can be examined. The focus on solutions can be monitored and maintained. Longer-term therapy or counseling is often recommended to address the past problems, as well as the ADD picture.

Let's take the example of Glenda. Glenda has been married ten years to Harry, and they have three kids and two Labrador retrievers. Glenda's ADD was undiagnosed until two years ago, when she was referred to our center for testing. Her tearful interview revealed a history of feeling stupid and inferior to her husband and even to her eight-year-old daughter, who had a better memory than her mom.

She had problems with discipline (of herself and her kids), and she sobbed that no one would help her change – they just complained about her all the time. In the interview, she also reported that her mother was an alcoholic and her father was frequently absent from the home. We commented that it sounded as if she had had some rough times, to which she soundly agreed, and we recommended testing.

We tested Glenda and diagnosed her as an ADD adult. Along with some other recommendations, we told her she might benefit from counseling – both individual and possibly family. She agreed to give it a try. We saw Glenda not too long ago in our office for a follow-up and she excitedly shared the results of the individual and family counseling. In the safety of the therapist's office, her husband had been able to share his concerns that she would not be able to take care of the family adequately because she was always forgetting things like important appointments and due dates for bills. He had also been afraid to share this for fear of Glenda losing her temper and exploding at the family. He had seen her mother's behavior several times and worried that Glenda would end up the same way.

With the therapist's care, each member of the family was able to express his and her secret worries and to participate in solving the problems in ways that respected the family unit and *still* worked very well, situation after situation. You see, it takes time to develop our behaviors and coping skills, whether they've been effective or not, and it takes time for us to change them. A skilled counselor can help instigate sharing, propose solutions and follow up with the individual or family member to ensure change.

Group 3

There is yet a third category of ADD adults that includes adults who have come from severely dysfunctional families where alcoholism, drug abuse, chronic disease, or physical, sexual, emotional abuse or neglect was present and untreated over an extended period of time. Based on material presented at the U.S. Psychiatric and Mental Health Congress (1996), it is estimated that roughly ten to twenty percent of ADD people whose symptoms persist into adulthood have significant impairment in their personal and professional lives. They may be severely learning disabled. They may also have more than one diagnosis, which complicates treatment strategies. All of these conditions seem to benefit from ongoing therapy wherein not only the ADD is addressed but the deeper issues are thoroughly explored as well. In some cases, the damage may be so severe that even with extensive counseling and medication, change is slow and almost imperceptible. This can be difficult for both the ADD client and the therapist, and progress must be measured using a different yardstick.

What Counseling Should Include

Counseling should include specific information about ADD and coping techniques, as well as an exploration of what the ADD person and his or her family has been doing that *works*! Remember, you have a right to know what is an ADD issue, what is a family issue (past or present), and which issues contain elements of both. The old saying, "If it ain't broke, don't fix it," applies here.

If "it ain't broke," the therapist should be clear in complementing and praising the behaviors and skills that work within the family or on the part of the individual. The therapist should definitely empower the individual and the family by pointing out their successes and the fact that they *have* made it! ADD is not an excuse for poor behavior; most individuals have some control over the level of empowerment and ability to change that they will give themselves.

There are many different types of therapy and therapists to choose from, for both short- and longer-term therapy. It is important that the therapist has a solid working knowledge of ADD and is willing to treat it as real, not just a fad. The goal of therapy is often to set the whole family line on a new course. We frequently see multiple generations showing the same behavior right down through the family lines. It is often stated that we can't change the cycle until we know we're in one. Therefore, when one family generation begins to deal with the ADD and any related problems, the generations that follow will definitely benefit from the insights and changes.

As a client, you have the right to ask about the therapist's background knowledge and orientation. It is reasonable to ask whether the therapist has experience working with ADD, what her hours of work and availability after hours are, what her fees are, and whether she has a cancellation policy. Sometimes changing therapists is an option to consider. Perhaps you or your family feel, after sincere effort, that you are not able to reach your optimal goals. It may be that a therapist with a different orientation would be more beneficial. You also have the right to discontinue therapy if, after giving it a chance, you feel that it is not providing what you are seeking.

Coaching: An Emerging Support System

There is a new development in the treatment of ADD beyond counseling, education, coping skills, and medication – it is called **coaching**. An ADD coach is a person who provides ongoing support and encouragement to the ADD adult, as well as helping him to keep on track and moving forward in his daily life. Often after a diagnosis of ADD, the adult feels that he should have been able to improve more quickly, get it all together more consistently, and lead his life more efficiently. Even ADD adults in therapy can get frustrated because therapists can only go so far.

For the ADD adult, there is often that immediate need, at home or at work, when the ADD adult really needs to talk with someone right then who understands and will help sort the problems out so he can move on.

A coach helps provide a supportive and encouraging environment wherein the adult can learn new behaviors and strategies to overcome difficulties, as well as to break things into manageable pieces and tangible action. The American Coaching Network has training, coaching and a newsletter. For more information on looking for a coach in your area or becoming a coach after being screened for eligibility, see the appendix.

New: Twelve-Step Groups for ADD Adults

Another emerging support system is the crossover of the twelve-step concepts and principles into the world of adults with Attention Deficit Disorder. There are now some ADD twelve-step programs/support groups being created to provide a structured arena in which to discuss ADD concerns, with low or no cost to the participants. It is hoped that the formation of twelve-step groups will allow the natural evolution of mentors to develop. Hopefully, this will decrease the need for even a paid "coach." Instead, it will be the ADD community developing resources within its own circle.

Summary

In closing, we encourage you to develop your own list of coping skills and resources as you go along in your ADD journey. Keep the list in a prominent place in your home or office so that you don't have to rely on your memory for solutions, and so that you can add to it when you come across a new idea. Please feel free to modify any of the suggestions we have offered in this chapter and to keep your eyes open for new information as it comes out. Don't forget to do your part in identifying and dissecting your problem areas so that you can create solutions that truly address the problem and not venture off on some wild goose chase. Make a personal decision about whether counseling would benefit you and/or your family. Look into coaching. Locate a twelve-step group for ADD. Remember, ADD is not a fad, and there is a growing body of information available to us – sometimes in the most unlikely places!

Chapter 15

ADD for Real

Over our years of working with clients we have developed a deep appreciation and respect for our ADD adults. We listen to their plights, we walk with them through diagnosis, we explore numerous coping tools, we consult with their physicians regarding medications and, once they are launched, we give them our blessings as they go on their way. We share their individual heartaches and successes. At times we are overwhelmed by their courage and strength. At other times we are delightfully amazed at some of the things they do to cope! Sometimes we help them develop a sense of humor about their particular ADD quirks, because they often come to us serious and distraught.

We are including several case profiles of ADD adults in our final chapter. Our purpose is two-fold: We have found that when a person is new to the ADD quest and is able to identify herself in case examples, it often provides a tremendous feeling of relief to know that she is not alone.

Secondly, for the ADD adults who are familiar with their condition, case profiles help them to understand that their own brand of ADD is not as rare or devastating as they may think. Instead, they can recognize that they are part of a much larger family – the family of ADD adults with all of their variations.

It is with love and empathy we present to you real-life stories of ADD adults. They don't all have happy endings, many of them are still stories in progress, but they are *ADD for real*.

The Case of The Porcupine Businesswoman
Description: *Female, workaholic, hot temper, disorganized*

Giselle is a thirty-eight-year-old businesswoman who is known as a workaholic, successful in her own business and fairly ambitious. She also has quite a temper and tries to cope with frequent, unexplained mood swings. At times, in direct contrast to her driving force mode, she appears confused, scattered and without focus. She was referred to our office by her therapist for an evaluation. Upon interviewing her, we observed that she was abrasive, frequently interrupted the interviewer and was very defensive about the possibility that she would have ADD. "After all, I graduated with my bachelor's and my master's degrees with honors – how can I have ADD?"

Test results confirmed the probability of ADD, and she was referred to a physician in the area who was knowledgeable about ADD. It took Giselle two weeks to get the courage to call for an appointment, a week to fill her prescription (under protest) and a month to start trying the medication. The results were astonishing and almost immediate; Giselle herself didn't feel much different, but her spouse, co-workers, and family began making little comments like, "Are you doing something different with your life? You seem much calmer," or "Do you realize that we just had a fifteen-minute conversation and you didn't interrupt me once?"

She began to notice that she could set goals for reading an article, starting a project, dashing off thank-you notes, and actually *finish* her goals! Despite the fact that she doubted the diagnosis at first, the proof was in the pudding, as they say, and she now reports that she wouldn't trade her medication/coping skills program for anything. At times, her ADD symptoms still pose a problem in her life, but she is much better equipped to problem-solve than before her condition was named and explained.

The Case of the Man with Three Briefcases
Description: *Male, disorganized and compulsive, difficulties processing*

Jim is a man with many concerns and problems. He is married with two children, works full time plus overtime, constantly feels overwhelmed, frustrated and behind. He was referred to us by his physical therapist, to whom he was deeply grateful for the enormous physical relief she had provided and her extensive compassion and expertise in the physical side of his condition. She was, however, concerned with some unexplained psychological aspects that would appear to benefit from our professional attention.

There had been some angry eruptions in the home that really had him worried. The oldest son was acting out quite a bit, and Jim himself alternated between being compulsively organized and completely disorganized. He often had difficulty with expressive language and was quite frustrated that he couldn't transmit the ideas from his extremely bright mind into the proper words. He desperately wanted to turn himself and his family around and was willing to seek help.

After some counseling and careful interviewing, it became apparent that Jim and possibly his oldest son, age eight, were struggling with ADD. Temper outbursts, processing difficulties, flooding and difficulty starting (and especially completing) projects were everywhere. The kitchen molding was half-completed, stacks of wood and materials for remodeling were all over the garage, and the kitchen cabinets had been "in progress" for three years. Needless to say, Jim's wife was at the end of her rope with the mess, especially since she took great pride in being able to keep house beautifully.

As Jim's pressures from work and home mounted, the number of briefcases he carried increased. Soon he came to our office with three briefcases to hold the most vital items in his life – these contained countless work materials, therapy notes and recommendations, gym clothes, his son's report cards, price quotes for various projects, a journal, a tape recorder, two baseball caps and tea bags. One of the briefcases was so heavy that Jim's chiropractor had concerns about him carrying it around.

We recommended that Jim be tested for ADD. He was eager to be tested, because if the results were affirmative that he had ADD, at least he would *know* what was "wrong" with him and the way he lived his life. Sure enough, Jim was diagnosed with ADD and his physician recommended medication. He was a great candidate for medication, since his tendency to chart and graph his progress, side effects and dosage made it very easy to monitor his case. We also tested and diagnosed his eight-year-old son with ADD, oversaw his placement on medication, and his report cards immediately began to show improvement.

While this case is still in the working stage, the prognosis for the family is outstanding and shows that when body work and mind work are combined with the proper diagnosis, the possibility of success often increases.

The Case of the Armchair Space Cadet
Description: *Female, processing problems which spanned elementary school through college, poor memory, depression, hypoactivity, tricky body chemistry*

Carlotta is a twenty-nine-year-old woman who came to our office after a particularly negative experience with another therapist who did not believe that body chemistry played any part in a person's psychological distress. The therapist believed that people somehow "willed" themselves unbalanced or crazy and should therefore take full and complete responsibility to "will" themselves normal again. By the time we met with her, Carlotta was feeling pretty crazy and very much like a failure, since she had yet to figure out how to "will" herself not to have her ADD traits.

Carlotta had had processing problems since elementary school and often didn't fully understand the instructions of her teachers. She was in a state of constant depression and anxiety, because it seemed as though all the other kids knew what was expected and just did it, while she still struggled with what exactly she was supposed to do. Carlotta decided early on that she had better begin cheating or she'd never make it. This pattern continued throughout high school and college, and she was quite adept at using cheating as a coping technique to get through school. She never knew about the Civil Rights Law or the ADA laws, so she never knew she had the right to special accommodations throughout school to make it fairer for her.

In addition to educational problems, Carlotta was also plagued with a poor, "Swiss cheese" memory, severe depression (caused by both internal and external sources), and a level of hypoactivity that made it difficult to get motivated to do much in her life. After we diagnosed Carlotta with ADD as an adult, we were able to make considerable headway in the area of whether or not she had "willed" herself to have ADD.

With a lot of education and conversation, she slowly began to make positive changes in her life. Incidentally, it also turned out that Carlotta had a particularly tricky body chemistry, which meant we worked closely with her physician to locate the correct combination of medications for her. At one point, she even changed physicians to locate one who would really listen to her when she said that her body responded to even subclinical levels of certain medications.

The Case of The Locked Freezer

Description: *Female, pack rat, impulsive, night owl, weak immune system*

Matilda was a bright and creative individual who worked very successfully in Hollywood as a costume designer for many years. She had been plagued with asthma since childhood but was able to keep it well under control by working closely with her doctor.

When she was thirty-five, she felt on top of the world and decided it was time to be her own boss and work on projects that she wanted to do, not projects she was assigned. She wanted to name her own hours so she could take advantage of the burst of creativity she typically felt at 2 or 3 a.m. This was the period when she became most inspired and could create costumes that were fabulous.

Matilda's career as a designer gave her a legitimate reason to collect small scraps of fabric with interesting textures, and bags of yarn and trim. Her new business was expanding, and, although she was happy with her success, she began to feel overwhelmed. As her stress increased, she began to collect more things. To her material and yarn she added interesting articles that she knew she would have time to read someday and recipes she would like to try someday. Because she was always short on time, she often couldn't clip out the article or recipe, so she saved the entire magazine or newspaper. Soon she had stacks of clutter everywhere. No matter how Matilda tried to sort and organize the piles, they continued to grow, almost as if they had a life of their own.

Soon she couldn't walk through her spare bedroom. Next, she filled up the room she used as an office, and the clutter continued to spread. It was at this point that the leader of Matilda's local packrat group sent her to our office for an ADD evaluation. She was identified as ADD and placed on a trial of medication. But, before she was regulated on any medication, catastrophe struck. Matilda's house was smack in the middle of the epicenter of the last California earthquake. After the shaking ended and she realized she was still alive, she saw that the contents of her kitchen cupboards had been tossed out into the middle of the floor. Her bedroom closet doors were open, and all her clothes were strewn across the room. All the paper and odds and ends that she had collected for years were tossed and scrambled. The entire house was an impossible mess.

The stress of the earthquake, the condition of her house and her demanding work schedule weakened her immune system. Matilda had a severe asthma attack and, in fact, it was touch and go if she would even live for about a week. After she was released from the hospital, she was weak and shaky. She couldn't even think about going home. Not only was her home a mess, but the dust and debris caused by the earthquake aggravated her asthma. The only thing that she could do was move in with a friend.

There is another facet of Matilda's personality that you must understand to grasp the overall picture of her life. She was extremely compassionate and an animal lover. She felt one of her missions in life was to rescue homeless dogs and cats that were hurt or abandoned and find them good homes. Over the years, Matilda had managed to find homes for over two hundred dogs – truly a remarkable record. During the process she typically had six or seven dogs (not to mention the eight cats and four bunnies) in her backyard. It was a given that she herself kept the dogs that were beyond placing, so as permanent residents she had a blind, twelve-year-old Shelty, a ten-year-old Silky Terrier who was partly crippled by his previous owner, and other assorted dogs who would be considered total rejects by most people. She loved them all dearly, and no matter what was happening in her life, she *always* made sure that they were well-fed and cared for. She lived in a quiet residential neighborhood and lived in constant fear that a mean-spirited neighbor might complain to the city about the number of animals she owned. She was very concerned about what she would do if this happened. What would happen to her beloved pets?

After the earthquake, one of Matilda's older cats, Sam, became ill. She took her carefully hoarded savings and took Sam to her long-time veterinarian so she would have the best care. Even so, Sam died in Matilda's arms. Now she had a new dilemma – what to do with Sam's body? She didn't have the money to bury Sam in the pet cemetery, and she refused to have her cremated, believing it was too unfeeling. She had read information at the vet's office that it was illegal to bury animals in your backyard, so she was stuck. Then she had a brainstorm. What do veterinarians do with animals who have died while waiting for the disposal service? They freeze them! This was the answer!

She lovingly wrapped Sam in her favorite blanket and placed her in the freezer. It wasn't until days later that she began to question what she had done. What if someone finds out? Will they think I am a horrible person? She began to feel ashamed of her impulsive decision and certainly never told anyone what she had done.

A few months later Duke, her favorite Silky Terrier, developed a kidney tumor. He died in her arms at the veterinarian's office. Once again she agonized over what to do with him. Finally, she wrapped Duke in his very own, freshly-laundered blanket and put him the freezer too. Many of her unplaceable animals were very old, and, over the next few months, she lost two more small dogs, a cat, a rabbit and two stray birds that she had tried to save. She continued to wrap each one carefully and place them in the freezer (just until she could afford a proper burial, you know). Of course, she carried a tremendous load of guilt and shame. She was worried someone would find out and wouldn't understand that she did it out of desperation and love. Another thought struck her. She had been ill and work was sporadic. What if she was unable to pay her electric bill and the power to the house (and the freezer) was cut off? What on earth would she do then?

Slowly, ever so slowly, Matilda became stronger. As she began to get a few small jobs, she was able to pay for regular asthma medication, and her overall health began to improve. She began to clean up her home little by little. Of course, for a pack rat the loss of any item is an emotional trauma, so it was slow going. She got a little more work, returned to our office and attended some of our support groups. She was able to get in touch with her doctor for some help with her medication.

She regained some of her strength and was making enough money to do something with her frozen animals, but what should she do? She called her local pet cemetery, not sure of the response she would get. The owner of the cemetery said she understood perfectly and they would certainly take the animals and arrange a proper burial. Matilda carefully unloaded the freezer, packed up her car and drove to the cemetery. She made sure all of her charges were buried, completed her good-byes to each of them and, after placing a single red carnation on each of their graves, drove away, tears streaming down her face.

Finally, her guilt over her pack rat syndrome and impulsive behavior in using her freezer to store her dead pets began to lift. Her health continued to improve, and she continued to chip away at the clutter in her house until she was able to return to her home. This time she hired a cleaning woman to keep the clutter manageable. She continued to work with our office and her doctor. She continued to acquire profitable design jobs and is now making a good income again. Her life is finally right side up, but what a struggle.

The Case of the Spray-Painted Man
Description: *Male, temper, Tourette Syndrome*

Mark's story begins way back in his childhood. It actually doesn't begin with Mark at all, but with his older brother, Alan.

Alan had a lot of difficulty in school. He couldn't seem to learn to read or do math. His behavior was outrageous. He would often yell things out in class, no matter how many times he was sent to the principal's office or put on detention. He also had a motor tic which took the form of violent shoulder shrugging. By the time he reached fifteen, his learning problems and his violent behavior were so severe that he was expelled from school. Rather than trying another high school and facing the same problems all over again, he went to work and managed to hold a job framing houses. He drank six beers after work daily to calm himself. He lived in a small trailer, all alone, but he was surviving. Alan was actually an adult with Tourette Syndrome (TS) which had never been diagnosed. Instead, he was viewed as a troubled adolescent and a "bad egg" throughout adolescence.

Mark, on the other hand, didn't exhibit severe learning problems or blurt out answers in class. The only hint that he might also be carrying the TS gene was a slight facial tic that made him look almost as though he was winking, but with both eyes at the same time. He hummed constantly, but under his breath so that it was barely audible.

He did have some discipline problems when he reached adolescence, but by that time his parents had had enough trouble with his brother that they put Mark in a small private school with a small class size and one-to-one help when it was needed. With this help, Mark made it through high school with good grades, and he had the courage to try college. He went to a certificate program in a community college in auto body repair and painting and obtained his AA and a certificate after a two-year course.

To everyone in his life – his family and his new girlfriend, who would soon move up to the status of fiancée and sport a beautiful diamond ring – his life looked solid and secure. Remember, no one in his family had any idea of his brother's TS or that Mark could be carrying the gene for it too, which, in fact, was made more probable because of his barely perceptible vocal and facial tics.

The trouble began for Mark when he found a job painting cars. The company was run by two partners who were constantly arguing about how Mark should do his

job. One partner would tell him to paint the car a certain way, and the other partner would come into the shop and tell him "No, that is not right. Do it this way."

He had no clue as to how to handle this situation. His level of stress definitely
increased, but he had a good-paying job and didn't want to leave. He had no way
of solving the problem and alleviating the stress. This was a very different situation
from the small, supportive atmosphere of his private school and also the support
provided by the community college. For the first time in his life he began to experience episodes of rage. He began to fantasize about smashing the car he was working on into a twisted scrap of metal.

As his stress increased, he began to fantasize about tying the two owners
together and suspending them from the metal roof of the shop. Next he fantasized
about tying them together, but throwing them off a bridge with their feet planted
in cement. Of course, he knew he really wouldn't do any of those things, but just
thinking about the possibility provided him with some relief.

After eight months of arguments between the owners, his stress reached the
breaking point. The final incident occurred when he had just completed some
body work and new paint on a red Corvette. He knew his work was excellent, and
he was proud of the results. One owner told him he did a good job; the other
owner appeared in the shop and demanded that he redo both back fenders.

This was all Mark needed. Still holding the paint compressor in his hand, he
turned it toward the owner and spray-painted him from his shoes to his shirt collar.
The owner was furious and came after him. Mark started swinging blindly and,
unfortunately, connected and broke the owner's nose. The owner, taking no responsibility for causing Mark's frustration, called the police and pressed charges. Mark
had very little money to pay for an attorney and was not well-represented in court.

Since his TS was still not diagnosed, he just looked like someone with a bad
temper. The understanding that he was dealing with a biochemical disorder that
caused his rages was never even considered. Mark, of course, lost this job. He had
trouble finding a second job, and, more importantly, his self-image began to
change. His sudden outburst of rage frightened him. If he was capable of that sort
of incident at work he wondered if it could it happen in his marriage.

Finally, Mark was referred to our office by a family friend. He was evaluated
and diagnosed with ADD and TS. His medication was difficult to adjust; in fact,
he fell into a category of adults that we label as having a "difficult body chemistry."
Even medicated, he continued to have rage attacks for months while his medication was changed and the dosage adjusted. He is still working on coping techniques that will work for him. Although he still has a long way to go, he now
understands that there is a clear pathway that will enable him to reach his goal.

The Case of the Mysterious Filing System
Description: *Female, hyperactive, compulsively neat, poor memory*

Althea is a thirty-five-year-old CPA who was quickly snapped up by one of the
"Big Six" accounting firms as soon as she passed her CPA exam. She is a workaholic, sharp and nothing, absolutely nothing, gets by her.

Althea was diagnosed as ADD in elementary school due to her hyperactivity.
Since she had no academic problems due to her ADD condition, she was never

placed on medication. In addition to the hyperactivity, Althea had a compulsively neat side to her personality. As a little girl, she would line up her Barbie dolls in a row. Her books were arranged from tall to short in her bookcase and her mother never, ever had to tell her to clean her room or pick up her clothes. In fact, her mother worried that Althea was not quite normal because she was just too neat.

Even as a little girl, it was obvious that Althea had a poor memory. She often forgot her school books or her lunch. Although she always completed her homework, she usually forgot to turn it in to her teacher. In adolescence, she was a straight-A student, but she had to study for an exam for days and add a final cramming session the night before the test as well. She began to recognize something must be wrong with her memory because she couldn't remember her fourth birthday party or the family vacation when she was six years old. When her friends talked about early events, she remained silent because her memories were gone. She would occasionally feel that she couldn't be very intelligent if she couldn't remember things, but she did make A's in school. This was very confusing.

As a go-getter at work, Althea realized that she needed to disguise certain traits, such as her poor memory and hyperactivity, if she was going to be successful. She practiced looking calm and serene at work. In long meetings she had a pad of paper in front of her and doodled to keep herself from jumping up and running out of the room. She managed to look calm on the outside, but no one realized that she was going one hundred miles per hour on the inside. What to do with her terrible memory took some thinking. Finally, she hit upon the idea of making three copies of everything that she needed to file. For example, if she needed to file an invoice regarding some plumbing repair work, she would file one copy under "R" for repair, one copy under "F" for Fred (the repairman), and the final copy under "P" for plumbing.

As the pace of her job picked up, she found that her stress level also increased. It became much more difficult to remain calm and to hide her poor memory. In desperation, she had to share her secret with her secretary, who promised to keep it private. Once her secretary realized how much trouble Althea was having with her memory, she began making the usual three copies for Althea, but insisted on keeping the original copy for her own files, as added protection.

Althea was coping well, until disaster struck in the form of Bill, a new supervisor who was totally disorganized and who thrived in the midst of clutter. In the work room, the copy room, the conference room, piles of papers and clutter began to appear. Althea was in trouble. Because of her compulsiveness, she couldn't think if any clutter was present, and she would stop whatever she was doing and clean up the clutter. Because she was unable to work in the clutter, she was unable to hide this problem. She was desperate for answers.

She finally saw a news program about ADD in adults and remembered that she had been labeled as hyperactive as a child. She called the office and made an appointment for an evaluation. She was diagnosed with ADD. Due to her stress level at work caused by Bill, she decided to give medication a try. Ritalin didn't work in her case, and her doctor next tried a prescription for Zoloft. After only three or four days the difference in her anxiety level was remarkable. As a surprising but welcome side effect, she found that her PMS, which lasted ten days out of each month and made her volatile and critical, disappeared. She decided that Zoloft made her life much easier and she chose to remain on the medication. After reading two or three of the current ADD books for adults, she felt that she had enough information that she could understand her own ADD pattern. With medication and her own self-education process, she was once again on top and moving ahead in her career.

The Case of the Self-Medicating Mixologist
Description: *Bright, impulsive, problems with drugs and alcohol*

Ed was referred to us by a therapist who worked primarily with drug and alcohol use and rehabilitation, but who also had some working knowledge of adult ADD. She referred Ed to our office for a formal evaluation and diagnosis because of his fascinating drug history.

Ed had intuitively known that there was something different about him, something wrong. As young as ten years of age, Ed began taking drugs out of his mother's medicine cabinet, just to experiment. Since his mother was a nurse, there were always pills around the house and no aversion to using medication. He would impulsively reach for pills in any combination, just to feel different. He discovered that niacin pills would make him feel flushed and different, and No-Doz® was a real find, since they made him feel great. He also got into a lot less trouble for forgetting to finish his homework.

When Ed reached high school, he had access to marijuana, alcohol and amphetamines. He found that when he used drugs, he could focus better and was more likely to complete his assignments. He became quite the artist at mixing the "proper" combinations, whether he had to study, go to sleep or work at his part-time job. In college, Ed had even more access to the medication combinations he was after – whether obtained legally through prescription or illegally on the streets, – but he was still on the endless search for just the right mix. His drug mixing finally came to the attention of his family, who urged him to seek help. He decided to be honest with his physician, who then referred him to a drug and alcohol counselor.

Ed was diagnosed with adult ADD. In taking his history, it turned out that he had also used sweets, coffee, cigarettes and "pep" vitamins in his amateur chemist role. Ed was started on one medication by his physician. After some trial runs, he ended up on specific dosages of two medications – a psychostimulant and an antidepressant. To date, he is three years clean of all other drugs, has graduated from college and will be getting married at the end of the year. This isn't to say that he doesn't have any problems, just that he must no longer try to solve them alone by second-guessing his body and the drugs' effects.

Do you see yourself? Do you see someone you know or love? Do you feel better?

Appendix

Resources

Advocacy Organizations (California)
Protection and Advocacy Inc. 100 Howe Avenue, Ste 185-N, Sacramento, CA 95825 800-
776-5746.

Books
Barkley RA. *Attention Deficit Disorder: A Clinical Workbook*. New York: The Guilford Press,
1990.

Barkley RA. *Attention-Deficit Hyperactivity Disorder: A Handbook for Diagnosis and
Treatment*. New York: The Guilford Press, 1990.

Comings DE. *The Gene Bomb*. Duarte, California: Hope Press,1996

Comings DE. *Search for the Tourette Syndrome and Human Behavior Genes*. Duarte,
California: Hope Press,1996.

Comings DE. *Tourette Syndrome and Human Behavior*. Duarte, California: Hope Press,1990.

Copeland ED. *Medications for Attention Disorders (ADHD/ADD) and Related Medical
Problems (Tourette's Syndrome, Sleep Apnea, Seizure Disorders): A Comprehensive
Handbook*. Atlanta, Georgia: Resurgens Press, Inc., 1991/1994.

Copeland ED and Love VL. *Attention Please! A Comprehensive Guide for Successfully
Parenting Children with Attention Disorders and Hyperactivity*. Atlanta, Georgia: SPI
Press, 1991.

Dornbush M and Pruitt S. *Teaching the Tiger: A Handbook for Individuals Involved in the
Education of Students with Attention Deficit Disorders, Tourette Syndrome or Obsessive-
Compulsive Disorder*. Duarte, California: Hope Press, 1995.

Ellis A, *New Guide to Rational Living*. North Hollywood, CA: Wilshire Press, 1977

Garber S, Garber M & Spizman R. *Beyond Ritalin*. New York: Villard Books, registered trademark of Random House, Inc. , 1996.

Gordon M and McClure FD. *The Down & Dirty Guide to Adult Attention Deficit Disorder.* New York: GSI Publications, Inc. ,1996.

Hallowell EM and Ratey JJ. *Answers to Distraction.* New York: Pantheon Books, 1994.

Hallowell EM and Ratey JJ. *Driven to Distraction.* New York: Pantheon Books, 1994.

Hartmann T. *Beyond ADD: Hunting for Reasons in the Past and Present.* Grass Valley, California: Underwood Books, 1996.

Keirsey D and Bates M. *Please Understand Me.* Del Mar, California: Prometheus Publishers, 1978.

Kramer PD. *Listening to Prozac.* New York: Viking, 1993.

Latham, PS and Latham PH. *Learning Disabilities and the Law.* Washington D.C.: JKL Communications, 1993.

Latham PS and Latham PH. *Attention Deficit Disorder and the Law: A Guide for Advocates.* Washington D.C.: JKL Communications, 1992.

Latham PS and Latham PH. *The ADD Adult's Pocket Guide to Anti-Discrimination Law: A simplified guide to understanding the laws that protect Attention Deficit Disordered Adults.* United Way of Virginia Peninsula: PADDA, the Peninsula Attention Deficit Disorder Association, 1992.

Nadeau K. *Adventures in Fast Forward: Life, Love, and Work for the ADD Adult.* New York: Brunner/Mazel, Inc., 1996.

Weiss G and Hechtman LT. *Hyperactive Children Grown Up.* New York: The Guilford Press, 1986.

Book Distributors/Publishers
A.D.D. Plus. 1095-25th Street S.E. #107, Salem, OR 97301, (503) 364-9163. Economical, practical books, tapes and videos for at-risk children, Adolescents and families, emphasizing ADD/ADHD, inbcluding Spanish Language materials.

A.D.D. Warehouse. 300 N.W. 70th Avenue, Ste. 102, Plantation, FL 33317, (305) 792-8960. Publishes and distributes books, videos and assessment instruments on attention deficit disorders and related problems.

Brunner/Mazel-Magination Press. 19 Union Square West, New York, NY 10003, (212) 924-3344. *Comprehensive Guide to ADD in Adults.*

Guilford Publications. 72 Spring Streetm New York, NY 10012, (212) 431-9800. Publishes best-selling books, award-winning videos and periodicals in psychology, child psychology and learning disabilities.

Brochures/Pamphlets
IAM Cares, Complying with the American with Disabilities Act: A Guide for Approaching Job Descriptions and Determining Qualifications. International Association of Machinist & Aerospace Workers Authorization by the US Department of Education, 1994.

Newsletters
ADDendum. Jaffe, P (ed.). No longer being published, but back issues may be available. c/o CPS, 5041-A Backlick Rd., Annandale, VA 22003

The ADDventurer. Publication of the Kitty Petty ADD/LD Institute, a non-profit corporation; published bi-monthly. 410 Sheridan Ave. Ste 339, Palo Alto, CA 94306

ADDult News. Johnson, MJ (ed.). Four quarterly issues; 2620 Ivy Place,Toledo, Ohio 43613.

ADD-Vantage. Myers, R (ed.). PO Box 29972, Thornton, Colorado 80229.

The ADDvisor. Mealear, L(ed.). A publication of the Attention Deficit Disorder Resource Center; published bi-monthly. PO Box 71223, Marietta, Georgia 30007.

The ADHD Report (Quarterly Newsletter).Barkley RA and Associates (eds.). Published six times a year by the Guilford Press, 72 Spring Street, New York, NY 10012

ChADDER. A semi-annual publication of Ch.A.D.D., a national support organization for information on attention deficit disorders. 499 Northwest 70th Ave, Ste 308, Plantation, FL 33317 (305) 587-3700.

Challenge: A Report on Attention Deficit Disorder. Koplowitz R (ed.); published six times a year by Challenge, Inc. PO Box 2277, Peabody, MA 01960

Child and Adolescent Psychopharmacology News. Kutcher S (ed.); published six times a year by the Guilford Press, 72 Spring Street, New York, NY 10012.

Journal of Attention Disorders. Connors CK (ed.); published by Multi-Health Systems, Inc. 908 Niagara Falls Blvd., North Tonawanda, NY 14120.

Protection and Advocacy Inc. Newsletter. Ordas R (ed.) 100 Howe Avenue, Ste 185-N, Sacramento, CA 95825. 800-776-5746.

Support Organizations
Ch.A.D.D.
    499 Northwest 70th Avenue, Ste. 308

Plantation, FL 33317
(305) 587-3700

Tourette Syndrome Association
42-40 Bell Boulevard, Bayside, NY 11361, (800) 237-0717

Training Organizations
ADD Impact Coaching. Nancy Rady, director. (617) 237-3508

American Coaching Network. Sue Sessman, director. (610) 825-9549

Bridge Associates, Inc. Coaching manual, products and kit. General information about programs and trainings. One Elm Street, Hyannis, MA 02601. (508) 790-1333

Haney, Madelaine Griffith. Coaches' training. (423) 524-9549

Bibliography

the AA Member-Medications and other Drugs: a Report From a Group of Physicians in AA [sic]. New York: Alcoholics Anonymous World Services, Inc., 1984.

Amen DG. Windows into the ADD Mind. Fairfield, California:Mindworks Press, 1995

Attention Deficit Disorder Medicine Linked to Cancer. *The World Today* (CNN) Transcript #1244, Segment #8, January 12, 1996. Quote from Velokoff, Drake Institute.

Ball SA, Carroll KM and Rounsaville BJ. Sensation Seeking, Substance Abuse, and Psychopathology in Treatment-Seeking and Community Cocaine Abusers. *Journal of Consulting and Clinical Psychology* 1994;62(5):1053-7.

Barkley RA. *Attention Deficit Disorder: A Clinical Workbook.* New York: The Guilford Press, 1990.

Barkley RA. *Attention-Deficit Hyperactivity Disorder: A Handbook for Diagnosis and Treatment.* New York: The Guilford Press, 1990.

Biederman J, Wilens T, Mick E, Milberger S, Spencer TS and Faraone SV. Psychoactive substance use disorders in adults with Attention Deficit Hyperactivity Disorder (ADHD): effects of ADHD and psychiatric comorbidity. *American Journal of Psychiatry* 1995(November); 152(11):1652-8.

Biederman J, Faraone SV, Spencer T, Wilens T, Mick E and Lapey KA. Gender differences in a sample of adults with with attention deficit hyperactivity disorder. *Psychiatry Research* 1994; 53(1):13-29.

Biederman J, Faraone SV, Spencer T, Wilens T, Norman D, Lapey KA, Mick E, Lehman BK and Doyle A. Patterns of Psychiatric Comorbidity, Cognition, and Psychosocial Functioning in Adults with Attention Deficit Hyperactivity Disorder. *American Journal of Psychiatry* 1993;150:1792-1798.

Biederman J, Newcorn J and Sprich S. Comorbidity of Attention Deficit Hyperactivity Disorder with Conduct, Depressive, Anxiety, and Other Disorders. *American Journal of Psychiatry* 1991;148(5):564-77.

Black C. *It Will Never Happen to Me.* Denver, CO: M.A.C. Printing and Publications

Division, 1981;rev. 1996.

Blum K, Braverman ER, Dinardo MJ, Wood RC, and Sheridan PJ, Prolonged P300 Latency in a Neuropsychiatric Population with the D_2 Dopamine Receptor A_1, Allele, *Pharmacogenetics 4* (1994): 313-322.

Bradshaw JE. *Homecoming*. New York, New York:Bantam Books, 1990

Bradshaw JE. *Healing the Shame that Binds You*. Deerfield Beach, FL:Health Communications, Inc, 1988

Cantwell D. ADHD Across the Life Cycle: Current Program in Diagnosis and Management. Hyatt Regency, La Jolla, CA May 31-June 2, 1996.

Comings DE. *The Gene Bomb*. Duarte, California: Hope Press,1996

Comings DE. *Search for the Tourette Syndrome and Human Behavior Genes*. Duarte, California: Hope Press,1996.

Comings DE, Comings BG. The Dopamine D_2 Receptor Locus as a Modifying Gene in Neuropsychiatric Disorders. *Journal of American Medicine* 1991;266:13.

Comings DE. *Tourette Syndrome and Human Behavior*. Duarte, California: Hope Press,1990.

Comings DE. Blood Serotonin and Tryptophan in Tourette Syndrome. *American Journal of Genetics* 1990; 36:418-30.

Comings DE, Gade R, Muhleman D et al. Exon and intro variants in the human tryptophan 2,3-dioxygenase gene: potential association with Tourette Syndrome, substance abuse and other disorders. *Pharmacogenetics* 1990;6:307-18.

Copeland ED. *Medications for Attention Disorders (ADHD/ADD) and Related Medical Problems (Tourette's Syndrome, Sleep Apnea, Seizure Disorders): A Comprehensive Handbook*. Atlanta, Georgia: Resurgens Press, Inc., 1991/1994.

Copeland ED and Love VL. *Attention Please! A Comprehensive Guide for Successfully Parenting Children with Attention Disorders and Hyperactivity*. Atlanta, Georgia: SPI Press, 1991.

Copps SC. *The Attending Physician, Attention Deficit Disorder: A Guide for Pediatricians and Family Physicians*. Atlanta, Georgia: SPI Press, 1992.

Dornbush M and Pruitt S. *Teaching the Tiger: A Handbook for Individuals Involved in the Education of Students with Attention Deficit Disorders, Tourette Syndrome or Obsessive-Compulsive Disorder*. Duarte, California: Hope Press, 1995.

Dowling D. Ritalin alert. *Seventeen Magazine* 1996(February); p. 62.

Dunnick JK and Hailey JR. Experimental Studies on the Long-Term Effects of Methylphenidate Hydrochloride. *Toxicology* 1995 (Nov. 30): 103(2): 77-84.

Eyestone LL and Howell RJ An Epidemiological Study of Attention Deficit Hyperactivity Disorder and Major Depression in a Male Prison Population. *Bulletin of the American Academy of Psychiatry and the Law (BAR)* 1994;22(2):181-93.

Faigel HC. Attention Deficit Disorder in College Students: Facts, Fallacies, and Treatment. *American Journal of College Health* 1995; 43(4): 147-55.

Garber S, Garber M & Spizman R. *Beyond Ritalin.* New York: Villard Books, registered trademark of Random House, Inc. , 1996.

Goldstein S and Goldstein M. *Managing Attention Deficit Disorders in Children: A Guide for Practitioners.* Hanover, NJ:John Wiley & Co., 1996.

Gordon M and McClure FD. *The Down & Dirty Guide to Adult Attention Deficit Disorder.* New York: GSI Publications, Inc. ,1996.

Graph on Ritalin Production from 1975 to 1995. *New York Times,* May 15, 1996

Greenhill LL. Pharmacologic Treatment of Attention Deficit Hyperactivity Disorder. *Psychiatric Clinics of North America* 1992(March); 15: 1-25.

Greenhill, LL and Osman Betty B (eds.). *Ritalin: Theory and Patient Management.* New York: Mary Ann Liebert, Inc., 1991.

Guffrey DG. Ritalin: What Educators and Parents Should Know. *Journal of Instructional Psychology* 1992;19(3):167-169.

Hallowell EM and Ratey JJ. *Answers to Distraction.* New York: Pantheon Books, 1994.

Hallowell EM and Ratey JJ. *Driven to Distraction.* New York: Pantheon Books, 1994.

Hartman T. *Beyond ADD: Hunting for Reasons in the Past and Present.* Grass Valley, California: Underwood Books, 1996.

Hartman T. *Hunters in a Farmer's World.* Grass Valley, CA:Underwood Books, 1993.

IAM Cares, Complying with the American with Disabilities Act: A Guide for Approaching Job Descriptions and Determining Qualifications. International Association of Machinist & Aerospace Workers Authorization by the US Department of Education, 1994.

Kassebaum G and Chandler SM. Polydrug Use and Self Control Among Men and Women in Prisons. *Journal of Drug Education* 1994;24(4): 333-50.

Keirsey D and Bates M. *Please Understand Me*. Del Mar, California: Prometheus Publishers, 1978.

Koepp AH. Insurance Coverage for ADD Becomes State Law. *Challenge, Inc.* 1993;7:4

Kolata G (quote from Biederman). Boom in Ritalin Sales Raises Ethical Issues, *New York Times*, May 15, 1996.

Kramer PD. *Listening to Prozac*. New York: Viking, 1993.

Kwasman A, Tinsley BJ and Lepper HS. Pediatrician's Knowledge and Attitudes Concerning Diagnosis and Treatment of Attention Deficit and Hyperactivity Disorders. A national survey approach. *Archives of Pediatric and Adolescent Medicine* 1995. 149(11):1211-6.

Latham, PS and Latham PH. *Learning Disabilities and the Law*. Washington D.C.: JKL Communications, 1993.

Latham PS and Latham PH. *Attention Deficit Disorder and the Law: A Guide for Advocates*. Washington D.C.: JKL Communications, 1992.

Latham PS and Latham PH. *The ADD Adult's Pocket Guide to Anti-Discrimination Law: A simplified guide to understanding the laws that protect Attention Deficit Disordered Adults*. United Way of Virginia Peninsula: PADDA, the Peninsula Attention Deficit Disorder Association, 1992.

Leland J. A Risky RX for Fun. *Newsweek Magazine*, October. 30, 1995. p. 74.

Leventhal BL and Sallee FR. Mastering Challenges with ADHD and Comorbid Conditions. U.S Psychiatric & Mental Health Congress Conference and Exhibition; San Diego, CA. November 15, 1996.

Maugh TH. UCI Scientists Link Attention Deficit to Gene. *Los Angeles Times*, May 1, 1996.

McWhorter K. *College Reading and Study Skills*. New York: Harper Collins Publishers, 1992.

Miller D and Blum K. *Overload, Attention Deficit Disorder and the Addictive Brain*. Kansas City, Missouri:McMeel, 1996

Miller RD and Metzner JL. Psychiatric Stigma in Correctional Facilities. *Bulletin of the American Academy of Psychiatry and the Law (BAR)* 1994; 22(4): 621-8.

Nadeau K. *Adventures in Fast Forward: Life, Love, and Work for the ADD Adult*. New York:

Brunner/Mazel, Inc., 1996.

New York Times, Federal Agency Issues a Mild Caution on a Hyperactivity Drug. January 13, 1996. P. 8.

Psychiatry/Education's Ruin – Destroying Lives (1993).Church of Scientology Citizens' Commision for Human Rights, (800) 869-2247.

Reisinger J. A Visual Guide to ADD: Seeing Through the Haze of Attention Deficit Disorder. A discourse to explain and encourage more to see the "A" in the "D" student. Destined for Jail. (1996) Unpublished.

Thompson LL, Riggs PD, Mikulich SK and Crowley TJ. Contribution of ADHD symptoms to substance problems and delinquency in conduct-disordered adolescents. Journal of Abnormal Child Psychology 1996(June); 24(3):325-47

Tracy-Weber C. Asperger Syndrome, A New Kind of Learning Disability, *CAPED (California Post-Secondary Educators) Communique.* Spring 1995. California

Volkow ND, Ding Y, Fowlder JS, Wang G, Logan J, Fatley JS, Dewey S, Ashby C, Lieberman J, Heitzmann R and Wolf AP. Is methylphenidate like cocaine? Studies on their pharmacokinetics and distribution in the human brain. *Archives of General Psychiatry*, 1995; 52:456-463.

Weiss G and Hechtman LT. *Hyperactive Children Grown Up*. New York: The Guilford Press, 1986.

Wender PH. *The Hyperactive Child, Adolescent, and Adult: Attention Deficit Disorder Through the Life Span*. New York, NY:Oxford University Press, 1987.

Zametkin AJ, Nordahl TE, Gross M, King AC, Semple WE, Rumsey J, Hamburger S and Cohen RM. Cerebral Glucose Metabolism in Adults with Hyperactivity of Childhood Onset. *New England Journal of Medicine* 1990; 323:1361-66.

Index

Drake Institute 212
dream state sleep 82, 142
Driven to Distraction 193, 205, 239
drowsiness 233
drug abuse (*see* abuse, drug)
drug baby 26, 33
Drug Enforcement Agency (DEA) 216, 228
dyes 221-2
dyscalculia 59-61, 230
dysgraphia 59-61, 230
dyslexia 41, 59-61, 197, 207, 230

E
ear infection 202
eating disorders (*see also* addiction, food) 132-3, 142
Edison, Thomas 37, 169
education v, vii, 24, 26, 34, 39-40, 57-8, 65, 68, 70, 72, 85, 101, 107, 128, 147, 149-51, 163, 165-8, 180-2, 184, 188-9, 195, 197-8, 213, 215-6, 238, 241, 251, 253, 257, 263
educational history 14-5, 17, 29-30, 124, 194, 197-9
educational jargon 59
Educational Testing Service (ETS) 68
EEG 195
ego 41-2, 48, 154, 195
Einstein, Albert 280
electrical activity 22
electroencephalogram (*see* EEG)
electroshock 197
elementary school 1, 5, 7, 9, 44, 57-60, 65, 70, 72, 106, 147, 157, 167, 171, 176, 199-200, 202, 204, 230, 238, 257, 261
Ellis, Dr. Albert 249
employee v, 44, 103, 117, 121-2, 160, 169-91, 237, 242-3
employer v, 44-5, 61, 164, 169-91, 203
employment/work history 17, 197, 199-200
emotion 4, 17, 73, 103, 113-5, 125, 145-6, 150, 155, 161, 189, 197, 210, 213, 259
emotional abuse (*see* abuse, emotional)
energy iii, vii, 18-9, 36, 45, 49, 80, 83, 87, 98-101, 103, 109-10, 112, 116, 122, 125, 127, 170-1, 175, 207, 214, 223, 225, 243
Enhancing the Concept 78, 80
entrepreneurs 36, 108, 169
enuresis 202
ephedrine 221
espresso 129, 236
Excedrin® 129
exercise 16, 18, 54, 85, 107, 121-2, 127-9, 209-10, 236-7, 240, 250
Expressive Language Disability 114
extroversion 103-4

personal history 32-3, 48, 55, 65, 72, 118, 164, 197-201, 207, 209, 251, 263

pharmacy 28, 211-2, 214, 217, 221-2, 231

Pharmacotanixx 235

Ph.D. 63, 72, 120, 182

physical abuse (*see* abuse, physical)

physical activity 1, 18, 250

physical assault (*see* abuse, physical)

physically handicapped 170

physical state 97, 149, 242-4, 248-50

physician 19, 31, 53, 60, 120, 130, 146, 149, 169, 176, 194, 200, 205, 209-17, 220-2, 224, 226, 228, 231, 237, 239, 241, 248, 255-60, 262-3

Physicians Desk Reference (PDR) 215

piperidine ring 221

pituitary dysfunction 215

planning iii, 21, 103, 116, 131, 140, 142, 210

Please Understand Me 103

police 8, 10, 102, 131, 148, 154, 156, 162-3, 261

polygenetic 25, 206

Positron Emission Tomography (PET) 23, 27, 206-7, 209

post-doctoral program 71

pot (*see* marijuana)

potential, failure to reach 1, 7, 14, 25, 41-2, 62, 70-2, 108, 177, 207

powerlessness 137, 144

pregnancy 26, 33, 172, 198, 205

premarital counseling 103, 107

Premenstrual Syndrome (PMS) 239, 262

prison (*see* jail/prison)

problem behavior (*see* behavior, problem)

processing problems 7, 9, 11-2, 15, 35, 38, 41-2, 55, 60-1, 70-1, 75, 104, 155, 160, 174-5, 178, 198, 204, 219, 224, 226, 237, 241, 256-7

procrastination 18, 44-5, 87, 174, 243

Prozac 228-32, 234-5, 239

PSAT 68, 71

psychiatry 2, 23, 25, 28, 48-9, 137, 153, 181, 194-6, 204, 207, 209, 213-20, 227, 231, 234-6, 240, 252

psychoeducational history 30, 68

psychoeducational testing (*see* testing, non-medical)

psychology v, 28-9, 33, 49, 120, 132-3, 153, 194, 196, 203, 207, 212-4, 256-7

psychologist, clinical 188, 196, 203

psychologist, educational 2, 196, 203

psychologist, school 33, 212

psychostimulants 61, 122, 129, 211, 213, 215, 217, 219-20, 223-6, 227-8, 230, 234, 236, 239, 263

puberty 35, 47, 161

publicity 29, 211, 220

R

race 26, 34

radioactive material 206

rage 11, 17, 30, 38, 49-50, 101-2, 111, 113-5, 117, 119, 121, 123, 125, 153-4, 157-8, 160-1, 183, 219, 229, 232, 234, 237, 239, 248, 261

rapid eye movement (REM) 82

Ratey 205, 210, 217, 224, 238

reading 9, 12, 41-2, 57-60, 62-4, 70, 77-8, 80, 84-5, 89-91, 114, 155, 158-60, 163, 165, 168, 176, 194, 199, 204, 230, 238, 250, 256

rebound effect 223-4

receptors 22, 229

recidivism 135-6, 164

recovery program 131, 135, 137-9, 145, 147-51

Refreshing Your Memory 78, 81-2

registration, early or priority 65

rehabilitation 133, 135, 262

Rehabilitation Act 28, 188-90

rehabilitation programs 162, 164-7

rehearsal 77, 79

relapse 135, 137-8, 146-8, 150-1, 164

relationship history (*see* personal history)

relaxation 9, 33, 43, 74, 147-8, 217, 250

religion 136

report cards 1, 14, 71-2, 199, 256-7

resentment 101, 112, 142, 145, 182, 247

Resource Specialist Program (RSP) 58-9, 62

retrieval 47, 77, 79, 175, 182

Richwood Pharmaceuticals 227

rigidity 17-8, 47, 139, 174, 188, 191

Ritalin 29, 122, 208, 211-5, 217, 220-8, 230, 236-7, 262

ritalinic acid 221

Ritalin SR 221-2

role-playing 107

rudeness 38, 98-9, 154, 173

S

Sallee 153, 228

sarcasm 100, 120

SAT 8, 68-71, 168

Say No to Drugs 211

school, dropping out 10, 16, 26, 40, 58-9

school history (*see* educational history)

school phobia 58

science (*see also* medical science) v, 27, 33, 36, 39, 63, 124, 205-7, 218, 234

secretaries 11, 18, 38, 41, 44, 46, 60, 105, 108, 174, 179, 262

seizure 214, 228

Order Form

1. Books:

Quantity   Amount

Tourette Syndrome and Human Behavior
_____   1S Softback $39.95   _____

Search for the Tourette Syndrome and Human Behavior Genes
_____   8H Hardback $34.00   _____
_____   8S Softback $29.95   _____

***The Gene Bomb   Does Higher Education and Advanced
Technology Accelerate the Selection of Genes for Learning
Disorders, ADHD, Addictive and Disruptive Behaviors?***
_____   9H Hardback $29.95   _____
_____   9S Softback $25.00   _____

RYAN — A Mother's Story of Her Hyperactive-Tourette Syndrome Child
_____   2S Softback $9.95   _____

What Makes Ryan Tick? A Family's Triumph over TS and ADHD
_____   10S Softback $14.95   _____

Hi, I'm Adam - A Child's Book about Tourette Syndrome
_____   4A Softback $4.95   _____

Adam and the Magic Marble
_____   4B Softback $6.95   _____

Hi, I'm Adam + Adam and the Magic Marble
_____   4C Both together $11.50   _____

Echolalia - An Adult's Story of Tourette Syndrome
_____   5A Softback $11.95   _____

***Don't Think About Monkeys - Extraordinary Stories by
People with Tourette Syndrome***
_____   6A Softback $12.95   _____

***Teaching the Tiger - A Handbook for Individuals Involved
in the Education of Students with Attention Deficit Disorder,
Tourette Syndrome or Obsessive-Compulsive Disorder***
_____   7A Softback $35.00   _____

***A.D.D. Kaleidoscope - The Many Facets of Adult Attention
Deficit Disorder***
_____   8A Softback $24.95   _____

Subtotal for Books   _____

2. Tax: **California residents please add 8.25% sales tax** _____

3. Mailing and Handling:

☐ Fourth Class: $4.00 lst item $1.00 each additional item
☐ U.P.S. Ground: $6.00 lst item $1.00 each additional item
☐ U.P.S. Air: $10.00 lst item $2.00 each additional item   _____

Total ▄▄▄▄▄▄

Name: _____

Address: _____

City: _____ State:_____ Zip: _____

Country (if other than U.S.A.): _____

Check Enclosed _____   **or**   Visa ___ Mastercard ___

CC#_____ Expiration Date _____

send to: ☐┬○ **Hope Press** P.O.Box 188,
                    Duarte, CA 91009-0188

or Fill out this form with credit card # and FAX it to 626-358-3520

or Order by phone **1-800-321-4039** — 24 hr service

[Foreign buyers outside North America please: a) send bank check in U.S. dollars, or b) order by credit card with charge in U.S. dollars, or c) FAX in the form. For surface mail add $6.00 shipping for first book and $1.00 for each additional and allow 4-6 weeks. For air mail add $25.00 shipping and $2.00 for each additonal book and allow 1 week.]

for more details on each book visit our web site: **http://www.hopepress.com**

Order Form

1. Books: <u>Quantity</u>   <u>Amount</u>

Tourette Syndrome and Human Behavior
_____   1S Softback $39.95   _____

Search for the Tourette Syndrome and Human Behavior Genes
_____   8H Hardback $34.00   _____
_____   8S Softback $29.95   _____

***The Gene Bomb   Does Higher Education and Advanced
Technology Accelerate the Selection of Genes for Learning
Disorders, ADHD, Addictive and Disruptive Behaviors?***
_____   9H Hardback $29.95   _____
_____   9S Softback $25.00   _____

RYAN — A Mother's Story of Her Hyperactive-Tourette Syndrome Child
_____   2S Softback $9.95   _____

What Makes Ryan Tick?   A Family's Triumph over TS and ADHD
_____   10S Softback $14.95   _____

Hi, I'm Adam - A Child's Book about Tourette Syndrome
_____   4A Softback $4.95   _____

Adam and the Magic Marble
_____   4B Softback $6.95   _____

Hi, I'm Adam + Adam and the Magic Marble
_____   4C Both together $11.50   _____

Echolalia - An Adult's Story of Tourette Syndrome
_____   5A Softback $11.95   _____

***Don't Think About Monkeys - Extraordinary Stories by
People with Tourette Syndrome***
_____   6A Softback $12.95   _____

***Teaching the Tiger - A Handbook for Individuals Involved
in the Education of Students with Attention Deficit Disorder,
Tourette Syndrome or Obsessive-Compulsive Disorder***
_____   7A Softback $35.00   _____

***A.D.D. Kaleidoscope - The Many Facets of Adult Attention
Deficit Disorder***
_____   8A Softback $24.95   _____

Subtotal for Books _____

2. Tax: **California residents please add 8.25% sales tax** _____

**3. Mailing
and
Handling:**

☐   Fourth Class: $4.00 lst item $1.00 each additional item
☐   U.P.S. Ground: $6.00 lst item $1.00 each additional item
☐   U.P.S. Air: $10.00 lst item $2.00 each additional item   _____

Total ▬▬▬▬

Name: _____

Address: _____

City: _____ State:_____ Zip: _____

Country (if other than U.S.A.): _____ _____

Check Enclosed _____   **or**   Visa ___ Mastercard ___

CC#_____ Expiration Date _____

send to: ☐┬◯ **Hope Press** P.O.Box 188,
Duarte, CA 91009-0188

or Fill out this form with credit card # and FAX it to 626-358-3520

or Order by phone **1-800-321-4039** — 24 hr service

[Foreign buyers outside North America please: a) send bank check in U.S. dollars, or b) order by credit
card with charge in U.S. dollars, or c) FAX in the form. For surface mail add $6.00 shipping for first
book and $1.00 for each additional and allow 4-6 weeks. For air mail add $25.00 shipping and $2.00 for
each additonal book and allow 1 week.]

for more details on each book visit our web site: **http://www.hopepress.com**

Order Form

1. Books: Quantity   Amount

Tourette Syndrome and Human Behavior
_____   1S Softback $39.95   _____

Search for the Tourette Syndrome and Human Behavior Genes
_____   8H Hardback $34.00   _____
_____   8S Softback $29.95   _____

***The Gene Bomb   Does Higher Education and Advanced
Technology Accelerate the Selection of Genes for Learning
Disorders, ADHD, Addictive and Disruptive Behaviors?***
_____   9H Hardback $29.95   _____
_____   9S Softback $25.00   _____

RYAN — A Mother's Story of Her Hyperactive-Tourette Syndrome Child
_____   2S Softback $9.95   _____

What Makes Ryan Tick?   A Family's Triumph over TS and ADHD
_____   10S Softback $14.95   _____

Hi, I'm Adam - A Child's Book about Tourette Syndrome
_____   4A Softback $4.95   _____

Adam and the Magic Marble
_____   4B Softback $6.95   _____

Hi, I'm Adam + Adam and the Magic Marble
_____   4C Both together $11.50   _____

Echolalia - An Adult's Story of Tourette Syndrome
_____   5A Softback $11.95   _____

***Don't Think About Monkeys - Extraordinary Stories by
People with Tourette Syndrome***
_____   6A Softback $12.95   _____

***Teaching the Tiger - A Handbook for Individuals Involved
in the Education of Students with Attention Deficit Disorder,
Tourette Syndrome or Obsessive-Compulsive Disorder***
_____   7A Softback $35.00   _____

***A.D.D. Kaleidoscope - The Many Facets of Adult Attention
Deficit Disorder***
_____   8A Softback $24.95   _____

                                          Subtotal for Books   _____

2. Tax: **California residents please add 8.25% sales tax** _____

**3. Mailing
and
Handling:**
☐   Fourth Class: $4.00 lst item $1.00 each additional item
☐   U.P.S. Ground: $6.00 lst item $1.00 each additional item
☐   U.P.S. Air: $10.00 lst item $2.00 each additional item   _____

                                                    Total ▬▬▬▬

Name: _____

Address: _____

City: _____ State:_____ Zip: _____

Country (if other than U.S.A.): _____

Check Enclosed _____   **or**   Visa ___ Mastercard ___

CC# _____ Expiration Date _____

send to: ☐┬○ **Hope Press** P.O.Box 188,
                    Duarte, CA 91009-0188

or Fill out this form with credit card # and FAX it to 626-358-3520

or Order by phone **1-800-321-4039** — 24 hr service

[Foreign buyers outside North America please: a) send bank check in U.S. dollars, or b) order by credit
card with charge in U.S. dollars, or c) FAX in the form. For surface mail add $6.00 shipping for first
book and $1.00 for each additional and allow 4-6 weeks. For air mail add $25.00 shipping and $2.00 for
each additonal book and allow 1 week.]

for more details on each book visit our web site: **http://www.hopepress.com**

Order Form

1. Books: Quantity   Amount

Tourette Syndrome and Human Behavior
_____   1S Softback $39.95   _____

Search for the Tourette Syndrome and Human Behavior Genes
_____   8H Hardback $34.00   _____
_____   8S Softback $29.95   _____

The Gene Bomb   Does Higher Education and Advanced Technology Accelerate the Selection of Genes for Learning Disorders, ADHD, Addictive and Disruptive Behaviors?
_____   9H Hardback $29.95   _____
_____   9S Softback $25.00   _____

RYAN — A Mother's Story of Her Hyperactive-Tourette Syndrome Child
_____   2S Softback $9.95   _____

What Makes Ryan Tick? A Family's Triumph over TS and ADHD
_____   10S Softback $14.95   _____

Hi, I'm Adam - A Child's Book about Tourette Syndrome
_____   4A Softback $4.95   _____

Adam and the Magic Marble
_____   4B Softback $6.95   _____

Hi, I'm Adam + Adam and the Magic Marble
_____   4C Both together $11.50   _____

Echolalia - An Adult's Story of Tourette Syndrome
_____   5A Softback $11.95   _____

Don't Think About Monkeys - Extraordinary Stories by People with Tourette Syndrome
_____   6A Softback $12.95   _____

Teaching the Tiger - A Handbook for Individuals Involved in the Education of Students with Attention Deficit Disorder, Tourette Syndrome or Obsessive-Compulsive Disorder
_____   7A Softback $35.00   _____

A.D.D. Kaleidoscope - The Many Facets of Adult Attention Deficit Disorder
_____   8A Softback $24.95   _____

                                        Subtotal for Books   _____

2. Tax: **California residents please add 8.25% sales tax** _____

3. Mailing   ☐ Fourth Class: $4.00 lst item $1.00 each additional item
   and   ☐ U.P.S. Ground: $6.00 lst item $1.00 each additional item
Handling: ☐ U.P.S. Air: $10.00 lst item $2.00 each additional item _____

                                                    Total ▬▬▬▬

Name: _____
Address: _____
City: _____ State:_____ Zip: _____
Country (if other than U.S.A.): _____
Check Enclosed _____   **or**   Visa ___ Mastercard ___
CC#_____ Expiration Date _____

send to: ☐┬○ **Hope Press** **P.O.Box 188,**
                      Duarte, CA 91009-0188

or Fill out this form with credit card # and FAX it to 626-358-3520

or Order by phone **1-800-321-4039** — 24 hr service

[Foreign buyers outside North America please: a) send bank check in U.S. dollars, or b) order by credit card with charge in U.S. dollars, or c) FAX in the form. For surface mail add $6.00 shipping for first book and $1.00 for each additional and allow 4-6 weeks. For air mail add $25.00 shipping and $2.00 for each additonal book and allow 1 week.]

for more details on each book visit our web site: **http://www.hopepress.com**